The Cambridge Companion to An

Amy Beach was a pathbreaking composer and pianist who transcended the restrictions of nineteenth-century Boston to become America's most famous turn-of-the-century female composer and, later in her career, a prominent performing artist and promoter of music education. *The Cambridge Companion to Amy Beach* makes her life and music accessible to a new generation of listeners. It outlines her remarkable talent as a child prodigy, her marriage to a prominent physician twice her age, and her subsequent international acclaim as a composer and piano virtuoso. Analytical chapters examine the range of her musical output, from popular songs and piano pieces to chamber and symphonic works of great complexity. As well as introducing Beach's compelling music to those not yet familiar with her work, it provides new resources for scholars and students with in-depth information drawn from recently uncovered archival sources.

E. DOUGLAS BOMBERGER teaches musicology and piano at Elizabethtown College. He has published six books and numerous articles on music in the United States, and he served as subject editor for nineteenth-century music for the *Grove Dictionary of American Music* (2013).

Cambridge Companions to Music

Topics

The Cambridge Companion to Ballet
Edited by Marion Kant

The Cambridge Companion to Blues and Gospel Music
Edited by Allan Moore

The Cambridge Companion to Caribbean Music
Edited by Nanette De Jong

The Cambridge Companion to Choral Music
Edited by André de Quadros

The Cambridge Companion to the Concerto
Edited by Simon P. Keefe

The Cambridge Companion to Conducting
Edited by José Antonio Bowen

The Cambridge Companion to the Drum Kit
Edited by Matt Brennan, Joseph Michael Pignato and Daniel Akira Stadnicki

The Cambridge Companion to Eighteenth-Century Opera
Edited by Anthony R. DelDonna and Pierpaolo Polzonetti

The Cambridge Companion to Electronic Music
Edited by Nick Collins and Julio D'Escriván

The Cambridge Companion to the 'Eroica' Symphony
Edited by Nancy November

The Cambridge Companion to Film Music
Edited by Mervyn Cooke and Fiona Ford

The Cambridge Companion to French Music
Edited by Simon Trezise

The Cambridge Companion to Grand Opera
Edited by David Charlton

The Cambridge Companion to Hip-Hop
Edited by Justin A. Williams

The Cambridge Companion to Jazz
Edited by Mervyn Cooke and David Horn

The Cambridge Companion to Jewish Music
Edited by Joshua S. Walden

The Cambridge Companion to K-Pop
Edited by Suk-Young Kim

The Cambridge Companion to Krautrock
Edited by Uwe Schütte

The Cambridge Companion to the Lied
Edited by James Parsons

The Cambridge Companion to Medieval Music
Edited by Mark Everist

The Cambridge Companion to Music and Romanticism
Edited by Benedict Taylor

The Cambridge Companion to Music in Digital Culture
Edited by Nicholas Cook, Monique Ingalls and David Trippett

The Cambridge Companion to the Musical, third edition
Edited by William Everett and Paul Laird

The Cambridge Companion to Opera Studies
Edited by Nicholas Till

The Cambridge Companion to Operetta
Edited by Anastasia Belina and Derek B. Scott

The Cambridge Companion to the Orchestra
Edited by Colin Lawson

The Cambridge Companion to Percussion
Edited by Russell Hartenberger

The Cambridge Companion to Pop and Rock
Edited by Simon Frith, Will Straw and John Street

The Cambridge Companion to Recorded Music
Edited by Eric Clarke, Nicholas Cook, Daniel Leech-Wilkinson and John Rink

The Cambridge Companion to Rhythm
Edited by Russell Hartenberger and Ryan McClelland

The Cambridge Companion to Schubert's 'Winterreise'
Edited by Marjorie W. Hirsch and Lisa Feurzeig

The Cambridge Companion to Serialism
Edited by Martin Iddon

The Cambridge Companion to Seventeenth-Century Opera
Edited by Jacqueline Waeber

The Cambridge Companion to the Singer-Songwriter
Edited by Katherine Williams and Justin A. Williams

The Cambridge Companion to the String Quartet
Edited by Robin Stowell

The Cambridge Companion to Twentieth-Century Opera
Edited by Mervyn Cooke

The Cambridge Companion to Wagner's Der Ring des Nibelungen
Edited by Mark Berry and Nicholas Vazsonyi

The Cambridge Companion to Women in Music since 1900
Edited by Laura Hamer

Composers

The Cambridge Companion to Bach
Edited by John Butt

The Cambridge Companion to Bartók
Edited by Amanda Bayley

The Cambridge Companion to Amy Beach
Edited by E. Douglas Bomberger

The Cambridge Companion to the Beatles
Edited by Kenneth Womack

The Cambridge Companion to Beethoven
Edited by Glenn Stanley

The Cambridge Companion to Berg
Edited by Anthony Pople

The Cambridge Companion to Berlioz
Edited by Peter Bloom

The Cambridge Companion to Brahms
Edited by Michael Musgrave

The Cambridge Companion to Benjamin Britten
Edited by Mervyn Cooke

The Cambridge Companion to Bruckner
Edited by John Williamson

The Cambridge Companion to John Cage
Edited by David Nicholls

The Cambridge Companion to Chopin
Edited by Jim Samson

The Cambridge Companion to Debussy
Edited by Simon Trezise

The Cambridge Companion to Elgar
Edited by Daniel M. Grimley and Julian Rushton

The Cambridge Companion to Duke Ellington
Edited by Edward Green

The Cambridge Companion to Gershwin
Edited by Anna Celenza

The Cambridge Companion to Gilbert and Sullivan
Edited by David Eden and Meinhard Saremba

The Cambridge Companion to Handel
Edited by Donald Burrows

The Cambridge Companion to Haydn
Edited by Caryl Clark

The Cambridge Companion to Liszt
Edited by Kenneth Hamilton

The Cambridge Companion to Mahler
Edited by Jeremy Barham

The Cambridge Companion to Mendelssohn
Edited by Peter Mercer-Taylor

The Cambridge Companion to Monteverdi
Edited by John Whenham and Richard Wistreich

The Cambridge Companion to Mozart
Edited by Simon P. Keefe

The Cambridge Companion to Arvo Pärt
Edited by Andrew Shenton

The Cambridge Companion to Ravel
Edited by Deborah Mawer

The Cambridge Companion to the Rolling Stones
Edited by Victor Coelho and John Covach

The Cambridge Companion to Rossini
Edited by Emanuele Senici

The Cambridge Companion to Schoenberg
Edited by Jennifer Shaw and Joseph Auner

The Cambridge Companion to Schubert
Edited by Christopher Gibbs

The Cambridge Companion to Schumann
Edited by Beate Perrey

The Cambridge Companion to Shostakovich
Edited by Pauline Fairclough and David Fanning

The Cambridge Companion to Sibelius
Edited by Daniel M. Grimley

The Cambridge Companion to Richard Strauss
Edited by Charles Youmans

The Cambridge Companion to Michael Tippett
Edited by Kenneth Gloag and Nicholas Jones

The Cambridge Companion to Vaughan Williams
Edited by Alain Frogley and Aiden J. Thomson

The Cambridge Companion to Verdi
Edited by Scott L. Balthazar

Instruments

The Cambridge Companion to Brass Instruments
Edited by Trevor Herbert and John Wallace

The Cambridge Companion to the Cello
Edited by Robin Stowell

The Cambridge Companion to the Clarinet
Edited by Colin Lawson

The Cambridge Companion to the Guitar
Edited by Victor Coelho

The Cambridge Companion to the Harpsichord
Edited by Mark Kroll

The Cambridge Companion to the Organ
Edited by Nicholas Thistlethwaite and Geoffrey Webber

The Cambridge Companion to the Piano
Edited by David Rowland

The Cambridge Companion to the Recorder
Edited by John Mansfield Thomson

The Cambridge Companion to the Saxophone
Edited by Richard Ingham

The Cambridge Companion to Singing
Edited by John Potter

The Cambridge Companion to the Violin
Edited by Robin Stowell

The Cambridge Companion to Amy Beach

Edited by

E. DOUGLAS BOMBERGER

Elizabethtown College

Shaftesbury Road, Cambridge CB2 8EA, United Kingdom

One Liberty Plaza, 20th Floor, New York, NY 10006, USA

477 Williamstown Road, Port Melbourne, VIC 3207, Australia

314–321, 3rd Floor, Plot 3, Splendor Forum, Jasola District Centre,
New Delhi – 110025, India

103 Penang Road, #05–06/07, Visioncrest Commercial, Singapore 238467

Cambridge University Press is part of Cambridge University Press & Assessment,
a department of the University of Cambridge.

We share the University's mission to contribute to society through the pursuit of education,
learning and research at the highest international levels of excellence.

www.cambridge.org
Information on this title: www.cambridge.org/9781108845847

DOI: 10.1017/9781108991124

First published 2023

A catalogue record for this publication is available from the British Library.

Library of Congress Cataloging-in-Publication Data
Names: Bomberger, E. Douglas, 1958- editor.
Title: The Cambridge companion to Amy Beach / edited by E. Douglas Bomberger.
Description: Cambridge, United Kingdom ; New York, NY : Cambridge University Press,
2023. | Series: Cambridge companions to music | Includes bibliographical references and index.
Identifiers: LCCN 2023019806 (print) | LCCN 2023019807 (ebook) | ISBN 9781108845847
(hardback) | ISBN 9781108991124 (ebook)
Subjects: LCSH: Beach, Amy, 1867–1944. | Beach, Amy, 1867–1944 – Criticism and
interpretation. | Composers – United States – Biography. | Women composers – United
States – Biography. | Music – United States – 20th century – History and criticism. | Music –
United States – 19th century – History and criticism.
Classification: LCC ML410.B36 C35 2023 (print) | LCC ML410.B36 (ebook) |
DDC 780.92 [B]–dc23/eng/20230501
LC record available at https://lccn.loc.gov/2023019806
LC ebook record available at https://lccn.loc.gov/2023019807

ISBN 978-1-108-84584-7 Hardback
ISBN 978-1-108-96504-0 Paperback

Contents

List of Figures [*page* xi]
List of Tables [xii]
List of Music Examples [xiii]
List of Contributors [xv]
Acknowledgments [xviii]
Chronology [xx]
AMARIS WOLFE

PART I HISTORICAL CONTEXT [1]

1 Between Composer's Desk and Piano Bench: Amy Beach's Life and
Works [3]
E. DOUGLAS BOMBERGER

2 Amy Beach and the Women's Club Movement [22]
MARIAN WILSON KIMBER

3 "A Reality of Glorious Attainment": Amy Beach's MacDowell
Colony [38]
ROBIN RAUSCH

4 Amy Beach and Her Publishers [50]
BILL F. FAUCETT

PART II PROFILES OF THE MUSIC [69]

5 Amy Beach's Keyboard Music [71]
KIRSTEN JOHNSON

6 Songs of Amy Beach [93]
KATHERINE KELTON

7 "Worthy of Serious Attention": The Chamber Music of Amy
Beach [121]
R. LARRY TODD

8 The Power of Song in Beach's Orchestral Works [154]
DOUGLAS W. SHADLE

9   Choral Music   [180]
MATTHEW PHELPS

10   Beach's Dramatic Works   [201]
NICOLE POWLISON

PART III RECEPTION   [229]

11   Phoenix Redivivus: Beach's Posthumous Reputation   [231]
E. DOUGLAS BOMBERGER

Appendix: List of Works   [243]
Select Bibliography   [249]
Index   [260]

Figures

1.1 Wedding photo of Dr. and Mrs. Beach. [*page* 6]
2.1 Musicians Club of Women program for Beach's 1928 Chicago
     appearances. [28]
2.2 Composer Group of the National League of American Pen Women,
     1932. [30]
3.1 Amy Beach in the New Hampshire woods. [43]
10.1 Program and photo of *Cabildo* by Nan Bagby Stephens, 1930. [212]
10.2 Amy Beach diary entry for June 11, 1932. [215]

Tables

8.1 Amy Beach, orchestral works. [*page* 155]
8.2 Song allusions in Amy Beach's orchestral works. [161]

Music Examples

6.1   "Ecstasy," op. 19, no. 2, mm. 1–14.   [97]

6.2   "After," op. 68, mm. 71–78.   [101]

6.3   "Forget-me-not," op. 35, no. 4, mm. 55–59.   [101]

6.4   Richard Strauss, "Ständchen," op. 17, no. 2, mm. 10–12.   [106]

6.5   Beach, "Juni," op. 51, no. 3, mm. 7–8.   [106]

6.6   "The Lotos Isles," op. 76, no. 2, mm. 1–9.   [109]

6.7   "In the Twilight," op. 85, mm. 100–15.   [112]

7.1   Beach, "Sweetheart, Sigh No More," op. 14, no. 3, mm. 1–6.   [124]

7.2   Beach, *Romance*, op. 23, mm. bars 1–6.   [124]

7.3a Beach, Violin Sonata in A minor, op. 34/I, mm. bars 1–7.   [126]

7.3b Reduction.   [126]

7.4   Beach, Violin Sonata in A minor, op. 34/I, mm. 63–71.   [127]

7.5   Beach, Violin Sonata in A minor, op. 34/II, mm. 1–5.   [128]

7.6   Beach, Violin Sonata in A minor, op. 34/II, Più lento,
      mm. 1–3.   [129]

7.7   Beach, Violin Sonata in A minor, op. 34/III, mm. 14–15.   [129]

7.8a Brahms, Symphony No. 4, op. 98/IV, mm. 113–18.   [130]

7.8b Beach, Violin Sonata in A minor, op. 34/III, last six measures.   [131]

7.9   Beach, Violin Sonata in A minor, op. 34/IV, mm. 13–16.   [132]

7.10 Beach, Violin Sonata in A minor, op. 34/IV, mm. 47–51.   [132]

7.11 Beach, Violin Sonata in A minor, op. 34/IV, mm. 97–102.   [133]

7.12a Brahms, Piano Quintet in F minor, op. 34/I, mm. 1–4 and
      reduction.   [134]

7.12b Brahms, Piano Quintet in F minor, op. 34/I, mm. 12–16 and
      reduction.   [135]

7.13a Brahms, Piano Quintet in F minor, op. 34/IV, mm. 252–60.   [135]

7.13b Beach, Piano Quintet in F♯ minor, op. 67/I, mm. 1–24.   [136]

7.14 Reduction of Example 7.13b.   [137]

7.15 Beach, Piano Quintet in F♯ minor, op. 67/I, mm. 25–28.   [138]

7.16 Beach, Piano Quintet in F♯ minor, op. 67/I, mm. 73–79.   [139]

7.17 Beach, Piano Quintet in F♯ minor, op. 67/I, tetrachordal
      summary.   [139]

7.18   Beach, Piano Quintet in F♯ minor, op. 67/II, mm. 1–8.   [140]

7.19   Beach, Piano Quintet in F♯ minor, op. 67/III, mm. 311–14.   [141]

7.20   Beach, "An Indian Lullaby," op. 57, no. 3, mm. 1–4.   [143]

7.21   Beach, Theme and Variations, op. 80, Variation 1,
        mm. 37–43.   [144]

7.22   Beach, Theme and Variations, op. 80, Variation 5,
        mm. 51–54.   [145]

7.23   Beach, String Quartet, op. 89, mm. 1–14.   [146]

7.24a   Beach, String Quartet, op. 89, mm. 15–19.   [147]

7.24b   Beach, String Quartet, op. 89, mm. 263–74.   [147]

7.25   Beach, Piano Trio, op. 150/I, mm. 1–6.   [149]

7.26a   Beach, Piano Trio, op. 150/II, mm. 1–3.   [150]

7.26b   Beach, Piano Trio, op. 150/II, mm. 33–42.   [150]

 8.1   Comparison of the opening melodies of Beach's "Wouldn't that be
        Queer," op. 26, no. 4, and *Bal Masqué*.   [163]

 8.2   Comparison of the principal themes of (1) Dvořák's Symphony
        "From the New World," movement IV; (2) the opening of Beach's
        Piano Concerto, op. 45, movement I; and (3) Beach's song, "Jeune fille
        et jeune fleur," op. 1, no. 3.   [168]

10.1   *Eilende Wolken, Segler der Lüfte*, mm. 79–95.   [204]

10.2   *Jephthah's Daughter*, mm. 44–53.   [207]

10.3a   Habanera rhythm written in Amy Beach's "Notes on Creole Folk
        Music."   [219]

10.3b   *Cabildo*, The "Governor's Ball," mm. 294–301.   [219]

Contributors

E. DOUGLAS BOMBERGER is Professor of Music at Elizabethtown College, where he teaches music history and piano. His research explores nineteenth-century music of the United States and European-American transnational connections. His doctoral dissertation research on nineteenth-century American music students in Germany was supported by a fellowship from the Deutscher Akademischer Austauschdienst (DAAD). His book *MacDowell* (Oxford, 2013) received a subvention from the AMS John Daverio Fund. He served as nineteenth-century editor for the *Grove Dictionary of American Music* (Oxford, 2013) and has been elected president of the Society for American Music (2023–25).

BILL F. FAUCETT is the author of *Music in Boston: Composers, Events, and Ideas, 1852–1918* (Lexington, 2016), *George Whitefield Chadwick: The Life and Music of "The Pride of New England"* (Northeastern University Press, 2012), and other volumes. An experienced arts administrator and fundraiser, Faucett has held positions at the Raymond F. Kravis Center for the Performing Arts, the Florida Orchestra, and the David A. Straz Jr. Center for the Performing Arts. He is currently an advancement professional at the University of South Florida. Faucett is an independent scholar.

KIRSTEN JOHNSON has recorded the complete piano works of Amy Beach in a four-CD set, including many world premieres and unpublished works available only in manuscript. Her championing of American piano music also includes two discs of Florence Price's piano pieces (Guild, 2022); and the complete works of Arthur Foote (Delos), James Hewitt (Centaur), and Benjamin Carr (Centaur). Dr. Johnson earned her Doctor of Musical Arts from the University of Missouri–Kansas City under a Kemper Doctoral Fellowship. Her doctoral research became the basis of her first CD: *Këngë: Albanian Piano Music*. Dr. Johnson later researched Dmitri Kabalevsky's music, making the first recording of Dmitri Kabalevsky's *Three Preludes for Piano*, op. 1, which she discovered in a Paris library and then edited for publication. For more information on Dr. Johnson's music and recordings, please visit www.kirstenjohnsonpiano.com.

KATHERINE KELTON has enjoyed an eclectic singing career that has included solo recital and oratorio work, in addition to extensive professional choral singing. Her CD, *Amy Beach: Songs* (Naxos, 2004), has introduced Beach's songs to a worldwide audience and contributed to their regaining their rightful place within the body of art song literature. Formerly Associate Professor of Music at Butler and Pittsburg State Universities, she received DMA and MM degrees in Applied Voice from the University of Texas at Austin. She has been active in the National Association of Teachers of Singing on the national level and has been a contributor to *American Music, American Music Teacher,* and *Classical Singer Magazine*, among other publications. In addition to her advocacy for Amy Beach's songs, Kelton's work focuses on phonetics and vocal composition.

MATTHEW PHELPS is Minister of Music at West End United Methodist Church in Nashville, Founder and Artistic Director of Vocal Arts Nashville, the Artistic Director of Collegium Cincinnati, and a faculty member at Lipscomb University. He has performed as a pianist, organist, and conductor throughout the nation. Dr. Phelps has presented and performed at conferences of the American Choral Directors Association, the Hymn Society, the American Guild of Organists, and the National Pastoral Musicians. His critical edition of Amy Beach's *Grand Mass in E-Flat Major* is published by A-R Editions.

NICOLE POWLISON received her master's and doctoral degrees in historical musicology from Florida State University. Dr. Powlison's research interests also include the history of opera in the United States, the history of music publishing, music history pedagogy, ludomusicology, and music of the medieval and Renaissance eras. She lectures on popular music, American music, music research skills, and other topics in musicology at the University of Maryland, and she is a professional arts administrator for nonprofit music organizations in Northern Virginia.

ROBIN RAUSCH is Head of Reader Services in the Music Division at the Library of Congress in Washington, DC. She has published on the history of the MacDowell Colony in *Very Good for an American: Essays on Edward MacDowell* (Pendragon, 2017); *The Grove Dictionary of American Music*, 2nd edition (Oxford, 2013); *Women in the Arts: Eccentric Essays in Music, Visual Arts, and Literature* (Cambridge Scholars Publishing, 2010); *A Place for the Arts: the MacDowell Colony, 1907–2007* (The MacDowell Colony, 2006); and *American Women: A Library of Congress Guide for the Study of*

Women's History and Culture in the United States (Library of Congress, 2002).

DOUGLAS W. SHADLE is Associate Professor of Musicology at the Vanderbilt University Blair School of Music. He is the author of *Orchestrating the Nation: The Nineteenth-Century American Symphonic Enterprise* (Oxford, 2016) and *Antonín Dvořák's New World Symphony* (Oxford, 2021). With Samantha Ege, he is coauthoring a biography of composer Florence B. Price for Oxford University Press's Master Musicians Series.

R. LARRY TODD is Arts and Sciences Professor at Duke University. Among his books are *Mendelssohn: A Life in Music (Felix Mendelssohn Bartholdy: Sein Leben, seine Musik), Fanny Hensel: The Other Mendelssohn*, and, with Marc Moskovitz, *Beethoven's Cello: Five Revolutionary Sonatas and Their World*. He has published essays on topics ranging from Obrecht, Haydn, and Mozart to the Mendelssohns, Schumanns, Liszt, Joachim, Brahms, Richard Strauss, and Webern. A former fellow of the Guggenheim Foundation, he edits the Master Musician Series for Oxford University Press and has issued with Nancy Green the cello works of the Mendelssohns (JRI Recordings).

MARIAN WILSON KIMBER is Professor of Musicology at the University of Iowa. Her research has explored issues related to historiography, gender, performance, and musical reception. Wilson Kimber's numerous publications have treated Felix Mendelssohn, Fanny Mendelssohn Hensel, women's musical activities, and the role of poetic recitation in concert life. Her book, *The Elocutionists: Women, Music, and the Spoken Word* (University of Illinois Press, 2017) won the H. Earle Johnson Subvention from the Society for American Music. Wilson Kimber is a founding member of the duo Red Vespa, which performs comic spoken word pieces by women composers.

Acknowledgments

Editing the *Cambridge Companion to Amy Beach* has been a joy and a privilege because of the dedication of the contributors. Each of them approached the task with enthusiasm for the subject and flexibility when challenges arose. They each brought unique perspectives and disciplinary orientations to their assigned topics, resulting in essays that are uniquely suited to the varied aspects of Beach's long and fruitful career. I am also grateful to Kate Brett and her colleagues at Cambridge University Press for supporting this project and seeing it to completion in a professional manner.

All of us who value the music of Amy Beach are indebted to the research pioneers who make our work possible. Adrienne Fried Block's numerous writings, especially her award-winning biography, *Amy Beach, Passionate Victorian* (1998), established the scholarly foundation on which this study rests. Barbara White and William Ross of the University of New Hampshire's Milne Special Collections Library created a peerless collection of archival source materials for us to consult. The list of new recordings of Beach's music grows each year, owing in equal part to dedicated performers and receptive record companies.

I am grateful to Elizabethtown College for several sources of funding. A faculty grant supported research visits to New Hampshire in 2021 and 2022 as well as numerous day trips to the Library of Congress. The college's Summer Creative Arts and Research Program (SCARP) was crucial in completing the manuscript preparation in summer 2022. Amaris Wolfe, the SCARP recipient, was very helpful in a variety of tasks from database searching to proofreading. She demonstrated a special skill in preparing musical examples. My colleagues and students in the music department have afforded many opportunities to present my findings in seminars as well as to perform Beach's works in campus concerts.

This book was written under the shadow of the coronavirus pandemic, and the research has made us grateful for the printed music and secondary literature available online or through interlibrary loan but also acutely aware that many important documents relating to Beach and her music are available only as archival sources. We are deeply indebted to Robin

Rausch, Paul Sommerfeld, and their colleagues at the Library of Congress Music Division, along with Bill Ross at the Milne Special Collections Library at the University of New Hampshire, for fielding questions during the shutdown and for allowing us to visit their research collections as early as possible in the summer of 2021. We must also acknowledge that without the heroic work of health care workers in our communities and research scientists at pharmaceutical companies, we would not have been able to enjoy this window of availability.

Finally, I wish to acknowledge that the reason for my ongoing interest in and advocacy for Amy Beach has always been her compelling music. I thank Marmaduke Miles, whose recital of Beach's solo piano works in the University of North Carolina's Hill Hall ignited a flame that has burned ever since. I am grateful to my piano teachers, including Marvin Blickenstaff and Bradford Gowen, who coached me on Beach works that were previously unfamiliar to them but related to the Romantic piano literature they knew. I appreciate the willingness of my piano students, particularly Anthony Beer and Sarah Palatnik, to immerse themselves in Beach's works and perform them publicly. I am grateful to David Sariti and Emily Derstine, who helped me internalize the Violin Sonata through their performances with me. Most importantly, I cannot express enough gratitude to my wife, soprano Teresa Bomberger, whose countless performances of Beach's solo songs have given me insights into the beauties of this music that are only matched by her insightful critiques of my attempts to express those beauties in writing.

Chronology

September 5, 1867	Amy Marcy Cheney is born in Henniker, New Hampshire, to Clara Imogene (Marcy) Cheney and Charles Abbott Cheney.	
1871	Clara Cheney allows her child to sit at the piano for the first time. Amy Cheney is able to pick out tunes and harmonize them from memory. Starting at age six, mother and daughter hold lessons in their home three times a week.	"Mamma's Waltz"
1876	Amy Cheney begins piano study with Ernst Perabo. Mentors recommend that Amy be sent to Europe, but her mother declines.	"Air and Variations" (1877) "Minuetto" (1877) "Romanza" (1877) "Petite Waltz" (1878)

By Amaris Wolfe.

1881	Cheney begins to study harmony with Junius Welch Hill at Wellesley College. She takes lessons for only one year.	
1882	Cheney ends her study with Perabo and begins study with Carl Baermann, a pupil of Liszt. Amy also begins to educate herself on counterpoint and orchestration by examining works of prominent composers such as J. S. Bach.	
October 24, 1883	Amy Cheney gives her official debut, performing in Alfred P. Peck's Anniversary Concert in Boston.	
January 9, 1884	Cheney's first public recital is given at Chickering Hall in Boston.	"A Rainy Day" (1884)
February 1885	Cheney's composition, "With Violets," is published by the Arthur P. Schmidt Company.	"With Violets," op. 1, no. 1 (1885)
March 28, 1885	Amy Cheney performs Chopin's Concerto in F minor, op. 21, in her debut with the Boston Symphony Orchestra.	

December 2, 1885	At age 18, Amy Marcy Cheney is married to Henry Harris Aubrey Beach, a prominent Boston physician. In accordance with Henry's wishes, Amy limits her public piano performances and turns to composing under her married name, Mrs. H. H. A. Beach. The couple reside at 28 Commonwealth Avenue in Boston.	*Valse Caprice*, op. 4 (1889) Grand Mass in E-flat major, op. 5 (1890) "Empress of the Night," op. 2 (1891)
February 7, 1892	The Handel and Haydn Society of Boston performs Beach's first major work, the Grand Mass in E-flat major, op. 5.	*Festival Jubilate*, op. 17 (1891) *Sketches*, op. 15 (1892)
May 1– October 30, 1893	Several of Beach's works are performed at the World's Columbian Exposition in Chicago.	"Ecstasy," op. 19, no. 2 (1893) *Romance*, op. 23 (1893)
November 21, 1894	Beach begins composing the first movement of her "Gaelic" Symphony, basing many of the work's themes on Gaelic folk tunes.	*Ballade*, op. 6 (1894) *Bal Masqué*, op. 22 (1894)

October 31, 1896	The Boston Symphony Orchestra performs Beach's "Gaelic" Symphony, op. 32, under Emil Paur's baton. This work is met with outstanding success.	"Gaelic" Symphony, op. 32 (1896) *Three Shakespeare Songs*, op. 37 (1897)
April 7, 1900	Amy Beach premieres her Piano Concerto in C-sharp minor, op. 45, with the Boston Symphony Orchestra.	Sonata in A minor for Piano and Violin, op. 34 (1899) *Three Browning Songs*, op. 44 (1900)
February 8, 1905	Amy Beach premieres her *Variations on Balkan Themes*, op. 60, a large-scale work for solo piano.	*Variations on Balkan Themes*, op. 60 (1904) *The Sea-Fairies*, op. 59 (1904) Service in A, op. 63 (1906)
June 28, 1910	Henry Harris Aubrey Beach dies of infection following a fall.	*Four Eskimo Pieces*, op. 64 (1907) *The Chambered Nautilus*, op. 66 (1907) Quintet for Piano and Strings, op. 67 (1907)
February 18, 1911	Amy Beach's mother dies.	
September 5, 1911	Newly widowed, Amy Beach sets sail for her European tour, where she promotes her own music outside the United States for the first time.	

1911–1914	Amy Beach's compositions are met with popularity in Germany, especially her larger works.	
September 18, 1914	Shortly after the outbreak of World War I, Amy Beach arrives in New York after her three-year tour.	
February 1915	Amy Beach begins renting an apartment in New York City, leaving her residence at 28 Commonwealth Avenue behind.	
1915–1916	Beach continues to travel and perform throughout the United States, mainly California.	*Panama Hymn*, op. 74 (1915)
February 1918	Amy Beach relocates to Hillsborough, New Hampshire, along with her aunt and cousin.	
Summer 1921	Beach begins her visits to the MacDowell Colony in Peterborough, New Hampshire. She would stay at the Colony periodically over the next twenty years. Beach divides her time between the Colony, her New York apartment, and her two homes.	*Hermit Thrush Pieces*, op. 92 (1921) *From Grandmother's Garden*, op. 97 (1922)

1925	The Society of American Women Composers is founded. Beach serves the organization as president until 1928 and honorary president until 1932.	
June 18, 1928	Amy Beach receives an honorary master's degree from the University of New Hampshire. The university president later expresses regret that the university did not award her an honorary doctorate instead.	*The Canticle of the Sun*, op. 123 (1928) *Christ in the Universe*, op. 132 (1931)
June 18, 1932	Beach completes her one-act opera, *Cabildo*, op. 149.	*Cabildo*, op. 149 (1932)
April 23, 1934	Beach is summoned to the White House by Eleanor Roosevelt to accompany soprano Ruth Shaffner.	
April 17, 1936	Beach is invited to perform at the White House again with Shaffner.	
March 19, 1940	Amy Beach's last performance takes place in Brooklyn with violinist Carl Tollefsen and cellist Willem Durieux. Shortly after, doctors forbid her to play piano due to deteriorating health.	Trio, op. 150 (1939)

November 27–28, 1942	A festival is held in honor of Beach's 75th birthday at the Phillips Gallery in Washington, DC. Bashka Paeff's plaster bust of Beach is displayed, and several concerts entirely comprised of Beach's compositions are performed.	
December 27, 1944	Amy Marcy Cheney Beach passes away of heart disease in her New York apartment, attended by Ruth Shaffner.	*Pax nobiscum* (1944)

PART I

Historical Context

1 | Between Composer's Desk and Piano Bench

Amy Beach's Life and Works

E. DOUGLAS BOMBERGER

> I have literally lived the life of two people – one a pianist, the other a writer. Anything more unlike than the state of mind demanded by these two professions I could not imagine! When I do one kind of work, I shut the other up in a closed room and lock the door, unless I happen to be composing for the piano, in which case there is a connecting link. One great advantage, however, in this kind of life, is that one never grows stale, but there is always a continual interest and freshness from the change back and forth.
>
> – Amy Beach[1]

The eighteenth-century ideal of a master musician equally skilled as performer and composer – exemplified by Bach, Haydn, and Mozart – became increasingly rare in the nineteenth century. Despite noteworthy exceptions like Mendelssohn, Liszt, and Rachmaninoff, most musicians specialized in one or another aspect of musical production, and their choices were reinforced by the expectations of critics and audiences. In assessing the life and career of Amy Marcy Cheney Beach (1867–1944), it is enlightening to view her as one of those rare individuals who achieved fame as both a performer and a composer. The decision to vacillate between composer's desk and piano bench was not entirely her own, but it is crucial to a complete understanding of her significance.

Beach's origin story – like those of Mozart and Mendelssohn – centers on her role as a child prodigy. Her mother reported that the precocious child had a repertoire of forty tunes before her first birthday, and that she could improvise a simple harmony to her mother's melody before her second birthday. She exhibited early evidence of perfect pitch, along with a synesthetic association of colors with pitches and keys. This association was so strong that as a toddler she cried if adults sang a song that she knew in a different key than she had learned, and as a six-year-old she transposed a piano piece up a step to accommodate for an out-of-tune piano at a friend's house.[2]

In a 1914 article entitled "Why I Chose My Profession," Beach recalled that her mother, "who was a fine musician and wanted to raise one," subscribed to Gerald Stanley Lee's "top bureau-drawer principle" of education, in which a student's motivation is stimulated by keeping a desired object just out of reach.[3] In her case, this meant that the family piano, which Clara Cheney played often, was off limits to her daughter Amy during her toddler years. The future composer and pianist was obsessed with music and thought about it constantly, but she was limited to singing until the age of four or five, when a visiting aunt granted her access to the instrument. Amy was then able to play the songs that she had been singing and to improvise accompaniments as she had seen her mother do. When she was six, her mother consented to giving her lessons, and by the age of seven, her playing of a Beethoven sonata and Chopin waltz was sufficiently advanced that her parents received offers from several music managers. These were declined, and Amy's public performances were curtailed.

The family moved from her birthplace of Henniker, New Hampshire, to Chelsea, Massachusetts, around 1871, and from there to Boston in 1875. This opened a new world of educational possibilities, and Amy had the opportunity to study piano with professional teachers, first Ernst Perabo (1845–1920) and later Carl Baermann (1839–1913). Both had been trained in German conservatories, and it may have been they who reportedly advised Beach's parents to send her abroad for a European musical education. By this time, German musical education had become the preferred professional training for any American who could afford it,[4] but again Amy's parents refused to consider this course of action.

Adrienne Fried Block explored the motivations and results of the restrictions placed on Amy's musical opportunities by her parents. She argued that the "top bureau-drawer principle" was an outgrowth of Protestant religious practices in child-rearing, and that her parents' decisions prioritized Amy's eternal salvation over her musical development.[5] There is an additional explanation, however, that may have unconsciously played into their deliberations.

Amy's parents, Charles Abbot Cheney (1844–95) and Clara Imogene Marcy Cheney (1845–1911), were members of the Progressive Generation (born 1843–59), whose worldview was shaped by the political polarization and harrowing losses of the Civil War. When they became parents, this cohort of Americans prioritized home comforts and security over adventure and risk. Their children, known as the Missionary Generation (born 1860–82), grew up in the 1870s loved and protected in ways that would not be replicated until the Baby Boomer childhood of the 1950s. When the

Missionary Generation reached adulthood, full of confidence and accustomed to having their wishes fulfilled, they set out to change the world as missionaries, civic leaders, and reformers. These generational characteristics help to explain Clara's need to restrict her daughter's public activities as well as Amy's desire for a public career.[6]

Beach's recollection of the next stage of her life is telling. She wrote, "When I was sixteen, I was allowed to make my début in Boston. I played the Moscheles G minor concerto with a large orchestra. Life was beginning!"[7] This October 1883 debut, so long deferred, was an unalloyed triumph. The *Boston Transcript* gushed:

> She is plainly a pianist to the manner born and bred. Her technique is facile, even and brilliant; her use of the pedal exceptionally good. But fine as her technical qualifications are, it is the correctness and precocity of her musical understanding that must, in the end, most excite admiration. Much natural musical sentiment must, of course, be taken for granted; but the purity and breadth of her phrasing, the intelligence with which she grasps the relation of the several parts of a composition to the whole, show how thoroughly musical her training must have been. That she does not play like a woman of forty need not be said. The ineffable charm of her playing is that perfect youthful freshness, directness and simplicity of sentiment which belongs to her age, but which one very rarely finds so utterly free from the little awkwardnesses which are also wont to characterize immaturity.[8]

Praise like this can open doors for a young performer, and now that her parents' permission had been granted, Amy played frequently in solo recitals, chamber music, and concerto performances throughout the Boston area. On March 28, 1885, she debuted with the Boston Symphony Orchestra under the baton of Wilhelm Gericke in the Chopin Concerto in F minor, op. 21, earning praise for her sensitive interpretation of this notoriously challenging work. A month later, she famously impressed America's leading conductor, Theodore Thomas, when he conducted her in a performance of the Mendelssohn Concerto. He assumed that a seventeen-year-old girl would not be able to handle the brisk tempo of the finale, but when she heard his slow tempo, she "swung the orchestra into time," to the amusement of all present.[9] She proved herself equally adept at solo recitals and chamber music, making inroads with the most prominent musicians in Boston's close-knit professional circle.[10] It seems that in her teens she already possessed the technique, artistic sensitivity, and fearlessness that are the essential ingredients of a successful performance career. She also possessed unusually large hands, with broad palms and very long thumbs, as shown in Figure 1.1.

Figure 1.1 Wedding photo of Dr. and Mrs. Beach. Box 17 envelope 15, Amy Cheney Beach (Mrs. H. H. A. Beach) Papers, 1835–1956, MC 51, Milne Special Collections and Archives, University of New Hampshire Library, Durham, NH.

But on December 2, 1885, Amy's career trajectory shifted dramatically with her marriage to Dr. Henry Harris Aubrey Beach (1843–1910). Their engagement had been announced in the Boston papers in mid-August, but it is unclear how the two met.[11] A prominent surgeon at Massachusetts General Hospital and lecturer at Harvard University who was actively building a private practice treating Boston's wealthiest and most socially connected residents, Beach was a 42-year-old widower when he married the 18-year-old Amy. She moved into his home at 28 Commonwealth Avenue, Boston's exclusive, tree-lined counterpart to New York's Park Avenue. She immediately took his name, and for the rest of her life was known in the United States as "Mrs. H. H. A. Beach." Her new home came with a staff of servants, allowing her to devote all her time to music and her husband. The spacious second-floor music room contained a grand piano, ample shelf space for her growing collection of books and scores, and a bay window facing north onto the trees of Commonwealth Avenue. A reporter who described the room in 1897 noted, "A quaint empire desk inlaid in various light woods tells the place where all Mrs. Beach's best and most serious work has been done, and it is considered a family friend and treasure."[12]

Dr. Beach's position in Boston society was worth protecting, which may help to explain – but not justify – the stipulations he placed on his young bride. She was not to play concerts for money, but rather to donate her fees to charitable causes. During the twenty-five years of their marriage, she averaged one solo recital per year, often advertised prominently as a benefit for a specific charity. She was allowed to accept invitations to play chamber music or concerto performances with orchestra more often, but again the fees were donated to charity. She was also not to teach piano lessons, which were associated with working women of a lower class. She was expected to serve as hostess on social occasions as appropriate for a female member of Boston's elite Brahmin set. These stipulations clearly changed her status in the city. When Amy played the Mozart Concerto in D minor with the Boston Symphony Orchestra on February 20, 1886 (less than three months after her marriage), she donated her fees to the free-bed fund of the Massachusetts General Hospital, and her concert two weeks later was for the "kindergarten entertainment at Mr. Robert Treat Paine's."[13] The *Boston Transcript* review of the BSO concert was considerably less specific about her playing than that of the previous year. The reviewer stated: "Mrs. Beach, who was enthusiastically received by the audience, played it very beautifully indeed; especially fine was her playing of the Romanza (second movement); she struck the true keynote of Mozart's grace." He then went on a lengthy diatribe about the cadenza chosen for the performance, without another word about her playing.[14] The impression is of a reviewer who does not wish to say too much.

Again, Amy found her career path circumscribed by a member of the Progressive Generation. If Dr. Beach restricted her performance career, however, he had bold plans for her compositional career. It is unclear why he saw potential in her as a composer, since at the time of her marriage she had published only two songs with piano accompaniment. "The Rainy Day" (published by Oliver Ditson in 1883) was a setting of a Longfellow poem whose vocal line begins with a direct quotation from the third movement of Beethoven's "Pathetique" Sonata, op. 13, transposed from C minor to F minor. "With Violets," op. 1, no. 1 (Arthur P. Schmidt, 1885) was a setting of a poem by Kate Vannah dedicated to the opera star Adelina Patti. Dr. Beach also had intimate knowledge of a third song, however: on

January 16, 1885, he had sung her unpublished song "Jeune fille, jeune fleur" on a recital of voice students of Mr. L. W. Wheeler.[15] These songs are pleasant and sentimental but do not show the maturity and technique that reviewers had praised in her piano playing. More to the point, they contain no inkling of the large-scale works that would eventually become her most distinctive creations. Nonetheless, the couple agreed that she would devote the bulk of her time to composition rather than performance. As an added incentive, she was allowed to keep the publication royalties her compositions generated.[16]

Beach's composition training had been limited to one year of harmony and music theory lessons with Junius Welch Hill (1840–1916). In 1885, Amy's parents had consulted the recently appointed conductor of the Boston Symphony Orchestra, Wilhelm Gericke (1845–1925), who recommended that she learn composition by studying scores of European masters rather than studying with a composition teacher.[17] After her marriage, Henry urged her to follow the same course. A conscientious student, she acquired the best books available on orchestration and counterpoint, along with a substantial collection of scores. These she studied carefully to develop the skills she would need to go beyond songwriting. It is a testament to her discipline and innate talent that her autodidactic approach yielded remarkable results and gave her the tools for a successful compositional career. In later years, she gave credit to her husband and mother for developing her into a composer:

When Dr. Beach and I were married, he felt that my future lay in composition, and very often he and I would discuss works as I was preparing them. He might differ as to certain expressions and so would my mother, with the result that I had two critics before facing a professional critic. And Dr. Beach would be very impartial and hard-boiled.[18]

The following twenty-five years saw Beach's most productive period of compositional activity and a steady trajectory of growth. Her first major work – which will be discussed in the chapter by Matthew Phelps – was a setting of the Latin Mass for choir, soloists, and orchestra. The work was premiered by the Boston Handel and Haydn Society on February 7, 1892, a reflection of the Boston musical establishment's support for their home-town composer. Her next major work was a symphony that made extensive use of Irish folk themes. Known as the "Gaelic" Symphony, it was written in the shadow of American debates over musical nationalism spurred by the New York residency of Antonín Dvořák from 1892 to 1895 and was premiered by the BSO on October 31, 1896. This performance elicited a much-quoted note of appreciation from her fellow Boston composer George Whitefield Chadwick, who confirmed her position in the inner circle of local musicians: "I always feel a thrill of pride myself whenever I hear a fine new work by any one of us, and as such you will have to be counted in, whether you will or not – one of the boys."[19] The experience she gained in orchestrating her symphony prepared her for her next orchestral work, the Piano Concerto in C-sharp minor, completed and performed with the BSO in 1900. These two works will be analyzed in Douglas Shadle's chapter on the orchestral works.

Beach enjoyed a fruitful relationship with the Kneisel Quartet and its first violinist, Franz Kneisel (1865–1926). She performed major chamber works with them, including the Schumann Piano Quintet, op. 44, in 1894 and the Brahms Piano Quintet, op. 34, in 1900. Her familiarity with these works, along with her relationship with Kneisel, informed the composition of her Violin Sonata, op. 34 (1896), and Piano Quintet in F-sharp minor, op. 67 (1907). Both are serious works whose virtuosity is used not for empty display but for the exploration of serious thematic connections. Beach's engagement with the European cosmopolitan tradition in these works will be the subject of Larry Todd's chapter on the chamber music.

The major works that Beach wrote and premiered between 1892 and 1907 represent much more than the determined efforts of an autodidact. Beach (and by extension her principal patron, her husband) directly confronted the assertions of George P. Upton in his influential 1880 book *Woman in Music*. Writing five years before Beach's marriage, Upton acknowledged that women had successfully created serious works of painting, poetry, and fiction but had achieved nothing comparable in music:

[W]ho is to represent woman in the higher realm of music? While a few women, during the last two centuries, have created a few works, now mostly unknown, no woman during that time has written either an opera, oratorio, symphony, or instrumental work of large dimensions that is in the modern repertory. Man has been the creative representative."[20]

He went on to assert that the proper role of women in music was as muse to great men. In the home at 28 Commonwealth Avenue, this hierarchy was reversed, as Dr. Beach played the role of muse and his wife created works in the major cosmopolitan genres that Upton had declared to be the province of men alone because of their ability "to treat emotions as if they were mathematics, to bind and measure and limit them within the rigid laws of harmony and counterpoint."[21] Beach's choral, orchestral, and chamber works put the lie to Upton's claim that women lacked the intellectual facility to plan and create works of integrity in these genres. Of her husband's role in her compositional development, Beach later recalled,

> It was he more than any one else who encouraged my interest upon the field of musical composition in the larger forms. It was pioneer work, at least for this country, for a woman to do, and I was fearful that I had not the skill to carry it on, but his constant assurance that I could do the work, and keen criticism whenever it seemed to be weak in spots, gave me the courage to go on.[22]

As Beach produced ever more ambitious concert works in the major genres of Western music, she continued to broaden her pianistic repertoire in her annual benefit recitals. These events sometimes included her own piano works, but their primary focus was European solo piano literature from the Baroque to Romantic eras. During the 1890s and 1900s, she composed a steady stream of shorter solo works with programmatic titles, including the Four Sketches, op. 15 (1892) and the Trois morceaux caractéristiques, op. 28 (1894). Curiously, she never composed a piano sonata, but in 1904 she produced a solo piano work that was a worthy companion to her major works in other genres. The Variations on Balkan Themes, op. 60 (1904), is a 30-minute compendium of virtuoso techniques that introduces and develops four songs shared with her by a missionary to Bulgaria. The poignancy of the first of these songs, "O Maiko moyá," inspired some of her most evocative pianistic writing. Her extensive catalog of piano compositions is explored in Kirsten Johnson's chapter.

The preceding works demonstrate that Beach took seriously the imperative of composing in the major concert genres, but it was her solo songs that gained her a national following. In a 1918 interview, she explained how her composition of songs differed from her work on more "serious" genres:

> I write, primarily, for instruments – my song writing I have always considered rather as recreation. When I am working on some larger work, as when I was writing my piano Concerto, I will occasionally find myself tiring – "going stale," as they say. Then I just drop the larger work for the day and write a song. It freshens me up; I really consider that I have given myself a special treat when I have written a song. In this way I have written about a hundred songs.[23]

As Katherine Kelton discusses in her chapter, Beach's art songs spanned the entirety of her career and drew from a vast array of textual sources. At their best, they contain tuneful melodies that lie well in the voice, supported by piano accompaniments that enhance but do not overpower the vocal lines. Her early song "Ecstasy," op. 19, no. 2 (1892), was so successful that its royalties financed the purchase of a vacation home in Centerville on

Cape Cod.[24] Several of her song sets strike a balance between the serious aspirations of her instrumental works and the lighter tone of her parlor songs, most notably the *Three Shakespeare Songs*, op. 37 (1897), and the *Three Browning Songs*, op. 44 (1900). Her setting of Elizabeth Barrett Browning's poem "When soul is joined to soul," op. 62 (1905), illustrates her Romantic penchant for communicating emotion through harmony in procedures reminiscent of her contemporaries Wolf and Mahler.

As Beach's reputation grew, she found herself in demand as a composer for women's events at international expositions outside of the Boston area. She was commissioned to write *Festival Jubilate*, op. 17, for the 1893 World's Columbian Exposition in Chicago as well as a *Hymn of Welcome*, op. 42, for the 1898 Trans-Mississippi International Exposition in Omaha, Nebraska. She would later be called upon to write a *Panama Hymn*, op. 74, for the 1915 Panama–Pacific International Exposition in San Francisco. These occasional pieces were too specific to have a significant afterlife, but they reflected her reputation as a leading American composer.

Beach's growing stature in Boston circles and her national reputation were materially aided by the support of Arthur P. Schmidt (1846–1921), a German immigrant who made his fortune as a music publisher in Boston. Schmidt was so grateful for the opportunities afforded him in the United States that he made a practice of promoting American composers, even when their works were not highly remunerative.[25] He was also a patient of Dr. Beach who was grateful for the medical care he received. The extensive correspondence between the publisher and the two Beaches demonstrates a close friendship as well as an important professional relationship.[26] Schmidt was Amy's sole publisher during her twenty-five-year marriage, and his carefully prepared editions of nearly all the works she composed during this era contributed to her growing reputation. He afforded her the courtesy of multiple proofs, allowing her to develop high standards and an assiduous skill at proofreading. In 1906, he published a handsome 134-page booklet with a biographical essay by the eminent music theorist Percy Goetschius (1853–1943), a complete work list, and extensive excerpts from positive reviews.[27] She used this pamphlet frequently for publicity purposes in the following years. Bill Faucett's chapter chronicles the importance of Schmidt to her early career as well as her subsequent turn to other publishers.

The death of Beach's husband on June 28, 1910, brought an end to her comfortable life in Boston society and initiated a series of events that proved transformational for the rest of her life. Adrienne Fried Block's detective work has demonstrated that Beach was not a wealthy widow, as was generally assumed. She speculates that – unknown to Amy – the couple may have been living beyond their means, as Dr. Beach left her only a small inheritance, including the heavily mortgaged house on Commonwealth Avenue. Within a short time, she dismissed the servants and moved with her ailing mother to the Hotel Brunswick. In October, Beach declined Schmidt's offer of an advance on future royalties, writing instead:

Whatever can come from the sale of my compositions will be a <u>great</u> help to me, until I am strong enough to take up other musical work. Therefore I shall appreciate gratefully any increase of advertising or other placing of my work before the public that you may see fit to undertake.[28]

In a subsequent letter freighted with symbolic as well as practical significance, Beach offered to return the works of art that Schmidt had given to her husband as gifts over the years of their friendship.[29] He refused to take them back, but there is no evidence that he acceded to her wishes for increased advertising of her works.

Her mother's death on February 18, 1911, deepened her grief while paradoxically removing the last impediment to a new life, and she took a bold step in that direction by sailing for Europe on September 5, 1911, her forty-fourth birthday. She had never been out of the country before, and she sailed with the intention not of taking a grand tour but rather of reestablishing her career as a performer. She lived for the next three years in the Pension Pfanner in Munich, the same hotel as soprano Marcella Craft (1874–1959), who had accompanied her on the transatlantic crossing. Dr. and Mrs. Beach had known the Indiana-born Craft since her days as a vocal student in Boston in 1898; now she was a leading singer with the Bavarian Opera, where she had sung under the direction of Richard Strauss. Beach spent her first year soaking up the culture by attending concerts and playing in private gatherings at which Craft introduced her to prominent German and expatriate American musicians.

By the fall of 1912, Beach had engaged a concert manager, who scheduled a series of concerts for her under the name of Amy Beach. She later described to an interviewer her reluctance to drop her husband's name after so many years, but the decision was made in the interest of promoting her to a European public that had no knowledge of her husband or his position in Boston society.[30] In the fall of 1912 she played her Violin Sonata on chamber concerts in Dresden and Leipzig to encouraging reviews. On January 17, 1913, she performed an entire concert in Munich, again playing the Violin Sonata and two sets of songs, along with songs by Brahms and piano solos by Bach, Beethoven, and Brahms (Block notes that this was a program of "the four B's").[31] The reviews of this concert and another five days later on which she played her Piano Quintet with the Munich Quartet were mixed, as critics struggled to assess her work as composer and performer. Her playing was deemed technically brilliant but lacking in tonal warmth. Her chamber works – the lengthy and virtuosic Violin Sonata and Piano Quintet – were praised for their artistic aspirations, while her songs were criticized for being pleasant, accessible, and unworthy of her talent.

Nevertheless, it was the songs that piqued the interest of the public, and she wrote several letters to Schmidt asking him to send more copies of her songs to European distributors so that she could capitalize on their new-found popularity. Schmidt had established a branch office in Leipzig, Germany, in 1889 and had actively promoted the works of Edward MacDowell and other American composers there for decades. In 1910 he had sold the rights to his European catalog to B. Schott's Söhne, perhaps explaining why he was unresponsive to Beach's pleas for better support. The correspondence tapered off in 1913 without satisfying her demands.[32] From 1914 to 1921, Beach's new works were published by G. Schirmer, a New York rival to Schmidt.

Beach continued to expand her reach that spring with concerts and private performances in Breslau, Meran, and Berlin, all of which were reported in the American music journal *The Musical Courier*. At a Berlin gathering hosted by the journal's European correspondent Arthur Abell, she made the acquaintance of American conductor Theodore Spiering, whose advocacy proved decisive in the following year.

The fall 1913 concert season allowed Beach to hear her major orchestral works performed by three German orchestras. Concerts in Leipzig on November 22 and Hamburg on December 2 both featured her "Gaelic" Symphony and Piano Concerto. Her performance of the concerto with Spiering and the Berlin Philharmonic took place in the Prussian capital on December 18. After each of the three concerts, critics lavished praise on her playing and compositions. There were none of the complaints about her tone quality that she had received in chamber concerts the previous year, perhaps a reflection of the power and strength needed to project the solo part of a piano concerto. Her compositions were universally praised, and the words of the eminent critic Ferdinand Pfohl after her Hamburg performance proved useful for publicity materials for years to come. He characterized her as

a possessor of musical gifts of the highest kind, a musical nature touched with genius. Strong creative power, glowing fancy, instinct for form and color are united in her work with facile and effortless mastery of the entire technical apparatus. To this is added charm of poetic mood, delicacy and grace of melody, and a gift for rich, soulful harmonization.[33]

Beach's European stay had been extended from an initial plan of one year to a third year with no definite end in sight. The entry of Germany into World War I on August 1, 1914, however, forced the cancellation of a planned tour of Europe that fall, and although she remained in Munich for another month, she reluctantly sailed for America, arriving in New York on September 18.[34] During her absence, the musical press had publicized her activities regularly, and she was about to discover the value of a European reputation with American audiences.

Beach returned immediately to Boston, where she received a warm welcome from friends and many potent reminders that her professional standing had grown rather than shrunk during her three-year absence. She was greeted by a standing ovation when she played for 700 persons at the Boston MacDowell Club on November 18. An all-Beach concert on December 16 (the first of many that would be given throughout the country in the years ahead) brought out Boston's musical and social elite. But despite – or perhaps because of – the many memories of her Boston years, Beach chose to leave her home and take up residence in New York instead. She relinquished the calm and settled life that her parents and her husband had envisioned for her, opting instead to travel the country, with the bustling musical center of New York as her home base.

During the next few years, Beach finally achieved her childhood dream of making her living as a touring piano virtuoso. Thanks to the reputation she had burnished in Europe, along with the efforts of a competent manager, she could state in a December 1914 interview, "I have now enough dates to be quite satisfied, especially as I want some of my time left for composition."[35] She crisscrossed the country, playing with major orchestras, accompanying singers in lieder recitals, and playing for the innumerable music clubs that formed such an important part of urban social life in the early twentieth century. Continuing her association with world's fairs, she was commissioned to write her *Panama Hymn*, op. 74, for the Panama–Pacific International Exposition in San Francisco in 1915, and she was honored with two "Mrs. H. H. A. Beach Days" by the Panama–California Exposition in San Diego on June 28, 1915, and May 2, 1916. One commentator called her the "lion of the hour" in February 1915.[36]

Owing to the decades she had spent at the quaint inlaid empire desk in her music room at 28 Commonwealth Avenue, Beach had an extensive list of works to offer in concert. She was widely regarded as America's leading female composer, and she had compositions in various genres that could suit nearly any recital or concert setting. As a consequence, she now played primarily her own works, which in turn helped promote sales of the musical scores. Her songs were perennial favorites, and her playing of her solo piano compositions earned accolades from amateur club members and professional critics alike. The Violin Sonata and Piano Quintet were featured on chamber concerts, while her "Gaelic" Symphony was played by prominent orchestras, including twice by Leopold Stokowski's Philadelphia Orchestra.

But none of her compositions was as personally gratifying as her Piano Concerto in C-sharp minor, op. 45. After its April 1900 premiere with the Boston Symphony Orchestra, the work had languished, with just one subsequent performance (this time in a two-piano arrangement with Carl Faelten) in Boston on February 17, 1909. She revived the work with great success on her German concerts, after which it became a staple of her American tours during the mid-teens. She played it with at least five major orchestras, in Los Angeles, Chicago, Boston, Minneapolis, and St. Louis. In these performances, she truly attained the ideal of the Romantic pianist–composer who was thoroughly skilled in both disciplines. Chicago reviewer Stanley K. Faye wrote of her performance there:

Her concerto commands admiration equally with respect, for with its spirited construction, its fearlessness, and its triumphant force is combined a richness of material that is unusual. The composer has been prodigal of melody, bringing interesting incidents into the progress of the different movements with as much care and as good effect as she attains in the handling of the massed orchestra and the solo instrument. As a pianist Mrs. Beach will satisfy most people who demand that a woman play the piano like a man. The virile force with which she attains to an enormous tone is remarkable, the more so because she does not merely pound the piano but seeks for effects with the pedal. Her technic is superb. The one mighty descending passage almost at the end of the finale would in itself induce enthusiasm.[37]

As she approached her fiftieth birthday, she was clearly at the height of her pianistic powers, and the large, muscular hands that were evident in the marriage photo with Dr. Beach allowed her to compete on equal terms with the Chicago Symphony Orchestra.

This invigorating new career path – deferred since her teens – lasted for only three years. In part because of wartime restrictions, but primarily because of the need to care for a terminally ill cousin, Beach drastically curtailed her concert engagements and took over the management of her own career in February 1918. For the next two years she lived in Hillsborough, New Hampshire, and restricted her performances to nearby venues. Though she returned tentatively to touring in the early 1920s after the death of her cousin, she never rekindled the frenetic pace she had embraced after her return from Europe in 1914.

The decade of the 1910s began and ended with personal tragedy, but it had given Beach the opportunity to pursue her dream of a performance career. The demands of that career meant that her compositional output was reduced significantly. Although she wrote several virtuoso piano works and some of her most compelling songs during her time in Germany, she lacked the time and space for concentrated efforts in composition after returning to the United States. In the summer of 1921, a new source of inspiration reinvigorated her compositional activities and resulted in the second most productive period of her life.

Marian MacDowell (1857–1956), widow of the eminent composer Edward A. MacDowell (1860–1908), had turned their farm in Peterborough, New Hampshire, into an artist's colony in 1907. After declining several previous invitations, Beach finally agreed to spend a month as a fellow of the colony in 1921. There, in an isolated cabin in the New Hampshire woods, she found the conditions that had been lacking for artistic creation in the previous decade, and she released a flood of new compositions. Block attributes this inspiration to the fact that "in the following five years, nearly fifty works appeared (opp. 83–117), twice as many as in the previous ten years."[38] Her pattern was to compose or sketch new works during her summer residencies at the colony and to revise, perform, and publish them during the winter seasons. She returned to the colony nearly every summer until declining health forced her to discontinue her residencies in 1941. Robin Rausch's chapter discusses the fruitful interaction between Beach and Marian MacDowell.

The solitude of the MacDowell Colony was crucial to Beach's renewed productiveness, but the natural surroundings also proved to be an important source of inspiration. Among the works created during the summer of 1921 were a pair of impressionistic piano pieces incorporating the song of the hermit thrush. This native bird was an insistent visitor to Beach's cabin, and its triadic song forms a striking counterpoint to the dreamy textures of the first piece, "A Hermit Thrush at Eve," op. 92, no. 1. Continuing in the impressionistic vein, Beach also wrote a set of five piano pieces entitled *From Grandmother's Garden*, op. 97. These evocative works are harmonically adventurous and emulate the pianistic textures of Debussy and Ravel. Both of these sets were published by the Arthur P. Schmidt firm, now under the leadership of Henry Austin since the death of the founder on May 5, 1921.

The compositions of the 1920s also included several of the large-scale works that had been vital to her early career but absent during the 1910s. Her *Suite for Two Pianos Founded upon Old Irish Melodies*, op. 104, was an expansive virtuoso work of 106 pages. It was dedicated to the duo piano team of Rose and Ottilie Sutro, who featured it on their tours of the United States and Europe. *The Canticle of the Sun*, op. 123, was a twenty-five-minute choral setting with orchestral accompaniment of a text by St. Francis of Assisi. It proved to be enduringly popular with both amateur and professional choirs, especially at churches in New York City. The *Quartet for Strings in One Movement*, op. 89, was begun in 1921 and completed during a visit to Italy in 1929. Block notes that this work is the most modern and tonally unstable of Beach's works, perhaps inspired by the Italian composer Gian Francesco Malipiero (1882–1973), but certainly influenced by the sparse textures of Inuit melodies she worked into the composition.[39]

Following the loss of her remaining close family members in the early 1920s and the reduction of her touring activities, Beach increasingly expanded her engagement with musical organizations. She helped establish a Beach Club for music students in Hillsborough, New Hampshire, part of the nationwide movement of music clubs. She took leadership roles in the Mu Phi Epsilon music sorority as well as the Music Teachers National Association. Her extensive association with the National League of American Pen Women led to the founding of a Society for American Women Composers, for which she served as the first president in 1925. Her work with these organizations is chronicled in Marian Wilson Kimber's chapter.

After more than a decade in New Hampshire, Beach relocated in the fall of 1930 to New York City. There she spent her winters living at the American Women's Association Club House, filling her time with practicing, performing, and attending concerts. Summers were divided between the MacDowell Colony and her home in Centerville. She was surrounded by a circle of younger female professional musicians who provided companionship and musical collaboration. Perhaps most important to her musical life during this decade was her close association with David MacKay Williams (1887–1978), organist and choirmaster of St. Bartholomew's Episcopal Church. He and the church's soprano soloist, Ruth Shaffner (1897–1981), were close friends and active supporters of Beach, who wrote numerous sacred works for the services. Religion had long been important to her, and the combination of musical stimulation and religious solace at St. Bart's allowed her to become, in Block's words, "virtually a composer in residence."[40]

Beach continued to derive inspiration from her summers at the MacDowell Colony throughout the 1930s. Her still-formidable piano skills were a valuable support during chamber music evenings at the colony, and she appreciated the associations she made with younger artists in various fields. Among the most fruitful was her connection with novelist and playwright Nan Bagby Stephens (1883–1946), who wrote the libretto to Beach's 1932 one-act opera, *Cabildo*. Stephens was a native of Atlanta, Georgia, whose works focused on Southern themes and often featured African American actors. As discussed in Nicole Powlison's chapter, the opera was a reworking of Stephens' 1926 play of the same title set in New Orleans during the early nineteenth century. The opera was premiered in Atlanta on February 27, 1945, two months after Beach's death.

Beach developed serious heart problems in 1940, causing her to end her performing career and virtually all travel for the last four years of her life. She was forbidden by her doctor from all piano playing, an ironic bookend to a life that began with her mother's forbidding of the family piano. She was remembered fondly by her fellow MacDowell colonists, and she received several important honors, even as World War II raged in Europe. On May 8, 1940, she was honored with a testimonial dinner and concert at Town Hall, attended by about 200 persons. Two months later, *Musical Quarterly* published a lengthy article by Burnet C. Tuthill, which summarized her career and praised her compositions.[41] Though acknowledging that the music of the American Romantic composers was out of style at the time, he urged performers to revisit it in search of unanticipated beauties. In November 1942, a two-day festival in honor of her seventy-fifth birthday was presented at the Phillips Gallery in Washington, DC, by violinist Elena de Sayn. The programs featured a representative sampling of her most important compositions, with emphasis on the chamber works.

After months of declining health, Beach died on December 27, 1944, surrounded by friends in the Hotel Barclay. The *New York Times* published a generous obituary in which she was designated "most celebrated of American women composers."[42] It listed several of her compositional "firsts" and described in detail some of the highlights of her performing career. In death as in life, Beach was remembered as both an accomplished pianist and a trailblazing composer. Not surprisingly, the obituary is devoted primarily to her nineteenth-century career, with scant mention of her recent activities. As the United States entered the final months of World War II, musical tastes had shifted decisively away from Romanticism, and the music of Amy Beach would need to wait for a more receptive generation to rediscover it later in the century.

Notes

1. Quoted in John Tasker Howard, *Our American Music* (New York: Crowell, 1931), 346.
2. These and other anecdotes were recorded in an eleven-page handwritten manuscript by her mother, Clara Imogene Cheney, dated February 26, 1892, box I:58, "Biographical Writings and Notes," MacDowell Colony Records, Manuscript Division, Library of Congress. Amy Beach's own selection of childhood stories may be found in, "Why I Chose My Profession," *Mother's Magazine* 9, no. 2 (February 1914): 7–8; reprinted in *Music in the USA: A Documentary Companion*, ed. Judith Tick (New York: Oxford, 2008), 323–29.
3. Beach, "Why I Chose," 7.
4. For a history of this phenomenon, see E. Douglas Bomberger, "The German Musical Training of American Students, 1850–1900," PhD diss., University of Maryland, 1991; UMI 92–25,789.
5. Adrienne Fried Block, *Amy Beach, Passionate Victorian* (New York and Oxford: Oxford University Press, 1998), 5–7.
6. An introduction to generational theory may be found in William Strauss and Neil Howe, *Generations: The History of America's Future, 1584–2069* (New York: William Morrow, 1991), particularly pages 217–27 and 233–46, on the Progressive and Missionary Generations respectively. This book and a second, entitled *The Fourth Turning*, have been justifiably criticized for using past historical trends to predict the future, but their analysis of this time period is enlightening.
7. Beach, "Why I Chose," 326.
8. "Mr. Peck's Anniversary Concert," *Boston Evening Transcript*, October 25, 1883, 1. This verdict is confirmed by numerous reviews of the concert preserved in Cheney's scrapbook, pp. 2–5, box 12, Amy Beach Collection, University of New Hampshire. In particular, the unsigned article in the *Boston Advertiser*, October 25, 1883, goes into extensive detail on the specifics of her technique.
9. Beach, "Why I Chose," 326.
10. In a letter to her future husband, the prominent pianist Dr. William Mason gave a frank assessment of the seventeen-year-old Amy in October 1884: ". . . Miss Cheney whom I heard play and who certainly impressed me as being a young lady of remarkable talent and attainments. She has a strong, firm and at the same time elastic touch which evinces strength of character and at the same time she plays 'musikalisch' as the Germans express it." Letter from William Mason to Dr. H. H. A. Beach, October 3, 1884, box 3, folder 1, Beach Collection, University of New Hampshire.

11. The announcement read, "The engagement – not unexpected – of Dr. H. H. A. Beach and Miss Amy Marcy Cheney is announced." *Boston Globe*, August 16, 1885, 12. As clarified in Mason's letter in the previous footnote, Dr. Beach had taken an interest in Amy since at least October of the previous year. The simple wedding service, officiated by Rev. Phillips Brooks, was described in "Table Gossip," *Boston Globe*, December 6, 1885, 13.

12. A. M. B., "America's Chief Woman Composer," *Chicago Times-Herald*, November 28, 1897. Detailed descriptions of this music room are found in this article and in Edith Gertrude Kinney, "Mrs. H. H. A. Beach," *The Musician* 4, no. 9 (September 1899): 355.

13. "Music and Drama," *Boston Globe*, February 28, 1886, 13.

14. "Boston Symphony Orchestra," *Boston Evening Transcript*, February 23, 1886, 1.

15. Program, box 16, folder 2, Beach Collection, University of New Hampshire. The song was later published with the revised title "Jeune fille et jeune fleur," op. 1, no. 3.

16. For an in-depth analysis of the pros and cons of this arrangement, see Block, "Two Ways of Looking at a Marriage," Chapter 5 of *Amy Beach, Passionate Victorian*, 42–53.

17. Block, *Amy Beach, Passionate Victorian*, 38–41.

18. H. A. S., "At 74, Mrs. Beach recalls her first Critics," *Musical Courier* 123, no. 10 (May 15, 1941): 7.

19. Letter from Chadwick to Beach, November 2, 1896, autograph book, p. 68, box 1, folder 19, Beach Collection, University of New Hampshire.

20. George P. Upton, *Woman in Music* (Boston: J. R. Osgood, 1880), 19.

21. Upton, *Woman in Music*, 22.

22. Letter to Mrs. Edwin H. Wiggers, August 24, 1935, P.E.O. Archives, New York; quoted in Block, *Amy Beach, Passionate Victorian*, 48.

23. Quoted in Hazel Gertrude Kinscella, "Play No Piece in Public When First Learned, Says Mrs. Beach," *Musical America* 28, no. 19 (September 7, 1918): 9.

24. Block, *Amy Beach, Passionate Victorian*, 98–99.

25. For discussions of Schmidt's role in American music history, see Adrienne Fried Block, "Arthur P. Schmidt, Music Publisher and Champion of American Women Composers," in *The Musical Women: An International Perspective*, vol. 2, *1984–1985*, edited by Judith Lang Zaimont, Catherine Overhauser, and Jane Gottlieb (Westport, CT: Greenwood Press, 1987): 144–76, and Wilma Reid Cipolla, "Arthur P. Schmidt: The Publisher and His American Composers," in *Vistas of American Music: Essays in Honor of William K. Kearns*, ed. Susan L. Porter and John Graziano (Warren, MI: Harmonie Park Press, 1999), 267–81.

26. For an illustration of the active role that Dr. Beach played in his wife's career, see the letter from Beach to Schmidt dated March 12, 1905, box 303, folder 3, Arthur P. Schmidt Collection, Library of Congress. Beach gives suggestions to

the publisher on strategies to ensure a "friendly audience" for performances of Amy's *Sea-Fairies*, op. 59.

27. [Percy Goetschius], *Mrs. H. H. A. Beach* (Boston: A. P. Schmidt, 1906).
28. Beach to A. P. Schmidt, October 1, 1910, box 303, folder 6, Schmidt Collection.
29. Block, *Amy Beach, Passionate Victorian*, 178.
30. Block, *Amy Beach, Passionate Victorian*, 183.
31. Block, *Amy Beach, Passionate Victorian*, 184.
32. Box 303, folder 7, Arthur P. Schmidt Collection.
33. Quoted in Block, *Amy Beach, Passionate Victorian*, 187.
34. Block, *Amy Beach, Passionate Victorian*, 194–97.
35. Quoted in "Mrs. Beach in the West," *Musical Courier* 69, no. 23 (December 9, 1914): 13.
36. Emilie Frances Bauer, "Music in New York," *Musical Leader* 29, no. 5 (February 4, 1915): 122.
37. Stanley K. Faye, "Erudition Rules Symphony Program," *Chicago Daily News*, February 5, 1916.
38. Block, *Amy Beach, Passionate Victorian*, 223.
39. Block, *Amy Beach, Passionate Victorian*, 234–41.
40. Block, *Amy Beach, Passionate Victorian*, 258. Beach's relationship with this church and its musicians is discussed in detail on pages 257–59.
41. Burnet C. Tuthill, "Mrs. H. H. A. Beach," *Musical Quarterly* 26, no. 3 (July 1940): 297–310.
42. "Mrs. Beach Dead; Composer, Pianist," *New York Times*, December 28, 1944, 19.

2 | Amy Beach and the Women's Club Movement

MARIAN WILSON KIMBER

On the evening of June 5, 1906, women from all over the United States gathered at the Armory in St. Paul, Minnesota, a building that held 3,000 people. There they were treated to a concert of women composers performed primarily by professional musicians.[1] On the concert program, dominated by European composers, were multiple pieces by the American, Mrs. H. H. A. Beach, including several compositions she had arranged for cello and her cantata, *Sea-Fairies*, op. 59. *Sea-Fairies* had recently been commissioned by and was dedicated to Boston's Thursday Musical Club.[2] Many of the performers on the Minnesota program, among them soprano soloist Jessica De Wolf and two pianists, were members of St. Paul's Schubert Club, founded in 1882; Elsie Shawe, who had helped to arrange the entire event, was its past president.[3] The concert took place at the eighth biennial meeting of the General Federation of Women's Clubs (GFWC), a national organization made up of over 5,000 women's groups.

That the 1906 performance of Amy Beach's recent music was made possible by multiple women's organizations is emblematic of much of the composer's career. Beach's position as America's foremost woman composer initially came about because she produced two large-scale compositions, her Mass, op. 5, and her "Gaelic" Symphony, op. 32. The success of these works, performed by leading musical ensembles, suggested that she had transcended the musical restriction of women to the domestic sphere, the space in which they were encouraged to compose only songs and piano music, and that her music would henceforth be heard in the public world dominated by men. Yet this position, achieved at the beginning of the composer's professional life, overlooks the roles of women's organizations and women musicians in her ongoing success.[4] Beach's life paralleled the rise of women's clubs in America, and the movement played an important role in the way that her career unfolded. That a composer of her stature was active in numerous gendered musical communities underscores the multiple ways in which such clubs served as the American infrastructure for women musicians during this period. For Beach, clubs were not only a place for her to appear as a professional pianist and to present her music, but also a source of commissions and, more broadly, they represented an audience interested in purchasing and performing her music. Some groups in which Beach was involved provided her with a community that was social as well as musical; they were made up of like-minded women, some of whom became her collaborators. Because of Beach's special cultural position, she was viewed as an important leader and a role model for other women in music. Her appearance at events organized by women validated them and legitimized their activities, and clubs took full advantage of Beach's fame and status.

Although late nineteenth and early twentieth-century women's clubs had a major role in suffrage, temperance, labor reform, and other social movements, their widespread influence on American music is frequently overlooked. Women often justified their collective entrance into public activity as "municipal housekeeping," merely extending their domestic care into the civic arena, and some music clubs' activities – organizing community singing, providing scholarships, or outreach to settlement houses – served to overshadow the opportunities they provided for musical professionals. Clubs have been discounted due to the supposed "amateur" status of their members, though the amateur/professional distinction is often artificial when it comes to women's organizational networks, which Karen Blair has described as shaping "the context in which professionals marketed their artistic wares."[5] Women's club members generally performed music for each other without pay; despite some clubs' demanding audition requirements, their semiprivate nature and the race, gender, and class status of the participants caused them to be publicized in the society pages rather than newspapers' entertainment sections.[6] Yet some clubs, particularly in urban areas, could be quite substantial in size, and those that had paying but nonperforming "associate" members functioned like a concert series, either through scheduled performances of members or through bringing leading professional artists to their city to appear before large audiences. That many clubs are now perceived to have been "amateur" in nature is largely due to assumptions related to the gender of their members; many clubwomen were, in fact, professionals, including music teachers or church musicians. Clubs not only provided opportunities for women musicians, some of whom were very accomplished, but also served to connect professional and amateur musicians by linking private teachers with potential students and creating audiences before which professionals could perform.[7] Clubs across America were sometimes named for successful female composers (including Beach herself, but most often French composer Cécile Chaminade), suggesting that not all women were content with their supposed "amateur" status.[8] Clubs thus served as important venues for women whose access to the larger musical world was made more difficult by their gender. Not only did clubs provide opportunities locally, but also the large networks created through the meetings and publications of two federations, the General Federation of Women's Clubs (GFWC), founded in 1890, and the National Federation of Music Clubs (NFMC), established eight years later, shaped the careers of Beach and many other women musicians; the National League of American Pen Women (NLAPW) was particularly influential for women composers. Beach recognized "the value of women's clubs as a factor in the development of our country" early in her career; in an 1898 article in *The Etude*, she noted that "American audiences display a power of judgment in marked advance of that shown fifteen years ago" due to clubs' "unceasing toil" in cultivating "a true appreciation of great music and musicians."[9]

The earliest women's clubs were literary societies and study groups for self-improvement, though they clearly had a social function as well. As a young married woman in the 1890s, Beach was a member of such clubs, and though they were not specifically related to music, many featured music in their meetings as a matter of course. Adrienne Fried Block has described Beach's involvement in an unnamed lunch club, and in 1894 the composer became a founding member of New Hampshire's Daughters, a fifty-member club of women who, like her, had been born in the state.[10] The group combined literary, social, and charitable work, and each of its regular programs was organized by women born in the same New Hampshire county.[11] Both of Beach's clubs contained more notable writers than musicians; novelists Margaret Deland and Sarah Orne Jewett were members of the lunch group, and writer Kate Sanborn served as the first president of New Hampshire's Daughters. Although Beach's marriage purportedly prevented her from undertaking a public career, in 1897 she could be heard performing her own songs with Mrs. Heinrich Unverhau between recitations and talks on the state's history before 200 fellow clubwomen at the Hotel Vendome, followed by a tea.[12] That this occasion was semiprivate and perceived as less than fully professional made it socially acceptable for a musician of Beach's gender and class. In 1900 the club hosted the New Hampshire Federation of Women's Clubs, and Beach's two new Browning settings, "The Year's at the Spring" and "Ah, Love, But a Day!," were sung by Margaret Murkland. Originally commissioned by the Boston's mixed-gender Browning Society, the two songs would become staples of women's clubs' repertoires.[13]

When she lived in Boston, Beach became well known among men's clubs, women's clubs, and clubs made up of both genders. Several clubs programmed concerts entirely of her music after the turn of the century, including the Chromatic Club, founded by Edward MacDowell, the Amphion Club (a male vocal ensemble), the College Club, and the Thursday Morning Musical Club; both the latter club and the Chromatic Club made Beach an honorary member.[14] However, even before Beach began to make appearances at clubs outside of New England, her reputation preceded her. The premiere of her Mass with the Boston Handel and Haydn Society in 1892 was reported in pro-suffrage women's journals and was the subject of a paper at a meeting of the Women's Press Association in San Francisco in 1892.[15]

Beach's appearance at the Women's Musical Congress of the World's Columbian Exposition in Chicago in 1893 undoubtedly helped solidify her national reputation among women's organizations. The impetus for the NFMC, of which Beach was a member, is frequently attributed to Rose Fay Thomas' address, "The Work of Women's Amateur Musical Clubs," at that gathering. Beach's *Festival Jubilate*, op. 17, had been commissioned for the dedication of the Woman's Building, and she returned to the Chicago Congress for three performances, so she, along with over 1,000 other women, presumably heard Thomas' address.[16] When the Federation was formally established five years later, the women gathered at Chicago's Steinway Hall read a letter from Beach before moving on to their musical program.[17] The composer maintained close ties with the group as it grew into its national role, particularly after 1911 when her husband and mother had died and she undertook a more active professional career. The Federation's magazine, *Musical Monitor*, frequently reported on Beach's activities, including those in Europe, and published notices of her availability as a composer-pianist, citing the leading orchestras with which she had appeared. One article profiled Beach's manager, M. H. Hanson, who arranged her European appearances with soprano Marcella Craft, noting that he had taken special interest in music clubs.[18] Beach seems to have used the *Monitor* deliberately to keep her name before the club members, for in 1917 it published a letter from her merely describing the landscape in New Hampshire where she was working during the summer.[19]

The National Federation provided Beach with numerous performing opportunities, and she sometimes presented her own music at its biennial meetings. She appeared at the 1915 NFMC meeting in Los Angeles, playing her Piano Concerto with the Los Angeles Symphony Orchestra; her music was also heard on a choral program, and the Brahms Quintet performed her Piano Quintet.[20] In the teens, Beach assisted in judging NFMC competitions, and she appeared before clubs in Chicago, Milwaukee, Detroit, Pittsburgh, Philadelphia, Boston, and elsewhere. Beach was less involved with the larger GFWC than with the NFMC, though she did appear at its June 1922 meeting in Chautauqua, New York, performing her own compositions as well as music by Marion Bauer and Marion Ralston. As it was typical practice for the GFWC to mix music in with its lectures, the composer followed addresses on "woman and moral idealism" and "woman and public health." Beach also made one of her numerous appearances promoting the MacDowell Colony, which received much financial support from women's clubs, appearing with Marian MacDowell and performing compositions she had composed while in residence there.[21] After attending the GFWC's meeting, Beach was impressed enough with the organization to agree to become head of its Aid to American Musicians Committee, though she largely served as a figurehead in order to bring notice to its work.[22]

Although the compositions that clubwomen most often performed were Beach's songs and character pieces for piano, her other works were programmed by them as well. The rise of female string players resulted in violin being the third most common performance medium in clubs, behind voice and piano.[23] Many of Beach's songs, like those of other American composers of the period, were published with violin obbligato, and although cellists were less frequently part of women's clubs, a few featured violoncello.[24] Thus, Beach's Two Songs, op. 100, from 1924, were scored for an ensemble of the most widely available women's club members: soprano, violin, cello, and piano. More importantly, many clubs had women's choruses that could perform the thirty compositions Beach produced for that ensemble as well. Some works resulted from clubs' commissions, such as *The Rose of Avon-town*, op. 30, by the Caecilia Ladies' Vocal Society of Brooklyn, and *The Chambered Nautilus*, op. 66, by Victor Harris, the conductor of the St. Cecilia Club of New York.[25] *Sea-Fairies* was probably the most performed of the larger works, and women's clubs' programs frequently featured the two choral arrangements Beach did of her most popular songs, "The Year's at the Spring," and "Ah, Love, But a Day!"

Clubs were also important as audiences for Beach's largest works. Longtime music critic Charlotte Mulligan, who founded Buffalo's formidable Twentieth-Century Club, reported that "through the instrumentality of a musical club of women" the "Gaelic" Symphony "was secured for presentation" by the Buffalo Orchestra in 1897 and that "at the matinee it was most interesting to see one club, then another, come down the aisle and take reserved seats."[26] Likewise, the 1901 performance of Beach's Symphony by the Baltimore Symphony on an all-women composers' program came about because of the organization, United Women of Maryland.[27] Even when Beach's musical appearances were in conjunction with larger professional ensembles, women's clubs in cities where she performed served as additional venues for recitals and as social hosts, housing her and providing receptions. For example, in 1915, when Beach appeared at the Panama–Pacific International Exposition in San Francisco to hear her *Panama Hymn*, op. 74, sung at its opening ceremonies, she was received by the wealthy Century Club, where she was treated to a play by four of its members.[28] In November 1928, when the Women's Symphony of Chicago programmed two movements of the "Gaelic" Symphony, Beach stayed in the home of composer Phyllis Fergus, who was a Symphony board member and president of the Musicians Club of Women. The Club's published program of Beach's ten-day residency lists a series of social and musical events (see Figure 2.1). The composer was hosted by not only the Musicians Club of Women but also the Melodist Club, the MacDowell Society and the Cordon Club, Mu Phi Epsilon, and Pro Musica.[29] Thus, the club network greatly enhanced Beach's opportunities. As Beach's invitations to appear with leading orchestras faded in the 1920s in the era of Modernism and jazz, she continued to appear before women's organizations.[30]

Beach's compositions also figured heavily in the educational agendas of American women's clubs, which aspired to create a culture of American music on par with that of Europe. The advertisements of Beach's longtime publisher, Arthur P. Schmidt, marketed Beach's music and that of other American composers to clubs. Not only did Schmidt's notices in the *Musical Monitor* indicate that he had women's compositions available, but they sometimes grouped pieces by possible club program themes, such as nature or "inspirations from the poets."[31] Many clubs included Beach as they worked to familiarize themselves with women composers, such as the Woman's Club of Evanston, Illinois, which in 1900 heard a presentation on Beach along with reports about Clara Schumann, Fanny Hensel, Cécile Chaminade, Jessie Gaynor, and others.[32] However, particularly after World War I, nationalism, more than gender, shaped clubs' study and performance agendas. Clubs regularly studied what they perceived to be America's music history and performed the music of its composers; thus, Beach's music appeared alongside that of Edward MacDowell, George Whitefield Chadwick, Ethelbert Nevin, Charles Wakefield Cadman, and many others. Beach's national identity made her the ideal figure to represent the success of both American music and women's musical efforts.

CHICAGO MUSICAL ORGANIZATIONS HONOR
MRS. H. H. A. BEACH

NOVEMBER 21ST, 11 A.M.
Melodist Club—*Program and Luncheon*

NOVEMBER 21ST, 2:30 P.M.
Iota Alpha Chapter of Mu Phi Epsilon National
Sorority—*Program and Tea.*
ILLINOIS WOMEN'S ATHLETIC CLUB

NOVEMBER 25TH, 8:15 P.M.
The Woman's Symphony of Chicago—*Presents The
GAELIC SYMPHONY by Mrs. Beach at its first concert,*
EIGHTH STREET THEATRE

NOVEMBER 26TH, 2:30 P.M.
The Musicians Club of Women—*Presents Mrs. Beach,
assisted by club members, in a program of her compositions.* STUDEBAKER THEATRE

NOVEMBER 27TH, 7 P.M.
MacDowell Society of American Musicians—*Guest of
Honor at Banquet Given by Cordon Club.*
CORDON CLUB

NOVEMBER 28TH, 12:30 P.M.
The International Society for Contemporary Composers—Pro Musica. *Luncheon.* AUDITORIUM HOTEL

NOVEMBER 30TH, 4 TO 6 P.M.
Reception at Lyon & Healy's—*Sponsored by the*
MUSICIANS CLUB OF WOMEN. *Musicians Club Room.*

Figure 2.1 Musicians Club of Women program for Beach's 1928 Chicago appearances. Box 16, folder 27, Amy Cheney Beach (Mrs. H. H. A. Beach) Papers, 1835–1956, MC 51, Milne Special Collections and Archives, University of New Hampshire Library, Durham, NH.

When the GFWC prepared publications to assist members with their musical educations, Beach was included. In 1919 Ida Gray Scott, head of "Club Development in Music," published a suggested year-long program for clubs in the *General Federation Magazine*, the ninth program of which was devoted to Beach; the plan was circulated and republished regionally, such as in the *Illinois Club Bulletin*.[33] The same year, Mrs. William Delaney Steele of the GFWC Department of Music reported circulating 4,800 copies of a list of available materials; a tiny pamphlet providing a brief overview of Beach's career into the 1910s found in the GFWC's archives probably dates from around this time.[34] Three years later the Music Department sent out 20,000 study club outlines of monthly programs, so information about Beach was able to circulate widely.[35] The leading figure in the General Federation's ongoing music initiatives in the 1920s was the music chair, Anne Shaw Faulkner [Oberndorfer]. Faulkner's book *What We Hear in Music*, designed to be used with Victor Recordings, presented Beach's "Ah, Love, But a Day!" and "The Year's at the Spring," both of which had been recorded, as evidence that music could be popular and also represent the classical music tradition.[36] The book went through a dozen editions.[37] Faulkner's article, "American Women in the World of Music," published in *Better Homes and Gardens* in 1925, concentrated heavily on Beach, noting that both songs were "bestsellers,"[38] and they also appeared on lists of compositions for the music appreciation classes sponsored by women's clubs and schools. In 1936, Beach gave scores of her compositions, including her major works for women's voices, to the General Federation's circulating music collection. The GFWC's loan program had been providing copies of Beach's pieces to clubs around the country since at least 1925; also available was a six-page typed report about the composer's achievements.[39] In the 1930s, Beach was the woman composer best represented in the GFWC's music brochure, which listed suggested programs containing over twenty of her compositions.[40] The frequent appearance of Beach's music on club programs, whether amid works of other Americans or on events devoted entirely to her, demonstrates the success of the two Federations' efforts. The honors and accolades from women's groups continued to the end of Beach's life. In 1941, to celebrate its half century, the General Federation named Beach on a list of fifty-three women who "represented the great strides made by women in the last fifty years."[41] At its Atlantic City meeting that year, the Federation's huge National Jubilee Chorus, made up of clubwomen from among its two million members, sang "The Year's at the Spring."[42]

Beach was also an important figure for the National League of American Pen Women (NLAPW), an organization for professional writers, artists, and composers founded in 1897 by female journalists.[43] Musicians were the smallest component of the group, but by 1922 when Beach began to attend the League's national meetings it had fifty composer members;[44] in the 1930s, its total membership was 2,000 women in fifty-three branches, located in almost every state.[45] During her early years with the League, Beach also served as the first president of the Society of American Women Composers, probably founded at the Pen Women's 1924 meeting, perhaps because there were limited opportunities for performance of members' works at their national conferences. Beach had larger ambitions for the very small Society, made up of only around twenty members; she wrote that it might "come to mean much in the future of American music if we go about the work in the right way."[46] In 1925, while Beach was both Society president and the Pen Women's National Music Chairman, the League sponsored its "First Annual Festival of Music of the American Woman Composer" at its Washington, DC, meeting. The Society presented a series of chamber music concerts in New York before it disbanded in 1932, reportedly due to financial difficulties stemming from the Depression.[47] Although the Society is frequently cited as significant in historical accounts of women composers, there were many more concerts of music by women presented by the Pen Women after its demise.

Beach must have found the company of so many other professional female composers stimulating, though she remained the leading figure among them (see Figure 2.2). She had been the Pen Women's honored

Figure 2.2 Composer Group of the National League of American Pen Women, 1932. Back row, left to right: Reah Jackson Irion, Margaret McClure Stitt, Pearl Adams, Phyllis Fergus, Bonita Crowe, Marianne Genet, Annabel Morris Buchanan, Helen Matthews De Lashmutt, Josephine Forsyth, Gena Branscombe, and Louise Crawford. Front row: Francesca Vallejo, Amy Beach, Grace Thompson Seton (NLAPW president), Dorothy DeMuth Watson, Mary Carr Moore, Mary Howe, and Dorothy Radde Emery. Louise Crawford Papers, Iowa Women's Archives, University of Iowa Libraries, Iowa City.

guest as early as 1922, and she became an expected feature of their Washington meetings;[48] her 1938 plans to go to France were publicized, as if to alert members in the United States that she would *not* be attending their conference. For the 1934 meeting, music chairman Phyllis Fergus arranged six days of concerts billed as a "Golden Jubilee" in honor of Beach's fifty years in music. Beach performed the piano parts for her compositions on an evening concert – including *Sea-Fairies* – and appeared on a radio broadcast. The high point of the week was a recital in the East Room of the White House for First Lady Eleanor Roosevelt; four hundred tickets were issued to attendees.[49] It took several letters to convince the First Lady and the White House staff, and part of Fergus' approach was to emphasize that the League would be honoring Beach: "Mrs. Beach is no longer at our call as she has wont to be. She is older and we cherish the time she comes to us. With the Cherry Blossoms in April – it is easy to think of her great music to the 'Year[']s at the Spring.'"[50]

Whether it was linking one of Beach's best-known songs to Washington's flowering trees that enticed Mrs. Roosevelt to grant permission for a "short entertainment" is unclear; however, Fergus obviously recognized that the senior composer was important to her request. In July 1935 Beach's music was featured in another series of Pen Women concerts in Chautauqua, New York, a festival of six musical events "Honoring American Women Composers."[51] Fergus again arranged a Pen Women's concert featuring Beach at the White House in April 1936, at which the composer performed her piano music and spoke about the MacDowell Colony.

Just as the NFMC worked to create junior clubs for children in the 1920s, establishing over 2,300 of them by the final year of the decade, Beach was likewise concerned about children's musical education and involved in musical outreach to young people.[52] Not only did she compose piano works appropriate for younger players, but in 1922, with the help of the music club in her mother's hometown of Hillsborough, New Hampshire, she also sponsored two "Beach clubs" for local children of different ages.[53] Beach was also involved with the Music Teachers National Association (MTNA), although it was not primarily a women's group. She initially served as an advisory member to the group's Association of Past Presidents ca. 1918–20. In the 1930s, she published three essays in their journal, including versions of presentations she gave at their national conferences in Detroit in 1931, Washington, DC, in 1932, and Philadelphia in 1935. She was elected to serve as one of the directors on the organization's executive committee from 1933 to 1935, and her songs sometimes appeared on the Music Teachers National Association's contest repertoire lists.[54]

Beach's position as a role model for younger women lasted from her early years to the end of her life. In 1899, she was initiated as an honorary member of the women's fraternity, Alpha Chi Omega, by the Zeta chapter of the New England Conservatory. Beach "remembered" the group when she performed her Concerto with the Boston Symphony, presumably supplying tickets for the event; she also produced "A Song for Class Day" for them.[55] Beach's membership in another collegiate group, Mu Phi Epsilon, apparently came about through her visits to Chicago, as its publications indicate that she was a member of the Iota Alpha chapter of the Chicago Musical College. In 1922, she entertained young chapter members at the home of Mrs. Albert J. Ochsner, former president of the NFMC.[56] Beach's association with Mu Phi Epsilon appears to have continued, as in 1933 she was hailed as "Aunt Amy" in an article in their publication, *The Triangle*, which described how "splendid citizenship is her constructive influence everywhere."[57] Beach was an honorary "aunt" to some of the composers she knew through organizations such as the NLAPW as well, and they viewed her as a mentor. While Beach's connections to groups such as Mu Phi Epsilon may not have been as important to her social and professional lives as those described previously, they were yet another audience who might teach and perform her music; Alpha Chi Omega subsidized the building of a studio at Beach's beloved MacDowell Colony.

Beach's memberships were not just a way for her to be part of national women's networks, but also represented local means for music-making and sources of companionship. For example, she had an ongoing relationship with the Hillsborough Music Club and performed there while living in the town. In the last decade and a half of her life, Beach's professional connections centered on a group of women who became the focus of her personal life when she settled in New York City. Then in her sixties, Beach often took a maternal role among the younger women musicians in her immediate circle, whose use of "Aunt Amy" signified their friendship and true intimacy. Of Beach's closest "nieces" or "children," the most prominent figures were the mezzo-soprano Lillian Buxbaum, the soprano Ruth Shaffner, the pianist Virginia Duffey, and the violinist Eugenie Limberg; collectively the performers represented the typical scorings that had been heard in women's music clubs for decades. Beach called this circle of young women her "kittens" and preserved hundreds of letters to and from them.[58] Shaffner, Duffey, and Limberg came to live at the American Women's Association (AWA) Clubhouse, which served as Beach's New York home. In her years in the building on West 57th St. and later when the AWA moved to 48th St., Beach was able to socialize with some of the other women residents and to concertize for them. Beach arranged for Duffey and Limberg to pay for their room and board at the AWA (and to have access to better practice rooms) by performing short concerts there. The pair performed Beach's Violin Sonata and recruited others to assist them in presenting her larger chamber works as well.[59] In 1935, Beach became a member of P.E.O., a sorority to which Ruth Shaffner belonged, and Beach, Duffey, and Limberg frequently performed brief recitals together for the New York chapter.[60] Although P.E.O. supports women's education, it has never been formally associated with music. Nonetheless, in 1944 Beach composed a song, "Ballad of the P.E.O.," for the group, just as she had for Alpha Chi Omega decades before.

When Beach first met Ruth Shaffner, she was a soloist at St. Bartholomew's Episcopal Church where the composer was a longtime attendee, and the dramatic soprano frequently sang her sacred music there. Shaffner came to be one of Beach's closest friends and a regular partner in her concert life, performing her songs on over 200 recitals in the 1930s, including at the two White House performances.[61] Beach's effusive letters to her friend reveal the deep regard she had for the singer's talents; she enthusiastically complimented Ruth's wonderful performances, heaping praise on her singing, her perfect diction, her looks and demeanor, and her "spiritual force." Shaffner also functioned as Beach's surrogate family in her declining years. The two women spent holidays and vacations together and traveled to England together in 1936. Shaffner was at Beach's bedside when she passed away in 1944.[62]

Lillian Buxbaum was also a member of Beach's female circles during the final two decades of her life. Beach praised her friend's singing highly, and Buxbaum became one of the composer's musical collaborators in club settings in New England. Although Buxbaum's relationship with Beach was not specifically related to club activities, as a part-time singer, wife, and mother, she was the kind of female musician who frequently made up women's music clubs' memberships. Buxbaum's first appearance singing Beach's music was on a program for the Women's City Club of Haverhill, Massachusetts, in 1924. She sang on the radio with Beach in Boston in 1931 and was one of two singers who performed with the composer at a Music Guild lunch for the renowned French pedagogue Nadia Boulanger in 1937, as well as on other occasions.[63] However, the women's relationship was also deeply personal, with Lillian and her husband Isidore functioning as family members for Beach, assisting her with acquiring groceries and in undertaking travel, and helping to arrange for her frequent moves from New York City to Centerville, Hillsboro, and the MacDowell Colony as she aged.[64] The depth of their intimacy and Beach's regard for Buxbaum's longtime friendship is apparent from her will, which provided Lillian with her Centerville home.

Beach's singular position as the best-known American female composer of her era, whose name still regularly appears amid those of the Second New England School and other leading male figures, has made it possible to overlook the tremendous networks of women musicians who supported her throughout her life and whose countless activities contributed to her success. Though Beach made breakthroughs by composing in major genres, and her large-scale music was performed by professional male ensembles, organizations typically understood as "nonprofessional" that were founded and maintained by women, growing into national prominence during her lifetime, were equally if not more important to her career. Groups such as the GFWC, the NFMC, and the NLAPW provided Beach with ongoing performance opportunities at which she could promote her own music. The amateur and professional female musicians of the GFWC and the NFMC made up thousands of clubs across the country at which Beach's music was regularly studied and heard. Beach's stature made her the ideal figure around which women's clubs could shape their promotion of American composers, simultaneously emphasizing individual female creativity and casting women's music as a national good. In turn, Beach's remarkable success validated their efforts to make women central to American musical life.

Notes

1. General Federation of Women's Clubs, *Eighth Biennial Convention, Official Report* (Chicago: The Federation, 1906), 265–66.
2. Andrew Thomas Kuster, Introduction to Amy Beach, *The Sea-Fairies, Opus 59*, Recent Researches in American Music 32 (Madison, WI: A-R Editions, 1999), ix.
3. Sondra Wieland Howe, "Elsie Shawe, Music Supervisor in St. Paul, Minnesota (1898–1933)," *Journal of Research in Music Education* 52, no. 4 (Winter 2004): 331–32.
4. Lili Fae Tobias has made this point in "'All My Heart, in This My Singing': Amy Beach and the Women's Clubs of New England," Senior Comprehensive Paper, Swarthmore College, December 6, 2018; accessed June 2, 2021; decomposedblog .wordpress.com/blog-feed/amy-beach/.
5. Karen J. Blair, *The Torchbearers: Women and Their Amateur Arts Associations in America, 1890–1930* (Bloomington: Indiana University Press, 1994), 4–5.
6. Linda Whitesett, "'The Most Potent Force' in American Music: The Role of Women's Music Clubs in American Concert Life," in *The Musical Woman*, vol. 3, ed. Judith Lang Zaimont et al. (Westport: Greenwood Press, 1991), 667.

7. See Linda Whitesett, "Women as 'Keepers of Culture': Music Clubs, Community Concert Series, and Symphony Orchestras," in *Cultivating Music in America: Women Patrons and Activists since 1860*, ed. Ralph P. Locke and Cyrilla Barr (Berkeley: University of California Press, 1997), 65–86.

8. Adrienne Fried Block, *Amy Beach, Passionate Victorian: The Life and Work of an American Composer, 1867–1944* (New York: Oxford University Press, 1998), 164.

9. Quoted in Mrs. Charles S. Virgil, "The Woman's Club a Factor in General Music Culture," *The Etude* 16, no. 5 (May 1898): 132.

10. Block, *Amy Beach, Passionate Victorian*, 110.

11. J[ennie] C. Croly, *The History of the Woman's Club Movement in America* (New York: H.G. Allen, 1898), 645–46.

12. "Mrs. Micah Dyer Presided," *Boston Globe*, January 18, 1897.

13. "From the Granite State," *Boston Globe*, October 26, 1897.

14. Block, *Amy Beach, Passionate Victorian*, 173.

15. Alma Alden, "Women's News," *Woman's Exponent* 20, no. 20 (1892): 152.

16. "They Develop Taste," *Chicago Tribune*, July 8, 1893, does not list Beach on this event, although other reports suggest she was to perform there.

17. Lucile Parrish Ward, *A Musical Heritage of 100 Years: A History of the National Federation of Music Clubs* (Greenville, SC: A Press, 1995), 59. Some clubs did contain men, but the organization became dominated by women.

18. "Interview with M. H. Hanson," *Musical Monitor* 6, no. 8 (April 1917): 454.

19. "Letter from Mrs. H. H. A. Beach," *Musical Monitor* 6, no. 12 (August 1917): 698.

20. "The Story of the Biennial," *Musical Monitor* 4, no. 11 (July 1915): 479.

21. General Federation of Women's Clubs, *Sixteenth Biennial Convention, Official Report* (Chicago: The Federation, 1922), 355–56, 630.

22. "30 Music Libraries Available to Clubs," *General Federation News* 5, no. 7 (January 1925): 12.

23. Judith Tick, "Passed Away Is the Piano Girl: Changes in American Musical Life: 1870–1900," in *Women Making Music: The Western Art Tradition, 1150–1950*, ed. Jane Bowers and Judith Tick (Urbana: University of Illinois Press, 1986), 328.

24. Maryann McCabe notes similar scorings by Mabel Daniels, Gena Branscombe, Helen Hopekirk, and some male composers in *Mabel Daniels: An American Composer in Transition* (London: Routledge, 2018), 210.

25. Block, *Amy Beach, Passionate Victorian*, 164–65, 169.

26. Charlotte Mulligan, *Buffalo Courier*, February 5, 1897, quoted in Percy Goetschius, *Mrs. H. H. A. Beach* (Boston: A. P. Schmidt, 1906), 103.

27. "Conzert zum Besten der 'Vereinigten Frauen von Maryland' in der 'Musik-Halle'," *Der Deutsche Correspondent*, March 15, 1901.

28. Leta Miller, "Fostering the 'Art of Forceful Speech': Music in the Century Club of California, 1888–1920," *Journal of the Society for American Music* 16, no. 3 (August 2022): 283.

29. Special Board Meeting May 28, 1928, Musicians Club of Women Minutes 1927–31, Chicago History Museum; Musicians Club of Women 1928 program,

box 16, folder 27, Amy Cheney Beach (Mrs. H. H. A. Beach) Papers, 1835–1956, MC 51, Milne Special Collections and Archives, University of New Hampshire Library, Durham, NH.

30. Block, *Amy Beach, Passionate Victorian*, 243.

31. See Adrienne Fried Block, "Arthur P. Schmidt, Music Publisher and Champion of American Women Composers," in *The Musical Woman: An International Perspective*, vol. 2, 1984–1985, ed. Judith Lang Zaimont, Catherine Overhauser, and Jane Gottlieb (Westport, CT: Greenwood, 1987), 145–76.

32. "Woman in Composition," *Music* [Chicago] 17 (February 1900): 431.

33. Ida Gray Scott, "A Year's Program for a Music Club," *General Federation Magazine* 18 (September 1919): 12; "Department of Music," *Illinois Club Bulletin* 12, no. 3 (March 1920): 27.

34. "Mrs. H. H. A. Beach," Sheet Music, Box 4, Women's History and Resource Center, General Federation of Women's Clubs Headquarters, Washington, DC.

35. "Report of Chairman of Music Division," *Sixteenth Biennial Convention, Official Report,* 353.

36. Anne Shaw Faulkner, *What We Hear in Music; a Course of Study in Music History and Appreciation*, 6th ed. (Camden, NJ: Victor Talking Machine Co., 1928), 359.

37. Terese M. Volk, "*What We Hear in Music*: Anne Shaw Faulkner's Music Appreciation Text, 1913–1943," *The Bulletin of Historical Research in Music Education* 20, no. 3 (May 1999): 157.

38. Anne Shaw Faulkner Oberndorfer, "American Women in the World of Music," *Better Homes and Gardens* 4, no. 4 (December 1925): 37.

39. "Gifts of Music from Mrs. Beach," *The Clubwoman, GFWC* (November 1936): 26.

40. *I am Music*, General Federation of Women's Clubs, Music Division, 1935–38, in Program Records, Women's History and Resource Center.

41. "53 Women Named as Leaders of Sex," *New York Times*, May 9, 1941.

42. Program, The National Jubilee Chorus, May 20, 1941, Women's History and Resource Center.

43. See Marian Wilson Kimber, "Female Composers at the White House: The National League of American Pen Women and Phyllis Fergus's Advocacy for Women in American Music," *Journal of the Society for American Music* 12, no. 4 (November 2018): 489–91.

44. Mrs. J. Harry Cunningham, "Wanted – A Policy," *The Pen Woman* 1, no. 4 (Winter 1921): 241.

45. Laurine Elkins-Marlow, "'Music at Every Meeting': Music in the National League of American Pen Women and the General Federation of Women's Clubs, 1920–1940," in *Politics, Gender, and the Arts: Women, the Arts, and Society* (London: Associated University Presses, 1992), 187.

46. Beach to Fannie Charles Dillon, September 26, 1925, Dillon Collection, University of California Los Angeles Research Library Special Collections, quoted in Block, *Amy Beach, Passionate Victorian*, 246.

47. Laurine Elkins-Marlow, cited in Dorothy Indenbaum, "Mary Howe: Composer, Pianist and Music Activist" (PhD diss., New York University, 1993), 194.

48. Program, Silver Jubilee and First Biennial Convention of League of American Pen Women, April 24–29, 1922, National League of American Pen Women Archives, Pen Arts, Washington, DC.

49. The League's *Bulletin* reported that "our hostess stayed throughout the program which was surely tribute enough for anyone." Clyde Burke Millspaugh, "Here and There at the Convention," *Official Bulletin* 10, no. 9 (June 1934): 3.

50. March 19, 1934, Phyllis Fergus to Eleanor Roosevelt, box 444, 1934 A–G Eleanor Roosevelt Papers, FDR Presidential Library and Museum, Hyde Park, New York.

51. Program for *Chautauqua Music Festival Honoring American Women Composers*, July 26–29, 1935, National League of American Pen Women, Green Mountain Branch Scrapbook, University of Vermont Library Special Collections, Burlington, VT.

52. Blair, *The Torchbearers*, 52.

53. Block, *Amy Beach, Passionate Victorian*, 244.

54. "Music Teachers National Association," *Music Educators Journal* 21, no. 4 (February 1935): 14.

55. Spicie Bell South, "Zeta," *The Lyre* 5 (March 1901): 505; Nancy Nitchman Leonard, *The History of Alpha Chi Omega Fraternity: The First 25 Years* (August 14, 2019), 61; accessed June 2, 2021; issuu.com/alphachiomega/docs/alphachiomega_the1st25years-1.

56. "Iota Alpha, Chicago Musical College," *The Triangle of Mu Phi Epsilon* 16, no. 3 (May 1922): 244.

57. Phyllis Fergus, [untitled], *The Triangle of Mu Phi Epsilon* 28 (February 1933): 85, in National League of American Pen Women, Green Mountain Branch Scrapbook, [152], University of Vermont Library Special Collections, Burlington, VT.

58. The correspondence with Buxbaum and Shaffner may be found in boxes 2 and 3, Amy Beach Papers, University of New Hampshire. Numerous letters to Limberg are housed in box 27, Adrienne Fried Block Papers, University of New Hampshire. Further correspondence from all four women may be found in box 1, Walter Jenkins Papers, University of New Hampshire.

59. Block, *Amy Beach, Passionate Victorian*, 256, 262.

60. Block, *Amy Beach, Passionate Victorian*, 261.

61. Block, *Amy Beach, Passionate Victorian*, 259–60.

62. Block, *Amy Beach, Passionate Victorian*, 283, 295.

63. Block, *Amy Beach, Passionate Victorian*, 247, 259, 285.

64. Block, *Amy Beach, Passionate Victorian*, 248, 282.

3 | "A Reality of Glorious Attainment"

Amy Beach's MacDowell Colony[1]

ROBIN RAUSCH

On July 9, 1921, Amy Beach wrote to her publisher, the Arthur P. Schmidt Company, asking them to send a selection of her scores to the MacDowell Colony in Peterborough, New Hampshire, where she was working as a resident artist for the first time. "I have promised to contribute some of my music to the Tea Room, which opens on Friday, the 15th, to be sold for the benefit of the Colony, among books, etc. written by people who have worked here," she wrote. The Nubanusit Tea Room was a new venture at the MacDowell Colony. It offered refreshment to the tourists who motored through the area during the summer months, while providing information about the Colony and its artists in hopes of gaining new supporters. Beach concluded her letter to the Schmidt Company with enthusiasm for her first Colony experience: "I am having a wonderful month of work here, and love the place beyond words."[2]

Founded in 1907, the MacDowell Colony embodied Edward MacDowell's dying wish to turn his New Hampshire farm into a gathering place for creative artists, where they could work undisturbed in a community of their peers. The plan was but a vague idea when the composer became ill. Marian MacDowell, the composer's wife, established the Colony shortly before her husband's death to prove to him her commitment to the project. She was a talented pianist who had once been MacDowell's student. For almost four decades, she managed the Colony from June through September, and then traveled the country during the off-season, promoting the Colony and playing her husband's music as only she could.[3]

The MacDowell Colony became an important part of Amy Beach's life. Facilitated by her friendship with Marian MacDowell, Beach held eighteen residencies at the Colony between 1921 and 1941. She worked well there. Inspired by the woodland setting and the uninterrupted solitude of a studio of her own, her time at the MacDowell Colony guaranteed productivity. Beach felt a great debt to the Colony, which she repaid by becoming one of its fiercest supporters.

Amy Beach was twenty-one years old, in her third year of marriage, and living at 28 Commonwealth Avenue when, in the fall of 1888, Edward and Marian MacDowell returned to the United States from living abroad and settled in Boston. The MacDowells lived in Boston for the next eight years. While it is easy to imagine Beach and the MacDowells moving in the same musical circles during this time, the existence and extent of a friendship between Beach and the couple remains speculative. There are no known letters or other documents from these years that suggest that Beach knew either Marian or Edward MacDowell. Later in her life, Beach remembered her acquaintance with Edward MacDowell as "slight" and recalled only "two occasions when we met."[4] The sole evidence of a possible acquaintance is an undated letter Beach preserved in her scrapbook from Edward's mother Fanny, written on stationery of the Copley Square hotel in Boston. Fanny writes: "My dear Mrs. Beach I send back the jar & napkin. The broth was the most delicious I ever ate – will you accept the roses with my deepest gratitude to your dear husband for his care of me. Faithfully always Fanny D. MacDowell."[5]

The earliest known correspondence between Beach and Marian MacDowell dates from 1906, a year after the national press publicly announced Edward MacDowell's tragic illness and deteriorating condition.[6] Beach had long admired MacDowell's music, and now she intentionally included it on her recitals in support of the ailing composer. In a letter dated November 27, 1906, Beach discusses plans for two upcoming programs. She also offers encouragement to Mrs. MacDowell in her decision to teach the coming winter: "There are so many people who would naturally go to you for the best understanding of your husband's music, that I feel sure of your success in a unique field." In closing, Beach expresses her admiration for Marian's "great courage" in the face of difficult circumstances. "It is needless to assure you again of the deep sympathy which Dr. Beach and I feel for you in this terrible experience. You are much in our thoughts, as you must be in those of all people to whom the music of your dear one has meant many, many hours of happiness."[7]

Edward MacDowell died January 23, 1908, leaving Marian MacDowell a widow at age fifty. Two years later, on June 28, 1910, Henry Beach died. Amy Beach was forty-two. Neither woman had children. Widowhood conveyed a freedom to start life anew, unfettered by the prevailing strictures of marriage. Marian MacDowell styled herself the matriarch of what would become America's premiere artist colony. Amy Beach pursued life as an itinerant concert artist and composer, and she became celebrated as the Dean of American Women Composers.

The paths of Amy Beach and Marian MacDowell did not cross for several years after their husbands' deaths. Beach cared for her ailing mother until she died in February 1911. This double loss of both her husband and mother, occurring so close in time, proved the catalyst that led Beach to head to Europe, where she traveled and performed for the next three years. During this time, Marian MacDowell focused on the growth and development of her fledgling Colony. From 1910 to 1914, she produced a series of summer pageants and music festivals to publicize the Colony and draw new talent and supporters. The first of these productions was the 1910 Peterborough Pageant, an outdoor drama that used Edward MacDowell's music in a retelling of the town's history. A phenomenal success, it garnered national press coverage and was the impetus for Mrs. MacDowell's first lecture–recital tours.[8] World War I eventually brought an end to these summer Peterborough productions. The growing conflict made it increasingly dangerous for Amy Beach to remain abroad. She returned to the United States in September 1914.

Beach's success overseas buoyed her career back home. In 1915, her tour schedule took her to the West coast, where she heard her *Panama Hymn*, op. 74, performed at the Panama–Pacific International Exposition in San Francisco. Her music was featured at the 1915 biennial meeting of the National Federation of Music Clubs in Los Angeles, June 24 through July 3, and included a performance of her piano concerto, with the composer at the piano. California feted her, and Beach maintained a base there for over a year. In 1916, she came back East for good and moved to Hillsboro, New Hampshire, seven miles from her girlhood home of Henniker and roughly twenty miles due north of Peterborough and the MacDowell Colony.

Beach's return to New Hampshire coincided with the launch of an endowment campaign to secure the financial future of the MacDowell Colony. By now, it was recognized as a critical success. But financial stability remained elusive. As the Colony approached its tenth anniversary in 1917, Marian MacDowell was nearing sixty. She did not know how much longer she could continue her grueling lecture–recital schedule. In the fall of 1916, appeals for support began to appear in newspapers and popular music magazines. These often portrayed the MacDowell Colony as a uniquely American institution, with an important role in fostering a national cultural identity. Writing in *The Musical Courier* of September 7, 1916, composer Carl Venth suggested: "If ever a real national American art is born, and I believe the time is near, the ideal conditions for a demonstration of genius loci are offered in Peterboro, which in a very short time should mean as much to America as Bayreuth means to Germany or Stratford-on-Avon to

England." He considered the MacDowell Colony "a national asset of the greatest value" and believed it was "the duty of every musical organization and of every woman's club to take a share in supporting this splendid effort."[9]

Amy Beach's name first appears in the annual reports of the MacDowell Colony in 1917, listed among the contributors to the endowment fund "raised by Mrs. MacDowell." This was the first of many donations that she made annually thereafter. And when Marian MacDowell invited the National Federation of Music Clubs to hold their 1919 biennial meeting in Peterborough, Beach performed on the program, playing her *Suite Française* in a special recital at the Peterborough Town Hall on July 2.[10]

Amy Beach came to work at the MacDowell Colony as a resident artist in 1921, at Marian MacDowell's personal invitation. By then, the Colony had nineteen studios that accommodated close to fifty artists per season. Most were chosen by an admissions committee from close to 300 applications. Beach, however, was always invited by Marian MacDowell. In the early years Marian chose all the artists. As Colony founder and resident manager, she continued to have great latitude in extending invitations to artists of her choosing. While Beach benefited from her friendship with Marian MacDowell, the Colony benefited as well. Beach was an established composer at the height of her career, and her presence lent the still-young institution a certain prestige.

A typical day at the MacDowell Colony started with a communal breakfast in Colony Hall, a refurbished barn that served as the social hub of the Colony. Artists then headed to their assigned studios for a day of uninterrupted work. A cardinal rule stated that no artist should disturb another while at work in their studio unless they had been invited. Lunch baskets were quietly delivered to studio doors at midday. At the end of the day, residents relaxed in Colony Hall, where a rousing game of cowboy pool was routine after the evening meal. Beach worked in the Regina Watson studio exclusively when she was in residence. The studio was built in memory of the composer and beloved piano teacher from Chicago, Regina Watson, funded by her friends and former students.[11] Designed in the neoclassical style, it remains one of the largest studios at the Colony, and at that time served as both a music studio and a small recital space for informal performances.

A basic tenet of Colony life was Edward MacDowell's belief in the correlation between the arts. He thought that artists from different disciplines had much to learn from one another, and a Colony residency brought together a unique group of visual artists, writers, and composers each season. During the summer of 1921, Beach met poet Edwin Arlington

Robinson (1869–1935), a regular at the Colony who became a friend, and sculptor Bashka Paeff (1889–1979), who years later sculpted a bust of the composer. Writer Padraic Colum (1881–1972) was translating old Irish songs and introduced Beach to the tune she later arranged in her piano piece "The Fair Hills of Éiré, O," op. 91. Beach encountered the poet Katharine Adams and set two of her poems, "The Moonpath" and "I Shall Be Brave." Marion Bauer (1882–1955) was also in residence that summer and composed her "Prelude in D major," for the left hand alone, the first of her *Six Preludes*, op. 15, which she dedicated to Beach.

By Beach's own account, her first season at the Colony was magical. It was the summer of the infamous hermit thrush that sang so insistently that Beach transcribed the bird's song and wrote two piano pieces based on the melody: "A Hermit Thrush at Eve" and "A Hermit Thrush at Morn," op. 92. She annotated the manuscript of "A Hermit Thrush at Morn" with a statement of authenticity: "These bird calls are exact notations of hermit thrush songs, in the original keys, but an octave lower, obtained at MacDowell Colony, Peterborough, N.H."[12] Beach began performing these pieces that fall and implored her publisher to expedite publication. "If you can only do two of the piano pieces early in the year, I should prefer the two Hermit Thrush pieces, as the interest in them is really remarkable everywhere I play them, either in public or private. They appeal to the musician and bird-lover alike, and I am constantly asked when they are to appear in print."[13] The pieces count among her most popular piano works. In 1998, critic David Wright singled them out for praise in an article on Beach's music for the *New York Times*: "In this music, Beach does for the Romantic piano piece what Ives did for the symphony: express human longings for nature and the divine through a polytonal mix of natural and artful sounds. Such discourse came readily to these successors of the New England Transcendentalists."[14]

Beach told the hermit thrush story often when she spoke about the MacDowell Colony. It captures perfectly the inspiration that she found in nature and illustrates the ideal environment that the Colony provided for her creative work. The studios were strategically situated on the grounds, almost 500 acres, tucked into the woods and far enough apart to ensure that Beach had what she most needed to compose: "silence in solitude." Beach elaborated on this idea in a speech she gave to the Music Teachers National Association in 1932, on the occasion of the twenty-fifth anniversary of the MacDowell Colony. "It is not merely the absence of noise or any other distracting influence. It is the actual communication which we receive from some source outside ourselves, which can only reach us through 'the innermost silence.'"[15] In her speech, Beach twice mentions *The Garden of Vision*, a book by

L. Adams Beck, published in 1929. Lily Adams Beck was a pseudonym of Canadian author Elizabeth Louisa Moresby (1862–1931). Moresby traveled throughout Asia and lived in the East most of her life. She was a devout Buddhist and published on themes of Eastern culture and philosophy under the pseudonym L. Adams Beck. Beach quotes from *The Garden of Vision*: "To live with lovely things is not a part of the Cosmic Law, but the whole of it when rightly understood. For art and true spirituality are one." Later in her speech, she quotes from it again: "Why do the spiritually minded seek solitude? Because Divinity sits in solitude, weaving happy spells." This comes from a paragraph that begins: "Nature holds the secret, for Nature is not the veil of the Divine but Divinity itself and being so can interpret man's own divinity to him."[16] We do not know how Beach became acquainted with *The Garden of Vision*, but the ideas it espoused, equating art and spirituality, and nature and divinity, clearly spoke to her. Beach had spent a decade's worth of summers at the MacDowell Colony when she made this speech, and it is evident that her Colony experience shaped her personal artistic credo.

At the MacDowell Colony, Beach found that "music poured out of her that had been all but dammed up." Beach's biographer, Adrienne Fried Block, has documented the increase in Beach's productivity that dates from her early residencies. In the five years following her first residency, Beach wrote nearly fifty works (opp. 83–117), doubling her output from the previous ten years. Almost all of Beach's music going forward was written or sketched at the MacDowell Colony.[17] Figure 3.1 shows her in the idyllic atmosphere that came to mean so much to her.

Figure 3.1 Amy Beach in the New Hampshire woods.

In the summer of 1922, Marian MacDowell and Amy Beach presented a joint program at the biennial convention of the General Federation of Women's Clubs, held in Chautauqua, New York, from June 20 to 30. The women's club movement was vitally important to the success of both Amy Beach and the MacDowell Colony. There were clubs across the country, in towns big and small, all of them with potential audiences ready to lend their support to the latest cause. In the years following World War I, one of those causes was American music. The backlash against German music and musicians that surfaced during World War I, and lasted long after, resulted in a new appreciation for American composers and their music. American music was featured at the convention in a series of "Hearing America First" programs.[18] In what was called "one of the outstanding programs," Mrs. Edward MacDowell spoke about the MacDowell Colony and appealed to her listeners for financial aid to make it a permanent institution. She followed her talk with a performance of eight works by her late husband, and then introduced Mrs. H. H. A. Beach. Beach spoke about her Colony experience and played three pieces she had composed there the previous summer: her two hermit thrush works and "The Fair Hills of Éiré, O," op. 91.

Around this time Beach became involved in the National League of American Pen Women and led the formation of the Composers' Unit within the organization in 1924. That summer Dorothy DeMuth Watson, the League's convention chairwoman, paid a visit to the MacDowell Colony, where both Beach and Mrs. MacDowell showed her around. Watson spearheaded what was billed as "the first annual festival by American woman composers" in 1925, held in conjunction with the League meeting in Washington, DC. The three-day festival, April 28 to 30, featured several works by Beach: her songs "A Mirage" and "Stella Viatoris," op. 100, and her choral pieces "Peter Pan," op. 101, and *The Sea-Fairies*, op. 59. The composer accompanied all the performances. On the final day of concerts, Mrs. Edward MacDowell was featured on the program, giving a "Tribute to the American Woman Composers."[19] There is no doubt that Marian's speech was specific to the MacDowell Colony, which was welcoming women artists in all disciplines from its earliest years. Some of the women composers who held residencies before Beach include Helen Dyckman, Mabel Daniels (1878–1971), Margaret Hoberg (1890–1948), Frances Marion Ralston (1875–1952), Ethel Glenn Hier (1889–1971), and Marion Bauer. During Beach's tenure at the Colony, she mentored many of the young women composers in residence, who called her "Aunt Amy" at Beach's request. When the Society of American Women Composers was founded later in 1925, roughly half of the founding members had spent time at the MacDowell Colony.[20]

Many of these women composers held multiple, consecutive residencies at the Colony. Summer in Peterborough became an annual routine; it was a second home where they came to do their creative work without the distractions or responsibilities of daily life. Musicologist Denise Von Glahn elaborates on this idea of the Colony as a second home when she writes about "nature as a summer home." Von Glahn notes that "unmediated access to all of nature remained an elusive experience for women in the early years of the twentieth century." The MacDowell Colony provided "an opportunity to engage with nature in ways denied them in their more urban and busy lives."[21] Too often, escaping the city during the summer was an option only for those with the financial means to do so. While Colony artists were asked to pay a nominal daily fee toward room and board, there were stipends and fellowships available to anyone in need of assistance. The only requirement for acceptance was talent. The support that the Colony extended to women composers was unprecedented at this time.

As soon as Beach was eligible, she joined the Allied Members of the MacDowell Colony, an alumni group of Colony artists first organized in 1911, to "promote the general welfare of the Colony, preserve its traditions, and perpetuate the ideals upon which it was founded."[22] With the launch of the endowment campaign, the Allied Members were increasingly involved with fundraising. Beach spoke eloquently about the Colony on formal programs and organized benefit performances, such as the concert that was held on Saturday, March 7, 1925, in Washington, DC. Billed as "the first formal recital of her compositions in Washington," Beach was assisted by composer and pianist Mary Howe and soprano Gretchen Hood. The concert featured the Washington, DC, premiere of Beach's *Suite for Two Pianos Founded upon Old Irish Melodies*, op. 104. All musicians donated their services "to the cause of the famous MacDowell colony."[23]

By the 1930s, Marian MacDowell's failing health prevented her from touring any longer, and her loyal network of clubwomen was diminishing. The Colony marked its twenty-fifth anniversary in 1932, facing the economic consequences of the Great Depression along with the rest of the world. Beach, in her aforementioned speech to the Music Teachers National Association that year, appealed for support with this clarion call: "It rests with us all, who appreciate the value of that to which we have devoted our lives, to see that this flag of our country's art-life never touches the ground!"[24] The Colony survived the Great Depression, only to face devastation when a hurricane made a rare new England landfall in September 1938. Beach headed for Peterborough as soon as she could to check on her dear friend and assess the damage. The buildings held up remarkably well, with only minor repairs needed. But downed trees were everywhere. The Colony was forced to close in 1939 for the first time in its history. With clean-up costs estimated at $40,000, Marian MacDowell wasted no time. She assembled a team of lumbermen, built a sawmill on the property, and began fundraising. In an undated letter, likely from January 1940, Beach writes: "Dearest friend, Just a look at you, and the sound of your voice would coax the bark off a tree! I cannot be happy a moment In beginning the new year, without sending something to help even a little in the heroic work you are doing in your own heroic way."[25]

The Colony reopened in the summer of 1940, but without Amy Beach. She had fallen ill in late March with bronchitis and was diagnosed with a serious heart condition. On May 14, 1940, Beach wrote to Marian MacDowell, updating her friend on her medical condition:

the bronchial condition is practically normal, but the heart is weak and therefore everything must be cut down to its lowest terms at present, so far as exertion is concerned. Now – of course that rules out the Colony for June!! It hurts to write this more than you can ever know, but you must know the facts and then be able to pass on the bliss that would have been mine to someone else.[26]

A year later she published a letter to the editor of *The Musical Courier*, an appeal for MacDowell Colony Aid in the name of her "Hermit Thrush," to repair the chimney on the Regina Watson studio.[27] Beach returned to the MacDowell Colony one last time in 1941, but she suffered a bout of extreme weakness caused by her heart condition and was unable to stay.

In her final years, Beach split her time between New York and Centerville, Massachusetts. Just weeks before the composer's death, playwright Esther Willard Bates reported on her recent visit to Beach at the annual meeting of the Allied Members of the MacDowell Colony, which occurred each December in New York City: "She was sitting up in bed with a lovely pink jacket on and said in a firm voice, 'Give them all my love, my very dear love, my very best love; be sure to give them my love.'"[28] Seriously ill by this time, Beach had managed to call Marian MacDowell only a few days earlier, surprising her friend. Marian paid one last visit before Amy Beach died on December 27, 1944.

Amy Beach left the rights to her music to the MacDowell Colony, a gift that earned thousands of dollars each year in royalties and performance fees for roughly a decade after her death. The money was deposited into a special Amy Beach Fund. Amounts declined substantially in later years as Beach's music lost favor and the fund was subsumed into the Colony's general operating budget. But Beach biographer Adrienne Fried Block notes "a startling change" that occurred in the early 1990s. Performance and recording fees increased greatly; income from Beach's music tripled between 1992 and 1995. In the early twenty-first century, Beach's music continues to earn income for the MacDowell Colony. In 2022, royalties averaged $2100 annually over the last five years, a remarkable feat considering so much of her music is now public domain. No doubt, Amy Beach would have been elated to learn that almost eighty years after her death, her music continues to support her beloved MacDowell Colony.[29]

Notes

1. The title quotation comes from Mrs. H. H. A. Beach, "The Twenty-Fifth Anniversary of a Vision," in *Proceedings of the Music Teachers' National Association*, twenty-seventh series (Oberlin, OH: MTNA, 1933), 47. In July 2020, the MacDowell Colony dropped the word "Colony" from its name and is known today simply as MacDowell. This chapter retains the earlier usage, MacDowell Colony, which is how it was known during Amy Beach's lifetime.

2. Amy Beach to The Arthur P. Schmidt Co., July 9, 1921, box 303, folder 10, A. P. Schmidt Company Archives, Music Division, Library of Congress.

3. For more information on the history and development of the MacDowell Colony, see Robin Rausch, "The MacDowells and Their Legacy," in *A Place for the Arts: The MacDowell Colony 1907–2007*, ed. Carter Wiseman (Lebanon, NH: University Press of New England, 2006), 50–132.

4. Amy Beach to Richard Angell, April 7, 1938, cited in "MacDowell References," typescript, box 25, folder 5, Adrienne Fried Block Papers, MC 227, Milne Special Collections and Archives, University of New Hampshire Library, Durham, NH. The original is in box 4, the Edward MacDowell Papers, Columbia University.

5. Fanny D. MacDowell to Mrs. Beach, "Monday," Autograph album, box 1, folder 19, Amy Cheney Beach (Mrs. H. H. A. Beach) Papers, 1835–1956, MC 51, Milne Special Collections and Archives, University of New Hampshire Library, Durham, NH. The letterhead reads "Copley Square Hotel, F. S. Risteen & Co." The hotel was opened in the summer of 1891 and sold to another owner after Risteen's death in 1903.

6. E. Douglas Bomberger, *MacDowell* (New York: Oxford University Press, 2013). See especially chapters 18 and 19.

7. Amy Beach to Marian MacDowell, November 27, 1906, box 42, folder 16, Edward and Marian MacDowell Collection, Music Division, Library of Congress.

8. For more on the 1910 Peterborough Pageant, see Robin Rausch, "American Bayreuth: The 1910 Peterborough Pageant and the Genesis of the MacDowell Colony" in *"Very Good for an American": Essays on Edward MacDowell*, ed. E. Douglas Bomberger (Hillsdale, NY: Pendragon Press, 2017), 195–212.

9. Carl Venth, "Peterboro," *The Musical Courier* 73, no. 10 (Sept. 7, 1916): 21.

10. The full title of this work is *Les rêves de Colombine: Suite française*, op. 65 (1907).

11. Regina Watson (1845–1913) studied with Franz Liszt and Karl Tausig in Europe and was a member of ASCAP. The effort to build a studio in her memory at the MacDowell Colony was spearheaded by Elizabeth Sprague Coolidge, a former pupil.

12. For an essay on these two works along with edited scores, see E. Douglas Bomberger, "Amy Marcy Cheney Beach" in *Women Composers: Music Through the Ages*, vol. 6, *Composers born 1800–1899: Keyboard Music*, ed. Sylvia Glickman and Martha Furman Schleifer (New York: G.K. Hall, 1999), 351–70. The manuscripts are in box 25, folders 27 and 28, A. P. Schmidt Company Archives, Music Division, Library of Congress.

13. Beach to The Arthur P. Schmidt Co., November 17, 1921, box 8, folder 10, A. P. Schmidt Company Archives, Music Division, Library of Congress.

14. David Wright. "A Lady, She Wrote Music Nonetheless," *New York Times*, September 6, 1998, p. AR23.

15. Beach, "Twenty-Fifth Anniversary," 45–48.

16. L. Adams Beck, *The Garden of Vision: A Story of Growth* (New York: Cosmopolitan Book Corp., 1929), 225, 232; quoted in Beach, "Twenty-Fifth Anniversary."

17. Adrienne Fried Block, *Amy Beach, Passionate Victorian: The Life and Work of an American Composer, 1867–1944* (New York: Oxford University Press, 1998), 223–24.

18. G. B., "American Music and Composers Loudly Acclaimed at Chautauqua Convention of the G. F. of M. [sic] C.," *The Musical Courier* 85, no. 1 (July 6, 1922): 24.

19. "Woman Composers' Festival," *The Sunday Star*, Washington, D.C., April 26, 1925, Part 3, 5. The Woman Composers' Festival Programs are also included.

20. The founding members of the Society of American Women Composers who had MacDowell Colony connections were Beach, Marion Bauer, Gena Branscombe (1881–1977), Mabel Daniels, Ethel Glenn Hier, Mary Howe (1882–1964), Frances Marion Ralston, Helen Sears, and Louise Souther. Gena Branscombe did not hold a residency until 1945, but she participated in the 1914 summer music festival. Mary Howe was introduced to the Colony by Amy Beach and first worked there in 1926; she later held a leadership position in the organization as a board member.

21. Denise Von Glahn, *Music and the Skillful Listener: American Women Compose the Natural World* (Bloomington: Indiana University Press, 2013), 15.

22. Minutes of Allied Membership meeting, July 22, 1911, Box I:69, Allied Membership, minutes of meetings, 1911–1936, MacDowell Colony Records, Manuscript Division, Library of Congress.

23. "Music in Washington," *The Sunday Star, Washington, D.C.*, March 1, 1925, Part 3, 5.

24. Beach, "Twenty-Fifth Anniversary," 48.

25. Amy Beach to Marian MacDowell, [January 1940?], box 42, folder 16, Edward and Marian MacDowell Collection, Music Division, Library of Congress.

26. Amy Beach to Marian MacDowell, May 14, [1940], box 8, Marian MacDowell Papers, Manuscript Division, Library of Congress.

27. "Mrs. H. H. A. Beach Asks MacDowell Colony Aid," *The Musical Courier* 123, no. 7 (April 1, 1941): 7.

28. Minutes of Allied Members of the MacDowell Colony meeting, December 16, 1944, box I:69, Allied Membership, minutes of meetings, 1937–1953, MacDowell Colony Records, Manuscript Division, Library of Congress.

29. Block, *Amy Beach, Passionate Victorian*, 297. Current figures are from MacDowell Finance Director, Andrew Zimmerman, email to Robin Rausch, June 3, 2022.

4 | Amy Beach and Her Publishers

BILL F. FAUCETT

"The cause of American music has many great champions."
Walter L. Coghill, general manager
The John Church Company (1923)[1]

Amy Beach's music was printed and distributed by a dozen publishers during her lifetime. Her compositions – melodic, imaginative, deftly fashioned, and often supplied with evocative titles and imbued with a popular appeal – were an irresistible commodity for businessmen astute enough to recognize their value. And in her day, there were plenty of those. Beach's principal publishers were Boston's Arthur P. Schmidt Company (by far her most important partnership), G. Schirmer, Inc. (New York), the Theodore Presser Company (Philadelphia), the Oliver Ditson Company (Boston), and the John Church Company (Cincinnati).[2] Several other firms combined to release a small number of her works, some of which rank among Beach's best.

Beach came of age at a time when advances in printing technology and business administration combined to give composers unprecedented visibility and access to a lucrative music market. Following the Civil War, the already flourishing publishing business proliferated. Technological innovations were matched by increased business efficiencies and advances in the mutable art of advertising. In the music publishing industry, as in other fields of commerce, heightened attention was paid to the customers' wants. This was, after all, the era during which the phrase "The customer is always right" gained currency.

Beach's publishers were acutely in touch with their times. As art music in America began to blossom in the second half of the nineteenth century, a cohort of American composers, including Beach, emerged. Publishers were eager to support them at home and abroad, often even at a financial loss. After the turn of the century, especially as the Great War approached, Germany's favorability in the US sank. Esteem for native composers swelled, and many publishers were eager to assert the Americanness of their respective firms.

Beach got to know some of her publishers personally, and, as they passed from the scene, she became familiar with their successors, those family members or business associates who carried on their firms' missions. Not all were musicians, but they were well versed in their trade and genuine in their determination to serve the musical public. As William Arms Fisher, an early historian of music publishing in America, observed, "Business routine and ability, both essential to success, develop with experience, but the great music publishers were primarily great music-lovers."[3] While access to information about Beach and some of her publishers is currently limited, the exploration of her relationships with these "great music lovers," to the extent they can be known, sheds significant light on her music and career.

The Arthur P. Schmidt Company

No small part of any publisher's attraction to Beach was her enormous versatility. When the Arthur P. Schmidt Company began issuing Beach's music, its principal, Arthur Schmidt, could not have imagined her resourcefulness. Among the first dozen Beach works circulated by Schmidt are five sets of songs, including one vocal duet (opp. 1, 2, 10, 11, and 12); three keyboard pieces (opp. 3, 4, and 6), the first of which was a cadenza to Beethoven's Piano Concerto No. 3, which Beach performed to acclaim in 1888 with the Boston Symphony Orchestra; three sacred choral compositions (opp. 5, 7, and 8), including her Grand Mass in E-flat major (op. 5); and *The Little Brown Bee*, a lighthearted secular chorus for women's voices (op. 9). A similar cornucopia of Beach's compositional riches – in all, some seventy works – would be made available exclusively from the Schmidt Company for the next twenty-five years.

When Beach's first works rolled off his press, Schmidt was still a new name in Boston's competitive music business. A German immigrant with about twenty years of US residency, Schmidt established in 1876 a small retail outlet on Winter Street in downtown Boston. He was an ambitious man by nature, and the following year he began to issue his own publications. The effort to reach the burgeoning middle-class consumers of music compelled Schmidt to move his operation in 1889 to Boylston Street in Boston's tony new Back Bay. During this time, Schmidt was also gaining a reputation abroad; he had successfully established relationships and sales outlets in Germany, and he was increasing the distinction of his company by publishing noteworthy works by celebrated composers on both sides of the Atlantic Ocean. As the century turned, the Schmidt Company could boast brisk sales and an expansive catalog of 6,000 compositions, including many by Beach.[4]

# # #

Beach's partnership with Schmidt dates to at least 1885, when on December 2 she married Dr. H. H. A. Beach, a prominent Boston surgeon who was not only Schmidt's personal physician but also a dear friend.[5] Earlier in the same year, Schmidt had published Beach's song, "With Violets," op. 1, no. 1. While there may well have been some cheerleading by the good doctor, Beach had already begun making a name for herself in Boston's musical circles. At her Boston Symphony Orchestra debut on March 28, 1885, she had played Chopin's Concerto in F minor, op. 21. The *Boston Daily Advertiser* critic marveled at her technique, which "has acquired that inexplicable something."[6]

The decades-long partnership between Beach and Schmidt was largely constructive. Schmidt esteemed women composers – before publishing Beach's music, he had churned out works by Helen Hood, Clara Kathleen Rogers, and Helen Hopekirk[7] – and he was sensitive to the values of his customers, many of whom were women. By all accounts, Schmidt was a formidable corporate leader, and he could provide composers with decent financial returns by squeezing from a composition every ounce of profit. Beach's song, "Ah, Love, But a Day," the second number from her popular *Three Browning Songs*, op. 44, provides an excellent example. When it appeared in 1900, one could purchase it in at least five different versions for various voices. Other renderings appeared over the years: a duet arrangement for mezzo-soprano and baritone (1917); a version with an optional violin part (1920); and an arrangement for women's chorus (1927). Schmidt also routinely published "Song Albums," or compilations of previously released songs by various composers that were grouped together and sold at bargain prices.

Schmidt's attention to detail endeared him to many composers, including Beach. She and her husband were "simply overjoyed" with the design and layout of her piano work, *Summer Dreams*, op. 47 (1901), which they considered "strikingly attractive."[8] But if Schmidt's publications were aesthetically appealing – the printing was routinely clear, the spacing was often generous, and splashes of color gave energy to the whole – he recognized that "second editions were rare" and demanded notational accuracy.[9] A careful proofreader himself, on occasion he hired additional ones to ensure exactness. This was a level of service to the composer that would have been unheard of at other publishing houses. And, once a piece was published, Schmidt did not hesitate to send gratis copies to newspaper and journal editors who could review them and to musicians who could perform them.[10]

To the aforementioned characteristics may be added Schmidt's impeccable reputation for honesty. The scrupulous Edward MacDowell hailed the Schmidt Company as "thoroughly reliable and in every way solid and respectable," and insisted that the proprietor was "a thoroughly <u>honest</u> man."[11] Upon his retirement in 1916, Schmidt received a loving cup from composer-admirers whose written testimony acknowledged his "unselfish work in [*sic*] behalf of the American composer."[12] Schmidt by now was reckoned a "pioneer publisher of American music."[13]

# # #

There were other reasons to esteem Schmidt's business ingenuity. Although Beach was just getting into the composing trade, her publisher had already shown a remarkable devotion to the cause of American music. John Knowles Paine's Second Symphony, published by Schmidt in partnership with a Hamburg firm, had appeared in 1880, and Arthur Foote's String Quartet, op. 4, in 1884. Wilma Reid Cipolla has noted that Schmidt brought out relatively few large chamber and orchestral works compared to his enormous catalog of small works – songs, choruses, selections for piano, and the like.[14] But he nevertheless thought that by bringing major instrumental works to market, in both the US and in Europe, he could accomplish two goals: first, he would bestow on his company a necessary corporate identity; second, he would bolster composers native to his adopted country. Schmidt was a grateful patriot – critic Philip Hale called him "wholly American in feeling and in speech"[15] – but he knew that both of these goals invited peril.

As for the former aim, Schmidt made plain his belief that publishers required conspicuous markers of what, or in whom, they believed. "The aim of every firm," he calculated, "must be to secure something which is a specialty in its particular line."[16] To forge his corporate distinctiveness, Schmidt threw in with the almost completely unknown "American Composer." In so doing, he forged an original "brand identity," a gambit for which alone he may be considered a trailblazer among publishers. On the second point, Schmidt's advocacy added luster to the reputations of his stable of American composers – whose leading avatars, besides Beach, were Paine, Foote, MacDowell, and George Whitefield Chadwick – but it did so at his own considerable financial risk. Schmidt is known to have taken a publishing subvention in at least one instance – from Paine's widow, who wished to see her husband's *Oedipus tyrannus*, op. 35 (1881), in print – but more often he footed the printing bills himself. Hale reflected that "Cautious in some respects, [Schmidt] had faith in the American composer, when some other publishers were unwilling to run the risk of pecuniary loss." Hale deeply admired Schmidt's bold "willingness to publish compositions of long breath" – that is, works that might have staying power in an emerging American canon – "for which he knew there would be no adequate return."[17]

# # #

Much has been made of a possible rift between Beach and Schmidt, one that perhaps led to her rejection of the Schmidt Company following the publication of *Three Songs*, op. 71, in 1910. Beach's biographer Adrienne Fried Block has speculated that Dr. Beach's death in June of the same year may have closed the door on her relationship with Schmidt. Her mother's illness and death just eight months later no doubt contributed to their disaffiliation.

Yet another reason for the separation may have been Schmidt's brusque manner, which composer Mabel Daniels once referred to as "bluster."[18] But Hale, in his Schmidt obituary, critiqued the publisher's demeanor: "A man of strong convictions and decided opinions, he was at times aggressive in the expression of them, so that those who did not know him well took a wrong view of his character." Surely Beach knew Schmidt well enough to know that he was, as described by Hale, "sympathetic and generous"; he ultimately strikes one as a man not so much prone to intemperateness as one who could drive a hard bargain and would not hesitate to refuse unprofitable work.[19]

In truth, Beach's production had slowed long before 1910. Although in 1907 Schmidt published three of her finest delicacies – *Eskimos, Four Characteristic Pieces*, op. 64, and *Les rêves de Colombine: Suite française*, op. 65, both for piano; and *The Chambered Nautilus*, op. 66 – over the next three years, 1908 to 1910, just four new works appeared in print: the Quintet for Piano and Strings in F-sharp minor, op. 67, and three song sets (opp. 68, 69, 71). This represents a sharp decline in her published output.

# # #

Beach's spate of family tragedies had but one positive result: she was able in September 1911 to embark on a long-awaited Grand Tour of Europe, from which she returned to the US in September 1914. During three years away, she had intermittent, mostly productive communications with Schmidt. Topics of their correspondence included routine business matters – Beach provided various mailing addresses for the forwarding of royalty payments, and she was careful to keep Schmidt aware of her concert calendar and the resulting reviews.

Nevertheless, Beach grew increasingly dissatisfied with Schmidt. His European operations – the Leipzig branch that opened in 1889 and the English outlets that appeared following the passage of the sweeping International Copyright Law of 1891 – were a windfall to American composers who now had unprecedented visibility in musically mature nations. But Block has posited that while Schmidt had been a strong advocate for American music in Europe, his post-1901 overseas efforts had been comparatively lackluster.[20] He retained a corporate presence in Germany, but by 1906 he had virtually abandoned the British market.[21] It has been further asserted that Beach's bond with Schmidt may have been tested by his inability, or perhaps unwillingness, to keep European distributors supplied with her music during her travels.[22] One imagines that here Schmidt's age might have come into play. By the time Beach arrived in Europe near the end of 1911, her publisher, a man already sixty-five years old and within five years of retiring, may have simply lost his zest for peddling music overseas.[23]

Of course, there may have been other reasons for Beach's renunciation of her first publishing partnership. She had profited from it in innumerable ways, but the fierce relational chill that had now descended would take more than a decade to warm. Until then, Beach was finished with the Arthur P. Schmidt Company.

G. Schirmer, Inc.

Over the course of the next thirty years, until her death in 1944, Beach contracted with a number of other firms to publish eighty-five compositions. The first among them was the house of G. Schirmer, Inc., which took fourteen (16%) of her post-European compositions, most between 1914 and 1918. There are seven song sets (opp. 72, 73, 75, 76, 77, 78, 124); five choral works, including three sacred (opp. 74, 76, 78) and two secular pieces (opp. 74 and 82); the *Theme and Variations for Flute and String Quartet*, op. 80; and the *Prelude and Fugue* for piano, op. 81.

Electing to publish her works with G. Schirmer was not a gamble, for the brand was well respected. The founder and patriarch was Gustav Schirmer, Sr. (1829–93), a German immigrant whose entire life was devoted to the music business. Schirmer pursued his career at several New York City music houses, and he bought an interest in one of them in 1861. Within five years he was its sole owner. By the 1880s, sons Rudolph (1859–1919) and Gustave, Jr. (1864–1907), both highly educated and musically inquisitive, were deeply invested in the industry. Gustav's nephew, E. C. Schirmer (1865–1958), apprenticed at the firm in the late 1870s; he would go on to work at several G. Schirmer spinoff companies – including Boston Music Company – before establishing his own concern.[24] In later years, G. Schirmer, Inc., would be headed by another namesake, Gustave Schirmer (1890–1965), grandson of the founder.

# # #

Beach's recently acquired European bona fides may have endeared her to G. Schirmer's current president, Rudolph Schirmer, who, before matriculating to Princeton and then Columbia Law, had been formally schooled in Weimar, Germany. There he had become acquainted with none other than the great Franz Liszt.[25] Schirmer's affinity to German culture perhaps accounts for Beach's first two publications with the firm, each titled *Two Songs* (opp. 72 and 73), which comprise four songs in the German language.

Rudolph alone had borne the weight of leadership since the passing of his brother, but he oversaw a number of triumphs during his tenure as president. He was at the helm when in 1914 G. Schirmer opened its new publishing facility on Long Island, "the largest and most modern establishment of its kind in America."[26] A year later he introduced *The Musical Quarterly* and appointed as its first editor Oscar G. Sonneck, who resigned from the Library of Congress and the Music Division he had founded. Through the years, as employees moved between posts at G. Schirmer and the Library of Congress, one editorialist quipped that the Library "is an appanage of the Schirmer publishing firm."[27]

Schirmer, like all successful business professionals, was enterprising. One cost-saving ingenuity made big news in the industry. It was reported in 1916 that G. Schirmer would trim the size of its standard sheet music from 10½ × 13¾ inches to 9 × 12 inches, which would result in a 40 percent savings of paper "to the publisher's advantage." It was hailed as "one of those innovations which, when made, causes one to wonder why it was not thought of long ago."[28] It was expected that many competing publishers would follow suit.

Like Arthur Schmidt, Rudolph Schirmer took pride in his stable of American composers, artists whose careers "have become indissolubly connected with his own in American musical history."[29] Besides Beach,

Rudolph's American roster included Henry Hadley, John Alden Carpenter, Charles T. Griffes, and many others.

Health concerns compelled Rudolph to retire from active management in 1916. Given that nine of Beach's fourteen compositions published by G. Schirmer, Inc., date from 1914 to 1916, her rapport with the firm may have existed principally through Rudolph. Certainly, when he died in 1919, the sense of loss was considerable. Rudolph was roundly praised for his activities on behalf of American composers, for "in matters of real art he did not hesitate to subordinate commercial considerations to the higher cultural aspects of an enterprise." Music was vital to Rudolph's life; his vocalist wife sang a Beethoven selection at his deathbed.[30]

# # #

Following the flurry of issuances from G. Schirmer, Beach's published output again plunged. From 1917 to 1920, just three works sprang from Schirmer's press: the *Three Songs,* op. 78 (1917), the *Prelude and Fugue* for keyboard, op. 81 (1918), and the *Theme and Variations for Flute and String Quartet,* op. 80 (1920). Beach published nothing in 1919; and just one gem – the song "Mine Be the Lips," op. 113 – was published in 1921, although not by Schirmer.

Much of this stagnation can be attributed to the times. While the 1918 appearance in the United States of the Spanish flu contributed to interruptions in business operations – trade magazines routinely reported on contagion in the music industry – it was less significant than the menace of war. When the US joined the European war effort in April 1917, commerce struggled; the economy rebounded only two years later. G. Schirmer had by then been taken over by Rudolph's nephew, Gustave Schirmer, whose corporate ambitions gave shorter shrift to the promotion of art music. Popular music was on a meteoric rise, and it was another imposing factor with which the American composer of art music had to reckon. Instruments were at the forefront of public enthusiasm following the 1918 armistice: "Not for a generation or more has there been such an unprecedented demand for pianos and players [i.e., player-pianos]."[31] As concerns the latter, the writer exclaimed that "the demand for this class of instrument surpasses all belief."[32] Naturally, sheet music was required by America's new pianists, and "up-to-date, sentimental, novelty, jazz, rag, blue and shimmie songs" were flooding the American market.[33] Gustave took steps to secure G. Schirmer's place in popular music. He signed composers of middlebrow songs to exclusive contracts and expanded the company into Cincinnati, Memphis, Chicago, New Orleans, and Los

Angeles, although he wisely dumped the company's less profitable stake in the phonograph-selling business.

America's postwar boom – during which one economist reported that Americans "went on a spree that has never been equaled in history"[34] – resulted in skyrocketing inflation. Dwindling demand for increasingly expensive goods ushered in the depression of 1920, which had predictable effects on manufacturing and unemployment. The music business was not spared, but fortunately the economic woes were short-lived. The Roaring Twenties – no great boon to art music composers – soon rushed in.

Besides financial considerations, the music industry also had to grapple with adverse American attitudes toward Germany. Many composers, Beach included, considered Germany a sort of musical homeland, and some publishers thought likewise; it was a view that had the potential to cause trouble. It is likely not a coincidence that Rudolph Schirmer's withdrawal from company affairs had coincided with the upsurge in resentment against Germans as American involvement in the Great War became a reality. Many businesses, including publishing firms, publicly distanced themselves from Germany. One editor took pains to inform readers of G. Schirmer's domestic loyalties: "All its shareholders are American, and the company has no German connections or affiliations of any sort."[35] Declarations of this variety were not unique. At the 1921 death of Arthur P. Schmidt, an obituarist insisted the publisher was "a German of the old school, abhorring Prussian militarism and Prussian arrogance."[36]

Beach was seemingly torn on the matter. Although she abandoned the composition of German songs during the period of the Great War, she also had not been inspired to write any new patriotic ones.

The Houses of Presser, Ditson, and Church

As the depression ebbed, Beach contracted with the Theodore Presser Company, which published thirteen (15%) of her post-1914 compositions; most of them date from 1922 to 1925, although a few appeared later. Company founder Theodore Presser (1848–1925) was a competent musician who sought collaborations with composers. In his youth, Presser's brother had befriended Stephen Foster, and the three serenaded neighbors in their native Pittsburgh.[37] Composer George Whitefield Chadwick was also a close friend. Presser and Chadwick occasionally roomed together in Boston in the 1870s. They did likewise later, when both were students at the Royal Conservatory in Leipzig, Germany.[38]

What would one day be Presser's publishing empire began in 1883 with the founding in Virginia of his educational magazine, *The Etude*. Shortly afterward he moved the business to Philadelphia and added retail operations. *The Etude* featured copious amounts of music in its pages, and soon Presser began to publish those works in individual leaves. An aggressive publishing regimen, combined with the rapid acquisition of other, smaller firms, yielded impressive results. In 1908, the Theodore Presser Company could boast a catalog of 7,000 compositions, 119 employees, and circulation of *The Etude* at 135,000.[39]

A surprising number of Beach's compositions with Presser are religious in character. Several of her five songs or song sets are sacred, including "Spirit Divine," op. 88, "Jesus my Saviour," op. 112, and *Around the Manger*, op. 115. Presser also published four sacred choral works (opp. 84, 95, 96, 98), as well as her *Te Deum*, op. 84, and the secular "Peter Pan," op. 101, for women's voices. But instrumental works were not neglected; there are three works for keyboard (op. 87, a rare unnumbered selection, and op. 128) published respectively in 1923, 1928, and 1932.

Theodore Presser died in 1925, after which Beach published just two more compositions with his company.[40]

# # #

Beach published nine (10%) of her post-European compositions with the distinguished Oliver Ditson Company starting in 1921 – eight were brought out in the 1920s; one outlier appeared in 1934. They included three piano selections (opp. 102, 116, 119); four choral works, three sacred (opp. 103, 109, 115) and one secular (op. 140); and two songs (opp. 113 and 120). In what may have been an act of nostalgia, Beach was actually returning to – not debuting with – Ditson, for the company can claim credit for publishing Beach's first printed work, "The Rainy Day" (1883), a song with words by Henry Wadsworth Longfellow.

Beach's long-awaited return to Ditson may have been prompted by its striking corporate prowess. When Oliver Ditson died in 1888, a succession of leaders followed until 1907, when his son, Charles Healey Ditson, was named president. Charles, who had been leading his own firm in New York City, became president, but the Boston operations were run by Clarence A. Woodman, a company veteran.

Woodman was an innovative businessman. Under his leadership, Ditson's retail stores were redesigned, and advertising became far more aggressive, both in print media and onsite at various storefronts. The Ditson Company was a leader in creative window displays, which often spotlighted visiting artists, events and holidays, upcoming concerts, or local musical celebrities.[41] For example, Beach's *From Six to Twelve*, op. 119 – a delightful keyboard suite that includes "Canoeing," "Boy Scouts March," and "A Campfire Ceremonial" – reflected the company's support of the Boy Scouts, which was the subject of an elaborate window layout in 1923.[42]

Any composer would have admired Ditson's attention to its customers and to music dealers around the country. Woodman spoke regularly on matters related to customer service, and in 1921 the company's sales booklet titled "Ditson Service" offered tips to the sales force and advised "the music buyer as to how he may best satisfy his needs."[43] To that end, Ditson published a wide variety of popular, art, and educational music. Among the most progressive of Ditson's projects was the partnership with the Aeolian Company to produce recordings connected to some of its publications, including Clarence G. Hamilton's *Music Appreciation* (1920) and Karl W. Gehrkens's *Fundamentals of Music* (1924).[44] The company's geographic reach might also have convinced composers to sign with Ditson. Operations were imposing in Boston, New York, Chicago, and London, and the war hastened the company's foreign interests "to increase wondrously" – vital new markets even included Japan and Australia, both of which were proving profitable.[45]

As with the other publishers examined thus far, the Oliver Ditson Company was eager to validate its Americanness. It established the unabashedly patriotic *Red, White, and Blue* series, a "comprehensive catalogue of representative American songs," which were "bound to become camp favorites" among the troops.[46] Following the 1918 armistice, Woodman said, "I feel that we are justified in adopting a slogan for the future: 'The American Composer First.'" He further predicted that the expansion of the American music project would be "a dominating factor" across the globe.[47] Industry leader John C. Freund later called the Ditson Company "a distinctly American concern," one that was "among the very first to hold out a helping hand to the American composers – woman as well as man."[48]

# # #

John Church (1834–90) was already employed at the Oliver Ditson Company when in 1859 he partnered with Mr. Ditson for a half-interest in a Cincinnati music retail operation. Church bought Ditson's share a decade later, and he became the sole owner of what was later named the John Church Company. Celebrated for publishing music in a variety of styles – from Sousa's marches to hymns by the revivalists Dwight Moody and Ira D. Sankey – the firm was also known for its informative periodical, *Church's Musical Visitor* (1871–97), an out-West response to Boston's *Dwight's Journal of Music*.

Church died in 1890, and leadership of the company eventually fell to his son-in-law, R. B. Burchard. Perhaps Burchard's most astute business man-euver was the promotion in 1919 of Walter L. Coghill to the position of general manager of the Church Company's New York City–based publica-tion headquarters. Coghill had been a loyal employee since 1897 and was admired in the trade. Following a quarter-century of steadfast service, he was made a member of the company's board of directors in 1922.

Coghill was an effective advocate for his profession, and, as a representative of the Music Publishers Association of the United States, he often spoke at industry conventions. Coghill variously addressed "The Best Manner of Advertising"; the "Advantages of a Sheet Music Department to Piano and Talking Machine Retailers"; and best practices for the introduction of sheet music departments in general stores. Keeping an eye on developments in technology, Coghill also commented on extracting "royalties from broadcast-ing music through wireless methods."[49]

When made general manager, Coghill promised a "vigorous cam-paign" of sheet music selling, as he believed strongly in the cause of American music.[50] Marketing campaigns soon touted the John Church Company as "The House Devoted to the Progress of American Music."[51] Under Coghill's auspices Church published six compositions (7%) of Beach's post-European output. All appeared in 1924 and 1925, by which time the company had settled on a savvy sales strategy: its music would be supplied with "fanciful headings" and that "never-to-be-despised virtue, melody." Among the pieces Beach submitted were four keyboard works: the *Suite for Two Pianos Founded upon Old Irish Melodies*, op. 104; *Old Chapel by Moonlight*, op. 106; the far less fancifully titled *Nocturne*, op. 107; and *A Cradle Song of the Lonely Mother*, op. 108. Beach's compositions obviously comported nicely with Coghill's imperatives.

Schmidt Redux and Beach's Other Publishers

When Arthur P. Schmidt died in 1921, the encomia poured in. Composer Arthur Foote remarked that Schmidt's work was of "far-reaching import-ance"; critic Philip Hale cited his "sympathetic and generous" character; and a writer for *The Musical Courier*, echoing a sentiment MacDowell sounded three decades earlier, claimed that the publisher's "dealings with the composers . . . were scrupulously upright and honest."[52]

Beach gradually renewed her relationship with the Arthur P. Schmidt Company following his death. One could surmise that her appreciation of Schmidt's character and accomplishments had rebounded over time and were renewed at his passing; a more cynical view posits that he was now simply out of the way. In any event, Beach was ready to return to the Schmidt Company. Its new owners, who had taken over the management at Schmidt's 1916 retirement, were Harry B. Crosby, Henry R. Austin, and Florence J. Emery. Beach informed them that "It has been about 4 years since I have sent anything for publication in any direction, owing to many and various circumstances beyond my control," and that she was prepared to resume business dealings.[53] It is difficult to know the Schmidt Company's corporate priorities with certainty, but one was clearly a reconnection to Beach. Although the new managers responded that "difficulties of production" and "very unsettled conditions" prevented the company from making too many promises, they nevertheless went on to publish a whopping twenty-six (30%) of Beach's post-1914 compositions, nineteen of which were published after 1927.[54]

The earliest fruits of her revivified activities with Schmidt are three keyboard compositions (opp. 83, 91, and 92) and her song "In the Twilight" (op. 85), all of which left the presses in 1922. An additional three keyboard selections (opp. 97, 111, and 130) appeared through 1932. Beach's production of ten choral works, including her laudable *Canticle of the Sun* (op. 123), is noteworthy because seven of them are sacred. The remaining works are songs or song sets, several of which are also sacred. Among the secular works, we see that Beach has returned to ethnically influenced works with her arrangement of a traditional song, "On a Hill: Negro Melody" (without opus number). Schmidt also published her *Two Mother Songs* (op. 137), a subgenre that she had long found enthralling but which by now was considered old-fashioned.[55]

The Schmidt Company's desire to re-sign Beach may have been part of an ongoing strategy to emphasize the company's close connection to the American composer. Just after the Great War, Schmidt published two volumes of music by composer and signer of the Declaration of Independence, Francis Hopkinson. The initial installment, *The First American Composer* (1919), was "used extensively this season on the concert stage." The second volume, *Colonial Love Lyrics* (1920), was "quite as interesting musically as the first collection."[56] As for Beach, the Schmidt Company surely calculated that putting out works by America's greatest woman composer would be a feather in its artistic and marketing cap.

Beach corresponded with Schmidt principals throughout the twenties and thirties. One 1935 letter from Henry Austin demonstrates a cordial working relationship, although his friendly eye rarely strayed from the company's bottom line. He again groused about the company's current "slow rate of production," which was more likely a slow rate of sales caused by the Great Depression. Austin plainly wished to reissue some of Beach's older works, but he suggested that, rather than commissioning costly new engravings, a more fiscally prudent solution would include utilizing existing printing plates for reprints and depleting Beach inventories that were still sitting in company warehouses. Beach was probably unsurprised when Austin made clear that the publishing of new works for which there was no current market would have to be put on hold.[57]

# # #

Beginning in the 1930s, Beach published a few miscellaneous compositions with a number of firms. Many of them are respected names: Silver Burdett (Boston), H. W. Gray (New York), C. C. Birchard (Boston), and others. By far the most important of Beach's later publishers was Composers Press, led by Charles T. Haubiel (1892–1978). Haubiel, a pianist and composer of marked ability, was Beach's colleague at the MacDowell Colony. In 1935, he founded Composers Press explicitly for the purpose of putting out American works. Four Beach compositions appeared from Haubiel's press between 1938 and 1942, including her *Five Improvisations*, op. 148; the Trio for Piano, Violin and Violoncello, op. 150; *Pastorale* for Woodwind Quintet, op. 151; and the sacred song, "Though I Take the Wings of Morning," op. 152 (from Psalm 139). Although serious and contemporary in their conception, like most of Beach's oeuvre, these compositions are attractive and accessible.

Haubiel's press was a perfect match for Beach's 1930s compositional style, which had veered toward Modernism. Publishing music likely to have been eschewed by more mainstream publishers, Haubiel's operation was a collective; composers had to share the financial risks, and Beach had skin in the game.[58] Freed from the concerns of editors and the constraints of practical commerce, she could produce works whose appeal to profit-oriented publishers and general audiences might have been limited. Besides that, Beach was no doubt relieved that, at the Composers Press, it was unnecessary to gild her works with "fanciful titles."

Conclusion

What do we learn, then, from an investigation of Beach's publishers and an exploration of her relations with them? First, it is clear that Beach ably navigated personal ties to her publishers throughout her career. The available record demonstrates that while her husband was alive, Arthur P. Schmidt was perforce her go-to publisher. Beach's decision to take up with other publishers was only possible following Dr. Beach's passing. But while her connection with Schmidt may well have been the result of her husband's association with him, there are hints that Beach's future publisher relationships were based on more than corporate preeminence. Given a few facts – that Beach's work with G. Schirmer Inc. ended at approximately Rudolph Schirmer's death; and that her resumption of publication with the Arthur P. Schmidt Company occurred only after Schmidt's passing; and that her stint with the Theodore Presser Company ended at approximately Presser's death – there is every reason to believe that Beach's choices of publishers were generally guided by close personal connections. This is especially true of her later collaborations with Charles Haubiel and his Composers Press.

Second, music by Beach published before her European sojourn – that is, her pre-Great War works offered by Schmidt – represent an eclectic collection of genres, including vocal and instrumental compositions. But after the war, her published output comports with the narrower needs of her publishers, which – with the single exception of op. 80, the aforementioned *Theme and Variations for Flute and String Quartet* – did not include instrumental music other than works for keyboard until 1939. Schmidt and Schirmer had a market for her secular songs, as well as her choruses, both sacred and secular. Oliver Ditson benefited mostly from her keyboard works and sacred choral works. The Church Company focused its attention on her catchy keyboard pieces. And Presser considered her sacred compositions – songs and choruses – most favorable to his catalog. We cannot be certain whether Beach ever conversed with her publishers on the notion of putting out new works she might have wished to compose for orchestra or chamber ensemble. Although no more orchestral pieces appeared, she wrote several chamber works that remained unpublished for decades. Perhaps following the war, Beach simply acceded to the realities of a market that esteemed music in its smaller and more popular forms, ones that were not only more accommodating to home and church musicians but also more susceptible to profitability.

It is worth noting, thirdly, that all of Beach's major publishers were hugely concerned with perceptions of their own Americanism. Those firms founded by Germans were especially eager to tout themselves as American companies whose composers included Americans. Even if they did not seek to publish characteristically American music, per recipes supplied by Dvořák and others, Beach's publishers nevertheless were compelled to voice their strong support of native talent.

Finally, it is fascinating to discover that the men who published Beach's music were by and large considered extraordinary individuals, and that their tangled corporate interrelationships continued unabated through the mid-twentieth century. The John Church Company was acquired by the Theodore Presser Company in 1930. Two years after Charles Ditson's 1929 death, Presser added the Oliver Ditson Company to its empire. The Arthur P. Schmidt Company persevered until 1960, when it was purchased by the Illinois-based Summy-Birchard Company. And G. Schirmer, Inc., survived intact until 1968.

During a brief publishing renaissance in the 1990s, small and scholarly presses saw in Beach's compositions exactly what earlier publishers had seen in her works during her lifetime, but there was also an undeniable attraction to her personal odyssey. In a profession dominated by men, a young woman sought a career as a concert pianist. She was then directed toward composition, a field in which she struggled through self-guided learning, limitations wrought by marriage, family tribulations, wars, depressions, and the persistent vagaries of the music market and its related commercial considerations. It was to Beach's extreme good fortune that, for most of her professional life, she persevered in partnership with publishers – themselves music-lovers – who recognized her genius.

Notes

1. "Mr. Coghill's Earnest Plea," *The Music Trades* 65, no. 6 (February 10, 1923): 8A.
2. For data on Beach's publications, this overview relies on the "Appendix: Catalog of Works" provided by Adrienne Fried Block in her biography, *Amy Beach, Passionate Victorian* (New York: Oxford University Press, 1998), 300–9.
3. William Arms Fisher, *One Hundred and Fifty Years of Publishing in the United States, 1783–1933* (Boston: Oliver Ditson, 1933), 124.
4. See "Publisher Arthur P. Schmidt: Quarter-Centennial Anniversary," *Musical Courier* 43, no. 14 (October 2, 1901): 34.

5. Block, *Amy Beach, Passionate Victorian*, 49.

6. "Music and the Drama," *Boston Daily Advertiser*, March 30, 1885, 4.

7. Wilma Reid Cipolla, "Arthur P. Schmidt: The Publisher and His American Composers," in *Vistas of American Music: Essays in Honor of William K. Kearns*, edited by Susan L. Porter and John Graziano (Warren, MI: Harmonie Park Press, 1999), 269.

8. Beach to Schmidt, October 12, 1903; quoted in Cipolla, "Arthur P. Schmidt," 277.

9. Schmidt to Henry Austin, March 16, 1908; quoted in Cipolla, "Arthur P. Schmidt," 280.

10. Adrienne Fried Block, "Why Amy Beach Succeeded as a Composer: The Early Years." *Current Musicology* 36 (Fall 1983): 50–51, 55.

11. MacDowell to Doris Raff, January 12, 1889, and April 24, 1890 (MacDowell's emphasis); quoted in E. Douglas Bomberger, "Edward MacDowell, Arthur P. Schmidt, and the Shakespeare Overtures of Joachim Raff: A Case Study in Nineteenth-Century Music Publishing," *Notes* 54, no. 1 (Sept. 1997): 13, 19.

12. See "Publisher Schmidt Presented with Loving Cup," *Musical Courier* 72, no. 7 (February 17, 1916): 26. Beach was not among the signers of the note to Schmidt.

13. Cipolla, "Arthur P. Schmidt," 265, 281.

14. Cipolla, "Arthur P. Schmidt," 267.

15. Philip Hale, "Arthur P. Schmidt," *Boston Herald*, May 7, 1921, 12.

16. Schmidt to Max Kutschmann, December 9, 1908; quoted in Cipolla, "Arthur P. Schmidt," 275.

17. Hale, "Arthur P. Schmidt," 12.

18. Quoted in Block, *Amy Beach, Passionate Victorian*, 186.

19. Hale, "Arthur P. Schmidt," 12.

20. Block, *Amy Beach, Passionate Victorian*, 185; also Wilma Reid Cipolla, "Marketing the American Song in Edwardian London," *American Music* 8, no. 1 (Spring 1990): 86.

21. Cipolla, "Marketing the American Song," 92.

22. Block, *Amy Beach, Passionate Victorian*, 185.

23. Block, *Amy Beach, Passionate Victorian*, 185.

24. See "E. C. Schirmer Formed in Boston," *The Music Trades* 62, no. 25 (December 17, 1921): 196.

25. "Rudolph E. Schirmer Dies," *Musical Courier* 79, no. 9 (August 28, 1919): 34.

26. "Rudolph E. Schirmer Dies," 34.

27. [Untitled editorial notice], *Musical Courier* 83, no. 23 (December 8, 1921): 20.

28. Untitled editorial notice, 20.

29. "Rudolph E. Schirmer Dies," 34.

30. "Rudolph E. Schirmer Dies," 34. The Beethoven selection is unidentified.

31. "A 'Musical Christmas' has been the Dominating Note of Trade in Boston," *The Music Trades* 56, no. 26 (December 28, 1918): 17.

32. "A Musical Christmas," 17.

33. "Harris Ready for the New Year," *The Music Trades* 57, no. 1 (January 4, 1919): 34.

34. Roger W. Babson, "Business IS Recuperating – Get Your Share!" *The Music Trades* 61, no. 18 (April 30, 1921): 1.

35. "Trade Jottings," *Musical Opinion & Music Trade Review* 40, no. 475 [London] (April 1917): 443.

36. "A. P. Schmidt Dies," *The Music Trades* 61, no. 20 (May 14, 1921): 161.

37. Chris Yoder, "Theodore Presser, Educator, Publisher, Philanthropist: Selected Contributions to the Music Teaching Profession in America" (PhD dissertation, University of Illinois at Urbana-Champaign, 1978), 55.

38. Chadwick named his eldest son, Theodore, after Presser.

39. Yoder, "Theodore Presser," 66.

40. As of this writing, the Theodore Presser Company collection at the Library of Congress, comprising 600 boxes of materials, "is not processed, is housed off-site, and does not yet have a finding aid." It is unavailable to researchers. Communication to the author from Dr. Paul Allen Sommerfeld, Music Division, Library of Congress, July 15, 2020.

41. See for example: "Ditson Co. in [Charles Wakefield] Cadman Tie-Up," *The Music Trades* 66, no. 22 (December 1, 1923): 58.

42. "Oliver Ditson Co. Shows Two Seasonable Displays," *The Music Trades* 65, no. 25 (June 23, 1923): 39.

43. See Ditson advertisement, *The Music Trades* 61, no. 25 (June 18, 1921): 46.

44. See "Aeolian Co. to Issue Lists of Duo-Art Recordings for Use in Connection with Music Text Books," *The Music Trades* 66, no. 19 (November 10, 1923): 58.

45. "Foreign Business Grows," *The Music Trades* 56, no. 9 (August 31, 1918): 15.

46. "Ditson House is Aiding Soldiers," *The Music Trades* 56, no. 12 (September 21, 1918): 35.

47. "Manufacturers See Prosperity Ahead," *The Music Trades* 56, no. 25 (December 21, 1918): 45.

48. J. C. F. [John C. Freund], "The Ditson Company," *The Music Trades* 66, no. 12 (September 22, 1923): 12.

49. Coghill's addresses were compiled from various notices. On the American Museum of Musical Art, see "Convention of Music Publishers in New York," *The Music Trades* 61, no. 25 (June 18, 1921): 47.

50. "Coghill Heads Publication Dept.," *The Music Trades* 57, no. 16 (April 19, 1919): 49.

51. See the advertisement in *The Music Trades* 57, no. 23 (June 7, 1919): 177.

52. See Arthur Foote and Katherine Foote Raffy, *Arthur Foote, 1853–1937: An Autobiography* (Norwood, MA: Plimpton Press, 1946), 51–52; Hale, "Arthur P. Schmidt," 12; and *Musical Courier* 83, no. 5 (August 4, 1921): 20.

53. Beach to the Schmidt Company, October 18, 1921; quoted in Jeanell Elizabeth Wise Brown, "Amy Beach and her Chamber Music: Biography, Documents, Style" (DMA dissertation, University of Maryland College Park, 1993), p. 39.

54. Schmidt Company to Beach, November 14, 1921; quoted in Brown, "Amy Beach," 51–52.
55. "In Defense of Jazz Music," *The Music Trades* 61, no. 13 (March 26, 1921): 50.
56. "Francis Hopkinson's Songs Much Programmed," *Musical Courier* 79, no. 24 (December 25, 1919): 35.
57. Austin to Beach, November 27, 1935; quoted in Elizabeth Moore Buchanan, "The Anthems and Service Music of Amy Beach Published by the Arthur P. Schmidt Company" (M. A. Thesis, American University, 1996), p. 117.
58. See Block, *Amy Beach, Passionate Victorian*, 286.

## PART II

Profiles of the Music

5 | Amy Beach's Keyboard Music

KIRSTEN JOHNSON

Amy Beach was a prolific composer for the piano. As a teenager, she had a blossoming career as a concert pianist curtailed by her mother, who did not wish her to tour, and her husband, who encouraged her to compose. Beach herself wrote that while she made the switch to focusing on composition upon her marriage at the age of eighteen, she, at the time, had thought herself "a pianist first and foremost."[1] This aptitude as a pianist comes through in her piano compositions: Beach wrote fluidly for the piano, knowing the instrument intimately herself. Her pieces range from simple, more pedagogic works, through to character pieces and virtuosic works requiring an advanced piano technique. This chapter will explore Beach's prodigious oeuvre for piano solo, concluding with a brief discussion of her pieces for organ, piano duet, and two pianos.

The Early Piano Pieces

Beach's musical gifts were obvious from an early age: she was singing before she could speak, had perfect pitch, and had a remarkable musical memory. Her mother kept her away from the family piano until she was four, as she did not want Beach to have the life of a musical prodigy. *Mamma's Waltz*, her earliest extant piece for piano, along with *Snowflake Waltz* and *Marlborough Waltz*, were "written in her head" while visiting her grandfather's farm in Maine.[2] Beach herself notated *Mamma's Waltz* several years later in the manuscript that survives, with the annotation, "Composed at the age of four years."[3] *Mamma's Waltz* is in simple rondo form, with two interspersed sections contrasting with the opening material.[4]

Beach's mother limited her time at the piano and began to teach her piano formally only at the age of six. By seven, Beach was playing Bach fugues, Chopin waltzes, and a Beethoven sonata, as well as performing in public. She was offered contracts by several concert managers, all turned down by her parents. In 1875 her family moved to Boston, and in 1876 Beach began to study privately with the pianist Ernst Perabo, who taught at the New England Conservatory of Music.

Several pieces survive from this period. *Menuetto* (1877), *Romanza* (1877), and *Air and Variations* (1877) were all written when Beach was ten years old. *Menuetto* is a precursor of the *Menuet italien*, op. 28, no. 2. The first half of the piece is in rounded binary form, followed by the main theme presented in the parallel minor. A short harmonic progression leads to the final phrase, a restatement of the theme that ended the binary section. *Romanza* shows Beach experimenting with modulation as she moves skillfully from the opening key of D major into F-sharp major eight bars later.

Air and Variations is a larger work and evidence of Beach's technical development as a pianist. The theme is first presented simply in A minor. The variation that follows requires repeated-note facility in the right hand. The second variation moves into F major with sextuplet patterns and then returns to A minor for an energetic *presto* variation. A final variation, with the melody in the left hand accompanied by groups of four running up and down the keyboard, brings the set to conclusion.

Petite Valse (1878) is a charming waltz in D-flat major, a forerunner of the *Danse des fleurs*, op. 28, no. 3. Beach uses a structural organization similar to *Menuetto*: a binary form is followed by a move to the parallel minor, with a nicely handled modulatory sequence back to a statement of the opening melody in D-flat major.

Moderato, an undated piece in handwriting similar to the pieces just mentioned, so perhaps of a similar date, survives in manuscript with a single bar at the bottom of the first page lost due to a torn corner (completed by the author on her recording of this piece).[5] The mood Beach creates with *Moderato* is magical: the static writing, with a rising arpeggio in the first part of every bar leading to longer melodic notes, and subtle shifts of harmonic color come together to form a miniature gem.

In 1882, Beach began studying piano in Boston with Carl Baermann, a pupil of Liszt's. Her mother permitted her to make her debut in 1883 at the age of sixteen with Ignaz Moscheles's Concerto No. 2 in G minor in Boston's Music Hall. Beach performed as a recitalist and concerto soloist in and around Boston for the next several years, though her mother did not allow her to tour extensively, nor would she permit her to go to Europe for further study.[6]

Piano Pieces Composed After Her Marriage

Upon her marriage in 1885, Amy Marcy Cheney became Mrs. H. H. A. Beach. Her husband did not wish for her to accept performance fees, but he did allow her to play in aid of charities and encouraged her development as a composer. Beach's next surviving work for piano is an excellent *Cadenza* (1887, published 1888) written for the first movement of Beethoven's third piano concerto.[7] Nine pages in length, it uses scales, octaves, and trills to explore Beethoven's motives in a most effective manner, requiring virtuoso technique.

Beach's next solo work, *Valse Caprice*, op. 4, was premiered in 1889 by the composer herself. The figuration of the opening introduction is as if a curtain is being raised at a ballet. And then the dance begins. Beach decorates the melody with light grace notes, lending an improvisatory and capricious air to the work. The piece was championed by the pianist Josef Hofmann (1876–1957), who used it frequently as an encore.

Beach uses her song, "O my luve is like a red, red rose," op. 12, no. 3, as a basis for her wonderful *Ballade*, op. 6 (published 1894). Following a brief introduction, the melody enters, accompanied with flowing triplets between the hands. After setting out the theme, Beach begins again, initially in D-flat minor, with the melody in the left hand. The decoration in the right hand becomes more elaborate and passionate, with beautiful piano writing. An *Allegro con vigore* ensues, portraying Robert Burns' words of the third stanza of Beach's art song: "Till a' the seas gang dry, my dear; And the rocks melt wi' the sun; I will luve thee still, my dear; While the sands of life shall run."[8] Bold and tempestuous, this builds in a fervor of emotion to a climax. From the sustained unison octaves emerges a pianississimo *Lento*, a quasi-cadenza on the opening melody. The material from both sections is combined, building to a final statement of the theme in large chords and octaves. Utterly depleted, *Ballade* winds down, fading into the distance, ending exquisitely still.

Sketches, op. 15 (published 1892), is a four-movement work, each piece preceded with a line of poetry. The first, "In Autumn," is annotated, "Feuillages jaunissants sur les gazons épars" ["Yellowed leaves are scattered on the grass"], an excerpt from a poem by Alphonse de Lamartine. In F-sharp minor, it is jaunty and light, reminiscent of Schubert. At the beginning of the second piece, "Phantoms," Beach quotes a line by Victor Hugo: "Toutes fragiles fleurs, sitôt mortes que nées" ["All the fragile flowers die as soon as they are born"]. "Phantoms" is in 3/8, in ABA form, with an emphasis on the second beat of the bar, lending a mazurka-like feel.[9] "Dreaming" quotes another excerpt by Hugo, "Tu me parles du fond d'un rêve" ["You speak to me from the depths of a dream"]. It opens with triplet figuration between the hands, which continues throughout, with long notes conveying the melody. Another quotation from Lamartine is used under the title of the virtuosic final piece, "Fireflies": "Naître avec le printemps, mourir avec les roses" ["To be born with the spring, to die with the roses"]. Passages in double thirds in the right hand convey the flitting of fireflies as they light up the night sky. This piece was played by Ferruccio Busoni, Josef Hofmann, and Moritz Rosenthal, giving evidence of the spread of Beach's works during her lifetime.

Bal Masque, op. 22 (1893, published 1894), is a waltz in the Viennese tradition. It demonstrates Beach's affinity with the form, having heard her mother play Strauss waltzes at the piano from her infancy. In ABA form, the first section is preceded by a short introduction establishing the key of G major. The middle section in E-flat major is warmer and more intimate in sound. Beach decorates the "A" material in the restatement of the theme, imitating various woodwind instruments in her working of the material. Her orchestral arrangement of this work is discussed in Chapter 8.[10]

Trois morceaux caractéristiques, op. 28 (1894), opens with "Barcarolle," a lovely evocation of a boat-song. In 6/8 time, the undulating left-hand accompaniment provides an ongoing support for the *cantabile* melody. Set in ABA form, the middle section introduces a new melody in the left hand, which is developed expansively with full chords. After reaching a climax, Beach backs away, with a *tranquillo* setting of this melody ushering in an embellished restatement of the opening theme. The second piece, "Menuet italien," is an expanded version of Beach's childhood *Menuetto*. Beach uses much of the same material, but in a more complex way, adding passing tones and secondary lines. It is a larger work: there is now a middle section in C minor, with artfully written passagework decorating the line. "Danse des fleurs," marked *Tempo di Valse*, is the final *morceau*. In D-flat major, the opening theme dances between the hands. The second theme, with a longer line, is beautifully presented in the key of C-sharp minor. Clever motivic development, requiring pianistic dexterity, builds to a climax before Beach returns to the opening melody to finish lightly.

Some Pedagogic Pieces

Often the line is blurred between pedagogic and concert repertoire, epitomized by Beach's two sets of pieces for "children." While they may be less complex than her longer and technically challenging larger works, the pieces are worthy and appealing as concert program fillers or encores. It takes a master to write simply but effectively, and Beach shows her skill in these charming, delicate, and nuanced pieces.

Children's Carnival, op. 25 (1894), is a set of miniatures that depict a carnival festival using characters whose roots lie in the Italian commedia dell'arte. The set opens with a march, "Promenade": the procession of entertainers through city streets. Next is "Columbine," a quiet piece inspired by the character of a young woman, sometimes portrayed as the lover of Harlequin. "Pantalon," the next movement, is based on the eponymous character, an older man who is often cast as the father of Columbine. "Pierrot and Pierrette" follows, a gentle waltz in two parts, each section repeated. Pierrot and Pierrette are two clowns: Pierrot is desperately in love with Pierrette, but she falls in and out of love with him. "Secrets" is a lovely *andantino* with the melody hidden between the hands, a duet of two voices juxtaposed on different parts of the beat. *Children's Carnival* concludes with "Harlequin," the acrobat of the menagerie, conveyed in a quick, light melody that dances around the keyboard.

Children's Album, op. 36, was written in 1897,[11] the year after the premiere of Beach's "Gaelic" Symphony and the composition of Sonata in A minor for piano and violin. A suite of pieces in classic musical forms, it opens with "Minuet," a charming composition in three parts. The first section is in rounded binary form, followed by a trio and then the return of the opening section. The next movement, "Gavotte," harks back to the French court dance of the same name. In "Waltz," Beach sets a long melody over a waltz pattern in the left hand for this gentle reminiscence in ABA form. The fourth movement, "March," is a sprightly dance of dotted rhythms with the odd three-bar phrase thrown in to set the marchers off-kilter. A lively "Polka" ends *Children's Album*: marked *scherzando*, a sense of fun pervades as the phrases bubble one after the other.[12]

The Beginning of the Twentieth Century

Beach's first solo piano piece of the twentieth century is *Serenade* (1902), a beautiful transcription of Richard Strauss's *Ständchen*, op. 17, no. 2.[13] Beach's handling of Strauss's material transforms the original work in a highly compelling transcription for piano. She cleverly incorporates the sung line in among the rippling accompaniment, beautifully rendering Strauss's setting of the words by nineteenth-century German poet Adolf Friedrich von Schack. The opening stanza is in the same register as

Strauss's original, but the second verse is set down an octave by Beach, with occasional forays into the upper register of the piano to end vocal phrases. In the next section, when Strauss moves into D major, Beach begins with the melody in octaves in the bass of the piano to take the listener into "the twilight mysterious under the lime trees." The piece is mostly faithful to the original score except at the climax, where Beach expands the material in a most effective way: she includes extra bars of arpeggiation and doubles the duration of the vocal pitches, as well as adding a pianistic flourish at the end.

Beach had a keen interest in folk music, evidenced in many of her compositions, including the first of the *Two Compositions*, op. 54 (1903). "Scottish Legend" is an original melody, evocative of Celtic origins, rising thrice as it builds to a peak before a denouement to the tonic D minor. The solemnity of the first section is juxtaposed with the slightly more animated middle section, in D major. "Scottish Legend" concludes with a truncated restatement of the opening, marked *dolcissimo*. The second piece, "Gavotte fantastique," is based on the "Gavotte" of *Children's Album*, op. 36: Beach uses this as a springboard for a more advanced showpiece. Trills and octaves enhance the template already established to make this a fantastical tour de force.

Variations on Balkan Themes, op. 60 (1904), is one of Beach's seminal works for piano. Written in 1904, it is a substantial piece based on folk melodies that were introduced to Beach by Reverend William Washburn Sleeper and his wife, missionaries to Bulgaria. At a talk that Beach organized, Rev. Sleeper played some folk melodies that the couple had collected in their travels. Beach transcribed four of the melodies from memory several days after the presentation and used them as the basis for *Variations*, which she took just over a week to write.[14] Beach wrote an orchestral version of the variations in 1906, including an extra variation.[15] She revised the piano score of *Variations* in 1936 for her publisher, taking out repeats, transposing the funeral march and final statement into E-flat minor, and shortening the coda. Beach arranged the work for two pianos in 1937, using the 1936 version and including two extra variations. The following discussion is on the original version of 1904.[16]

The piece opens in C-sharp minor with a quiet chordal setting of the main theme, a Serbian folk melody entitled "O Maiko moyá."

O my poor country, to thy sons so dear,
Why art thou weeping, why this sadness drear?
Alas! thou raven, messenger of woe,
Over whose fresh grave moanest thou so?

Beach restates the last line again, "Over whose fresh grave moanest thou so?" painting an especially bleak picture of utter melancholy. Beach continues in C-sharp minor for the first three variations. Variation I is a canon, with the left hand following the right in imitation; the second variation is a grand expansion of the theme, marked *maestoso*, with three beats to the bar; and the third variation is a light *allegro* in duple meter. For the next variation, a *barcarolle*, Beach moves to B-flat minor: beautifully set in binary form, parallel thirds and sixths support the melody over a simple accompaniment. The fifth variation, in G-flat major, begins with the left hand alone. In the tenth bar the right hand enters with decorative trills. The next phrase, now in E-flat minor, is again for left hand alone, with the right hand joining in after eight bars in a descant trill.

Variation VI opens in F-sharp minor with another Balkan melody, "Stara Planina." Translated as "Old Mountain," Stara Planina is the mountain range that divides northern and southern Bulgaria. This folk tune acts as an introduction, "quasi-fantasia," to the actual variation on "O Maiko moyá," which is marked *Allegro all' Ongarese* [in Hungarian style]. As the sixth variation continues, Beach moves to F-sharp major and introduces a new melody, "Nasadil e dado" ["Grandpa has planted a little garden"]. This tune is taken into A major before returning to F-sharp minor to conclude the variation.

Beach returns to "O Maiko moyá" for variation VII, a slow waltz in E major. Variation VIII is a funeral march. There is a long introduction to the march based on the folk melody "Macedonian!" a mountain cry for help. "Macedonian" provides a desolate backdrop for the entry of a low trill, the rumble of which undergirds the funeral march. "O Maiko moyá" is stated simply in E minor, becoming grander and more tragic as the variation develops. The dotted rhythms of the march, coupled with full chords and tremolo in both hands, make the funeral procession a momentous occasion that builds to a climax before unraveling down to low trills in the bass of the piano, ending as quietly as it began.

An extensive cadenza follows, heralded by a quiet reflection on "Stara Planina." Lovely arpeggios and passages in thirds ensue, leading to a section alluding to the maestoso of Variation II. Octaves and massive chords usher in a grand presentation of "Stara Planina," which then winds its way down to a beautiful, still restatement of "Macedonian!" The opening theme returns, with Beach diverging from the original at the end of the third phrase, moving seamlessly into C-sharp major for the final cadence.

Beach's interest in folk music continues to be evident in her use of Alaskan Inuit tunes in *Eskimos*, op. 64 (published 1907, revised 1943).[17] The four pieces are based on melodies Beach found in a discourse by anthropologist Franz Boas (1858–1942).[18] "Arctic Night" opens starkly, with the melody "Amna gat amnaya" first in unison between the hands and then supported by lush harmonies. Beach references "Song of a Padlimio" as the second melody, with its distinctive outlining of a minor seventh chord. The sprightly energy of "The Returning Hunter" comes in contrast, again beginning simply with an Inuit melody of the same name before being harmonized. A second Inuit tune, "Haja-jaja," comes partway through, celebrating the nourishment brought by the returning hunter. In "Exiles," headed *lento con amore*, Beach sets the folk tune "Song of the Tornit" and later uses "The Fox and the Woman" as a second melody. "With Dog-teams" opens with "Oxaitoq's Song," then races ahead in a lively *presto* based on "Pilitai, avata vat," painting a brilliant picture of huskies skimming across a snowy landscape.

Begun in 1906, *Les Rêves de Colombine: Suite française*, op. 65, was completed in the spring of 1907, the same year in which she later finished her masterful Quintet for Piano and Strings in F-sharp minor.[19] In *Les Rêves de Colombine*, Beach takes the French pantomime character Columbine, usually depicted as the daughter or servant of Pantalon and in love with Harlequin, as her inspiration. Beach uses traditional forms (prelude – gavotte – waltz – adagio – finale: dance) in the organization of her suite of Columbine's dreams. In the first of these pieces, "La Fée de la fontaine," Beach has Columbine visualizing the fairy of the fountain. Beach remarked that it was about "a capricious, a fierce and sullen as well as gracious fairy." This is followed by "Le Prince gracieux," a gavotte that imitates a prince who has caught Columbine's eye dancing gracefully and lightly. The next piece, "Valse amoureuse," is a romantic waltz, where Columbine dreams of "a sweetheart with whom she is dancing."[20] Beach used material from her song, "Le Secret," op. 14, no. 2, as a basis for the waltz. This is followed by "Sous les étoiles," a slow serenade in which Columbine gazes at the stars and dreams of love. The final movement, "Danse d'Arlequin," opens with a snippet of "Valse amoureuse," and then Harlequin jumps in, whirling about in a light, high-spirited dance. A more dreamlike transition follows with arpeggiation between the hands, leading to material from the first movement. Harlequin then returns in his dance, building to a frenzied climax. Columbine is reminded of her sweetheart with material from "Valse amoureuse" before Harlequin finishes the movement with a flourish of his dance.

After Her Husband's Death

The second decade of the twentieth century was a pivotal time in Beach's life: her husband of twenty-five years died in 1910 and her mother died soon after, in February 1911. Later that year Beach left for Europe, not returning until 1914. Several of her piano pieces were written in Europe. The *Tyrolean Valse-Fantaisie*, op. 116, was begun in the Tyrol in 1911 and completed in Munich in 1914.[21] It was performed in Boston in December 1914 upon Beach's return from Europe and was published much later, in 1926. This concert piece begins in descending unisons, the bare bones of the fantasy melody, which soon emerges *pianissimo* in the right hand. Beach explores this simple motif sequentially, using extended harmonies and chromatic decoration. This improvisatory section ushers in the first waltz melody, related to the opening fantasy melody in the descending minor third outlined by the upper notes. The second waltz melody is the folk song, "Kommt ein Vogel geflogen." The two melodies are then combined, with the first waltz in the right hand and the second in the left. The third melody in this quasi-rondo form of waltz melodies is "Rosestock Holderblüh."[22] This tune is introduced on its own, then combined with "Kommt ein Vogel," before the return of the first melody. After a pause, Beach writes a grandiose section of full chords and octaves, which leads to a passage around the opening fantasy figure. "Kommt ein Vogel" is heard once again, accompanied by trills this time, before the music returns to the expansive chordal melody for more development. The opening material reappears, now introducing the coda – a masterfully constructed tour de force that includes all the main waltz themes in a final dance frenzy.

Prelude and Fugue, op. 81, was begun in 1912 during Beach's stay in Germany, performed in Boston in 1914, then published by Schirmer in 1918. The letters of Amy Beach's name (A. BEACH) inspire the piece, referencing Liszt's *Fantasy and Fugue on B-A-C-H* (1871), with four letters shared between Liszt's theme and Beach's (B flat, A, C and B natural [designated H in German]).[23] Notably, Beach studied with Carl Baermann, a pupil of Liszt's, in Boston from 1882 to 1885. In her work, Beach uses A-B-E-A-C-H both in opening the Prelude, written like a fantasy, and in the fugue subject. The prelude is sectional, and the theme is first presented in low octaves with sextuplet flourishes following in both hands. The theme is then set in full chords over sustained bass A octaves, marked *fortissimo*. This leads to a *dolce cantabile* section of development, first in arpeggiated figures, then in chromatic thirds, followed by more left-hand figuration accompanying the transposed theme in the right hand. A bombastic octave sequence follows, which builds to a climax followed by silence. Then beautiful *ppp* arpeggios in both hands usher in a quiet chordal reminiscence of the theme. Beach creates a very special moment, and in that mesmerizing stillness comes the fugue. In four voices, Beach presents the subject very simply with eighth-note accompaniment patterns. The tempo then becomes slightly faster, and a triplet underlying rhythm is introduced, with each voice again brought in in layers. The next section uses a sixteenth-note accompanying pattern with a lively countermelody, which is then developed. After a build-up using this material, Beach brings the whole piece down to *ppp*, with an octave ostinato pattern in the left hand (based on the countermelody) undergirding a choral development of the subject. This grows, and *maestoso* octaves of mounting fury lead to a grand statement of the theme in low octaves, the countermelody second subject in upper right-hand chords, and sixteenth-note octaves running between the two voices. Truly Lisztian in both technique and the way three hands are suggested but only two employed, Beach is in her finest compositional form writing the passagework that brings this work to culmination. It is an impressive concert work and one of her most important piano compositions.

Return to the United States

Having worked through her grief, traveled, and promoted her music through public performance, Beach came back to the US sure of herself and with newfound zeal for her work. Under management, she toured the country playing her chamber music, vocal pieces, piano solos, and the piano concerto. In 1916, Beach made her permanent base in Hillsborough, New Hampshire, the birthplace of her mother, living with her cousin and aunt. She had an article published in *The Etude* magazine later that year, detailing her perspective on piano performance and technique.[24] In it she advocated for intuition in interpretation: "one's technical equipment in any art should be sufficiently elastic to allow free adaptation in whatever direction our tasks lead us." She encouraged developing the tools of the trade: "Of course, we must have technic, and plenty of it. In order to express our own thoughts, or adequately those of others, we must first acquire a sufficient command of language." Beach was a natural pianist and was opposed to "hard and fast" rules in imposing particular techniques; indeed, the ultimate goal was to purvey musical meaning: "We must adapt the method used to each separate phrase, according to its musical and emotional significance." It is worth keeping that in mind in approaching her pieces – that she herself would wish pianists to become intimately acquainted with the notes, finding their own way of bringing the music to life. "Each one [piece] has its own story to tell, and the technic must be suited to the telling. Here we come to the real value of technic: a means of expression."

From Blackbird Hills, op. 83 (published 1922), subtitled "An Omaha Tribal Dance," is another adroit piece based on folk material. The Omaha are a Native American tribe of the American Midwest. *From Blackbird Hills* is based on a children's song, "Follow my leader."[25] It opens with the tune in duple meter, lively and quick, the melody first in the right hand and then in the left. This is followed by an *Adagio* that uses the same folk melody, but in an expanded rhythm with underlying harmonic development. The opening section returns but then falls into a sequential development that leads to a truncated return of the *Adagio*. A *presto* coda based on the opening of the piece brings *From Blackbird Hills* to a brilliant finish.

Fantasia fugata, op. 87 (published 1923), is a larger work, a concert fantasy based on the traditional prelude and fugue format. It opens with a flourish of octaves preceded by grace notes, a motive that later forms the basis of the fugue subject. Beach wrote that this gesture was inspired by Hamlet, "a large black Angora who had been placed on the keyboard with the hope that he might emulate Scarlatti's cat and improvise a fugue theme."[26] The extended opening section uses the grace note motif to explore harmonic sequences with arpeggiation. This section acts as a "prelude" to the more extensive fugal section that follows. In three voices, the fugue begins with underlying eighth-note rhythms supporting the theme. The next section uses sixteenth notes to develop the material sequentially. This is followed by a second theme, a rising subject with a somewhat jazzy rhythm, also presented in three voices. The earlier sequential development of the first theme returns, moving through different harmonies, to lead to a grand final statement of the fugal theme in left-hand octaves, followed by the second subject in right-hand octaves. *Fantasia fugata* ends with a tremendous final cadence, a satisfying conclusion to a well-crafted concert piece.

Beach penned a piano transcription of "Caprice" from *The Water-Sprites*, op. 90 (1921), originally written for flute, cello, and piano. Just under a minute long, Beach's transcription effectively amalgamates the three instrumental parts, with the right hand covering the running sixteenth figuration and some of the flute interspersions, and the left hand imitating the pizzicato cello line. The transcription is two bars longer than the original and deviates slightly toward the end, becoming in its own right a piece beautifully written for piano.[27]

The MacDowell Colony

In 1921, Beach began her long relationship with the MacDowell Colony, spending the summer composing at their retreat in Peterborough, New Hampshire. She found the quiet and closeness to nature inspiring and the contact with other artists, writers, and musicians at the Colony refreshing.

The Fair Hills of Éiré, O!, op. 91 (1922), takes as its melody the Irish American folk tune "Beautiful and Wide are the Green Fields of Erin," which Beach was introduced to by Padraic Colum while at the MacDowell Colony in 1921.[28] "Ban Chnuic Eireann O" begins: "Take a blessing from my heart to the land of my birth, And the fair hills of Eire, O!" Beach sets the melody first with a simple accompaniment, then she writes a quiet chordal triplet pattern for the right hand and lets the left take the melody. The piece becomes more virtuosic with thirty-second-note figuration introduced. The melody first comes in the middle voice, then in big chords with arpeggio sweeps in the left hand. A simple, evocative statement of the folk tune ends this lament for the homeland.

A Hermit Thrush at Eve, op. 92, no. 1, and *A Hermit Thrush at Morn*, op. 92, no. 2, were composed in 1921 at the MacDowell Colony. Beach writes in a footnote that the birdcalls "are exact notations of hermit thrush songs, in the original key but an octave lower," heard at the MacDowell Colony. At the top of *A Hermit Thrush at Eve* are lines by John Vance Cheney:

Holy, Holy! in the hush
Hearken to the hermit thrush;
All the air
Is in prayer.

The piece, in E-flat minor, begins in the depths of the piano and rises, with an undulating triplet pattern of great beauty emerging over an eighth-note accompaniment. The melody comes in, sweetly singing above the gentle movement, to create an atmosphere of utter tranquility, a prayerlike state suggested by the poem. The song of the thrush enters, freely notated in grace notes, floating on the dusk air. Beach brings the main tune back in, and then more thrush song, creating an absolutely gorgeous piece of music with profound depth. *A Hermit Thrush at Morn* quotes J. Clarke: "I heard from morn to morn a merry thrush sing hymns of rapture, while I drank the sound with joy." In D minor, this piece is written as a slow waltz. The thrush song is evident from the start, being part of the melodic impetus. It is in quasi-rondo form, with the second and fourth sections being more dramatic and developmental, moving through extended harmonies.

From Grandmother's Garden, op. 97, also written at the MacDowell Colony in 1921, is a suite of five pieces in which each movement represents a wildflower. The first, "Morning Glories," has fast arpeggiation between the hands with the melody set in the first note of each left-hand group as it sweeps up. The ripples depict the flower by the same name, which is fleeting and short-lived: the blossom usually lasts just for the morning. "Heartsease" is quiet and beautiful, painting a picture of the flower also known as Viola tricolor. The soothing melody comes three times, first in the middle register, then an octave lower, and finally in the right hand over a beautifully written descending bass line. "Mignonette" is translated "little darling" and is a plant with tiny, fragrant flowers growing on tall spikes. Yellowish white in color, its Latin name is *Reseda*, "to calm," and it was utilized by the Romans to treat bruises. Beach writes this exquisite little piece in the style of a minuet, apropos for its title, "Mignonette." "Rosemary and Rue" are flowers that connote remembrance. A nostalgic movement, Beach sets a gentle chromatic melody over a simple left-hand chordal pattern to represent rosemary. Beach uses rue for her second theme, written as a sustained melody in the left hand with quiet eighth-note accompaniment in thirds. "Honeysuckle" is a fast waltz, à la Chopin's *Minute Waltz*. Honeysuckle as a plant is a climber, with long tendrils that twine around anything handy. Beach twines the melody round and round, like the honeysuckle, in running right-hand patterns.

Two Pieces, op. 102, was published in 1924 and dedicated to Olga Samaroff (1880–1948). The first piece, "Farewell, Summer," has at the top lines that read, "O last of the free-born wildflower nation! Thy bright hours gone and thy starry crest: Three names are thine, and they fit thy station, Frost Flower, Aster and Farewell Summer, But Farewell Summer suits thee best!" The title of the piece, therefore, has a double meaning: it is saying goodbye to the summer months as well as depicting the flower of the aster family called Farewell Summer. Beach writes the first section of the piece in the style of a gavotte, with a light, playful character. The middle section is more introspective and marked *legatissimo*, with the melody in the middle voice and an eighth-note accompaniment in both hands lulling the listener in a dreamlike manner, remembering the days of the summer. The second piece, "Dancing Leaves," is exactly that, a cascade of leaves dancing in the autumnal breeze. Marking the tempo *molto vivace*, Beach uses chromaticism, a light accompaniment, and staccato patterns of parallel thirds and fourths to paint the picture perfectly.

One of the retreats at the MacDowell Colony, the Alexander Studio, provided inspiration for the *Old Chapel by Moonlight*, op. 106 (published 1924).[29] Crafted in stone, with arched windows and doorway, the building sits in the wooded landscape, much as the simple chorale tune that comes in the middle of the piece sits among the elegant parallel seventh chords that form the opening and closing sections.

Amy Beach's affinity with the piano as a performer comes through in her writing of *Nocturne*, op. 107 (1924).[30] The piece opens on the dominant octave and takes four bars of progression using seventh, diminished, and augmented harmonies to arrive at E major. The melody is introduced in the middle voice with low bass notes tolling the first beat of the bar and supporting chords on the second half of each beat. Beach moves the melody between the voices, building to an *appassionato* climax of full chords in both hands, making this a very wakeful "night piece" indeed! The dreams or passions of the night having subsided, the piece ends quietly in slumber.

A Cradle Song of the Lonely Mother, op. 108 (published 1924), is, as the title suggests, a lullaby from a mother who is lonely, caring for her baby on her own. The rocking accompaniment undergirds the melody that Beach develops freely in the right hand. This undulating motion subsides, and the middle section of the piece emerges *ppp*. A lovely pattern of two notes in the left hand against three in the right supports the new melody in the middle voice. Trills usher in the return of the opening theme, which becomes fuller and more decorated. The melody of the middle section returns as the coda in this most atmospheric piece.

From Olden Times, op. 111, a gavotte for piano, is unfortunately lost. The title is included on two lists of works, in Beach's own hand, as a manuscript and unpublished.[31]

By the Still Waters, op. 114 (1925), refers to Psalm 23: "The Lord is my shepherd; I shall not want. He maketh me to lie down in green pastures: he leadeth me beside the still waters . . ." Beach was baptized into the Episcopal church in 1910 several months after her husband's death. She wrote, "the greatest function of all creative work is to try to bring even a little of the eternal into the temporal life."[32] This piece is a tranquil portrayal of the still waters of Psalm 23 and the reassurance that comes later in the Psalm of one's soul being restored, with no fear of evil, and goodness and mercy pervading the rest of life.[33]

Another Set of Pedagogic Pieces

In 1922, Beach and two local teachers started a Beach Club for children in Hillsborough, NH.[34] She dedicated *From Six to Twelve*, op. 119, nos. 1–6 (1927), to "the Junior and Juvenile Beach Clubs of Hillsborough, N.H."[35] The pieces are character studies, with the titles indicative of the music that follows. The first and last, "Sliding on the Ice" and "Boy Scouts March," are in rondo form, with lively patterns depicting children frolicking on the ice and marching jauntily in step respectively. "The First May Flowers" is a simple waltz in ABA form. "Canoeing" conveys the gliding of a boat through water with the melody in longer notes surrounded by the moving water of broken chords. "Secrets of the Attic," in three-part form, has outer sections that whisper, "I have a secret . . .," and a middle section that insists it will not divulge the secret no matter what! "A Camp-fire Ceremonial" is solemn, with a low A gong sounding under the still chordal melody of the first and last sections. The middle section of the piece is perhaps the rite itself, conducted in moonlight in a circle around the campfire.

The Second European Visit

Beach visited Europe once again in 1926–27, beginning in Italy and finishing with six weeks in Paris. Her writing of *A Bit of Cairo* (published 1928) was perhaps influenced by seeing the Egyptian treasures at the Louvre and also by the success of the Harvard University–Boston Museum of Fine Arts Expedition to Egypt in 1927. The piece alludes to Debussy's *Golliwogg's Cake-walk* in the main theme and stylized accompaniment, with the opening jaunty melody taken through a myriad of keys.[36]

Three Pianoforte Pieces, op. 128, and *Out of the Depths*, op. 130, were both written at the MacDowell Colony in June 1928. The *Three Pianoforte Pieces* (published 1932) are dedicated to Marian MacDowell, wife of composer Edward MacDowell and good friend of Amy Beach. The pieces are reminiscent of the woods in Peterborough, New Hampshire, where the MacDowell Colony is located. Beach herself performed the pieces for Eleanor Roosevelt at a White House concert in 1936. The first, "Scherzino: A Peterboro Chipmunk," is a character piece with an energetic chipmunk scampering to and fro, up and down, in and out of the trees. The second, "Young Birches," impressionistic, with parallel fourths and extended harmonies, paints a picture of the breeze caressing the leaves of the birches, shimmering and calm. "A Humming Bird" finishes the set, with Beach using fast notes between the hands to capture the little bird flitting from flower to flower, collecting nectar in a blaze of color.

Out of the Depths, op. 130 (published 1932), carries the subtitle "Psalm 130," which begins, "Out of the depths I have cried unto thee, O Lord. Lord, hear my voice: let thine ears be attentive to the voice of my supplications."[37] The beginning of this piano piece evokes the hopelessness and cry for help that open Psalm 130. The development of this melody perhaps portrays verse five, "I wait for the Lord, my soul doth wait, and in His word do I hope." Beach builds to a climax of petition, with a flurry of notes adding weight to the plea for help. The piece ends quietly, in full submission to a greater will beyond human understanding.

Later Solo Works

A September Forest was most likely composed in 1930 during a stay at the MacDowell Colony.[38] The rising theme of the opening bars paints the picture of a quiet, beautiful woodland haven. The serenity and inner peace she must have felt at her retreat are revealed in the hymn-like melody that comes halfway through the piece. This melody builds to a *ff* climax of grandeur with full chords and resonating bass octaves. It then winds down to a simple restatement of the opening woodland theme. Beach used *A September Forest* as the basis for *Christ in the Universe*, op. 132, a vocal work with orchestra.

The Lotos Isles (c. 1930) is based on Beach's song of the same title for soprano and piano published in 1914 as Op. 76, No. 2.[39] The text for the song is from Alfred Tennyson's "The Lotos-Eaters." Beach writes an additional introduction and coda for her piano piece and only obliquely refers to the melody of the song. The piano piece uses the accompaniment pattern from the song, but here it is developed as melodic material. Also, the piano piece is in ¾ time, while the song is in 4/4. So, while there are strong similarities, the piano piece stands on its own as a work and is not a transcription of the vocal piece.

Beach arranged *Far Awa'*, the fourth of her *Five Burns Songs*, op. 43, for piano in 1936.[40] The song text is from Robert Burns' poem of 1788, "Talk of Him That's Far Awa'," and is about a woman longing for her sailor lover. In the piano version, Beach first states the vocal melody in the middle voice, with right-hand chords on the offbeat in syncopated accompaniment. The same melancholic tune is then presented in the top voice and developed sequentially with full chords that build to a climax. The loneliness of the woman left behind is captured beautifully, with the piece ending in quiet resignation after her plea for rest: "Gentle night, do thou befriend me, Downy sleep, the curtain draw; Spirits kind, again attend me, Talk of him that's far awa!"

The *Improvisations*, op. 148 (1937, published 1938), were composed by Amy Beach at the MacDowell Colony, writing to a friend that they were "really improvised" and that each "seemed to come from a different source." The first, in ternary form, atmospherically explores augmented and diminished harmonies, the phrases sequentially moving forward yet seemingly suspended in time. About the second improvisation Beach said she was remembering how she "many years ago sat with friends in an out-door garden outside Vienna and heard Strauss waltzes played."[41] The third is marked *Allegro con delicatezza* and consists of a playful melodic pattern over a light chordal accompaniment featuring extended harmonies with quartal implications. This is followed by a very slow piece of three long phrases, each beginning the same but then diverging in their quest, a pure G-flat major resolution being found only at the end. The last improvisation is a sort of *kujawiak*, a slow mazurka, with the emphasis in this piece being primarily on the second beat of the bar. The grandeur of the opening develops with broad chords and full use of the range of the piano, the *fff* climax subsiding into a *pp* restatement of the opening.

Music for Piano Duet

Allegro appassionata, Moderato, and *Allegro con fuoco* are three pieces Beach wrote for piano duet as a teenager.[42] With youthful exuberance, the theme from *Allegro appassionata* is later developed by Beach in her solo piece, "In Autumn," op. 15, no. 1. The second piece, *Moderato,* is marked "cantabile" and is beautifully introspective, evidencing Beach's early skill in harmonic nuance as she begins in D-flat major and deftly moves to G major before returning to the tonic. *Allegro con fuoco* is in 6/8, with a continual eighth-note pattern in the left hand undergirding a lyrical melody in the right.

Beach arranged *Largo,* the second movement of Beethoven's *Piano Concerto No. 1,* for piano duet as a gift to her husband on their second wedding anniversary, December 2, 1887.[43]

Summer Dreams, op. 47 (1901), is a set of six character pieces for piano duet. "The Brownies" refers to a girls' club of that name; "Robin Redbreast" "reproduces exactly the song of a robin"; "Twilight," marked *largo religioso,* is preceded by a poem by Beach's husband; "Katy-dids" is a light imitation of jumping grasshoppers; "Elfin Tarantelle" is a lively dance of the fairies in 6/8; and lastly "Good Night," a quiet closing piece.

Music for More Than One Piano

Variations on Balkan Themes, op. 60, for two pianos, as referenced earlier, was arranged in 1937 using the 1936 version and including two extra variations. Published in 1942, it is in two halves: both parts start with the theme and then are followed by a set of variations each.[44]

The score to *Iverniana for two pianos*, op. 70 (1910), is unfortunately lost, but there is evidence that it was later rewritten as Beach's *Suite for Two Pianos Founded upon Old Irish Melodies*, op. 104 (1924). This is a large-scale work in four movements. The first, "Prelude," is marked *Lento quasi una fantasia*. Exploratory in nature, there is beautiful interplay between the pianos with advanced technique required. "Old-time Peasant-dance" follows, an *Allegro con spirito* where the dance melody is presented in Piano II, with Piano I then entering with a second, more lyrical Irish melody. The third movement, "The Ancient Cabin," with trills, arpeggiations, scales, and octaves, is an expansive fantasy around its Irish folk melody. The concluding movement, "Finale," is a demanding piece, with the theme alluded to in introductory material, then set between the pianos in fugal fashion and effectively developed with compositional aplomb.[45]

Organ

The organ was used to accompany many of Amy Beach's choral compositions, but there is very little for solo organ. Beach wrote an organ version of *Far Awa'* in 1936, in the afternoon of the same day she wrote her piano arrangement (discussed earlier).[46] The organ version is very similar to the piano, though Beach here uses sustained pedal tones to underlay harmonic structures, and the left-hand accompaniment from bar 31 is more pressing, with continued emphasis on the offbeat.

Prelude on an Old Folk Tune ("The Fair Hills of Éiré, O!") (1942, published 1943) was based on the same Irish folk melody as her earlier piano piece, op. 91.[47] However, the organ work is a completely new setting of this melody, with expansive harmonies and much chromaticism in the accompaniment.[48]

Summary

Beach wrote, "I never remember when I didn't compose. ... Family anecdotes have it that I began at the age of four."[49] Music was a first language to Beach, and this innate ability to communicate musically comes throughout her entire oeuvre, from *Mamma's Waltz* to the *Improvisations*, op. 148. She heard music in her head; melodies naturally came to her and were not contrived. Beach's harmonic language developed from the simple progressions in her early keyboard work, through a broader romantic harmonic base, and then into more expressionistic tonalities. Her piano writing grew from basic Alberti bass patterns and chordal accompaniments to pieces requiring advanced piano technique and bravura performance. Throughout, Beach's love of melody shone through with long lines and overarching shape, making her music captivating, appealing, and listenable.

The keyboard works range from small character pieces to the large Balkan Variations, but what there isn't per se is a sonata, set of etudes, or series of preludes. Beach was a Romantic at heart and reveled in creating pictures with her music, using themes from nature, folk traditions, and the world around her to produce masterpieces. Her particular skill in shaping and developing melodies with rich harmonic language enabled Beach to paint snapshots of life as she experienced it, whether in the woods of New Hampshire or in the Tyrol, Austria. Beach's contribution to the keyboard literature is immense and should be celebrated for the wonderful treasure chest of piano gems that are a pleasure to hear and play.

Beach had her own keyboard voice – she was not trying to mimic the masters but brought to life music of her own making. She certainly was inspired by traditional forms such as waltzes, gavottes and minuets, and paid homage to the mainstay piano repertoire in contributing, for example, a beautiful *Barcarolle*, op. 28, no. 1, a passionate *Ballade*, op. 6, and an extraordinary *Prelude and Fugue*, op. 81. While similar to Liszt in being a composer/pianist, akin to Schumann in her character pieces, with technical writing versed in Chopin and expansive harmonies influenced by Brahms, Beach breathed into life music essentially her own, the synthesis of natural ability, schooled pianism, study of the masters, and disciplined dedication. Her wonderful keyboard music is testament to her greatness.

Notes

1. Mrs. H. H. A. Beach, "How Music Is Made," *Keyboard* (Winter 1942): 11.
2. Beach's own memories of her earlier years are included in this article: Amy Beach, "Why I Chose My Profession," *Mother's Magazine* 9, no. 2 (February 1914): 7–8; reprinted in *Music in the USA: A Documentary Companion*, ed. Judith Tick (Oxford: Oxford University Press, 2008), 323–29.
3. The original manuscripts of *Mamma's Waltz*; *Menuetto*; *Romanza*; *Petite Valse*; *Air and Variations*; and *Moderato* are held in the Amy Cheney Beach Collection, LaBudde Special Collections, University of Missouri–Kansas City. There are edited versions of *Mamma's Waltz*; *Menuetto*; *Romanza*; and Petite Valse in *The Life and Music of Amy Beach*, ed. Gail Smith (Pacific, MO: Mel Bay Publications, 1992), 20–29.
4. Beach's earliest works for piano are on Kirsten Johnson, *Amy Beach Piano Music, Volume One: The Early Years*, recorded 2007, Guild 7317, compact disc.
5. Kirsten Johnson, *Amy Beach Piano Music, Volume Two: The Turn of the Century*, recorded 2009, Guild 7329, compact disc.
6. Beach's personal recollections of her musical activities are included in "Why I Chose My Profession," 7–8.
7. Held in box 6, folder 31, Amy Cheney Beach (Mrs. H. H. A. Beach) Papers, 1835–1956, MC 51, Milne Special Collections and Archives, University of New Hampshire Library, Durham, NH.
8. Adrienne Fried Block, *Amy Beach: Passionate Victorian* (Oxford: Oxford University Press, 1998), 61–62.
9. For a detailed analysis, see: Edward D. Latham, "Gapped Lines and Ghostly Flowers in Amy Beach's "Phantoms," op. 15, no. 2," in *Analytical Essays on Music by Women Composers, Secular & Sacred Music to 1900*, eds. Laurel Parsons and Brenda Ravenscroft (New York: Oxford University Press, 2018), 229–42.
10. Regarding the orthography of this French term, both the piano manuscript in the Schmidt Collection in the Library of Congress and the published version of the piano piece omit the necessary accent in "masqué." The accent does appear in the orchestral version.
11. Recordings of Beach's pieces for piano composed at the end of the nineteenth century and into the beginning of the twentieth century are on: Kirsten Johnson, *Amy Beach Piano Music, Volume Two: The Turn of the Century*, recorded 2009, Guild 7329, compact disc.
12. Performance notes by Kirsten Johnson to *Polka* precede the score in *London College of Music Examinations: Piano 2018–2020, Grade 5* (London: LCM Publications, 2017), 21.
13. Amy Beach, *Serenade* (Boston: Arthur P. Schmidt, 1902).
14. Block, *Amy Beach: Passionate Victorian*, 122–26.

15. The precise date of composition is uncertain, as discussed in Hector Valdivia, "Amy Beach," in *Women Composers: Music Through the Ages*, vol. 8, *Composers Born 1800–1899: Large and Small Instrumental Ensembles*, ed. Sylvia Glickman and Martha Furman Schleifer (New York: G. K. Hall, 2006), 369–70.

16. For fuller background, and an analysis and comparison of the 1904 and 1936 versions, please see E. Douglas Bomberger, "Motivic Development in Amy Beach's *Variations on Balkan Themes*, Op. 60," *American Music* 10, no. 3 (Fall 1992): 326–47.

17. Adrienne Fried Block, "Amy Beach's Music on Native American Themes," *American Music* 8, no. 2 (Summer 1990): 141–66.

18. Franz Boas, *The Central Eskimo: Sixth Annual Report of the Bureau of Ethnology to the Secretary of the Smithsonian Institution, 1884–1885* (Washington, DC: Government Printing Office, 1888), 399–670. The other songs cited are also found in this source.

19. Beach's pieces for piano from 1907 to 1924 are included on Kirsten Johnson, *Amy Beach Piano Music, Volume Three: The Mature Years*, recorded 2011, Guild 7351, compact disc.

20. Arthur Wilson, "Mrs. H.H.A. Beach: A Conversation on Musical Conditions in America," *The Musician* 27, no. 1 (January 1912): 9–10. Quoted in Block, *Amy Beach, Passionate Victorian*, 127.

21. Amy Beach, *Tyrolean Valse-Fantaisie*, op. 116 (Boston: Oliver Ditson, 1926).

22. Block, *Amy Beach, Passionate Victorian*, 190–92.

23. Block, *Amy Beach, Passionate Victorian*, 189–90.

24. Amy Beach, "Common Sense in Pianoforte Touch and Technic," *The Etude* 34, no. 10 (October 1916): 701–2.

25. Alice Fletcher, *A Study of Omaha Indian Music* (Cambridge, MA: Peabody Museum of American Archaeology and Ethnology, 1893), 102.

26. Amy Beach, *Fantasia Fugata* (Philadelphia, PA: Theodore Presser Co., 1923), note on first page of score, box 8, folder 13, Amy Beach Papers, University of New Hampshire.

27. This piano transcription is found in manuscript in box 5, folder 35, Amy Beach Papers, University of New Hampshire.

28. Block, *Amy Beach, Passionate Victorian*, 222, 228.

29. Kirsten Johnson, *Amy Beach Piano Music, Volume Four: The Late Works*, recorded 2012, Guild 7387, compact disc.

30. Amy Beach, *Nocturne* (Cincinnati, OH: The John Church Company, 1924), in box 8, folder 3, Adrienne Fried Block Papers (Amy Cheney Beach), 1872–1960, Milne Special Collections, University of New Hampshire Library, Durham, NH, USA.

31. These two lists are found in box 4, folder 13, Amy Beach Papers, University of New Hampshire. One is a list of works by opus number; the other is a list of works in manuscript.

32. Quoted in Block, *Amy Beach, Passionate Victorian*, 230.

33. Amy Beach, *By the Still Waters*, op. 114 (St. Louis, MO: Art Publication Society, 1925).

34. Block, *Amy Beach, Passionate Victorian*, 244.

35. Amy Beach, *From Six to Twelve*, op. 119 (Boston: Oliver Ditson Co., 1927), in the Library of Congress.

36. Amy Beach, *A Bit of Cairo* (Philadelphia: Theodore Presser, 1928).

37. Amy Beach, *Out of the Depths*, op. 130 (Boston: Arthur P. Schmidt, 1932).

38. Amy Beach, *A September Forest* (manuscript), box 6, folder 13, Amy Beach Papers, University of New Hampshire.

39. Amy Beach, *The Lotos Isles* (manuscript), box 5, folder 26, Amy Beach Papers, University of New Hampshire.

40. Beach wrote at the top of the manuscript: "Studio MacD.C., about 9 am, September 17/36" and at the end, "Finished 10:45 am." Amy Beach, *Far awa'* (piano manuscript), box 4, folder 12, Amy Beach Papers, University of New Hampshire.

41. Block, *Amy Beach, Passionate Victorian*, 268.

42. Manuscript in the Amy Cheney Beach Collection, Box 1, Folder 2, UMKC. Now published as Amy Beach, *Three Movements for Piano Four-hands*, ed. Adrienne Fried Block (Bryn Mawr, PA: Hildegard Publishing Co., 1998).

43. Manuscript held in the Boston Public Library, Music Division. See also Block, *Passionate Victorian*, 49.

44. Bomberger, "Motivic Development," 326.

45. Block, *Amy Beach, Passionate Victorian*, 228–30 and 362n28.

46. Amy Beach, *Far awa'* (organ manuscript), box 5, folder 1, Amy Beach Papers, University of New Hampshire; original manuscript dated "afternoon of Sept. 17/36"; a diary note says this was revised in 1937 (Block, *Amy Beach, Passionate Victorian*, 377n15).

47. Amy Beach, *Prelude on an Old Folk Tune (The Fair Hills of Éiré, O')* (New York: H.W. Gray, 1943).

48. Block, *Amy Beach, Passionate Victorian*, 266.

49. Beach, "How Music Is Made," 11.

6 | Songs of Amy Beach

KATHERINE KELTON

Songs were the foundation of Amy Beach's musical world. Her mother reported that by the age of one, she could hum forty songs. By age two, she could sing harmony to any tune her mother sang. She insisted that her mother and maternal grandmother sing daily – but only songs she liked. Harmonizing with her mother's singing was a bedtime ritual. This love of singing led to mental composition of melodies, later harmonized during her first experiences playing the piano. It was natural that she felt all music-making was "singing," be it vocal or instrumental. Appropriately, her first publication was a song, and songwriting led to her initial fame as a composer. For decades after her death, she was best remembered for her songs. They are well crafted, most with singable melodies and integrated piano accompaniments, satisfying to both musicians and audiences.

Songs predominate her total compositional output. She composed them prolifically, even during the years she was occupied primarily with writing larger compositions. Between 1887 and 1915, several songs were published each year, almost all shortly after their composition. Performances by some of the United States' most prominent musicians furthered the songs' remarkable popularity and contributed to their quickly becoming standard concert, recital, and teaching repertoire. She and her primary publisher, Arthur P. Schmidt, worked diligently to promote the songs and ensure they stayed in print. Despite their popularity during her lifetime, they fell into neglect when ill health precluded her extensive travels and performances around the United States to promote them.

In the 1970s, despite a resurgence of interest in women composers, only two of her songs were available in print.[1] Renewed interest in her oeuvre focused primarily on her importance as the first successful American woman composer to create large-scale orchestral, choral, and piano works, leading to a revival of performances of her major works. Largely because it was not unusual for women of her day to compose in smaller forms, her songs remained in obscurity a bit longer. Only after several were reprinted in the mid-1980s did they begin to reclaim their well-deserved attention. As of this writing, almost all of her published songs in the public domain are available through www.imslp.org, and many songs have been republished in scholarly editions. Numerous autographs used by publishers to prepare printed editions are housed in the Library of Congress's A. P. Schmidt Collection (www .loc.gov/collections/a-p-schmidt-collection/).

Stylistic Characteristics

From 1880 to 1941, Beach composed 121 art songs with keyboard accompaniment, of which 111 were published during her lifetime. They demonstrate her exceptionally insightful understanding of texts, mastery of the form, and awareness of trends in current European musical styles. The assumption that Beach's songs are overly Romantic in nature, unnecessarily elaborate, and excessively sentimental has sometimes led to their cursory dismissal as being mere parlor songs. While those descriptions might be appropriate for many songs by her female contemporaries, Beach's songs were composed as art songs. Even though the vocal lines and accompaniments of some of her songs are complex and technically demanding, they were intended to be sung and played by both amateur and professional musicians.

She believed that the mission of all art is to uplift: "to try to bring even a little of the eternal into the temporal life."[2] She strove for musical expression people would understand, believing that songs should be inspired, creative, musical responses to texts – incorporation of both intellect and emotion.

Even though some critics have accused her of imitating other composers, or of composing in the style to which she had been most recently exposed, very few songs bear resemblances to those of her peers, a fact recognized early in her career. In a 1904 article on Beach's songs, critic Berenice Thompson wrote,

She is not a poet dreamer, nor are her instincts those of the morbid or fastidious impressionist. Her artistic personality is entirely distinct from the schools of the day. She is neither a disciple of Richard Strauss, nor an exponent of the peculiar theories of d'Indy, Debussy, and the other Frenchmen. Nor are her ideas affiliated with the decadence which programmatic music and the mixture of arts is bringing upon the music of the century.[3]

Any similarities between her songs and those of other composers are more a reflection of her manifold interests and experiences than of plagiarism. Several poem settings actually predate those of her contemporaries.

Other critics have implied that her songs are all more or less alike. Closer examination reveals that, while many songs share similarities in structure, sentiment, and methods of text setting, all are quite distinctive. A hallmark of her music is extensive use of chromaticism, rooted in the ideals of German Romanticism. The application of this chromaticism was increasingly implemented within the context of more modern musical idioms, including impressionism and quasi-atonalism.

Song composition played a major role in the development of her unique musical language, providing her with opportunities for small-scale experimentation incorporating a wide variety of musical influences. Their use within this small form was subtle and controlled in comparison with more obvious inclusion of increasingly modern musical influences in her larger works. Several quotations from her writings will provide a basis for understanding her goals in song composition.

"Music should be the poem translated into tone, with due care for every emotional detail."[4]

From earliest childhood, poetry was the foundation of Beach's songs. Well before she could read or write music, children's poems inspired spontaneous creation of accompanied songs. Memorizing texts came easily, as by age four, she was able to recite many long, difficult poems. This remarkable memory served her in good stead later in her method of songwriting: "In vocal music, the initial impulse grows out of the poem to be set; it is the poem which gives the song its shape, its mood, its rhythm, its very being. Sacred music requires an even deeper emotional impulse."[5]

"I believe that a composer, like anyone else, is influenced by what he studies and reads, because literature cannot fail to react upon artistic expression in any other form."[6]

Avid reading and continuing social contact with some of the United States' most esteemed writers refined her literary discernment. An eclectic taste in poetry is apparent in the wide range of authors whose texts she set. Her husband may have suggested settings of poems by historically significant authors, including Shakespeare and Burns, but the majority of the songs were settings of works by living authors, many of whom were friends. More than one-third of the texts were by female writers.

French and German poetry from anthologies, newspapers, and popular magazines inspired eleven German and seven French songs. These texts provided a means for experimentation with inclusion of elements of current trends in the styles of German *Lied* and French *chanson*, as well as an opportunity to hone her skills in text settings in those languages.

Much poetry of her early songs appealed to Victorian ideals and may seem dated today. She was drawn to poems about love and nature. Love song texts in the first person were most commonly from a female perspective. Other favorite topics were times of day (most frequently twilight or night), flowers, and birds. Several songs quote or are based on birdcalls, including "The Blackbird," op. 11, no. 3 (1889); "The Thrush," op. 14, no. 4 (1890); and "Meadowlarks," op. 78, no. 1 (1917).

"In vocal writing, the initial impulse grows out of the poem to be set; it is the poem which gives the song its shape, its mood, its rhythm, its very being."[7]

Beach fervently believed that in order to interpret a song effectively, a singer must fully understand a poem's meaning and character. To this end, she preferred that a song's text be printed on the page before the musical score, as she shared with her publisher in a 1908 letter: "A singer can get at a glance a better idea of the character of a song by this means than by a prolonged study of words scattered thro' [sic] several pages of music."[8] She expanded on her views of the importance of the text to interpretation in a 1916 article:

Each song is a complete drama, be it ever so small or light in character, and no two are interpreted in the same way. Even the quality of the voice may change absolutely in order to bring out some salient characteristic of the composition. Technical perfection may indeed be there, but so completely subordinated to the emotional character of the song that we lose all consciousness of its existence.[9]

"A composer must give himself time to live with what he is creating."[10] "It may happen that, for instance, that one has a 'perfect' theme for a song. . . . It is quite possible that the melodic line may not seem at all suitable for the voice . . . the original theme may develop into something quite different from the song that was first planned."[11]

Songwriting was recreation for Beach. When she felt a roadblock while working on a larger piece, she sometimes wrote a song, viewing it as a special treat: "It has happened to me more than once that a composition comes to me, ready-made as it were, between the demands of other work."[12] Her songs may have seemed to flow quickly and spontaneously from her pen, yet they often evolved unconsciously over a longer period of time, although this was not always the case.

"In writing a song, the composer considers the voice as an instrument, and that the song shall be singable should be the fundamental principle underlying its creation. Many an otherwise magnificent work lies on the shelf, unused, because it is not suitable for the voice."[13]

Example 6.1 "Ecstasy," op. 19, no. 2, mm. 1–14.

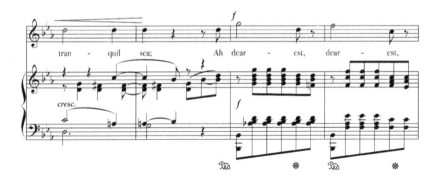

What makes most of Beach's songs so singable? Why do they practically sing themselves? The answer is most likely her remarkable sensitivity to languages' natural inflections, even though this may not be consciously perceived by the musician or listener. Her songwriting process began by careful contemplation of the poem to be set. After memorization, mental repetition of the words' spoken inflection led to the melody, phrase by phrase. The result: melodies that are musical representations of the text's natural inflections, as if the pitches of the spoken word were given musical notes (Example 6.1). Division of poetic lines into two- or three-measure phrases enhances the songs' singability as well.

It is worthwhile to consider the voice types Beach had in mind for each song. This can frequently be determined by a song's dedication. Most early songs were composed for light, high, female voices. Later in life, she favored large, dramatic female voices.

About 60 percent of the songs, most of which were for high voice, were published in only one key (much to the chagrin of those with lower voices). Because her musical response to poetry emerged in specific tonalities, with their associated timbres in both piano and vocal parts, it is preferable to sing them in their original keys. Even so, modern performers and audiences are not able to experience the exact, original, intended sonorities of the early songs, as pianos in Boston were tuned slightly lower in the late nineteenth century than they are today.

Most of her songs are in major keys, with F major, A-flat major, and E-flat major predominating. She perceived the latter two of these as blue and pink, respectively. Three lullabies composed for friends' newborn babies made use of these color associations, with blue for male and pink for female. Curiously, given her childhood aversion to music in minor keys, thirty-three of her songs represent ten different minor modes. With very few exceptions, songs in minor modes end with (sometimes quite abrupt) major cadences.

She was highly opposed to unauthorized transpositions of her songs, as her timbral intent would be obliterated. In order to fulfill and/or increase their demand, Schmidt requested transpositions of several songs (beginning with "Ecstasy" in 1893). Alternate keys were usually lowered by a minor third. Popularity of "Ah, Love, but a Day!" and "Shena Van" warranted three transpositions. Songs with expansive ranges and high *tessiture* not lending themselves to acceptable transpositions were published in one key, with alternate pitches for highest and/or lowest notes.

"A composer who has something to say must say it in a fashion that people will listen to, or his works will lie in obscurity on dusty shelves."[14]

Beach understood the publishing industry was purely a business matter, regulated by supply and demand. As her compositional career blossomed, she and Schmidt employed a variety of strategies to create broader demand for her music. Marketing efforts focused on songs and short piano pieces, music that would please the amateur musician and be performed frequently because of its accessibility. To appeal to this demographic, songs in foreign languages were published with English titles and singing translations printed above the original language, a common practice at the time.

Schmidt published notices and advertisements in newspapers and magazines. He also distributed his own promotional pamphlets containing effusive (sometimes misrepresentative) descriptions of Beach's songwriting prowess. He took advantage of publicity garnered by performances of her larger works by coordinating publication of her newest songs with those events. Their inclusion on subsequent high-profile concerts furthered sales. To satisfy and increase demand, arrangements of her biggest sellers were published with violin *obbligati* and for various combinations of voices.[15] "A Song of Liberty," op. 49, and "The Year's at the Spring," op. 44, no. 1, were issued in Braille (in 1922 and 1931, respectively).

Magazines offered another effective means for promoting songs. Several were composed expressly for them, usually published with an accompanying biography and/or interview. These songs are short, with simple melodies within limited ranges and easy accompaniments.

When programming Beach's songs, one should be aware that most of her early songs were composed as individual entities, with highly varying topics, usually unrelated. As soon as she had produced three to five songs, Schmidt published them in an opus, deciding on the order of the songs within the opus.

In 1891, after publishing eighteen of her songs, Schmidt assembled fourteen, issuing them as part of a series of song anthologies. All were subtitled "a Cyclus of Songs," even though none of them contained song cycles. Schmidt likely hoped these publications would increase profits, as customers wanting to purchase one or two songs might be likely to pay a little more to buy a collection that included songs that had not sold well singly. After publishing another thirty-nine songs, a second anthology of fourteen songs (also part of the "Cyclus" series) was issued in 1906. Plans for a third anthology in the 1930s never came to fruition due to high costs of printing during the Depression.

It is often misconstrued that since several of Beach's better-known songs are slow, they all share that trait. Actually, an equal number of fast and slow *tempi* are represented in her song output. All tempo designations are in Italian, most with added directives for their interpretation, commonly including the adverbs *espressivo* or *espressione*; *tranquillo* or *tranquillamente*.

Early songs exhibit somewhat of a formula for setting up a melody's climactic note, usually at or near a piece's end: an ascending vocal line leading to the highest tone is interrupted by descending movement, either stepwise or a skip, that precedes an ascending leap of at least a minor third to the high note. A song's highest (and either loudest or softest) tone is usually set on an open vowel ([a] or [ɔ], for example), sustained for one or two measures. She certainly sensed that these open vowels are the most conducive for optimum vocal resonance in singers' higher ranges. Frequently, though, the tone preceding the highest one is also on an open vowel. As these ascending intervals straddle singers' upper *passaggi*, it is more challenging to maintain forward placement than if the high note were preceded by a closed vowel (such as [e] or [i]). These highest tones and their accompanying chords were usually assigned sudden, extreme dynamic changes, sometimes *pianissimo*, but more often a jolting *forte* or *fortissimo*. Musicians should consider that these sustained tones were intended to have as much "life" as the preceding material, not beginning and maintaining the same dynamic from outset to completion. For effective interpretation, to give the music shape and carry expressive movement forward, *pianissimo* notes should begin as a slightly louder dynamic level than specified, making a decrescendo to the level indicated. As it can be strenuous for the singer to sing and sustain a loud tone "going nowhere" expressively for several measures, as well as unsettling to the listener to be bombarded by such an abrupt, loud dynamic change, the loudest notes should begin more softly than designated, making a crescendo to the indicated *fortissimo*.

Facility at the piano likely contributed to her technically challenging accompaniments. Continual use of octaves and complex chords with quite differing distributions of notes in quick succession requires long fingers and comfortable hand spans of more than an octave. Accompaniments rarely double vocal melodies. Occasionally during measures of rest between vocal phrases in earlier songs, what promises to be an effective counter-melody emerges, only to disappear at the voice's reentrance. Her preference for triple and compound meters (especially 6/8) facilitated the incorporation of repeated eighth note or triplet chords/figures to increase intensity and forward motion, a device also found in her solo piano works (Example 6.2). While used to great effect in several songs, its implementation for measures (or pages) at a time resulted in their monotonous similarities.[16] Endings of three chords or with ascending arpeggiated flourishes (often in sixths) became somewhat cliché (Example 6.3).

Clearcut variations in Beach's songs delineate three distinct compositional style periods. These correspond with three important periods of her life. The first style period begins with her first published work in 1883, "The Rainy Day" (composed 1880), and ends with the deaths of her husband and mother in 1910 and 1911, respectively. Songs composed in 1914 in Europe comprise a second style period. A third style period begins in 1916 and continues through 1941.

Example 6.2 "After," op. 68, mm. 71–78.

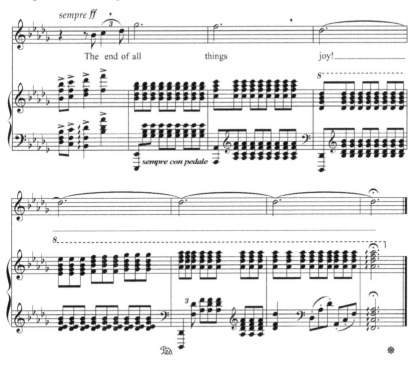

Example 6.3 "Forget-me-not," op. 35, no. 4, mm. 55–59.

A.P.S. 4282-5

First Style Period (1883–1911)

As a girl, and later as the wife of a socially connected, wealthy Boston surgeon, Beach had extensive time to devote to piano practice and composing, making this her most productive period of song composition.

She composed seventy-two songs during these thirty years, many of which became her best known. Notably, "The Rainy Day," her first published song, begins with a direct quotation of the first eight notes of the third movement of Beethoven's "Pathétique" Sonata, op. 13, transposed from C minor to F minor.

After marrying in 1885, her program of autodidactic musical study was supplemented inestimably by her husband's careful guidance. An amateur singer and accomplished pianist, Dr. Beach had extensive knowledge and appreciation of art song literature. He shared his expertise with Amy, introducing her to masterworks of song. This deepened her understanding of basic structural elements, including forms, text settings, sensitively crafted accompaniments, modulations, shaping of phrases, and appropriate ranges and *tessiture*.

Dr. Beach was also an amateur poet. Amy set seven of his poems, all composed within his lifetime and dedicated "To H," with authorship attributed to H. H. A. B. The first of these settings were the three op. 2 songs. They were certainly composed for him, as relatively low and limited ranges would have suited his baritone voice. She composed settings of his poems on his birthday (December 18), presumably as birthday presents. Manuscripts dated December 25 suggest that, after being given poems for Christmas, she made settings immediately.

It should be taken into account that late nineteenth-century pianos were usually tuned slightly lower than modern ones. The prevailing pitch standard in Boston from at least 1863 to 1900 was A = 435.[17] A = 440 was not officially adopted as the universal pitch standard until the International Standardizing Organization (ISO) meeting in London in May 1939.[18] As a result, many songs composed for medium voice may be deceptively difficult for today's amateur singers, as their highest notes fall slightly in voices' upper *passaggi*.

From the outset, strophic, modified strophic, and ternary forms predominated Amy Beach's song output. All but a handful follow this uniform pattern: minimally varied melodic material for repetitions of A sections are supported by accompaniments' substantially different harmonies. Most early songs are marked by expansive, flowing melodies and accompaniments that reflect the influence of contemporary European compositional styles.

Interspersed are several songs described as enjoyable, "if not fully apprehended at first hearing."[19] This type of song begins with four to eight measures of a memorable melody that subsequently evolves into a seemingly jagged chain of notes. This is caused by vocal parts' frequent extraction from (or burial within) their accompaniments' relentlessly changing harmonies. The voice sometimes provides counterpoint for the accompaniment or serves as an inner part to complete a complex chord. Rapidly changing harmonies rarely lead to predictable vocal entrances after measures of rests.[20] Several songs' introductions contain descriptive figures that are repeated between vocal phrases, yet the vocal lines that follow are disjunct and bear no correlation with an accompaniment's motive. Her usual sensitivity to natural speech inflection is absent in these songs.[21] These rambling, pianistic songs that lack perceptible melodies show no apparent compositional models. They bring into question her later statement that she always composed away from the piano.[22]

Vacillation between (often remote) tonalities necessitated the persistent use of accidentals (including frequent double sharps/flats) and enharmonic spellings (alternating between correct and incorrect spellings), making them difficult for an accompanist to read. Critic Rupert Hughes even described one of her more accessible songs as "bizarre."[23]

Prominent nineteenth-century American and European song composers generally employed evident melodies and sparse accompaniments with slow harmonic movement within conventional chord progressions. She hit her stride around 1894, composing increasingly marketable songs containing the streamlined accompaniments and flowing melodies for which she is best known.

The 1890s were her most productive years of songwriting, with publication of thirty-seven songs during the decade. Her first big seller was a modified strophic setting of her own two-verse poem, "Ecstasy" (1893). Its moderate range and simple, memorable melody in two-measure phrases (helpful for amateurs with limited breath control) made it appealing to the average musician. Its popularity prompted the first publication in an alternate key. The poem was included in *The Poetry Digest: Annual Anthology of Verse for 1939* (New York: The Poetry Digest, 1939). As most of the subsequent songs of this period are in this accessible style, the success of "Ecstasy" may have given her better insight into the type of song that might please the general public.

In his 1893 *Harper's Magazine* article, Antonín Dvořák proposed that in order to create a truly American art form, composers should incorporate "plantation melodies" and minstrel show music. The article prompted Beach's immediate *Boston Herald* rebuttal: the opposing idea that American composers should look to their own heritages for inspiration.[24] There is no evidence that they met personally during his 1892–95 stay in the United States, but she was clearly aware of his views and had thought deeply about them. Whether coincidental or not, it was around this time that Beach began inclusion of musical ideas reminiscent of traditional folk music of the British Isles, as evidenced by the stark contrast between her op. 12 (1887) and op. 43 (1899) settings of Robert Burns' poems. The 1887 songs number among the long, rambling, piano-heavy songs of her youth. In stark contrast, with inclusion of dotted rhythms and "Scotch snaps," the 1899 settings could be mistaken for folk songs. These songs appealed to the market: strophic with short, easily remembered melodies and simple accompaniments. The most popular of these, "Far Awa'!," was later published in six arrangements for various groupings of singers and instruments between 1918 and 1936.

Following the 1899 Burns songs' success, Beach employed the same formula for the highly successful "Shena Van," op. 56, no. 4 (1904), a setting of William Black's poem from his 1883 romance novel, *Yolande*. The melody's pentatonic melisma contributes to the song's folklike qualities, while a simple chordal accompaniment mimics a bagpipe with an open fifth drone. Similarities with Edvard Grieg's "Solveig's Song" suggest it might have been the model for "Shena Van."

Among the handful of Beach's most popular and enduring songs are the *Three Browning Songs*, op. 44 (1900), composed and dedicated to the Browning Society of Boston. Their high *tessiture* and manner in which vocal lines approach climactic high notes contribute to these being the most vocally demanding of her songs. "The Year's at the Spring" and "Ah, Love, but a Day!" are the best known and most frequently performed of the three. In 1932, "Ah, Love, but a Day!" was reportedly the popular choice in a nationwide survey of the most standard American songs.[25]

By far the most popular of her songs, "The Year's at the Spring," was a staple of recital repertoire throughout the first half of the twentieth century. She later recalled: "It was composed while travelling by train between New York and Boston. I did nothing whatever in a conscious way. I simply sat still in the train, thinking of Browning's poem and allowing it and the rhythm of the wheels to take possession of me."[26] She also recalled, "I had no writing materials with me, and so I went over and over it in my mind – learned my own composition by heart, so to speak, and as soon as I got to New York, wrote it down in twenty minutes. That, practically unchanged, was the song I gave them."[27]

Robert Browning's son was intensely moved upon hearing it, saying it could hardly be called a "setting:" the music and words seemed to form one entity; that one could not imagine anything more perfectly "married" than her music to his father's words.[28] Audiences' enthusiastic responses to it (and a length of less than a minute) often prompted singers to repeat it several times. Interestingly, it holds the distinction of being the first song transmitted over the telephone.[29]

Although published as no. 1 of op. 44, "The Year's at the Spring" is most effective at the end of the group when all three songs are performed together as a set. Its exuberance and animated tempo create a dramatic contrast with the two other songs' slower *tempi*, bringing the set to a jubilant end. This reordering (2, 3, 1) also preserves the intended harmonic progression.

Only in her first style period did Beach set French texts, with varying degrees of success. Of these seven, "Jeune fille et jeune fleur," op. 1, no. 3, and "Chanson d'amour," op. 21, no. 2, are more varied versions of the rambling, fast harmonic rhythm songs, as they contain occasional measures with slower harmonic rhythms supporting "melodies." These melodies appear as opening statements of verses or as short refrains. The four most appealing French songs show influences of the café chantant style of Charles Gounod and Eva dell'Acqua: "Le Secret," op. 14, no. 2 (1891); "Elle et moi," op. 21, no. 3 (1893); "Canzonetta," op. 48, no. 4 (1902); and "Je demande á l'Oiseau," op. 51, no. 4 (1903). Melodies reflecting the texts' inflection are absent in these songs, perhaps a result of her unfamiliarity with the language.

In contrast, the melodies of her eleven German songs are excellent examples of melodies mirroring their texts' spoken inflections. Both light-hearted songs and those with long, flowing melodies are among their number. They show her awareness of the most recent German song compositions, especially those of Hugo Wolf and Richard Strauss. Her admiration for Strauss' song "Ständchen" inspired her to compose a piano transcription in 1902. Around the same time, she produced the masterpiece, "Juni," op. 51, no. 3. Given her recent preoccupation with Strauss' song, one might expect to find similarities between their melodies (Examples 6.4 and 6.5).

The text's sole topic of blooming spring flowers is perfectly expressed through the melding of melody and accompaniment, which become increasingly effusive throughout the piece, ending with a burst of joy. Overutilized in some songs to the extent of being a trademark, implementation of repeated triplets in "Juni" is the precise element needed to heighten the song's intensity to its final chord.

Second Style Period (1914)

During most of her time in Europe from 1911 to 1914, a busy travel and performance schedule precluded time for composition. This lull was broken in 1914, her most prolific year of song composition. The ten

Example 6.4 Richard Strauss, "Ständchen," op. 17, no. 2, mm. 10–12.

Example 6.5 Beach, "Juni," op. 51, no. 3, mm. 7–8.

songs composed in Munich in May–June (opuses 72–73 and 75–76) comprise her second style period.

In September 1911, Beach sailed to Europe intending to establish a reputation abroad as a performer, thus promoting the sale of her works there. Her traveling companion, dramatic soprano Marcella Craft (1874–1959), was beginning the third year of her five-year contract with Munich's Bavarian Opera. Beach and Craft's friendship began in 1898 while Craft was a voice student at the New England Conservatory. Craft sang for Beach, who was immediately enamored with her voice. After moving to Europe in 1900, Craft sang in several Italian and German opera houses before being hired in Munich. She introduced Beach's songs to European audiences as early as 1903. Richard Strauss, the director of the *Bayrische Staatsoper*, often chose her to sing roles under his direction, including the title role in his *Salome*. Because Craft was well established in Munich, Beach chose it as her "home base" abroad. In addition to her own ties there, Beach benefited from Craft's musical and social connections with prominent public and musical figures in Europe.

As in the United States, programs of her larger instrumental works often included songs. Those large works received critical acclaim in Germany, but such was not always the case with her songs. Several critics expressed bewilderment about the songs' sentimentality in comparison with the high caliber of her works for larger forces. The 1914 songs show that she may have taken this criticism to heart. German audiences were accustomed to hearing vocal works by her European contemporaries, including Johannes Brahms, Hugo Wolf, Richard Strauss, Gabriel Fauré, and Claude Debussy. Rather than striving to rival such masters' work, she took another path. At last, she had freedom to develop her own musical aesthetic, unhindered by oversight, input, or advice from her husband and mother.[30] She left the complex Richard Wagner-influenced harmonies behind, resulting in simpler songs with leaner, less complex accompaniments. The four in German show influences of German folk songs.

After an extended trip to Italy for rest and relaxation in 1914, Beach returned to Munich, where she completed ten songs during the month of June, all published by G. Schirmer. Until this point, A. P. Schmidt had been her exclusive publisher for almost thirty years. Her exasperation with Schmidt's inability to keep European music stores stocked with her music led her to sign a contract with G. Schirmer the following month to publish future works.

In contrast with most earlier songs, these songs (and the majority composed afterward) served practical purposes. They were composed for singer friends, crafted to meet their needs for specific occasions and to display their greatest strengths. The 1914 songs were for performances at San Diego's 1915–16 Panama–California Exposition and for future tours. The eight songs of opuses 72–73 and 75 have simple melodies in limited ranges and uncomplicated accompaniments and are accessible to musicians of all levels. However, due to Schirmer's lack of large-scale marketing and restrictions in the publishing industry brought about by World War I, the delightful 1914 songs never received the widespread popularity of some of her earlier songs published by Schmidt.

The first of the 1914 songs, "Ein altes Gebet," op. 72, no. 1, shows similarities with Wolf's "Auf ein altes Bild," suggesting that it served as model. Parallels include structure, text, title, and use of a two-measure ostinato that introduces a mixture of major and minor modes, a device Beach used with increasing frequency for the rest of her career. The text's sentiment was clearly significant to her, as it returned in her choices of poems for two songs composed decades later: the necessity of faith in and total reliance on God's saving care.

Two folklike songs (op. 73) were composed for contralto Ernestine Schumann-Heink to sing at the San Diego Exposition, where her performances drew crowds in the tens of thousands. Schumann-Heink was a mother of eight; Beach's choice of German texts about familial topics complemented her public image of maternal devotion and domesticity.

A sense of playfulness and whimsy surfaces in the four op. 75 songs, commissioned by American mezzo-soprano Kitty Cheatham (1865–1946), known for her programs of folk music and children's songs. She was an early proponent of the African American spiritual, introducing many to both American and European audiences. These songs' medium, limited ranges, and straightforward accompaniments make them accessible to all musicians. These four short songs are perhaps Beach's most charming, in particular "The Candy Lion" and "A Thanksgiving Fable." Their unexpected punch lines always elicit giggles from the audience.

The final 1914 songs, "Separation" and "The Lotos Isles," op. 76, deviate from the folklike style of the previous eight. "Separation," composed for Marcella Craft, returned to the highly chromatic style of the less accessible early songs, with unpredictable vocal lines and thick accompaniments. Familiar repeated triplet chords make a final appearance, as after "Separation," Beach moved forward musically, "separating" herself from this style of composition.

"The Lotos Isles" bears no resemblance to any earlier songs. Alfred Tennyson's depiction of the drugged, floating, lethargic state induced by ingestion of lotos flowers provided a fitting musical canvas for her experimentation with impressionistic devices. She unified musical and poetic elements through a hypnotic melody, enveloped within a murmuring, dreamy accompaniment figure. A nebulous tonal center settles only at the end of the piece. Her inclusion of elements of the modern French style of Henri Duparc and Debussy marked a clear compositional pivot point (Example 6.6).

Example 6.6 "The Lotos Isles," op. 76, no. 2, mm. 1–9.

Third Style Period (1916–1941)

Her pattern of (practically) nonstop travel for performances, talks, and other appearances (along with the occasional respite) begun in Europe showed no sign of subsiding after her 1914 return to the United States. If anything, her demanding schedule intensified in 1915, leaving her scant time to compose. Returning to songwriting in 1916, she picked up where she left off stylistically with "The Lotos Isles." The definite break between the style for which she had become best known, and an increasingly more contemporary sound, defines a third style period (1916–41).[31] Musical ideas in this period became more compact and accompaniments less flamboyant. Her songs maintained their characteristic chromaticism yet emerged increasingly from contemporary musical trends rather than from late Romantic roots. Such musical elements included vacillations between major and minor modes; use of modal and quasi-modal scales; nonfunctional, ambiguous harmonies and tonal centers; extensive use of major–minor sevenths, half, and fully diminished seventh chords, and jazz harmonies. Although not serial music, use of all twelve scale degrees as a source of dissonance (chromatic saturation) in the introduction to the song "Birth" (1929), as well as her use of a whole-tone scale in the opening measures of the melody of "A Message," op. 93 (1922), demonstrates her openness to modernistic techniques. The majority of the thirty-two available songs from this period have memorable, singable melodies, underpinned by unexpected, chromatic harmonies reflecting the aforementioned elements. In more dissonant songs, ambiguous or restless tonal centers are clearly resolved in the final measures; usually ending with a cadence in a major mode. All are in English; all but two are settings of texts by contemporary authors.

For nineteen summers between 1921 and 1941, Beach composed (or made sketches for) almost all her compositions during summer months spent at the MacDowell Colony. Along with the Colony's peaceful atmosphere, intellectually stimulating interaction with some of the United States' most revered writers, artists, and composers precipitated a flood of creativity each year. New friendships with composers of the next generation led to reflection about modern trends in composition. Adrienne Fried Block notes that Beach's initial experiments with dissonant, nontonal harmonies began the year of her first stay at the Colony.[32]

Rather than on songwriting, her compositional efforts at the Colony focused on choral, keyboard, and chamber works, as well as her opera, *Cabildo*, resulting in an output of only thirty-nine songs in twenty-five years, slightly more than half the number composed in the thirty years of the first style period. Most of the thirty-one published songs were issued individually with separate opus numbers, rather than in groups. Manuscripts for three unpublished songs – "Mignonette," "My Love came through the Fields," and "A Light that overflows" – were not assigned opus numbers, nor are there copyright records for them.[33] The manuscript of "To One I Love," op. 135 (1932), is in private hands.

Inclusion of songs on her many performances and programs for various organizations and musical clubs introduced them to a wide range of audiences in towns of all sizes throughout the United States. Older songs were paired with her most recent works on these programs, focusing on the latter. An increasing number of speaking and performing appearances in the 1930s, as well as live performances of her music on local and nation-wide radio broadcasts, kept her in the public eye, prompting greater demand for her music. Sales of her newest works were thwarted by the outbreak of World War I, though, when paper and other shortages pre-cluded their expeditious publication. These production difficulties per-sisted through the Depression, further exacerbated by World War II. After A. P. Schmidt's death in 1921, his successor, Henry Austin, was often discouraging about possibilities of publishing her new songs, some-times questioning their marketability. His excuses and reluctance to issue or reissue her songs contributed to her contracting with other publishers (including Schirmer, Church, and Presser). It is conceivable that Austin's hesitancy to publish her most recent songs was due more to their inaccess-ibility to the average musician than to production problems. Despite his lack of interest in her most recent songs, he was eager to issue reprints of her most popular songs (all composed before 1905), also requesting they be arranged for various combinations of voices.

Until her death, Beach urged Austin persistently to publish her latest songs. As evidence of their merit, her letters frequently referenced success-ful performances of those in manuscript and their popularity with voice teachers. Always worded considerately, her letters reveal ever-increasing impatience. She was eager to have new songs copyrighted, lest they be plagiarized (a doubtful probability, given that those in question were of the "no perceptible melody" type).

Among the first pieces composed at the MacDowell Colony in 1921 was the dramatic song, "In the Twilight," op. 85. Typical of many third style period songs, its accompanimental device is more impressionistic in charac-ter than in harmonic structure. In some ways, harmonies are reminiscent of the first style period songs: quick movement from an initial tonality to other tonal areas by use of dominant sevenths and fully diminished chords, with a melody evolving from those harmonies. The poem tells of a fisherman's wife and child, watching a turbulent sea storm through a window at twilight, waiting for him to return from his day's work. The wife fears for her husband's fate. To enhance the text's ominous feeling, Beach set the song in F-sharp minor, one of her "black" keys. As the natural inflection of Henry Wadsworth Longfellow's masterfully chosen words create their own "text-painting," the majority of the musical interpretation was achieved by manipulating the keyboard's motif within the harmonic movement rather than through the vocal line. Expansion and contraction of this impressionis-tic pattern creates dramatic ebbs and flows, intensifying the text's sense of urgency, anxiety, and impending doom.

Example 6.7 "In the Twilight," op. 85, mm. 100–15.

The song's ending is the most unusual in Beach's vocal works, bearing a resemblance to the ending of Schubert's "Erlkönig." After building tension with tremolos for fourteen measures, a fermata precedes a German sixth chord, followed by an unaccompanied vocal line ending the song without the chord's resolution to reflect the text's final, unanswered question (Example 6.7).

"To me all music is sacred. . . . It is – and must be – a source of spiritual value. If it is not, it falls short of its function as music."[34]

At the 1926 New York City convention of the American Pen Women, Beach became acquainted with dramatic soprano Ruth

Shaffner (1896–1981), soprano soloist at St. Bartholomew's Church ("St. Bart's"), then the largest Episcopal church in North America. Schaffner invited Beach to attend a service there the next day to hear the composer's *Magnificat*. Highly impressed by both the choirs and organist/ choirmaster David McKay Williams's musicianship, she began regular attendance there when in New York. Both Shaffner and Williams became two of Beach's closest friends. Shaffner became Beach's most frequent collaborator, performing together hundreds of times throughout the United States.

Involvement with St. Bart's music program precipitated a flurry of sacred choral works and solo songs. Sacred music appealed to her more than anything she had previously done and became her favorite type of work. In a 1943 interview, she stated, "I find myself . . . turning more steadily toward so-called 'sacred' music. . . . It has not been a deliberate choice, but what has seemed a natural growth and a path which has brought me great happiness."[35] In a personal letter from a decade earlier, she had written, "There can be no greater experience than the act of entering into the great religious texts."[36]

A fortuitous incident on July 4, 1927, led to another of Beach's most significant relationships. Mezzo-soprano Lillian Buxbaum's (1884–1974) performance on a Boston radio station prompted Beach to telephone her that afternoon, to invite her to visit Centerville the next day. Buxbaum's acceptance led to a familial relationship between the two. Beach later regarded Buxbaum as a surrogate daughter. The two spent many summers together at Cape Cod and performed numerous concerts in New England. Like Shaffner, Buxbaum was a church soloist, serving at First Parish Church, Watertown, Massachusetts. Friendships with Shaffner and Buxbaum prompted composition of several pieces for their use in church services. Their needs and requests for sacred solos were met by Beach's increasing inspiration to compose them. To fit the rich timbres in these women's mid- to low ranges, some of these songs have lower *tessiture* than most earlier songs.

Unique among her songs is "On a Hill." Returning to the United States after a six-month trip to Europe in 1929, a chance shipboard encounter presented Beach with new musical material when a fellow passenger from Richmond, Virginia, shared a song "crooned to her by an old Mammy all through childhood."[37] (It was assumed to be an African American spiritual, although this has not been authenticated.) Beach said she had never been so pleased by a folk song. She provided the song with a simple, chordal, bare-bones accompaniment, varied harmonically (as was her practice) for each of its three verses. This unobtrusive accompaniment allows the listeners' ears to be drawn to the words and haunting, pentatonic melody. It was subtitled "Negro Lullaby" to set it apart from spirituals, which had recently inundated the market. Henry Austin of the Schmidt Company was discouraging about its sales potential, however, unless the prominent African American singer, Roland Hayes, would have interest in promoting it.[38]

Representative of Beach's later sacred solos are "I Sought the Lord," op. 142 (1937), and "Though I Take the Wings of Morning," op. 152 (1941), both composed at the MacDowell Colony and dedicated to Ruth Shaffner. They express the same sentiment as her earlier song "Ein altes Gebet": God's omniscience and omnipresence. These texts might well have brought her comfort as she faced the realities of aging and adjusting to giving up her performing career.

Composed following her 1940 heart attack, "Though I Take the Wings of Morning" is a setting of Robert Nelson Spencer's Psalm 139 paraphrase, taken from his *The Seer's House*.[39] The song shows influences of the African American spiritual, with chords vacillating between E minor and E major and use of alternating major and minor thirds in the melody. The accompaniment contains a rare example of vocal doubling. The final words of this, her final art song (and antepenultimate composition), are a poignant coincidence: "bid me then, be still."

Which were Beach's favorite songs? Those she frequently asked Austin to send to singers for specific performances provide clues. Almost all of the songs she requested after 1917 were composed early in her career. Several she repeatedly asked for had been long out of print. Songs selected for performances at retrospective concerts in honor of her seventy-fifth birthday in 1942 (all from the first style period) may indicate some favorites, those she felt were her most representative: "Ecstasy," op. 19, no. 2; "Villanelle: Across the World," op. 20; "My Star," op. 26, no. 1; "The Wandering Knight," op. 29, no. 2; "I send my heart up to Thee," op. 44, no. 3; and "June [Juni]," op. 51, no. 3. Those most consistently found on concert programs and mentioned in her correspondence were "Ecstasy," the *Browning Songs*, op. 44, and "Juni."

Despite the popularity of her works during her lifetime, after she was no longer physically able to tour and concertize to promote them, regard for most of her compositions, particularly the larger ones, declined quickly. Even though her later songs show her efforts to include more contemporary musical elements, the majority of her most well-known songs (from the first style period) were in the late nineteenth-century idiom, then regarded as old-fashioned and of little musical value. The author of her *Musical America* obituary described her later songs as not particularly original, having lost some of the melodic interest of her earlier works; certainly not an accurate assessment.[40] Restrictions in the publishing industry during World War II made reissuing out-of-print works difficult, leading to their quick neglect. By 1941, thirty-seven songs were unavailable. After Beach's death, Shaffner made efforts to keep New York music stores stocked with songs that were still in print. This number had dwindled to two by 1984.[41]

"There is enjoyment in every contact with beautiful song – in writing, singing, playing, or even thinking of it – and it brings to the listener a sense of discovery of a world in which serenity and contentment still reign."[42]

New generations of musicians and audiences are becoming familiar with Beach's songs as copyright expirations have made possible their inclusion in anthologies and their availability on the internet. They make a welcome re-addition to the body of American art song repertoire, as among their number one finds something for everyone: musicians of all levels of ability as well as audiences of varying levels of sophistication.

A quotation from the final published interview of Beach's life demonstrates her optimism in the face of the physical decline of old age and the tragedy of World War II. Fittingly, she expressed her optimism with the metaphor of singing:

We who sing have walked in glory.[43] What more can we say about singing than that? And was there ever a time when singing was more badly needed than now? Singing, not only with our throats but with our spirits. If we have no special voices, we can make our fingers sing on the keyboard or strings. The main thing is to let our hearts sing, even through sorrow and anxiety. The world cries out for harmony."[44]

Representative Songs and Difficulty Levels

First Style Period

Easy

"The Rainy Day"
"With Violets," op. 1, no. 1
"When far from Her," op. 2, no. 2
"Ecstasy," op. 19, no. 2
"Within thy Heart," op. 29, no. 1
"Sleep, Little Darling," op. 29, no. 3
"Dearie," op. 43, no. 1
"Scottish Cradle Song," op. 43, no. 2
"Far Awa'," op. 43, no. 4
"My Lassie," op. 43, no. 5
"Come, ah Come," op. 48, no. 1

"Go not too Far," op. 56, no. 2
"Shena Van," op. 56, no. 4
"Baby," op. 69, no. 1
"Hush, Baby Dear," op. 69, no. 2
"A Prelude," op. 71, no. 1

Medium

"Ariette," op. 1, no. 4
"Empress of Night," op. 2, no. 3
"Die vier Brüder," op. 1, no. 2
"Le Secret," op. 14, no. 2
"O mistress mine," op. 37, no. 1
"Take, O Take those Lips Away," op. 37, no. 2
"Fairy Lullaby," op. 37, no. 3
"Forgotten," op. 41, no. 3
"O were my Love yon lilac fair!" op. 43, no. 3
"The Year's at the Spring," op. 44, no. 1
"Canzonetta," op. 48, no. 4
"Ich sagte nicht," op. 51, no. 1
"Wir Drei," op. 51, no. 2
"Juni," op. 51, no. 3
"Je demande a l'Oiseau," op. 51, no. 4
"O Sweet Content," op. 71, no. 2

Difficult

"Dark is the Night," op. 11, no. 1
"Elle et moi," op. 21, no. 3
"Nachts," op. 35, no. 1
"Ah, Love but a day!" op. 44, no. 2
"I Send my Heart up to Thee!" op. 44, no. 3

Second Style Period

Easy

"Ein altes Gebet," op. 72, no. 1
"Grossmütterchen," op. 73, no. 1
"Der Totenkranz," op. 73, no. 2
"The Candy Lion," op. 75, no. 1
"A Thanksgiving Fable," op. 75, no. 2
"Prayer of a Tired Child," op. 75, no. 4

Medium

"The Lotos Isles," op. 76, no. 2

Third Style Period

Easy

"The Moonpath," op. 99, no. 3
"Around the Manger," op. 115
"The Host," op. 117, no. 2
"Song in the Hills," op. 117, no. 3

Medium

"In the Twilight," op. 85
"On a Hill"
"I Sought the Lord," op. 142
"May Flowers," op. 137
"Though I Take the Wings of Morning," op. 152

Notes

1. Desirée de Charmes and Paul Breed, *Songs in Collections: An Index* (Detroit: Information Service, 1966), supplemented by my own research in 1989. The songs were: "Meadowlarks," op. 78, no. 1, in *A New Anthology of American Songs: 25 Songs by Native American Composers* (New York: G. Schirmer, 1942), and "The Year's at the Spring," op. 44, no. 1, in Richard D. Row, *The Young Singer, Volume One, Soprano* (New York: Carl Fischer, 1965).
2. Mrs. H. H. A. Beach, "The Mission of the Present-Day Composer," *The Triangle of Mu Phi Epsilon* 36, no. 2 (February 1942): 72.
3. Berenice Thompson, "Music and Musicians: Mrs. Beach's Songs," *Washington Post*, January 17, 1904, p. E11.
4. Mrs. H. H. A. Beach, "The Enjoyment of Music," in Hazel Gertrude Kinscella, *Music on the Air* (Garden City, NY: Garden City Publishing Co., 1934), 25.
5. Benjamin Brooks, "The 'How' of Creative Composition: A Conference with Mrs. H. H. A. Beach," *The Etude* 61, no. 3 (March 1943): 151.
6. Quoted in Claire McGlinchee, "American Literature in American Music," *Musical Quarterly* 31, no. 1 (January 1945): 104.
7. Brooks, "The 'How' of Composition," 151.

8. Letter from Beach to the A. P. Schmidt Company, November 25, 1908, box 303, folder 5, A. P. Schmidt Company Archives, Music Division, Library of Congress.

9. Mrs. H. H. A. Beach, "Common Sense in Pianoforte Touch and Technic," *The Etude* 34, no. 10 (October 1916): 701.

10. Mrs. H. H. A. Beach, "How Music Is Made," *Keyboard* (Winter 1942): 11.

11. Brooks, "The 'How' of Composition," 208.

12. Brooks, "The 'How' of Composition," 208.

13. Beach, "The Enjoyment of Music," 24.

14. Beach, "How Music Is Made," 11.

15. Four of the songs that included string obbligati – "June," op. 51, no. 3; "Rendezvous," op. 120; "A Mirage," op. 100, no. 1; and "Stella viatoris," op. 100, no. 2 – have been republished with an introductory essay in Adrienne Fried Block, "Amy Beach (1867–1944)," in *Women Composers: Music Through the Ages*, vol. 7, *Composers born 1800–1899, Vocal Music*, ed. Sylvia Glickman and Martha Furman Schleifer (New York: G. K. Hall, 2003), 492–528.

16. For a discussion of this aspect of her piano accompaniments, see Adrienne Fried Block, *Amy Beach, Passionate Victorian: The Life and Work of an American Composer* (New York: Oxford University Press, 1998), 151 and 347n17.

17. A fascinating overview of pitch standards there can be found in Charles R. Cross, "Historical Notes Relating to Musical Pitch in the United States," *Proceedings of the American Academy of Arts and Sciences* 35, no. 22 (April 1900), 453–55.

18. Dr. G. W. C. Kaye, "International Standard of Concert Pitch," *Nature* 143 (May 27, 1939), 905. For a complete discussion of the evolution of Western pitch standards from the Renaissance through the twentieth century, see Bruce Haynes and Peter Cook, "Pitch," *The New Grove Dictionary of Music and Musicians*, 2nd ed., 29 vols., ed. Stanley Sadie (New York: Grove Dictionaries, 2001), vol. 19.

19. Burnet Corwin Tuthill, "Mrs. H. H. A. Beach," *Musical Quarterly* 26, no. 3 (July 1940): 298.

20. These early songs, published between 1887 and 1891, show her youthful inexperience in song composition. They include the popular "Hymn of Trust," op. 13; "Villanelle: Across the World," op. 20; French songs: "Jeune fille et jeune fleur," op. 1, no. 3, and both op. 21 songs, "Chanson d'amour" and "Extase."

21. Examples include "The Thrush," op. 14, no. 4, and "The Western Wind," op. 11, no. 2. These songs have relatively simple accompanimental motives that represent (respectively) the call of a wood thrush and a gentle breeze.

22. "unless it be an accompaniment that I want to try with the voice part, then I sometimes take it to the piano to see what changes are needed." Quoted in Harriet Brower, "Mrs. H. H. A. Beach: How a Composer Works," *Piano Mastery*, Second Series (New York: F. A. Stokes, 1917), 181.

23. Rupert Hughes, *Famous American Composers* (Boston: L. C. Page and Co., 1900), 430–32. In reviewing eleven of the fourteen songs in Schmidt's first anthology of Beach's songs (1891), Hughes stated: "Both the defects and effects of her qualities haunt Mrs. Beach's songs. When she is sparing in her erudition, she is delightful." He praised ten of the songs with such descriptions as "tender and graceful," "dainty and serene," and "of complete originality." His description of "A Secret" ("Le Secret," op. 14, no. 2) as "bizarre" is especially odd, given its lovely, flowing, singable melody. She quoted several of its measures in the third movement (a waltz) of her *Les Rêves de Columbine: Suite Française*, op. 65. It is plausible that Hughes's comment was in reference to "Extase," op. 14, no. 1.

24. This debate is discussed in Adrienne Fried Block, "Boston talks back to Dvořák," *Institute for Studies in American Music Newsletter* 18, no. 2 (1989): 10–11, 15.

25. Clipping file, Rebekah Crawford Collection, Manuscript Division, Library of Congress.

26. Quoted in "Among the Composers," *The Etude* 62, no. 1 (January 1944): 11.

27. Clare P. Peeler, "American Woman Whose Musical Message Thrilled Germany," *Musical America* 20, no. 24 (October 17, 1914): 7.

28. Letter from Emma Eames-Story to Beach, September 14, 1904, box 1, folder 5, Amy Cheney Beach (Mrs. H. H. A. Beach) Papers, 1835–1956, MC 51, Milne Special Collections and Archives, University of New Hampshire Library, Durham, NH.

29. Block, *Amy Beach: Passionate Victorian*, 207.

30. "The kindest, most helpful, and most merciless critics I ever had were my mother and my husband. How often they would make me work over a phrase – over and over and over! – until the flow of the melody and the harmonization sounded right." Quoted in Brooks, "The 'How' of Composition," 208.

31. "There are no absolute or eternal boundary lines in the expression of beauty and life. The underlying principles of truth live on, but the very momentum of the times in which we live is carrying us into new expression of them by new formulas of tone, color, and design." Quoted in Arthur Wilson, "Mrs. H. H. A. Beach: A Conversation on Musical Conditions in America," *The Musician* 17, no. 1 (January 1912): 9.

32. Block, *Amy Beach: Passionate Victorian*, 224.

33. Block, *Amy Beach: Passionate Victorian*, 371n25.

34. Quoted in Brooks, "The 'How' of Composition," 151, 209.

35. Brooks, "The 'How' of Composition," 151.

36. Letter from Beach to Mr. Weaver, May 30, 1932, box 2, folder 26, Beach Collection, University of Missouri, Kansas City.

37. Letter from Beach to Henry Austin of the Arthur P. Schmidt Company, June 3, 1929, box 303, folder 17, Schmidt Collection, Music Division, Library of Congress.

38. Letter from Austin to Beach, August 24, 1929, box 303, folder 17, Schmidt Collection, Music Division, Library of Congress. There is no evidence that Roland Hayes ever sang it.

39. Robert Nelson Spencer, *The Seer's House* (New York: C. Scribner's Sons, 1940).

40. "Mrs. Beach, Leading American Woman Composer, Dies at 77," *Musical America* 65, no. 1 (January 10, 1945): 24.

41. These were Anne L. and William D. Leyerle, *Song Anthology Two* (Geneseo, NY: Leyerle Publications, 1984) and Paul Sperry, *Songs of an Innocent Age* (Milwaukee, WI: Hal Leonard, 1984).

42. Kinscella, *Music on the Air*, 26.

43. The first line of her statement quotes a poem by Boston author Amy S. Bridgman (ca. 1865–1949). This poem (or at least part of it) was the basis of her choral piece, "We who sing have walked in glory," op. 140 (1930).

44. Quoted in "Among the Composers," 11.

7 | "Worthy of Serious Attention"[1]

The Chamber Music of Amy Beach

R. LARRY TODD

In memoriam Adrienne Fried Block

If relatively modest in quantity, the chamber music of Amy Beach comprised a significant body of work that confronted meaningfully the churning countercurrents animating her idiosyncratic musical style. She was a largely autodidactic composer steeped in traditions of European art music who nevertheless found ways to acknowledge her own American identity. She was a highly successful song composer who essayed the larger forms, and not at all timidly. She was a musician who, along with many of her contemporaries, lamented the relevance of Romanticism receding from the onslaught of twentieth-century modernisms. And she was a composer who, though "one of the boys,"[2] owing to her association with the Second New England School, worked energetically to promote the careers of other American women composers, even as she continued to publish her own music under the authorship of Mrs. H. H. A. Beach.

This last point bears emphasis, especially in approaching her chamber works. At the turn to the new century, the genre was still largely a male-dominated domain; relatively few women found their comfort zone while expending their aesthetic creativity on string quartets, piano trios, and all the rest. One has only to recall the experience of another gifted song composer, Fanny Hensel, who produced her sole string quartet in 1834 for private consumption, only to admit that, unlike her brother, who had already published two quartets, she had been unable to work through the unfathomable late quartets of Beethoven, and that in her view her larger compositions all too often died in their youth from decrepitude.[3]

Between Hensel and Beach, not many women composers invested substantially in chamber music. Among the few who come to mind was Clara Schumann, whose own Piano Trio in G minor, op. 17, dates from 1846, the year before Hensel died; following it by several years were the three Romances for violin and piano, op. 22, written for Joseph Joachim and figuring frequently in their concerts together.[4] The list of women after Clara Schumann who entered the lists of chamber music is not long. Three French composers who did were Cécile Chaminade (1857–1944), with a pair of piano trios; Marie Jaëll (1846–1925), with an estimable string quartet of 1875; and Louise Farrenc (1804–75), whose extensive chamber compositions range, most unusually, from duos all the way to a nonet. The Venezuelan pianist Teresa Carreño (1853–1917), to whom Beach dedicated her Piano Concerto and Violin Sonata, wrote a string quartet in 1896. English Dame Ethel Smyth (1858–1944), who studied in Leipzig, where she met Brahms, created two sonatas in 1880, both in A minor, for violin, op. 5, and for cello, op. 7, and both were fairly enveloped by the "Brahmsian fog."[5] Smyth's countrywoman Alice Mary Smith (1839–84) tested her mettle in piano quartets and string quartets. Finally, Swedish organist Elfrida Andrée (1841–1929) produced a violin sonata and a piano trio, quartet, and quintet, as well as string quartets.

Unlike most of the contributions of these predecessors, several of Beach's chamber works did receive noteworthy performances during her career in the United States and abroad, especially the *Romance*, op. 23; Violin Sonata, op. 34; and Piano Quintet, op. 67. Nearly all of Beach's chamber music appeared in print from her principal publisher, Arthur P. Schmidt, centered in Boston, with a branch in New York and international affiliation in Leipzig; only a few compositions were left in her musical estate for posthumous publication.[6] Chronologically, this repertoire falls into three groups, of which the first concentrated on works for violin and piano: the *Romance*, op. 23 (1893); Violin Sonata, op. 34 (1896); Three Pieces, op. 40 (1898); and *Invocation*, op. 55 (1904). In the second group, Beach explored a variety of other ensembles: Piano Quintet in F-sharp minor, op. 67 (1909); Theme and Variations for Flute and String Quartet, op. 80 (1920); Suite for Two Pianos, op. 70/104 (1924); and the one-movement Quartet for Strings, op. 89 (1929). The third and final group added two late works, the Piano Trio, op. 150 (1939), and *Pastorale* for wind quintet, op. 151 (1942).[7]

I

On May 1, 1893, having delivered a short address celebrating "the growth and progress of human endeavor in the direction of a higher civilization," President Grover Cleveland pressed a golden telegrapher's key to complete an electric circuit and activate 100,000 incandescent lights, launching the World's Columbian Exposition in Chicago. Among the technological innovations that enlightened, amused, and titillated fairgoers over the next six months – no fewer than some 28,000,000 visitors, a staggering two-fifths of the population of the United States – was the world's first Ferris Wheel (meant to rival the Eiffel Tower that had dominated the Parisian cityscape during the *Exposition universelle* of 1889), a moving sidewalk, the elevator, the phonograph, and the telephone. Among the practical inventions making their debut were the zipper and the dishwasher, the latter the brainchild of Josephine Cochrane.

She was just one of many women who made an impact at the fair. The Board of Lady Managers, whose president was Bertha Honoré Palmer, a wealthy Chicago socialite, had commissioned the Woman's Building, designed by the twenty-one-year-old architect Sophia Hayden, to show-case the "progress" of womankind. A number of women artists and sculptors displayed their work, among them Mary Cassatt, who, against the discouragement of her fellow impressionist Edgar Degas, contributed a 58 × 12-foot mural on the theme of the modern woman[8]; and the sculptor Enid Yandell, a pupil of Rodin, who created the caryatid that supported the roof garden. Amy Beach received a commission to compose a cantata, the *Festival Jubilate*, op. 17, performed by an orchestra and chorus directed by Theodore Thomas on the opening day before an audience of some 2,000 that thronged the Woman's Building.[9] Early in July, Beach returned to the Exposition to perform some of her piano pieces, the song "Sweetheart, Sigh No More" (the third of the Four Songs, op. 14), and the *Romance* in A major, op. 23, the last with Maud Powell, the first American violinist to enjoy an international concertizing and recording career.[10]

As Adrienne Block has suggested, the inspiration for Beach's first chamber work was, in fact, "Sweetheart, Sigh No More," though likely few at the time realized the connection.[11] Set to a text by Thomas Bailey Aldrich,[12] editor of the *Atlantic Monthly* from 1881 to 1890, this modified-strophic, sentimental love song falls into three sections (A, A', A") that progressively recall and expand to a climax the refrain-like line, "Sweetheart, Sigh No More," which concludes each of the three five-line stanzas. Here is the first stanza of Aldrich's poem and, for comparison, the beginnings of Beach's song and *Romance* (Examples 7.1 and 7.2).

It was with doubt and trembling,
I whispered in her ear,
Go, take her answer, bird on bough,
That all the world may hear,
Sweetheart, sigh no more!

Example 7.1 Beach, "Sweetheart, Sigh No More," op. 14, no. 3, mm. 1–6.

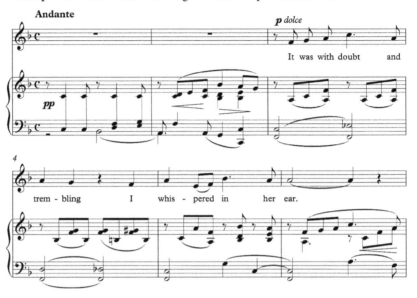

Example 7.2 Beach, *Romance*, op. 23, mm. bars 1–6.

Without much difficulty, one can perceive similarities between the two settings: they share, for instance, a rising melodic line defined rhythmically as three-eighths, dotted quarter, and eighth. That said, though, the *Romance* impresses as a recast version of the song. While the vocal line commences on its tonic keynote (f') and progresses through scale degrees 2, 3, and 5 (g', a', c"), the violin melody begins on its fifth scale degree (e') and climbs through scale degrees 6 and 7 (f♯', g♯') before reaching, via an appoggiatura on b', 8 (a'). What is more, the instrumental melody unfolds in three consecutively expanding gestures that span, in turn, a fifth (e'–b'), sixth (f♯'–d"), and seventh (a'–g♯"), presaging Beach's later manipulation and expansion of register in the concluding section of the piece, in which the violin plays its melody *beneath* the piano, which offers a murmuring accompaniment high above with *pianissimo* tremolos.

Like the song, *Romance* falls formally in three parts, though the second (*animato*) is sufficiently modulatory and developmental in character to suggest a contrasting middle section, yielding a ternary form (*ABA'*) for the whole, as opposed to the essentially strophic patterning of the original song. In the *B* section of the instrumental reworking, Beach explores third relationships, in particular the lower thirds F major and F-sharp major, more extensively than in the song, where the tonic F major is only briefly juxtaposed with D-flat and A-flat major, that is, thirds below *and* above the tonic. More subtle to trace is the relationship between the violin part and the vocal part. Initially, Aldrich's poetry does map conveniently onto the *Romance* so that, for instance, we may readily underlay "It was with doubt and trembling" beneath the violin entrance, encouraging us in effect to hear op. 23 as a *Lied ohne Worte*. But within a few bars, any imagined vestiges of a text disappear, while the music asserts its autonomous character as an abstract piece for violin and piano.

With the Violin Sonata, op. 34, Beach produced a major chamber work that freely acknowledged its nineteenth-century European roots – first and foremost, Brahms; to a lesser extent Liszt, in Beach's use of thematic transformation and certain piano figurations; Wagner, in her application of chromatically saturated textures, especially in the slow movement; and perhaps also Dvořák, in her intimations of folk music in the second-movement scherzo. The sonata dates from 1896, just months before the passing of Brahms in April 1897. From the outset, Beach's score absorbs the modally infused late style of Brahms; indeed, not insignificant portions of her sonata seem to privilege modal versus tonal formations and relation-ships. If we consider, for instance, just the keys of the four movements – A minor, G major, E minor, and A minor (ultimately ending in the parallel

Example 7.3a Beach, Violin Sonata in A minor, op. 34/I, mm. bars 1–7.

Allegro moderato (♩=120)

Example 7.3b Reduction.

major) – we see that the lowered seventh degree, a characteristic marker of the Aeolian mode, is tonicized in the second movement. In addition, several themes of the sonata tend to avoid the raised in favor of the lowered seventh scale degree and also feature the Phrygian half-step E–F, that is, in terms of the Aeolian mode, the fifth scale degree supported by its upper neighbor. As in the late music of Brahms,[13] these modal flavors afforded Beach viable alternatives to the well-trodden terrains of late nineteenth-century tonality, increasingly perceived, as the century's end neared, as having been stretched to its limits.

A case in point is the opening theme of the first movement, presented in stark *pianissimo* octaves, which analyze more convincingly as a modal rather than tonal gambit (Examples 7.3a and 7.3b). As the reduction in Example 7.3b illustrates, this theme divides the octave into the fifth and fourth (a–e'–a'), with the fifth scale degree embellished by its diatonic neighbor notes, d' and f'.

Significantly, Beach initially avoids the seventh scale degree; its first appearance occurs in bars 5 and 6, as the (lowered) g♮', an inner voice of the mediant C-major harmony. All these calculations have the effect of postponing until bar 14 the first, brief arrival of the dominant with its *raised* leading tone, G♯. But the onset of the *Animato* in bar 33, marking the transition to the second theme, now accommodates more compellingly a hybrid modal/tonal, if not tonal reading. Thus, the lowered seventh

Example 7.4 Beach, Violin Sonata in A minor, op. 34/I, mm. 63–71.

degree does return as a bass pedal point, but in tonal terms, as V/III, seemingly in order to prepare for a second theme in the mediant C major. Beach sidesteps this anticipated progression, however, so that when, moments later, the second theme emerges, it does so in a luminous E major, moving us securely into a tonal orbit around the dominant (Example 7.4).

The first movement offers other instances of modal/tonal exchanges, as at the end of the exposition, where the expected close in E major yields instead to a modally tinged E minor. Similarly, in the recapitulation Beach obviates the effect of the returning second theme in A major by recalling at the end of the movement its Aeolian opening, as if to remind us of the crepuscular, modal origins of the sonata. These modal/tonal ambiguities inform, too, the late music of Brahms, likely a primary influence on Beach's op. 34. One need look no further than the start of Brahms' Violin Sonata in D minor, op. 108 (1888), where our sense of "D minor" arguably rather suggests transposed Aeolian on D, with its lowered leading tone, C♮. Or, the beginning of the Clarinet Sonata in F minor, op. 120, no. 1 (1894), where the theme describes a descending form of the Phrygian mode transposed to F. Or, to choose three of Brahms' later compositions in A minor: the Intermezzo, op. 76, no. 4 (1878), Double Concerto, op. 102 (1887), and

Example 7.5 Beach, Violin Sonata in A minor, op. 34/II, mm. 1–5.

Clarinet Trio, op. 114 (1891), all of which highlight the lowered G♮ and thereby invoke the Aeolian mode.

As mentioned earlier, the second movement, in a ternary *ABA'* scheme, offers a scherzo in G major (with a trio in the parallel minor), thus elevating the natural seventh scale degree to prominence, but now in a tonal context. The scherzo does not exactly begin in G major, however. Rather, the first two bars describe a falling figure that outlines an A-minor triad in imitative counterpoint before pivoting toward G major (Example 7.5).

With the key signature of one sharp, this A-minor opening actually seems to draw on the transposed Dorian mode on A (i.e., A, B, C, D, E, F♯, G, A), which, through a simple process of rotation, readily transforms itself into G major, beginning in bar 3, where the bass of the piano establishes G as the tonal foundation. Beach's conceit thus links the scherzo to the first movement, so that its close in the Aeolian mode gives way, if only momentarily, to transposed A-Dorian before turning to a tonal organization and confirming G major as the key of the scherzo. Here the F♯, which replaces the F♮ of the first movement, is a critical pitch that plays two roles – first as the raised sixth of A to impart a Dorian character, and then as the leading tone to G major. In a similar way the spectral trio, putatively in the parallel G minor, creates enough tonal uncertainty through its use of the lowered seventh degree to tempt us to hear parts of it as G-Aeolian, or at least as a tonal/modal hybrid (Example 7.6).

These evocative mixtures are not dissimilar to what Chopin had explored in his Nocturne in G minor, op. 15, no. 3, of 1833, which similarly resists fitting comfortably within its assumed key, owing again to the prominence of the lowered seventh degree and strategic placement of chromatic pitches that challenge the tonal identity of the piece.

Chromaticism weighs heavily on the third movement (*Largo con dolore*) of Beach's sonata, one of her most heartfelt creations and the emotional

Example 7.6 Beach, Violin Sonata in A minor, op. 34/II, Più lento, mm. 1–3.

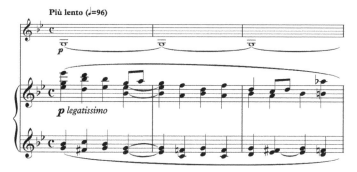

Example 7.7 Beach, Violin Sonata in A minor, op. 34/III, mm. 14–15.

high point of the work. Granted, the movement begins securely enough in E minor, but as we proceed further, the dense chromaticism more and more loosens the tonal moorings of the music, effectively setting us adrift in Wagnerian currents that evade tonal closure by means of strategically placed deceptive cadences. Example 7.7 illustrates one such cadence that seems intended to revisit the shifting tonal tides of *Tristan und Isolde*.

And yet, by the end of the *Largo* Beach again betrays her affinity to Brahms. The surprise turn to E major in the closing bars allows the composer to revive some modal associations that bring to mind the *Andante moderato* of Brahms' Fourth Symphony, op. 98 (1886), celebrated for its initial horn solo in the Phrygian mode, brought back in its closing bars, as shown in Example 7.8a.

Five bars from the end of her movement, Beach appears to allude in the high violin tessitura to this horn call, featuring the lowered sixth and

Example 7.8a Brahms, Symphony No. 4, op. 98/IV, mm. 113–18.

leading tone (C and D) as the piano climbs in gently quivering tremolos grounded in E major (Example 7.8b).

From this fading welter of sound we may extract a mixed mode on E (E–F♯–G♯–A–B–C–D–E), in which the first tetrachord supports E major, while the second favors a Phrygian hearing. As in Brahms' symphony, modal mixtures thus help to create a spellbinding, iridescent conclusion that plays at the borders between tonality and modality.

Just as Beach found a way to link the scherzo to the first movement, so too does she connect the finale to the slow movement, in this case through an energetic transition. Its purpose is to redefine the placid E-major close of the *Largo* as the invigorated dominant-seventh of A minor (V–V7–i). Here Beach draws on precedents of several nineteenth-century composers. One thinks, for instance, of the finale of Mendelssohn's Cello Sonata in D major, op. 58 (1843), or the complex finale of Brahms' Piano Quintet in F minor, op. 34 (1865), both of which use transitions to introduce their final movements. When Beach's first theme arrives thirteen bars into the finale,

Example 7.8b Beach, Violin Sonata in A minor, op. 34/III, last six measures.

we encounter a tonal/modal mixture that again may be read alternately in A minor or the Aeolian mode (Example 7.9).

Appropriately enough, this theme impresses as derived from the Aeolian theme of the first movement (cf. Example 7.3a), which partitions the octave into the fifth and fourth, the difference between the two themes being that in the finale, Beach partially fills in the fifth with a stepwise ascent to the third scale degree (A, B, C, E). Note also that the ornamentation of the fifth degree, E, with its upper neighbor, F, is now transferred to the busy tremolos of the piano accompaniment. Throughout the course of the finale,

Example 7.9 Beach, Violin Sonata in A minor, op. 34/IV, mm. 13–16.

Example 7.10 Beach, Violin Sonata in A minor, op. 34/IV, mm. 47–51.

Beach's primary theme undergoes metamorphoses not unlike the thematic transformations conjured by Liszt or what Arnold Schoenberg would later describe as the developing variations of Brahms. Thus, we may comprehend the lyrical second theme (Example 7.10) as a distant cousin of the opening theme – here Beach expands the original outline of a step and third (A B A C) slightly to accommodate a fourth (D E D G).

A more straightforward transformation of the first theme occurs in the fugato marking the beginning of the development (Example 7.11). In this case, Beach was perhaps recalling a similar procedure applied by Liszt in the fugato of his Piano Sonata (1853), the subject of which openly derives from the introductory bars of that work. But for the American theorist/

Example 7.11 Beach, Violin Sonata in A minor, op. 34/IV, mm. 97–102.

pedagogue Percy Goetschius, in the main Beach followed "the methods of development peculiar to Brahms."[14] Was Goetschius referring to how she developed her themes, how she applied modal mixtures, or perhaps to other techniques? He did not elaborate further, though as we shall see, Beach would find other opportunities to indulge her Brahmsian pursuits.

Her next two chamber compositions, the Three Pieces, op. 40 (1898), and *Invocation*, op. 55 (1904), are both small-scale creations that return us to the songlike character piece represented by the earlier *Romance*. Precious little is known about their inspiration or early history. Of the three titles for op. 40 – *La Captive*, *Berceuse*, and *Mazurka* – Nos. 2 and 3 refer to well-established genres through several common markers, whether the muted, rocking rhythms and stable pedal points of the berceuse, or the rustic gestures and drones of the Polish peasant folk dance. But in the cases of *La Captive* and *Invocation*, the sources for the titles remain unclear, so we are left to our own devices to interpret them. *La Captive*, at least, does encourage some speculation. It may be that here Beach was alluding to Victor Hugo's poem of the same name from *Les Orientales* (1829), a collection, in Graham Robb's pithy summary, "set in a Never-Never

Example 7.12a Brahms, Piano Quintet in F minor, op. 34/I, mm. 1–4, and reduction.

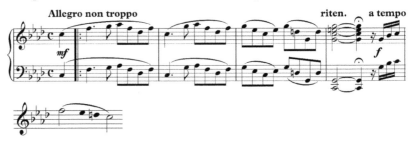

Land which resembled Spain, Algeria, Turkey, Greece and China, and called itself 'The East'."[15] Beach responded by restraining the violin part throughout to the G-string of the instrument, "freeing" this captive only in the final bars through an arpeggiated series of ethereal, ascending harmonics.

II

In 1908, when Beach turned to the vaunted genre of the piano quintet, she would have been intimately familiar with the exemplars of Robert Schumann (1842) and Brahms (1864), both of which she performed with the Kneisel Quartet, and probably also those of Franck (1879) and Dvořák (1887). All of these save the Dvořák use prominent cyclical thematic techniques, whereby material from the first movement reemerges in transformed guises in the finale (Schumann and Brahms) or second and third movements (Franck). Beach followed suit by recalling the mysterious prefatory *Adagio* of her quintet late in the finale, just before the coda, and spirited *Presto* leading to the radiant ending in F-sharp major. But in this case the construction of her *Adagio*, which unfolds a descending chromatic tetrachord (F♯, F♮, E, D♯, D♮, C♯), betrays the strong influence of Brahms' quintet, with which we may hear Beach's score to be in dialogue.

Beach would have noticed, for instance, that the initial bars of Brahms' op. 34 describe a tetrachordal Dorian descent from F through E♭, D♮, and C (Example 7.12a), and that subsequently the same perfect fourth is filled out chromatically (F–E♮–E♭–D♮–D♭, and C; Example 7.12b), a centuries-old topical reference to the lament (*passus duriusculus*).

This motive of the composed-out fourth provided Brahms with several options for later use in his quintet – for instance, the half-step D♭–C, highlighted especially in the jarring Phrygian cadence at the end of the

Example 7.12b Brahms, Piano Quintet in F minor, op. 34/I, mm. 12–16, and reduction.

Example 7.13a Brahms, Piano Quintet in F minor, op. 34/IV, mm. 252–60.

scherzo. Of particular relevance to Beach, though, was the second theme of his finale, also derived from the chromatic tetrachord, and the apparent inspiration for the first page of her quintet (Example 7.13).

In a remarkable transformation, Beach reworked this tetrachord, now transposed up a step to span the fourth F♯–C♯, into a new, tonally desta-bilized form. The reduction in Example 7.14 shows how.

She begins by assigning the violins and viola a stationary, high *pianis-simo* unison F♯ that seems to emerge *ex nihilo*, as if to assert that in the beginning was the unmediated, uninterpreted pitch F♯. Against it the piano erupts from below with a series of arpeggiated dissonances – first a French augmented-sixth chord, then a IV7 chord, and finally an embellished augmented triad, none of which clarifies our sense of F-sharp minor. The strings then repeat their unison, unharmonized pedal point and commence a craggy chromatic descent clearly modeled on the theme from Brahms' finale (cf. Example 7.13a). This descent actually overshoots its goal, for it

Example 7.13b Beach, Piano Quintet in F♯ minor, op. 67/I, mm. 1–24.

Example 7.13b (cont.)

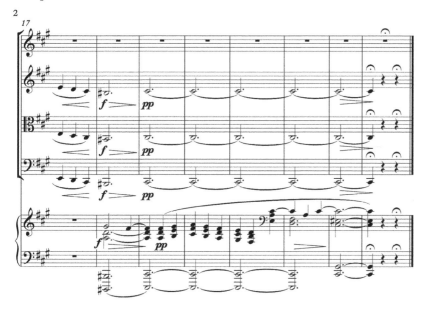

Example 7.14 Reduction of Example 7.13b.

extends the tetrachord by one step to fill out the tritone F♯–B♯. From this point, the downward stepwise motion continues in unison with the natural diatonic version of F-sharp minor before ultimately coming to rest on the dominant. The half cadence on C-sharp major is, notably, the only consonant moment in the slow introduction. In short, Beach has thwarted our sense of a tonic so that instead of an F♯-minor triad we hear just the pitch F♯, isolated and suspended in a high, rootless register, where it blends with the swirling dissonant arpeggiations accumulating below. From a tonal perspective, the effect of the whole *Adagio* is thus to begin *in medias res*, setting us down in an unpredictable sea of chromatic sonorities from which we slowly drift toward the relative stability of the dominant.

Example 7.15 Beach, Piano Quintet in F♯ minor, op. 67/I, mm. 25–28.

Notwithstanding her clear debt to Brahms, the abstract model behind Beach's *Adagio* is ultimately that of the historical slow introduction, traditionally understood to begin (securely) in the tonic and then to modulate and pause on the dominant, not infrequently via a stepwise descent, whether diatonic or chromatic.[16] By literally upending a stable opening on the tonic, Beach acknowledges the critical juncture at which tonality had arrived. Indeed, it is more than fitting that her quintet was exactly contemporary with another chamber work in F-sharp minor, the Second String Quartet, op. 10, of Arnold Schoenberg, which, ironically, *did* begin with a stable F♯-minor triad, though, of course, it would end with a phantasmagoric vision of Stefan George's poem "Ich fühle Luft von anderem Planeten" ("I feel a fragrance from another planet"), the new "pantonal" world that Schoenberg would fearlessly explore the very next year in his *Drei Klavierstücke*, op. 11.

Of course, Beach never committed to that *salto mortale*, though her modification of Brahms' tetrachord afforded her a viable way to explore a fully saturated chromaticism that, in turn, had direct implications for her understanding of tonal relationships. And so, the first theme of the exposition uses a variant of the tetrachordal figure in the first violin, with the tonic pitch now transposed to the deep bass of the piano, as if to grant it structural weight, even though Beach fills the space between with rustling, mostly dissonant piano sextuplets, few of which actually touch on the tonic harmony (Example 7.15).

Example 7.16 Beach, Piano Quintet in F♯ minor, op. 67/I, mm. 73–79.

Example 7.17 Beach, Piano Quintet in F♯ minor, op. 67/I, tetrachordal summary.

Eventually this first thematic group evaporates into diminished-seventh chords in the high register, and we proceed to the second theme, which, surprisingly enough, materializes in B major, that is, the subdominant (Example 7.16).

The new theme appears in the middle register of the piano in a texture reminiscent of Brahms' nostalgic use of the so-called three-hand technique.[17] Above we hear repeated statements of f♯''', the tonic pitch from the slow introduction that Beach now recasts as the fifth scale degree of the subdominant. She does not linger long before leading her new theme through a series of quick modulations that include the submediant D major, so that for a moment we might understand B major and D major as forming a pair of third-related tonalities. Nevertheless, the exposition does conclude in the subdominant, with references to the fourth B–F♯, and, again, the high treble f♯'''.

Now if we pause to consider the tonal trajectory of the exposition, we begin to apprehend its overarching unity. By modulating to the subdominant, instead of, say, the mediant or dominant, Beach reinforces the tetrachordal foundations on which this music rests. That is, the Ur-tetrachord of the Adagio, F♯–C♯ (extended through B♯ to the tritone) is complemented and "completed" in the exposition by its mirror tetrachord, B–F♯ (Example 7.17).

Taken together, the two symbolically span the total chromatic and help to explain the restless, searching quality of the quintet, which visits ever so

Example 7.18 Beach, Piano Quintet in F♯ minor, op. 67/II, mm. 1–8.

briefly any number of keys while minimizing if not avoiding altogether unambiguous statements of the tonic triad until the final cadence of the movement. For Beach, tonality is still understood as a teleological process – F-sharp minor is the goal of this movement and is ultimately attained in its closing bars, though the narrative of how she accomplishes that is anything but predictable, as most of the expected or familiar tonal anchoring points in the movement are weakened or occluded, if not removed.

It is well known that at an early age Beach displayed not only perfect pitch but pronounced signs of synesthesia, through which she associated particular keys with colors.[18] In her musical palette, F-sharp minor was a black key. In contrast, D-flat major, the key of the second movement of the quintet, aroused for her softer hues of violet. Perhaps not surprisingly, then, she created here a lushly romantic movement firmly centered on D♭, enharmonic equivalent of the C♯ of the first movement. The *Adagio espressivo* opens straightaway with a yearning theme in the muted strings, an eight-bar period that divides symmetrically into two four-bar phrases, the second stretched a bit by a brief metrical change from 4/4 to 6/4 (Example 7.18), as if to suggest an expressive *rubato*.

The theme appears subsequently in the piano, and then in the second violin a minor third above, in E major, before the cello introduces a second theme in B-flat minor, a minor third *below* the tonic. These third relationships return us to the realm of late Romantic tonality, as Beach rapturously redirects her gaze backward, to revive a fleeting, autumnal vision of the musical past from which she had first drawn her musical nourishment.

It remains then for the finale to reconvert the D♭ to C♯ in a brusque transition that launches the movement (*Allegro agitato*). The function of

Example 7.19 Beach, Piano Quintet in F♯ minor, op. 67/III, mm. 311–14.

C-sharp major as the dominant is now in focus and reinforced, so that the movement ultimately can conclude in F sharp, not in the veiled, chromatically clouded minor of the first movement, but in its triumphant major form. Along the way, Beach introduces and develops themes that derive from the tetrachord of the first movement, including, toward the end of the development, a fugato with a tonal answer that chisels out the telltale fourth, F♯–C♯, all in preparation for a dramatic ascent and pause. From the silence emerges once again the *Adagio* of the first movement, with the high, disembodied F♯''' suspended above. The final unwinding of the tetrachord then transpires in the spirited coda, where we hear in succession seven dissonant chords that accompany the chromatic descent F♯, E♯, E♮, D♯, D♮, C♯, and C♮ (Example 7.19).

Its continuation, ultimately moving through B to A♯, provides the final steps that convincingly affirm the tonal paradigm of dominant-tonic and bring this rich work to its close. All that remains unanswered is which color in the end supplants the black and violet of the first two movements.

III

Among Beach's least-known chamber work is the unjustly neglected *Suite for Two Pianos (Founded upon Old Irish Melodies)*, released in 1924 as her op. 104. We do not know for certain, but a reasonable hypothesis is that the composition at least drew upon an earlier two-piano work titled *Iverniana*, which Beach had performed in 1910. She went as far as to assign the opus number 70 to that duet, but never published it; subsequently the manuscript disappeared, and no trace has yet emerged. What has come down to us as the *Suite*, op. 104, is in four movements, two of which have programmatic titles: Prelude (E minor), "Old-Time Peasant Dance" (E minor), "The Ancient Cabin" (A-flat major), and Finale (E minor/major). The predominance of the key of E minor, use of the lowered seventh scale degree and pentatonic formations, and appearance of Irish folk melodies or imitations thereof recall the composer's "Gaelic" Symphony, premiered in Boston in 1896. In turn, that linkage encourages us to revisit briefly the celebrated controversy about American music precipitated by another symphony in E minor, Dvořák's "New World" Symphony, premiered in 1893 at the newly finished Carnegie Hall in New York.

In an interview appearing in the *New York Herald* on May 21, 1893, Dvořák had argued that the future of American music "must be founded upon what are called negro melodies." The pentatonic slow movement of his symphony was understood to simulate African American spirituals, and in fact its haunting English-horn melody would later enjoy an afterlife as the spiritual "Goin' Home." Nevertheless, among the early reactions to the "New World" Symphony were these private comments of Beach, who found Dvořák's music to "represent only the peaceful side of the negro character and life. Not for a moment does it suggest their sufferings, heartbreaks, *slavery*."[19] Dvořák later revised his views to take into account Native American music as a second repository of folk materials available to composers, and shortly before leaving the United States in 1895 to return to Prague went a step further: "It matters little whether the inspiration for the coming folk songs of America is derived from the negro melodies, the songs of the creoles, the red man's chant, or the plaintive ditties of the homesick German or Norwegian. Undoubtedly, the germs for the best of music lie hidden among all the races that are commingled in this great country."[20]

Unlike Dvořák, whose symphony "hinted at an exotic otherness that listeners were supposed to intuit as American,"[21] Beach confirmed her Gaelic/American sympathies by specifically labeling her symphony and citing several folk melodies excerpted from a series of articles about Irish music published in the Dublin-based *Citizen* of 1841.[22] Of interest to us here is that when composing the *Suite*, op. 104, she returned to the same source and chose four additional Irish melodies for reuse, one for each movement. In order of appearance, they are: 1) "Song of Sleep" (Lullaby), 2) Irish dance, 3) "Molly St. George," and 4) a traditional Irish fiddle tune.[23] Adapting them for her suite, Beach transposed three to different keys. The "Song of Sleep," transmitted in a tonally ambiguous setting oscillating between C minor and E-flat major, she reworked to E minor/major, but left unchanged the Irish dance in E minor. Then, she transposed "Molly St. George" a fourth above from E-flat to A-flat major, and the tune for her finale a fifth above from A minor to E minor, ending in E major. Three of the four movements thus privileged E minor, the

Example 7.20 Beach, "An Indian Lullaby," op. 57, no. 3, mm. 1–4.

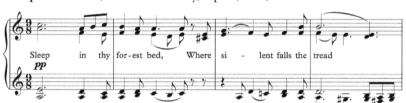

prevalent tonality of Dvořák's "New World" Symphony. In the case of the second movement ("Old-Time Peasant Dance"), Beach was perhaps intent upon providing an alternative to Dvořák's irrepressible symphonic scherzo, thought by some scholars to have been his musical realization of a Native American dance described in Longfellow's *Song of Hiawatha* (1855). In effect, Beach shifted the locale from the southern shore of Lake Superior for Dvořák's score to Gaelic "pagan mid-summer-nights' feasts" for her own, during which "the mad priests and votaries of Baal danced . . ., whirling round their bonfires."[24]

Though Beach often drew upon traditional materials from the "Old World" to celebrate local color – witness, for example, the piano *Variations on Balkan Themes*, op. 60 (1904) – she also explored music of the Alaskan Inuit natives in her search for an exotic American "Other."[25] Here Beach was allying herself with the so-called Indianist movement, which had produced visions of an "imaginary Native America steeped in an imaginary past"[26] in works such as Edward MacDowell's orchestral *Indian Suite*, op. 48 (1892),[27] and in the lecture-recitals and publications of Arthur Farwell, who founded the Wa-Wan Press in 1901 in an effort to promote composers who incorporated Native American musical materials into their work.

An early example of Beach's interest in the topic of Native American culture is her part song for female choir "An Indian Lullaby," op. 57, no. 3, of 1895. In this case, neither the text, which speaks of a soft forest bed of pine needles, nor the music, which begins in a lilting, modally colored A minor but ends in the parallel major, actually appears to draw on authentic Native American materials. Rather, the composition reflects the gaze of Amy Beach as she searches for an idealized American exoticism while still employing primarily Western musical techniques (Example 7.20).

Be that as it may, in 1920 Beach returned to her part song and reused it as the basis for her Theme and Variations for Flute and String Quartet, op. 80.

Example 7.21 Beach, Theme and Variations, op. 80, Variation 1, mm. 37–43.

Following the presentation of the part song by the string quartet, the flute enters with a brief cadenza that features augmented seconds, effectively identifying the instrument as the Native American protagonist (Example 7.21).

In the first variation the flute projects a high cantilena, like a spontaneous improvisation suspended above, while the string quartet adheres below more closely to the theme. There then follow a contrapuntal second variation and a third in the style of a slow, morbid waltz, both markers of Western musical topics, neither of which, however, fully engages the spectator-like flute. Only in the fourth variation, a fleet-footed scherzo for the string quartet that shifts the key signature from A minor to F-sharp minor, does the flute begin to sing strains from the original theme above the string ensemble, all preparatory to the emotional crux of the composition – the exquisite, searing fifth variation in F-sharp major. Here the flute finally enters fully into the conversation of the quartet, as Beach resorts to her most passionate, chromatic, late-Romantic style, matched in intensity possibly only by some passages in her Piano Quintet (Example 7.22).

Example 7.22 Beach, Theme and Variations, op. 80, Variation 5, mm. 51–54.

But, as if turning back from this unusual symbolic alliance of two different musical worlds, she then leads us through a foreshortened reprise of the scherzo to the *Tempo del Tema*, with its relatively monochromatic theme in A minor and cadenza-like response from the flute. The ultimate sixth variation brings one more Western "artifice," a fugue on a subject fashioned from a portion of the theme. Here the flute participates equally with the string quartet in dispatching a five-voice fugue, though its frenzied course toward A major is abruptly cut short. In the final page Beach comes full circle to the original modal theme and allows the flute to have the final comment with a hushed reference to its cadenza.

If the Theme and Variations offer an idealized meeting of two different musical cultures, a meeting admittedly still beholden to the Western musical hegemony, Beach progressed to the next step by directly integrating authentic Inuit melodies into a major chamber work, the one-movement String Quartet, finished in 1929.[28] This quartet was one of her few compositions she was unable to see through the press; indeed, not until 1994 did the first edition appear.[29] The result was a singular admixture of three modal Inuit melodies, each introduced against the backdrop of an intensely chromatic, dissonant language that also framed the composition in an introduction and coda best described, perhaps, as music in search of a tonal center. Ultimately Beach found it in the final cadence, in which an amorphous augmented triad slips almost imperceptibly into a G-major sonority, providing closure to this experimental work. The peripatetic

Example 7.23 Beach, String Quartet, op. 89, mm. 1–14.

fourteen-bar introduction, much of which returns in the coda, offers Beach at her most dissonant: these bookends represent her realization, as it were, of Schoenberg's *schwebende Tonalität*, or "suspended tonality." Here she explores a tonally decentered, weightless realm with eerie *pianissimo* altered chords – nearly all dissonant – and sliding chromatic lines that situate us somewhere in twentieth-century modernity and the crisis of tonality (Example 7.23).

When, after a brief silence, the first Inuit melody appears in the viola, it enters initially as unadorned monophony, as if some vision of a preternatural, uncorrupted past unaffected by musical modernity, before then being swept up in the swirling chromatic polyphony of the ensemble. Beach's strategy seems to be to contrapose the modern with the ancient – the European string quartet with its rich associations of contrapuntal thematic working out initially collides with the timeless, indigenous single-line music of the American Inuit. Thus, the third Inuit melody generates the subject of an unconventional fugue, the center of a symmetrical arch

Example 7.24a Beach, String Quartet, op. 89, mm. 15–19.

Example 7.24b Beach, String Quartet, op. 89, mm. 263–74.

form (Introduction *ABCB'A'* Coda) not unlike the paradigms employed by Bartók in his string quartets. And just as Bartók joins elements of folk music to a modernist style, so too does Beach create a new alliance of binary opposites – for instance, of modality vs. suspended tonality, or monophony vs. polyphony (Examples 7.24a and b).

But, in the end, the two sides meet halfway with a serene G-major sonority that at once resolves the accumulated dissonance of the whole and reimagines the limits of a modal musical universe, a compelling example of the new path Beach was beginning to explore in her later music.

IV

Beach would return to chamber music on two more occasions. The short *Pastorale*, op. 151, is a late recasting from 1941 for wind quintet of a modest earlier work for flute, piano, and cello. A far more substantial offering, one that conveniently summarizes the contrasting directions we have been tracing in her chamber music, is the Piano Trio in A minor, op. 150, composed in just two weeks in June 1938. In her diary Beach noted that she was creating the trio out of "old materials," and indeed the result arguably represents her most eclectic creation, incorporating, in Adrienne Block's estimation, "French modern, late Romantic, and folk elements, perhaps guided by narrative concerns."[30]

The first movement begins with swirling, *ppp* arpeggiations in the piano that project ambiguity in two ways. First, while the A-minor triad is embedded in the figurations, so too are the "outlier" pitches B, F, and D♯, creating a blurred, dissonant harmonic effect sometimes tending toward whole-tone formations, and indeed reminiscent of Beach's impressionist piano character piece of 1922, "Morning Glories," op. 97, no. 1. Second, the figure begins in the middle of a 3/4 bar, so that metrically speaking, we are not on *terra firma* until a bar and a half later, when the cello introduces the modal first theme on the downbeat in dotted halves (Example 7.25).

The more tranquil, expressive second theme follows in E-flat major (enharmonically D-sharp) and B major, two keys drawn from the anomalous pitches of bar 1 that again favor whole-tone associations, though on the local level Beach's harmonic language continues to drift in the chromatically saturated tonal style associated with post-Wagnerian tonality.

Perhaps this retrospective quality explains her decision to base the outer sections of the slow movement (*Lento espressivo*) on her setting of Heinrich Heine's "Allein," op. 35, no. 2 (1897), an intense composition that looks back to the lofty subjectivities of German Romanticism, with treatments of the same, trenchant verses by Schubert ("Ihr Bild" from *Schwanengesang*, 1828), Clara Schumann (op. 13, no. 1, 1844), and the young Hugo Wolf (1878). Heine's text concerns a portrait of a deceased lover who seems to come to life. Quite in opposition to Beach's nostalgic return to the German *Lied* in the "black" key of F-sharp minor (Example 7.26a) is the central portion of the movement, a playful scherzo in the parallel major, inspired by an Inuit melody, *The Returning Hunter* (Example 7.26b), that Beach had first explored in her suite for children, *Eskimos*, op. 64, no. 2, from 1907:

Example 7.25 Beach, Piano Trio, op. 150/I, mm. 1–6.

Example 7.26a Beach, Piano Trio, op. 150/II, mm. 1–3.

Example 7.26b Beach, Piano Trio, op. 150/II, mm. 33–42.

Beach thus pairs an art song with a vernacular folk song in a combination of a slow movement and scherzo, an arrangement that recalls Brahms' similar formal approach in the Violin Sonata No. 2 in A major, op. 100.[31]

Adrienne Block has surmised that the energetic finale was inspired by yet another Inuit melody, "Song of a Padlimio," which Beach could have discovered in a monograph by anthropologist Franz Boas, *The Central Eskimo* (1888).[32] Propelled by a compact ostinato figure spanning the thirds below and above A (**A–G♯–F♯–G♯–A–B–C♯–B**; note the reference to the F-sharp minor of the second movement), the movement features two themes, of which the first, in A major, appropriates pentatonic contours and syncopations pointing to folk song, while the second, in D-flat major, again lapses into Beach's lyrical, romantic vein.

In the end, it seems, Beach was content to juxtapose and celebrate musical opposites and to suggest, but not insist upon, their interrelationship as she pursued her distinctive vision of American music. It was a dynamic vision of leavening practices drawn from familiar nineteenth-century European music with relatively little explored but fertile resources of an American musical Other. It was, finally, one vision of many for the establishment of a viable twentieth-century American style that would combine elements of high art and vernacular traditions – a vision, to be sure, "worthy of serious attention."

Notes

1. William J. Henderson, in a review of Amy Beach's Violin Sonata in A minor, op. 34 (*New York Times*, March 29, 1899): "[Beach] has proved that it is possible for a woman to compose music which is worthy of serious attention."
2. This patronizing phrase comes from a letter George Chadwick wrote to Amy Beach congratulating her on the success of her "Gaelic" Symphony on November 2, 1896. Beach Autograph Album, box 1, folder 19, p. 68, Amy Cheney Beach (Mrs. H. H. A. Beach) Papers, 1835–1956, MC 51, Milne Special Collections and Archives, University of New Hampshire Library, Durham, NH, USA, quoted in Adrienne Fried Block, *Amy Beach: Passionate Victorian* (New York: Oxford University Press, 1998), 103. Later echoing Chadwick's assessment was the *Kansas City Journal* of April 5, 1916: "Mrs. Beach's Symphony . . . is a splendidly virile composition, betraying none of the weaknesses of feminism in an artistic sense."
3. See further, R. Larry Todd, *Fanny Hensel: The Other Mendelssohn* (New York: Oxford University Press, 2010), 178.

4. See Katharina Uhde and R. Larry Todd, "Contextualizing Clara Schumann's Romances," in *Clara Schumann Studies*, ed. Joe Davies (Cambridge: Cambridge University Press, 2022), 165–86.

5. In her recorded reminiscences of Brahms, Smyth later commented on the coarseness of his social manners – he lacked, she said, what the Italians termed "educazione," though she readily conceded that he possessed the "legitimate selfishness of genius." Ethel Smyth, "Recollections of Brahms," www .youtube.com/watch?v=8zbCRjA9wJ8, accessed June 11, 2021.

6. For details, see the catalogue of Beach's music in Jeanell Wise Brown, *Amy Beach and Her Chamber Music: Biography, Documents, Style* (Metuchen, NJ: Scarecrow Press, 1994), 360–62. The most significant chamber work that Beach did not see through the press was the String Quartet, begun at the MacDowell Colony in New Hampshire in 1921 and finished in Rome in 1929, but not released until 1994, in a critical edition by Adrienne Fried Block (*Music of the United States of America*, vol. 3, Madison, WI: A-R Editions).

7. Not included in these listings are the chamber arrangement for cello and piano of *Dreaming*, op. 15, no. 3, originally for piano solo, and four other unfinished compositions. For details, see Brown, *Amy Beach and Her Chamber Music*, 317–18.

8. See Wanda M. Corn, *Women Building History: Public Art at the 1893 Columbian Exposition* (Berkeley: University of California Press, 2011), 94–95.

9. Though not without some controversy in the planning stages. See Block, *Amy Beach, Passionate Victorian*, 77ff., and Ann E. Feldman, "Being Heard: Women Composers and Patrons at the 1893 World's Columbia Exposition," *Notes of the Music Library Association* 47, no. 1 (1990): 7–20.

10. A child prodigy, Powell had studied in Leipzig, and in Berlin with Joseph Joachim, before returning to the US. She was one of the first recording artists for RCA Victor.

11. Block, *Amy Beach, Passionate Victorian*, 83.

12. It appeared in 1890 in Aldrich's *Wyndham Towers*.

13. See R. Larry Todd, "Ancient Modes, Late Brahms," *Nineteenth-Century Music Review* 15 (2018), 421–42.

14. Percy Goetschius, "Mrs. H. H. A. Beach and Mademoiselle Cécile Chaminade: Their Works, 1: Mrs. H. H. A. Beach," *Musician* 4 (September 1899). Quoted in Block, *Amy Beach, Passionate Victorian*, 119.

15. Graham Robb, *Victor Hugo: A Biography* (New York: W. W. Norton & Co., 1997), 138. Beach may have known Berlioz's setting of *La Captive* for voice and orchestra, op. 12, from 1832. Also, in 1898, the same year as *La Captive*, Beach set two other Hugo poems, *Chanson d'amour* and *Extase*, in the Three Songs with cello obbligato, op. 21.

16. For some examples, see Peter Williams, "Some Thoughts on Mozart's Use of the Chromatic Fourth," in *Perspectives on Mozart Performance*, ed. R. Larry Todd and Peter Williams (Cambridge: Cambridge University Press, 1991), 204–27.

17. On the nineteenth-century tradition of this device, see R. Larry Todd, "Beyond Virtuosity: Joachim, Mendelssohn, Their Circle, and the Illusion of Three Hands" (forthcoming).

18. See Block, *Amy Beach: Passionate Victorian*, 10, and Jeremy Logan, "Synesthesia and Feminism: A Case Study on Amy Beach (1867–1944)," *New Sound* 46, no. 2 (2015): 130–40.

19. Amy Beach, "Music Reviews, Vol. 2," October 1894, box 4, folder 1, Amy Beach Papers, University of New Hampshire.

20. " Music in America," *Harper's Magazine* 90 (1895), 433.

21. Douglas W. Shadle, *Orchestrating the Nation: The Nineteenth-Century American Symphonic Enterprise* (New York: Oxford University Press, 2016), 252.

22. For further details, see Adrienne Fried Block, "Dvořák, Beach, and American Music," in *A Celebration of American Music: Words and Music in Honor of H. Wiley Hitchcock*, ed. Richard Crawford, R. Allen Lott, and Carol J. Oja (Ann Arbor: University of Michigan Press, 1990), 264–71.

23. *The Citizen, or Dublin Monthly Magazine* (1841), nos. 16, 6, 19, and 3 (pp. 320, 138, 368, and 66).

24. Ibid., 138.

25. See Adrienne Fried Block, "Amy Beach's Music on Native American Themes," *American Music* 8, no. 2 (1990), 144–66.

26. Michael V. Pisani, *Imagining Native America in Music* (New Haven, CT: Yale University Press, 2005), 204.

27. See further E. Douglas Bomberger, *Edward MacDowell* (New York: Oxford University Press, 2013), 193ff.

28. On the conflicting opus numbers for the quartet (70, 79, and 89), see Block, "Amy Beach's Music," 156.

29. See fn. 6.

30. Block, *Amy Beach, Passionate Victorian*, 272.

31. Beach briefly recalls her scherzo at the very end of the movement, so that we may represent the form as *ABA'(B')*.

32. See the preface to Block's edition of the Piano Trio (Bryn Mawr, PA: Hildegard Publishing Co., 1997).

8 | The Power of Song in Beach's Orchestral Works

DOUGLAS W. SHADLE

One of the most remarkable dimensions of Amy Beach's prolific career is that she composed so little orchestral music despite writing a string of pieces in rapid succession early in her career: *Bal Masqué* (1893), the "Gaelic" Symphony (1896), and the Piano Concerto (1900) – her only three major works for orchestra alone (see Table 8.1).[1] The symphony, in fact, prompted George Whitefield Chadwick, one of Boston's leading composers at the time of its premiere, to welcome Beach as "one of the boys" for having written such a "fine work."[2] Beyond this immediate praise, both the symphony and the concerto experienced a relatively high number of performances during Beach's lifetime compared to many analogous pieces by her contemporaries. Why no second effort in either genre? Why no tone poems, or even short concert overtures?

Perhaps the simplest explanation is that while orchestral writing might have been prestigious, it was not profitable. In the 1890s, securing commissions from orchestras was typically a fool's errand, as was seeking publication.[3] Biographer Adrienne Fried Block has explained, however, that Beach was among a small coterie of American composers of her generation who benefited from the generosity of publisher Arthur P. Schmidt. Sympathetic to the difficulties they faced in the international arena, Schmidt subsidized their large orchestral scores (including Beach's symphony) with receipts from music sold for home use.[4] Beach's relationship with Schmidt cooled after her husband's death in 1910, but this change cannot fully explain why she might have turned her efforts away from the orchestra since her published music remained in demand.[5]

Beach also faced the substantial hurdle of widespread bias against women. Though not an absolute barrier to staging her works, gender figured prominently in their reception, including in Chadwick's casual erasure when he called her "one of the boys."[6] In 1904, an astute critic named Berenice Thompson called out the obvious double standards Beach faced, noting,

Table 8.1 Amy Beach, orchestral works

Title	Instrumentation	Premiere
Bal Masqué	2(II=picc)2.2.2 – 4.2.0.0 – timp.perc (2) – harp – strings	December 12, 1893, Manuscript Society of New York
Symphony in E minor, "Gaelic," op. 32	2(II=picc)2.2(II=bcl).2 – 4.2.3.1 – timp.perc(1) – strings	October 30, 1896, Boston Symphony Orchestra
Piano Concerto in C-Sharp minor, op. 45	2(II=picc)2.2(II=bcl).2 – 4.2.3.1 – timp – strings	April 7, 1900, Boston Symphony Orchestra

Despite the apparent impossibility of the task for a woman, Mrs. Beach has composed a successful symphony in E minor, called "Gaelic." ... After listening to this work, nearly all of the critics forgot momentarily about "whistling girls," for they wrote such encomiums, as "This symphony stamps the composer as a writer of great ability," and that it is "full of strength and imagination." ... A great argument in its favor is that one of the critics who condemned the symphony after its first performance was loudest in its praise after the second hearing.[7]

And Thompson believed that Beach's best years as an orchestral composer were yet to come. "Mrs. Beach's talent finds its truest expression in large forms," she argued, and was "a striking exception in an age given over to miniature work." Urging Beach to persist against the negativity directed toward her gender, she added, "Her own instincts and predilections are those which will make for the most supreme accomplishments in her art. Her publisher, if he is a man of intelligence, will allow her genius full sway."

Beach, of course, did not take Thompson's advice and focused for the rest of her career on solo piano works, songs, and choral pieces – genres in high demand among women's music clubs.[8] On a practical level, she preferred to create in circles that appreciated her unconditionally without the constant barrage of sexism.[9] After her husband's death, moreover, she resumed touring as a concert pianist and often found herself too busy to compose in larger genres, once remarking that "I am too enthusiastic a traveler yet to settle down, too fond of my audiences to give them up."[10] But there is still more to the story than mere avoidance of a male-dominated orchestra culture and a restless spirit. Orchestras continued to perform Beach's music well into the twentieth century, after all.

Aesthetics also appeared to play a key role in Beach's move away from orchestral music. Thompson had encouraged Beach to continue subverting prevailing gendered attitudes that classed orchestral works as "masculine" and miniatures as "feminine."[11] But Beach herself developed distinct artistic priorities in her works that overturned this binary altogether. At their core, all three orchestral pieces are explorations of song, suggesting that song itself held pride of place in Beach's aesthetic outlook. By the 1890s, composers and critics had developed a wide-ranging discourse about the relationships between songs and instrumental music that informed Beach's approach to all three pieces and, as I argue here, helps explain her orchestral music's longevity as well as her lack of urgency in composing more. Viewing – and hearing – Beach's orchestral works with songs' centrality in mind ultimately offers a new framework for reassessing American orchestral music dating from her lifetime.

Song as Symbol

The incorporation of songs into instrumental music, whether through direct quotation or more subtle allusion, creates a rich (if slippery) symbolic matrix that offers listeners multiple layers for aesthetic and interpretive engagement.[12] While the practice has spanned at least two centuries, from Franz Schubert's "Trout" Quintet (1819) to Philip Glass' "Heroes" Symphony (1996), it reached an important crest during the 1890s in ongoing transatlantic discussions about the capacity of folk songs to suggest a national identity in instrumental works. Antonín Dvořák famously asserted in 1893, for example, that "the future music of [the United States] must be founded upon what are called negro melodies. . . . These are the folk songs of America, and your composers must turn to them."[13] Noting the ubiquity of the practice, he added, "All of the great musicians have borrowed from the songs of the common people." Yet, references to preexisting songs in instrumental music did not always point in the direction of national identity. Even composers known for writing so-called absolute music, such as Johannes Brahms, used song-based allusions to generate symbolic depth.[14] Indeed, referencing song in instrumental music was a pervasive stylistic strategy that heavily shaped the context in which Beach composed her orchestral works.

In the United States, the practice of referencing songs in instrumental works is nearly as old as the country itself. William Gibbons has shown that at least two generations of early American composers quoted "Yankee Doodle" for its "powerful symbolic value" – in this case, as a symbol of the nation.[15] Among orchestral writers, both Anthony Philip Heinrich (1781–1861) and Louis Moreau Gottschalk (1829–69) used a variety of patriotic songs, including "Yankee Doodle," for this very purpose.[16] Other early symphonists, notably William Henry Fry (1813–64) and George Frederick Bristow (1825–98), referenced songs that facilitated the construction of picturesque narratives – the Christmas hymn "Adeste Fidelis" in Fry's *Santa Claus: Christmas Symphony* (1853) and "Tallis's Evening Hymn" in a movement of Bristow's "Arcadian" Symphony (1872) meant to depict nighttime on the prairie.[17] By the latter part of the century, then, finding orchestral inspiration in song was certainly not out of the ordinary.

The specific use of folk songs to construct an American national identity emerged at mid-century in the piano music of Louis Moreau Gottschalk and blossomed across genres over the next several decades. Brooklyn composer Ellsworth Phelps's "Emancipation" Symphony (1880), for example, took inspiration from African-derived folk music but did not quote any songs directly.[18] John Broekhoven's *Suite Creole*, which premiered in Cincinnati in 1884, hewed more closely to Gottschalk's style by quoting Creole songs directly.[19] By 1893, when Dvořák made his famous argument that "negro melodies" would be the most suitable foundation for an American national style, such works had long been at the center of debates about the relationship between the folk and the national. Boston composer George E. Whiting's remarks at the 1884 Music Teachers National Association meeting typified the terms of debate:

There is one field of local color in this country, and which has been but little used, which I would like to call to the attention of composers. I refer to the melodies of the Creoles of the South and Cuba. Gottschalk is really the only American who has ever succeeded in producing compositions founded on subjects from his own land.[20]

The intensity of these discussions would only grow through the 1890s as commentators, including Beach herself, debated which folk music repertoires should be considered representative of American national identity.[21]

While these debates would certainly prove important for Beach in time, their prominence often obscured a parallel discourse about the relative artistic value of song references, regardless of their source. Failing to acknowledge the symbolic potential of direct quotation, critics often argued that it was tantamount to plagiarism or else signaled a lack of melodic creativity. Writing in 1873, one reviewer of Bristow's "Arcadian" Symphony called quotation "inartistic," adding that "the poverty of resource indicated by the borrowing practice, even in minor works, is aggravated in the symphony."[22] Of course, certain composers agreed with this sentiment since it granted artistic superiority – and true individuality – to those with a boundless gift for melodic writing. Dvořák himself explained that when he engaged with folk music, he attempted to transcend direct quotation with suggestive allusion, thus forging a piece solely from inner creativity. "I study certain melodies until I become thoroughly imbued with their characteristics," he said in an 1893 interview, "and am enabled to make a musical picture in keeping with and partaking of those characteristics."[23]

By the time Amy Beach sat down to write her first orchestral works in the 1890s, longstanding debates about the construction of national musical identity and the relative value of song references had converged in response to Dvořák's 1893 pronouncements. But she, among others, recognized that while national identity was a pressing political issue, the notion that song *could* symbolize national identity presumed the artistic desirability of instrumental song references in the first place. Writing in 1941, music historian Eileen Jackson (whose married name would later be Eileen Southern) maintained the power of this desirability by dividing certain folk-inspired orchestral works into two analytical categories: "Musical Works Containing Themes from Negro Folksong" and "Musical Works in the Negro Idiom."[24] More recent treatment of the same material has tended to elide the difference between "theme" and "idiom," thus blurring the artistic significance of direct song references in orchestral repertoire from the era.[25]

Song as Compositional Fundament

The deployment of song in an instrumental context presents distinct interpretive challenges for performers, listeners, and analysts. In some instances, the song's text might offer a clue about its meaning as a musical symbol. In others, the very removal of the text might illuminate other expressive dimensions of the tune that recast, or even thwart, the text's meanings. In others still, preexisting tunes might simply provide a source of creative inspiration irrespective of the text, with a motivic fragment serving as a point of departure for further musical elaboration and exploration. Among all three strategies, moreover, the song's presence in the score might range from wholesale quotation to nearly complete fragmentation. Beach's three orchestral works display virtually all the possible combinations at various moments, leading to a small but rich site for investigating how she might have perceived songs' value in an instrumental context.

Given Beach's expansive catalog of songs – nearly 150 – we can be reasonably certain that she held the genre in high esteem. It carried the potential to reach a large public through domestic and stage performances while offering composers distinct opportunities for honing their craft. "A small gem," she once claimed, "may be just as brilliantly cut as one weighing many carats."[26] Yet, vexingly, she left few direct clues about why song became such a fundamental element in her approach to large-scale instrumental works as well. Anna Poulin Alfeld has emphasized that Beach's avoidance of public remarks about self-borrowings in the symphony and the concerto strongly suggests that she wanted listeners to evaluate these pieces on "purely musical and compositional terms."[27] Nevertheless, other available evidence demonstrates that Beach approached the act of composition with certain methods that offer a fuller explanation of what these "purely musical and compositional terms" might have been.

In her later career, Beach's visibility as a leading composer afforded her many public opportunities to share ideas about the act of composition. For example, in a 1918 piece for *The Etude* called "To the Girl Who Wants to Compose," Beach divided the act into three distinct domains – the emotional, the intellectual, and the spiritual:

To begin with the emotional – which is the side of music most easily understood by the average human being – music plays an enormous part in our whole lives, from the lullabies which our mothers sing to us in our cradles to the funeral march played after we have reached the end of our earthly course. . . . Then there is the intellectual side. This can only be best understood by those who have entered in all seriousness into the composition of music in its most abstract forms. . . . Then there is what I have called the spiritual side of music. Of course, this has two aspects, the point of view of the listener, and that of the creator. There is music which uplifts us to a point far above and beyond the mere emotional plane.[28]

Twenty-five years later, again in *The Etude*, she described the ideal compositional process in much the same way:

The composer must have emotional and spiritual feeling to put into his work; he must achieve a comprehensible translation of his feeling through form; and he must have at his disposal a tremendous background of technical, musical craftsmanship in order to express his feelings and his thoughts. Thus, the craftsmanship, vital though it is, serves chiefly as the means toward the end of personal expression.[29]

Both formulations were conventional descriptions of the compositional process and in many respects echoed Joseph Haydn's well-known explanation from over a century earlier. As Haydn put it, he extemporized at the keyboard, "according to whether my animus was sad or happy, serious or playful," and then devoted his "entire effort toward elaborating and sustaining [a compelling idea] according to the rules of art."[30] Like Beach, he moved from emotion to idea to elaboration as technical skill hammered unbridled feeling into a meaningful musical shape.

Yet the nuances of Beach's first step – accessing an emotion – departed significantly from Haydn's fanciful improvisations. In one published explanation, she argued that memories of long-past events could erupt from the unconscious, creating "not only an art-form, but a veritable autobiography."[31] This observation traded in nineteenth-century tropes about the role of life experience in musical creativity that would have been foreign to Haydn.[32] In other commentary, she remarked that poetic texts often generated sufficient emotional sparks for composition. After procrastinating on a setting of a Robert Browning text, for example, she finally found inspiration while she "simply sat still on the train, thinking of Browning's poem, and allowing it and the rhythm of the wheels to take possession of me."[33] For Beach, ruminating on the emotional content of a song or text was a perfectly legitimate way to "get in the mood" for composing, even away from the keyboard.

Of course, a *spark* for composition and composition itself are two very different things – a sharp distinction that Beach understood all too well. On the advice of Boston Symphony Orchestra conductor Wilhelm Gericke when Beach was a teenager, her parents dissuaded her from pursuing formal training in composition, leaving her to figure it out for herself.[34] Beach was a uniquely successful autodidact from a young age because she possessed the ability to assimilate large amounts of musical information on a single hearing and could retain it with a prodigious memory. After her marriage in 1885, when she was only eighteen, her husband Henry curtailed her emerging career as a concert pianist, essentially compelling her to pursue composition even more vigorously but still without formal instruction.[35] Looking back in 1943, she explained that to learn her craft, she would write out music from memory and then compare it to the score while occasionally making certain manipulations to challenge herself.[36] At the same time, she cautioned that careful study was not sufficient for writing an effective composition. Study has "nothing to do with 'inspiration,'" she observed, "but provides the only means of enabling [a composer] to project 'inspiration' into the minds and hearts of listeners." The emotional spark was fundamental, and she sought that spark in songs.

Song in Beach's Orchestral Works

The pervasiveness of songs in Beach's orchestral works suggests that they served as her "sparks." Several previous scholars have tracked and analyzed the source material in this repertoire, and their collective findings are reproduced in Table 8.2 for easy reference. Drawing several strong

Table 8.2 Song allusions in Amy Beach's orchestral works

Location	Song	Source
Bal Masqué	"Wouldn't That Be Queer"	Beach, op. 26, no. 4 (1894)
"Gaelic" Symphony, I	"Dark Is the Night!"	Beach, op. 11, no. 1 (1890)
	"Conchobhar ua Raghallaigh Cluann"	*The Citizen* (1841)
"Gaelic" Symphony, II	"Goirtin Ornadh"	*The Citizen* (1841)
"Gaelic" Symphony, III	"Paisdin Fuinne"	*The Citizen* (1841)
	"Cia an Bealach a Deachaide Si"	*The Citizen* (1841)
"Gaelic" Symphony, IV	"Dark Is the Night!"	Beach, op. 11, no. 1 (1890)
Piano Concerto, I	"Jeune fille et jeune fleur"	Beach, op. 1, no. 3 (1887)
Piano Concerto, II	"Empress of Night"	Beach, op. 2, no. 3 (1891)
Piano Concerto, III	"Twilight"	Beach, op. 2, no. 1 (1887)

inferences from this analysis, Adrienne Fried Block has viewed Beach's engagement with songs in the symphony and the concerto through the lenses of national identity and autobiography, respectively, while giving the most interpretive weight to song texts from allusions in the concerto.[37] Sarah Gerk, Anna Poulin Alfeld, and E. Douglas Bomberger have challenged aspects of Block's interpretations by marshaling new evidence to reinterpret Beach's selection, structural placement, and compositional elaboration of material derived from song.[38] Despite the depth of these interpretations, the fundamental question, "Why song?" remains unaddressed. Zooming out from a detailed examination of the scores, my assessment here is that despite substantial differences between the three pieces on nearly every compositional level, the presence of song served as an intentional artistic binding agent that resonated with the public throughout Beach's lifetime.

Bal Masqué

Bal Masqué, Beach's first work for orchestra alone, was written as a prelude to a Boston revival of the musical theater piece *The Black Crook*, which had premiered in New York in 1866.[39] Beyond this utilitarian function, it was also an experiment in orchestration that formed a feedback loop in Beach's autodidactic process. Part of this effort involved eliminating the variables of a text and choir that had shaped her approach to the Grand Mass in E-flat major, op. 5 (1890), and *Festival Jubilate*, op. 17 (1892). In both earlier works, the texts themselves offered a significant emotional spark, while European works from the standard choral repertoire served as occasional models or templates.[40] In contrast, writing for orchestra alone presented an open field for emotional content, and she ultimately chose a comic text, "Wouldn't That Be Queer," by Elsie Jones Cooley, as a key source of inspiration:[41]

If the trees knew how to run up and down the hill,
If cats and dogs could talk and we had to keep still,
If the flowers should all try
like birds to sing and fly,
And the birds were always found,
Growing up out of the ground,
Dear, dear, wouldn't that be queer?

If the babies when they came were very old and tall,
And grew down instead of up to be quite young and small,
If the sun should come out bright
In the middle of the night,
And the dark should come and stay
When we knew that it was day,
Dear, dear, wouldn't that be queer?

Published in 1894 as op. 26, no. 4, Beach's waltz-like setting of this text, which rarely rises above a mezzo forte dynamic, is suitably whimsical, like a child whispering an imaginative secret. It is no surprise, then, that she could draw an emotional connection between the song and the socially topsy-turvy world of a nineteenth-century masked ball.[42]

Although *Bal Masqué* and "Wouldn't That Be Queer" share nearly identical melodies, Beach exploited the potential for smoother melodic shaping, more interesting counterpoint, and vivid coloration in her orchestral arrangement – variances that suggest she was attempting to draw more of the song's emotional content from the orchestra than she felt was possible in the vocal setting (Example 8.1). Regarding these types of transformations, she once observed, "When one sees how it *looks*, it is quite possible that the melodic line may not seem at all suitable for the voice. Its appearance (not its character) may suggest the violincello – the combination of violin and harp – and lo! the original theme may develop into something quite different from the song that was first planned."[43] In this case, the two versions display only subtle musical differences but share the same underlying emotional character despite the variance.

Riding a wave of positive reviews of Beach's large choral works, *Bal Masqué* was one of eight pieces programmed on the Manuscript Society of New York's opening concert of the 1893–94 season. Critics had widely

Example 8.1 Comparison of the opening melodies of Beach's "Wouldn't that be Queer," op. 26, no. 4, and *Bal Masqué*.

praised the Mass setting, particularly its orchestration and emotional alignment with the texts.[44] Unfortunately for Beach, however, they did not appreciate *Bal Masqué* – an unexpected misfire after the previous acclaim. William Thoms, for example, lamented that it "proved a disappointment to those familiar with the gifted Boston lady's larger achievements in works of a more serious character, which have led us to expect higher things from her pen than the sketch presented."[45] A writer for the *Evening World* said it "has a pretty theme" but dismissed it as "trivial."[46] The general audience, on the other hand, loved the piece so much that it reportedly "set the saltatorial nerves of the young people right on edge."[47]

The fact that Beach declined to share the source of her emotional spark – Cooley's text – can help explain the polarized reactions. With only the title and an unusual genre designation ("sketch") to guide expectations, critics familiar with her earlier work might have assumed it would contain elements appropriate for a tone poem: a narrative, inner drama, thematic transformations, and other displays of musical elaboration. When the piece ultimately reminded them of a "Strauss waltz" – a common refrain – the piece's "triviality" became a disappointment. Average listeners, on the other hand, took the title at face value and perceived the piece as Beach had intended it – as droll *accompaniment* to a masked ball, not a portrait of the ball itself. Hence dancing in their seats!

More broadly, the mixed responses to *Bal Masqué* show that a composer's intent to convey specific inner emotions with music is not self-revelatory. Disclosing this intent often relies on certain expectations generated with clues beyond the notes of the score: an epigraph, a genre designation, or a sheet music cover (to name a few examples). Would sharing the source of her inspiration have prompted dissatisfied critics to hear the piece differently? Either way, the electric audience reaction to *Bal Masqué* proved to be useful market research for Beach and Arthur P. Schmidt, who published the underlying song and an arrangement for solo piano a few months later while quietly leaving the orchestral "sketch" behind – save for an 1895 Boston Pops show led by Antonio de Novellis where the program specifically directed antsy audiences to "preserve silence during the performance of this number."

"Gaelic" Symphony

Beach greatly expanded her compositional engagement with song in her next orchestral work, the "Gaelic" Symphony in E minor, op. 32. With the conventional four-movement symphonic template at her disposal, she used several songs to generate large-scale formal structures in which the tunes take on a pervasive presence beyond direct quotations. Couching this procedure as a commandment for aspiring composers, she once remarked, "Learn to employ as much variety in form as possible. Above all things, avoid becoming stereotyped in the expression of melodic, harmonic, or rhythmic ideas."[48] The weighty demands of the symphonic genre – length, monumentality, cohesion, and variety – gave Beach an appealing sandbox for a kaleidoscopic treatment of intriguing emotional sparks. As with *Bal Masqué*, however, Beach's sources of musical inspiration were obscured at early performances, leading to substantial mishearings in the heated political context of its premiere.

Beach began writing a new symphony in January 1894,[49] just a month after the controversial world premiere of Antonín Dvořák's "New World" Symphony in New York – a long-awaited event that served as a capstone to a months-long public debate about folk song and American national identity. Like many of her contemporaries, Beach considered folk songs an especially abundant source of bare emotion that lent themselves well as sparks for compositional inspiration. But she also believed that the emotions they contained were not universally shared, or at least not universally accessible. In response to Dvořák's contention that "negro melodies" could inspire a distinctively American national style, she retorted that "if a negro, the possessor of talent for musical composition, should perfect himself in its expression, then we might have the melodies which are his folk-songs employed with fullest sympathy, for he would be working with the *inherited feelings of his race*."[50] She would later critique the "New World" Symphony on these very grounds in a private notebook, remarking that the piece "seems to me light in calibre and to represent only the peaceful, sunny side of the negro character and life. Not for a moment does it suggest their suffering, heartbreaks, *slavery*."[51] Regardless of the composer's ability to develop themes or create effective counterpoint – the "machinery," as she put it – a piece would fall short if it could not effectively convey the appropriate core emotions.

Beach believed that Anglo-American composers would stand a greater chance of merging craft and expression if they drew from their own folk heritage for compositional inspiration. "We of the North," she wrote in response to Dvořák, "should be far more likely to be influenced by old English, Scotch or Irish songs inherited with our literature from our ancestors, than by the songs of a portion of our people who were kept for so long in bondage, and whose musical utterances were deeply rooted in the heartbreaking griefs attendant upon their condition."[52] Previous scholarship has emphasized this statement's centrality in Beach's decision to compose a "Gaelic" symphony: it would be her version of a more appropriate – and more emotionally effective – vehicle of national expression than Dvořák's "New World."[53] Sarah Gerk has since made a convincing case that Beach's engagement with Irish folk music was as much transnational as national in character, arguing that the symphony is a "a complex example of late-century intertextuality, musical invention, and social statement that reflects the composer's nationality to some extent, but reaches far beyond it."[54] It seems all the more noteworthy, then, that the *emotional* content of folk songs sparked her decision to compose the symphony with a Gaelic character in the first place. In a 1917 interview, she explained,

I can ascribe no particular reason for my choice of Gaelic subjects for my first symphony other than having been attracted by some of the wonderful old tunes in a collection of Gaelic folk-music, which came under my observation. These tunes, of course, are of unknown origin and age, and like the folk-music of every race, sprang from the common joys, sorrows, adventures, and struggles of a primitive people. Their simple, rugged and unpretentious beauty led me to "take my pen in hand" and try to develop their ideas in symphonic form.[55]

True to her stated compositional method, she was plainly describing a spark arising from an emotional investment – and in this case, an investment aroused by folk song.

Although Beach had consulted printed sources of Irish folk songs to jump-start her composition and then used some of them as the principal themes in the symphony, the program notes distributed at the opening night concert obscured their origins as preexisting tunes. For example, she remarked on the "Gaelic folk-song character" of the first movement's closing theme, as well as the "strongly-marked Gaelic character" and "Keltic closing cadence" in the third movement's principal theme. The synopsis in the program also made no reference to Beach's source for the main themes in the first and last movements, her song "Dark Is the Night," op. 11, no. 1 (1889), which evokes the Irish American experience of a tumultuous oversea voyage and feelings of nostalgia.[56] As far as most listeners knew, the piece fell in the mold of other "national" symphonies that did not explicitly quote folk song, such as Felix Mendelssohn's "Scottish" or Frederic Hymen Cowen's more recent "Welsh" (1884), the inspiration for which the composer once described as "the recollections of my rambles, my broken-down old piano, the hymn-singing, and the honeymooners of the two years before."[57]

The "Gaelic" provoked a wide range of responses after its premiere, from fulsome praise to outright dismissal, with nearly all remarking on the composer's gender in some way.[58] Though less visibly, the ambiguity of Beach's source material also shaped these reviews. Believing that only the third movement quoted preexisting songs, a critic for the *Globe* observed that "most of [the themes] are new."[59] The second movement, the reviewer went on, "is thoroughly delightful, and pleased the audience most of all. The themes are deliciously melodious, and the graceful Siciliano is treated in the daintiest fashion imaginable." A writer for the *Daily Advertiser* also enjoyed the second movement but argued that it belied the work's title:

[The Scherzo] was entitled "Alla Siciliana," but was rather slow in the theme for a true Siciliana – the dance-song of the Sicilian peasantry is generally about allegretto in tempo, and is usually 6–8 rhythm. The melody, *not very Gaelic in character*, was very attractive, and was excellently played by the oboe, appearing afterwards upon the English horn.[60]

After hearing a repeat performance in Brooklyn a few weeks later, *New York Tribune* critic (and folksong expert) Henry Krehbiel left the hall unimpressed on precisely the same grounds:

She has called [the symphony] "Gaelic" and justified the epithet by the use of some melodies with Irish rhythms and turns, but the task of stamping the whole work with a spirit which would be recognized as characteristically Gaelic seems to have been beyond her powers. In this respect, as well as in the development of the national material the symphony falls short of Dr. Stanford's symphony called "Irish."[61]

Like his Boston counterparts, Krehbiel expected one approach – a symphony imbued with the *spirit* of Irish folk song – and, perhaps not knowing any better, was disappointed by a symphony imbued with *actual* Irish folk songs.

Would these critics have changed their tune knowing that the melodies with "Irish rhythms and turns" were direct quotations taken from printed Irish sources? Krehbiel's review, at least, suggests that expectations of originality ("the development of the national material") overshadowed the symbolic potential of song quotations for projecting a national identity.

These widely held expectations might explain why Beach ultimately shielded her sources from view at the premiere. At the same time, as in *Bal Masqué*, the absence of an explanation did not prevent listeners from making a strong emotional connection to Beach's music. The critic for the *Daily Advertiser* remarked that the second movement – the one allegedly lacking "Gaelic character" – "evoked the most spontaneous applause of all the movements" and compelled Beach "to bow her acknowledgments from her seat." Perhaps these listeners intuitively understood the final line of the song: "And now I and my own darling are married and live happy on what I earn every day" – a line that embodied the "common joys" expressed in Irish folk song.[62]

Piano Concerto

Of Beach's orchestral works, the Piano Concerto contains the most – and the most oblique – references to preexisting songs. Each movement contains transformations of melodic material drawn from her own art songs published about a decade earlier, rather than the wholesale quotations found in previous works. An analysis of the art song texts led Adrienne Fried Block to an autobiographical reading of the concerto in the 1990s, but her interpretation would have been even more inscrutable to Beach's original audiences at the work's 1900 premiere than the quotations in the "Gaelic" Symphony proved to be in the 1890s. Douglas Bomberger has offered a more historicist reading that places the concerto in direct dialogue with Dvořák's famous "New World" Symphony, which Beach had heard in Boston a few years earlier and had roundly critiqued in her private notebook.[63] Of course, like the "Gaelic" Symphony, the "New World" Symphony was itself inspired by song – folk song, to be more precise. Unlike Beach, Dvořák had attempted to evoke a folk idiom without direct reference to specific songs. Following Bomberger's lead, then, we might hear the conversation between Dvořák's symphony and Beach's concerto as her attempt to test the boundaries of quotation and allusion, song and idiom – a distinction that would continue to inform American orchestral composition well into the twentieth century.

The crux of Bomberger's revision of Block's interpretation rests on how to hear the principal theme of the concerto's first movement. Block presents the sinewy five-measure melody as an allusion to Beach's 1885 setting of a Chateaubriand text, "Jeune fille et jeune fleur," and notes the shared key, "serious affect," and "falling modal scales" of both excerpts.[64] The reference is thin but is buttressed by the secondary theme's more overt

Example 8.2 Comparison of the principal themes of (1) Dvořák's Symphony "From the New World," movement IV; (2) the opening of Beach's Piano Concerto, op. 45, movement I; and (3) Beach's song, "Jeune fille et jeune fleur," op. 1, no. 3.

allusion to another passage in the song.[65] Bomberger draws a convincing parallel between the concerto theme's melodic and rhythmic contours and those of the principal theme in the fourth movement of Dvořák's symphony. He argues further that Beach's manipulation of the theme later in the movement "improves" on the technical and emotional deficiencies she had noted in private comments about Dvořák. Considering all three melodies side by side – the song, the symphony, and the concerto – we might hear that the folklike character of each theme, conveyed by modality and an accompanying sense of timeless origins, serves as a clear expressive binding agent in keeping with the matrix of allusions shared across the pieces[66] (Example 8.2). In other words, rather than referencing folk songs directly, the theme's allusions construct a folk *idiom* inspired by a chain of song encounters.

The program note distributed at the concerto's premiere, given by the Boston Symphony Orchestra under Wilhelm Gericke with Beach at the piano, offers a rather dry technical analysis of each movement's form with no descriptions of the melodic character found in any of the work's several main themes. Presumably written by Beach herself, the note not only obscured the sources of her melodic ideas but concealed the work's abundant stylistic connections to Dvořák's "New World" and other inspirational models, such as Brahms' Second Concerto. While this framing presumably placed the concerto on an even technical playing field with similar pieces – an understandable desire for Beach, who would almost certainly have faced sexist accusations of plagiarism or derivativeness by disclosing her inspiration – the note's utter decontextualization left significant holes for listeners to fill with their own impressions of where the piece "fit" in the contemporary musical landscape.

And fill they did. A writer for the *Boston Transcript* complained loudly that Beach had attempted to do too much at once. "In this concerto," the critic observed,

[S]he has done pretty near everything that possibly can be done with pianoforte and orchestra; there is material – essential and ornamental – enough in it to make two concertos. It is overloaded with figural ornamentation and contrapuntal cleverness. To make some of her combinations effective and clear would take the skill of a Richard Strauss.[67]

Of course, perhaps Beach tacitly took these remarks as proof that she had outdone Dvořák's "machinery" in the "New World" Symphony! Yet the distinguished critic Philip Hale grumbled even more resolutely and left no room for a positive spin:

The concerto was a disappointment in every way. ... The themes were not distinguished; the development was too often vague and rambling; the moods, when there were moods, were those of other composers; thus the mood of the opening of the slow movement was palpably Wagnerian. ... There were notes, notes, notes; and where there were so many notes there were inevitably a few pretty passages; but there was little or no display of vital musical thought, proportion, skill in structure, or taste or brilliance in orchestral expression.[68]

Notably, Hale detected *something* noteworthy about the opening theme – the theme under scrutiny here – but dismissed the modality and asymmetry of its folklike idiom as "Wagnerian," a catchall epithet for any musical procedure that deviates from classical convention.[69]

But not all the critics hurled boulders. Writing for the *Courier*, Howard Ticknor specifically praised Beach's melodic gift and handling of melody as a structural unit. "Each year," he noted, "sees a fresher, richer and more spontaneous melody, alike in the simple salon songs and in works for the chamber, or the orchestral musician, while the variety, surety and strength of the instrumentation develop logically and agreeably, as was felt when her 'Scotch' symphony was presented."[70] Invoking symphony offered readers a small context for approaching repeat performances of the concerto, but Louis Elson pinpointed it with even greater precision in his review for the *Daily Advertiser*, worth quoting at length for its perceptiveness:

The whole first movement seemed rather indefinite at a first hearing; although there were many passages of much charm, there did not seem to be that coherency and clear scheme which one finds in the masterpieces; it was a case of the dove soaring with the eagles. ... The largo, although given on the house-programme as combined with the finale, was in reality a movement of itself. It treated a figure which reminded of the fate-figure in Wagner's trilogy (Cesar Franck has also developed this figure in his D minor symphony) and indicated a pensive melancholy. The finale seemed to us the best, most decisive and most original movement of the work. There were some phrases given in this that seemed to be in the vein of Dvorak's "American Symphony," although not suggesting plagiarism in the remotest degree. The entire movement was interesting and had many bold and striking contrasts.[71]

Although Elson made a connection between the concerto's fourth movement and Dvořák's symphony (rather than the first), his remarks indicated that a sensitive listener could ultimately detect Beach's ongoing efforts to develop an orchestral idiom that partook of songlike features, whether art song, folk song, or even Wagnerian vocal lines. And the audience? Elson remarked, "The public were in the friendliest mood and recalled the composer-pianist four times and also added floral tributes."

Beach's Orchestral Afterlives

Louis Elson's remarks about the concerto evidently left Philip Hale unmoved after a second hearing, but, more important, they opened the door to the possibility that Dvořák's symphony had in fact launched a new branch of orchestral writing – a branch that Beach had followed in both the "Gaelic" Symphony and the Piano Concerto. Over the next half century and beyond, dozens of composers – Henry Gilbert, Nathaniel Dett, Daniel Gregory Mason, Frederick Delius, William Grant Still, and Aaron Copland, to name only a few – followed Dvořák's lead by incorporating various folk song elements into their works. But while Dvořák had assiduously avoided direct quotation in favor of an idiomatic approach (save for a brief explicit allusion to "Swing Low, Sweet Chariot" in the symphony's first movement), many of these composers freely borrowed well-known melodic fragments and, in some cases, used entire songs as structural themes, much as Beach had in the "Gaelic" Symphony. These composers still risked accusations of plagiarism – William Dawson's 1934 *Negro Folk Symphony* is a noteworthy example[72] – but a critical mass of works with quotations signaled to audiences that the practice served a symbolic purpose beyond purely musical considerations. And this general relaxation rejuvenated Beach's orchestral works, much to her benefit.

The reception of Beach's orchestral music transformed dramatically after the turn of the century. Conductor Emil Paur, who had directed the "Gaelic" Symphony's premiere in 1896, returned to the work in 1905 with the

Pittsburgh Orchestra in a concert that also featured Beach at the piano in Saint-Saëns' Second Concerto. Audiences and critics alike loved the performance. Charles Boyd of the *Weekly Gazette* remarked that "the themes are decidedly melodious and their development is logical and sensible."[73] "Strange to say," he added, "the four movements met with almost uniform approval, though one would predict a preference on first hearing to the second movement, with its naïve siciliana and dainty scherzo" – the movement with the most explicit allusion. Another happy reviewer, evidently a fan of Richard Wagner, contradicted Krehbiel's assertion from a decade earlier that the work failed to project a Gaelic spirit:

Throughout the symphony one is strongly reminded of Wagner. Not that Mrs. Beach could be accused of plagiarism in the slightest degree, but her methods remind one of Wagner. . . . It has been said of Wagner that he had, in reality, only one small box of pearls, but that he understood how to arrange them, with such brilliancy and power, that one never tires of the variation. This might also be said of Mrs. Beach's work. The symphony is entitled "Gaelic," and it is truly wonderful how she *retains the quaint Irish atmosphere throughout the work.*[74]

This reviewer did not mention – and may not have known – that Beach's "pearls" were published folk songs but found that her treatment of the melodic ideas had captured the emotional content she wanted to convey. In return, Beach expressed her appreciation from the stage: "To say that I am pleased with the Pittsburgh audiences is but faintly conveying my delight at my reception here and the enjoyment I have found in the recitals."[75]

About a decade later, the Kansas City-based composer and conductor Carl Busch programmed Beach's symphony in an ambitious season-long series exploring national identity that included symphonies by Beethoven, Schumann, Franck, Glazunov, Sibelius, Svensen, Sinding, and Stanford. As one commentator remarked, Beach's inclusion would afford "interesting comparison," completing "in a becoming way this highly attractive and representative selection."[76] In advance of the concert, Busch's orchestra sponsored a class for audiences to hear an analysis of the symphony given by Sarah Ellen Barnes, a noted preconcert lecturer. And whatever she said must have worked. A reviewer for the *Kansas City Times* gushed about the piece's suggestion of a national identity brought on by folksong references:

The Beach symphony is a work of impressive beauty. . . . *While much of its material is of Scotch origin*, as the skirl of the bagpipes in the third movement and the mingling of austerity with sentiment in the second and last, the work is in reality more American than Scotch, and very much more universal than American. . . . An unprejudiced ear must concede that Mrs. Beach has written a symphony that is likely to live.[77]

And it would go on to lead a happy life alongside Beach until her death in 1944.

Meanwhile, Beach's concerto would also experience a significant critical rebound after its disastrous Boston premiere. Beach had taken the piece on a successful tour through Germany in 1913 and returned with it eighteen months later to great acclaim in a performance with the Los Angeles Symphony Orchestra.[78] One local reviewer, Luella Keller, was so enthusiastic that she declared, "This is perhaps the greatest feat an American woman has performed in the musical world, and will be long remembered by those who saw it."[79] The war in Europe had catalyzed nationwide interest in American compositions at this very moment, leading Beach and her concerto to be included on a program held at San Francisco's Panama–Pacific International Exposition in August 1915 that featured music by seven other Americans, including Frederick Stock, who doubled as the conductor of the Chicago Symphony Orchestra. Although Beach's performance received scant notice – and what notice it did receive was poor – Stock himself took up the piece in Chicago a few months later.[80]

The momentum from Los Angeles that had stalled in San Francisco ramped up again in Chicago, where Stock was already well known for programming music by a wide array of American composers.[81] Another budding composer, Eric DeLamarter, was enthralled after her performance. In a world now open to orchestral pieces inspired by song, he wrote in the *Chicago Tribune*:

Everything was thoroughly proper, O, thoroughly! yesterday afternoon at Orchestra Hall. . . . The concerto itself is frank and ingenious, *relying on its melodic facility and on its approved effects of the salon composer* – a work, to draw comparison, developed to the ultimate degree of finesse in scores like Saint-Saëns' G minor concerto, or the Grieg concerto. It is plausible in its orchestral setting, and as grateful under the fingers as it is in the ear.[82]

Although he did not detect (or at least did not mention) any of the folklike qualities permeating the first movement, the piece's debt to song was clear to him, as if he fully grasped her compositional process from the inside. A few weeks later, however, an enthusiastic reviewer in St. Louis, Richard L. Stokes, heard something particularly evocative – national sounds:

Still another American influence was shown in her free use of syncopation in the first movement. Despite its prevailing chromatic hues in melody, harmony, and counterpoint, *the concerto abounded in clearly discernible tunes*, for Mrs. Beach holds that the soul as well as the body requires its quota of sugar. The consequence is that although the work is technically most difficult – only a pianist and orchestra of the utmost expertness could perform it – there is also a fascinating popular appeal.[83]

Though not with Louis Elson's precision after the work's Boston premiere, Stokes was emphatically trying to make sense of a work that did not quite fit into a conventional orchestral idiom. DeLamarter had pointed toward Grieg as a suitable comparison, but the best words Stokes could divine were "American" and "popular" – just as Beach might have hoped.

Although opportunities for Beach to perform her concerto faded with time despite audiences' newfound admiration for it, the "Gaelic" Symphony practically became close to a canonical fixture as Beach earned a place as one of the country's most distinguished composers in any genre. Some of the symphony's most noteworthy performances during the later part of her career included those by Leopold Stokowski and the Philadelphia Orchestra (1915 and 1919), the Woman's Symphony Orchestra of Chicago under Ebba Sundstrom (1928 and 1934), Henry Hadley and the Manhattan Symphony Orchestra (1931), and the Women's Symphony Society of Boston under Alexander Thiede (1940). At a concert in Harrisburg, Pennsylvania, honoring Beach's seventy-fifth birthday in 1942, the local orchestra and its founder, George King Raudenbush, programmed the symphony as a keynote. It was a smashing success – one with a critical response that echoed DeLamarter in its vindication of Beach's song-based compositional approach. "While the symphony has all the richness and technical intricacies of an elaborate tapestry," a critic for the *Evening News* began,

Its charm is found in the total effect of wholesome simplicity. Solo instruments throughout the work give the effect of a narrator telling in a straightforward manner, "This is the way the sea rolls up on our North Irish coast" and "These are the songs our people sing when they are happy or sad." . . . Mrs. Beach says that her symphony is founded on folk music of the Gaelic people; but while these simple melodies are used freely and with the skill of a highly intelligent musician, they do not overshadow the compelling moods and descriptions which the composer has so deftly written into her work.[84]

By this time, Beach was freely sharing the symphony's folksong-based origins to guide listeners, ensuring they would make no mistake about what emotions she was trying to convey. That her themes were direct quotations had finally become a decided strength.

The Power of Song

The virtual disappearance of Beach's orchestral music in the period between her death and the sustained revival of the 1990s betrays the fact that Beach's orchestral music, written as a very early response to Dvořák's ideas, was in certain respects ahead of its time in the 1890s, only to find its stride in the 1910s. This curious asynchrony suggests that certain compositional values emerged in the decades after Dvořák's "New World" Symphony that rose and fell in tandem with Beach's orchestral music. As I noted in the opening of this chapter, one of the first rigorous scholarly investigations of orchestral music from this period that drew on Afrodiasporic folksongs, written by a graduate student at the University of Chicago in 1941, three years before Beach's death, noted:

> From the beginning [i.e., 1893], composers in this field of musical composition have been impelled by an earnest desire to use folk material but have had rather vague notions concerning the actual process. With the early composers, often a work in Negro idiom meant that a Negro folksong theme was set into a musical work which might be of contrasting style and no attempt was made to integrate the theme into the music. . . . As the years passed and the movement grew richer with experience, composers began to formulate definite ideas of how to incorporate Negro material into the composition. There emerged the general feeling that the Negro material should always be an integral part of the whole; a work in Negro idiom.[85]

Although the author, Eileen Jackson, focused her observations more specifically on compositions inspired by folk music of the African diaspora ("Negro folksong"), the more general compositional problem she described – how to integrate any song into a larger orchestral framework – had animated Beach's approach to orchestral composition from *Bal Masqué* through the Piano Concerto. In each case, and as Beach herself explained, song provided her with an appropriate emotional "spark" that she would then attempt to grow into glowing embers and eventually a roaring fire with the "machinery" of counterpoint, developmental variation, and other advanced technical procedures.

As luck would have it, this very problem came to animate an entire generation of composers. Some of these composers, as Jackson goes on to explain, hewed more closely to Beach's approach in the "Gaelic" Symphony by quoting songs, possibly hiding their origins, and working the melodic material sufficiently to retain the underlying emotional depth of the source tune. Others attempted to transcend their source material, as Beach was able to do in the first movement of the concerto with her invocation and transformation of Dvořák's theme. Just as a critical mass of composers threw their proverbial hats into the arena of this style, Beach returned from Germany and was able to show that she had already created workable solutions to a seemingly vexing compositional challenge. Her work could then hold its own alongside an entire generation of composers who were tackling similar stylistic problems, many of whom, such as Texan Radie Britain (1899–1994), have likewise remained absent from most histories of American concert music from this period despite stunning popularity.

By 1944, Beach's "Gaelic" Symphony and Piano Concerto certainly would have sounded very old-fashioned next to Aaron Copland's folksy but angular *Appalachian Spring* or even Florence Price's cinematic *Songs of the Oath*, both of which date from that time. Yet the persistent vitality of Beach's orchestral works during the three decades prior to her death signals that conductors, critics, and audiences valued *something* in this music that not only allowed it to remain on concert programs but also convinced Beach that writing new orchestral music might be self-defeating. That *something* was a kernel of song clothed in the garments of conventional symphonic structures. With two successful, popular, and idiomatically current pieces always at the ready, why would Beach risk disrupting a sterling compositional reputation with something new? Perhaps, ironically, song had made her orchestral career.

Notes

1. The choral-orchestral works are discussed in Chapter 9, and the dramatic arias with orchestral accompaniment are discussed in Chapter 10.
2. Letter from Chadwick to Beach, November 2, 1896, autograph book, p. 68, box 1, folder 19, Amy Beach Collection, University of New Hampshire, quoted in Adrienne Fried Block, *Amy Beach, Passionate Victorian* (New York: Oxford University Press, 1998), 103.
3. See Douglas W. Shadle, *Orchestrating the Nation: The Nineteenth-Century American Symphonic Enterprise* (New York: Oxford University Press, 2016).
4. On Beach's relationship with Schmidt, see Block, "Arthur P. Schmidt, Music Publisher and Champion of American Women Composers," *The Musical Woman*, vol. 2: *1984–1985*, ed. Judith Lang Zaimont, Catherine Overhauser, and Jane Gottlieb (Westport, CT: Greenwood Press, 1987): 159–63; on the publishing climate more generally, see E. Douglas Bomberger, "Edward MacDowell, Arthur P. Schmidt, and the Shakespeare Overtures of Joachim Raff: A Case Study in Nineteenth-Century Publishing," *Notes* 54, no. 1 (September 1997): 11–26.
5. Block, *Amy Beach, Passionate Victorian*, 185–86, and Block, "Arthur P. Schmidt," 162–63.
6. Block, *Amy Beach, Passionate Victorian*, 101–3.
7. Berenice Thompson, "Music and Musicians: Mrs. Beach's Larger Works," *Washington Post*, January 24, 1904.

8. Block, *Amy Beach, Passionate Victorian*, 163–65.

9. See Marian Wilson Kimber, "Women Composers at the White House: The National League of American Pen Women and Phyllis Fergus's Advocacy for Women in American Music," *Journal of the Society for American Music* 12, no. 4 (November 2018): 477–507.

10. Quoted in Block, *Amy Beach, Passionate Victorian*, 203.

11. See George P. Upton, *Woman in Music* (Chicago: A.C. McClurg and Co., 1892 [1886]), 18–22.

12. See Christopher Reynolds, *Motives for Allusion: Context and Content in Nineteenth-Century Music* (Cambridge, MA: Harvard University Press, 2003), 1–17 and 177–81.

13. [James Creelman], "The Real Value of Negro Melodies," *New York Herald*, May 21, 1893.

14. See Dillon Parmer, "Brahms, Song Quotation, and Secret Programs," *19th-Century Music* 19, no. 2 (Autumn 1995): 161–90.

15. William Gibbons, "'Yankee Doodle' and Nationalism, 1780–1920," *American Music* 26, no. 2 (Summer 2008): 246.

16. Gibbons, "'Yankee Doodle,'" 256–59.

17. See Shadle, *Orchestrating the Nation*, 97–98 and 174–75.

18. Shadle, *Orchestrating the Nation*, 206.

19. See Douglas W. Shadle, *Antonín Dvořák's New World Symphony* (New York: Oxford University Press, 2021), 80–82.

20. Quoted in Shadle, *Antonín Dvořák's New World Symphony*, 79.

21. Shadle, *Antonín Dvořák's New World Symphony*, 91–112, and Adrienne Fried Block, "Boston Talks Back to Dvořák," *Institute for Studies in American Music Newsletter* 18, no. 2 (1989): 10–11, 15.

22. "Philharmonic," *Brooklyn Daily Eagle*, February 10, 1873.

23. "For National Music," *Chicago Tribune*, August 13, 1893.

24. Eileen Stanza Jackson, "The Use of Negro Folksong in Symphonic Forms" (MA thesis, University of Chicago, 1941).

25. See, for example, Adrienne Fried Block, "Dvořák's Long American Reach," in *Dvořák in America, 1892–1895*, ed. John C. Tibbetts (Portland, OR: Amadeus Press, 1993), 158–81, and Maurice Peress, *Dvořák to Duke Ellington: A Conductor Explores America's Music and Its African American Roots* (New York: Oxford University Press, 2003).

26. "How Mrs. Beach Does It," *Musical Courier* 71, no. 1 (July 7, 1915): 25.

27. Anna Poulin Alfeld, "Unsung Songs: Self-Borrowing in Amy Beach's Instrumental Music" (MM thesis, University of Cincinnati, 2008), 97.

28. Beach, "To the Girl Who Wants to Compose," *Etude* 36, no. 11 (November 1918): 695.

29. Beach, "The 'How' of Creative Composition," *Etude* 61, no. 3 (March 1943): 151.

30. Quoted and translated in Mark Evan Bonds, *The Beethoven Syndrome: Hearing Music as Autobiography* (New York: Oxford University Press, 2020), 24.

31. Beach, "To the Girl Who Wants to Compose," 695.

32. See Bonds, *The Beethoven Syndrome*, 157–61.

33. Beach, "The 'How' of Creative Composition," 151.

34. Block, *Amy Beach, Passionate Victorian*, 38–41.

35. Block, *Amy Beach, Passionate Victorian*, 47–48.

36. Beach, "The 'How' of Creative Composition," 208; for more on the details of Beach's methods, see Block, *Amy Beach, Passionate Victorian*, 54–56.

37. Block, "Dvořák, Beach, and American Music," in *A Celebration of American Music: Words and Music in Honor of H. Wiley Hitchcock*, ed. R. Crawford, R. Allen Lott, and Carol J. Oja (Ann Arbor: University of Michigan Press, 1990), 256–80; Block, *Amy Beach, Passionate Victorian*, 131–45.

38. Sarah Gerk, "'Common Joys, Sorrows, Adventures, and Struggles': Transnational Encounters in Amy Beach's 'Gaelic' Symphony," *Journal of the Society for American Music* 10, no. 2 (May 2016): 149–80; Alfeld, "Unsung Songs"; E. Douglas Bomberger, "Rewriting Dvořák: The Power of Allusion in the Beach Piano Concerto," paper delivered at the conference American Women Composer-Pianists, University of New Hampshire, September 16, 2017, and forthcoming in the conference proceedings.

39. Although the Boston run of the show began in September 1893, Beach's music was first performed there on January 1, 1894, a few weeks after the work's New York premiere; see "Boston Theater Attractions," *Boston Globe*, January 2, 1894, and "Salvini in 'Zamar,'" *Boston Post*, January 3, 1894.

40. On the genesis of these two works, see Block, *Amy Beach, Passionate Victorian*, 63–85.

41. Cooley was a Michigan writer who, like Beach, had given up her career as a teacher when she married, enabling her to focus more intently on literary endeavors; see Peter Simonson, *Refiguring Mass Communication: A History* (Urbana: University of Illinois Press, 2010), 101.

42. The emotional connection is also evident in the work's middle section, which shares a melody with Beach's "Pierrot and Pierrette" from *Children's Carnival*, op. 25, for solo piano, also written at the same time; see "Beach's *Bal Masqué* in Boston Performance," Women's Philharmonic Advocacy, last modified August 19, 2018, https://wophil.org/beachs-bal-masque-in-boston/.

43. Beach, "The 'How' of Creative Composition," 151.

44. See C[harles] F[rederick] Dennée, "Musical Matters," *Boston Daily Advertiser*, February 8, 1892; "Handel and Haydn," *Boston Globe*, February 8, 1892.

45. "The Manuscript Society Concert," *American Art Journal* (December 16, 1893): 189.

46. "Manuscript Society's Concert," *New York Evening World*, December 13, 1893.

47. "Manuscript Society of New York," *Musical Courier* 27, no. 25 (December 30, 1893): 35.

48. "How Mrs. Beach Does It," 25.

49. The pencil sketches of the "Gaelic" Symphony are housed in box 5, folders 5–8, of the Beach Collection at the University of New Hampshire. She began with the second movement, which contains the notations "Jan. (?) 1894" on p. 1 and "Finished March 22nd 1894" on p. 32.

50. "American Music," *Boston Herald*, May 28, 1893; emphasis added.

51. "Music Reviews, v. II," pp. 33–34, box 4, folder 1, Amy Beach Collection, Milne Special Collections, University of New Hampshire at Durham, quoted in Block, *Amy Beach, Passionate Victorian*, 88.

52. "American Music," *Boston Herald*, May 28, 1893.

53. Shadle, *Orchestrating the Nation*, 251–56.

54. Gerk, "'Common Joys, Sorrows, Adventures, and Struggles,'" 176.

55. Caryl B. Storrs, "Program Notes," *Minneapolis Tribune*, December 13, 1917; the phrase "take my pen in hand," incidentally, is a subtle allusion to Walt Whitman's reflection on the creative process in "What Think You I Take My Pen in Hand," in which the sad departure of two dear friends – an acutely emotional experience – proved to be more of a poetic inspiration than nature or urban expanse.

56. Gerk, "'Common Joys, Sorrows, Adventures, and Struggles,'" 171–72.

57. Frederic H. Cowen, *My Art and My Friends* (London: Edward Arnold, 1913), 127.

58. See Block, *Amy Beach, Passionate Victorian*, 100–3.

59. "Campanari Soloist at the Symphony Concert," *Boston Sunday Globe*, November 1, 1896.

60. "Musical Matters," *Boston Daily Advertiser*, November 2, 1896; emphasis added.

61. "Musical Comment," *New York Tribune*, March 29, 1897. Stanford's symphony, incidentally, also quotes folk songs directly.

62. "The Native Music of Ireland," *The Citizen* 3 (April 1841): 260.

63. Bomberger, "Rewriting Dvořák."

64. This song was published as op. 1, no. 3, in 1887, but as noted in Chapter 1, it was performed from manuscript by her future husband, Dr. H. H. A. Beach, in a recital on January 16, 1885.

65. See Block, *Amy Beach, Passionate Victorian*, 132–35.

66. Though not folk poetry, Chateaubriand's text for "Jeune fille" has a distinct archaic quality captured in Beach's modal setting.

67. "Music Hall: Boston Symphony Orchestra," *Boston Transcript*, April 9, 1900.

68. Philip Hale, "Symphony Night," April 15, 1900.

69. See Shadle, *Antonín Dvořák's New World Symphony*, 46–50.

70. "Music," *Boston Courier*, April 7, 1900.

71. [Elson], "Symphony Concert," *Boston Daily Advertiser*, April 9, 1900.

72. See Shadle, *Antonín Dvořák's New World Symphony*, 157–59.

73. Charles N. Boyd, "Mrs. H.H.A. Beach in a Dual Role," *Pittsburgh Weekly Gazette*, December 30, 1905.

74. "Mrs. Beach Was Well Received," *Pittsburgh Press*, December 30, 1905; emphasis added.

75. "Lauds Mr. Paur and Orchestra," *Pittsburgh Weekly Gazette*, December 31, 1905.

76. "Music and Musicians," *Kansas City Star*, June 13, 1915.

77. "Played the Beach Symphony," *Kansas City Times*, April 5, 1916.

78. See Walter S. Jenkins, *The Remarkable Mrs. Beach, American Composer*, ed. John H. Baron (Detroit, MI: Harmonie Park Press, 1994), 71–80, and Block, *Amy Beach, Passionate Victorian*, 346n24.

79. Luella Keller, "Enthusiastic Climax of Music Festival," *Monrovia Daily News*, June 29, 1915.

80. See "Noted Composers Wield Baton," *San Francisco Chronicle*, August 2, 1915, and Redfern Mason, "Composers of America Display Art," *San Francisco Examiner*, August 2, 1915.

81. See Dena J. Epstein, "Frederick Stock and American Music," *American Music* 10, no. 1 (1992): 20–52.

82. Eric DeLamarter, "Chicago Symphony at Orchestra Hall," *Chicago Tribune*, February 5, 1916; emphasis added.

83. Richard L. Stokes, "Mrs. H.H.A. Beach Triumphs as Composer and Pianist," *St. Louis Post-Dispatch*, January 13, 1917; emphasis added.

84. "Orchestra and Melchior Please," *Harrisburg Evening News*, November 18, 1942.

85. Jackson, "The Use of Negro Folksong in Symphonic Forms," 5.

9 | Choral Music

MATTHEW PHELPS

Introduction

On a spring day in New York City, I was in the catacombs of St. Bart's on Park Avenue. In a room filled with canned goods to feed the homeless, my friend Paolo Bordignon (organist and choirmaster of St. Bart's) and I were moving pallets of tomatoes and peaches to uncover shelves of neglected music. We found another piece by Amy Beach with each can of fruit we moved.

The dust on the boxes confirmed just how hidden these treasures were. On numerous occasions, my friend exclaimed, "I can't believe this. I had no idea this was down here." We found multiple copies of sacred choral works by Beach, in perfect condition, bound years ago by a professional binder, sharing space next to canned goods.

Even in an age of online repositories, these discoveries were exciting. Beach's choral works are carefully cataloged through extensive scholarship, most notably by Adrienne Fried Block and Jean Reigles; however, that does not mean they are accessible. It is even less likely you have heard a performance of them. Paolo and I looked at each other in amazement and wondered how this could be the case.

It is easy to blame it on changing tastes, but that has not affected the works of other notable Victorians from the late nineteenth and early twentieth century. Plenty of writing seeks to answer this question through sociological constructs, namely the place of women in classical music and upper-class family life during the turn of the twentieth century. Over the last generation, research into Amy Beach's works has sought to correct this, yet several of her choral works remain inaccessible. For whatever reason, a lack of familiarity is often endemic to Amy Beach's experience as a composer.

"I had no idea this was down here" sums it up perfectly.

Historical Context

At the turn of the century, the landscape of choral music in America gave Beach an ample breeding ground for her compositions. American singing societies such as the Cincinnati May Festival, the Apollo Club of Chicago, the Mendelssohn Club of Pittsburgh, and the Handel and Haydn Society of Boston all came of age in or around Beach's lifetime. These were undoubtedly informed or inspired by the numerous choir festivals in England. Much of the standard oratorio repertoire performed during this time was either written for or made prominent by festivals in Birmingham, Leeds, Norwich, and the famous Three Choirs Festival in Gloucester. While Beach may not have participated directly in one of these, she likely benefited from their influence – whether assimilating these scores in her self-directed study or through the inspiration these choral organizations and their concerts provided. Moreover, the Industrial Revolution in America produced a class of people with new-found wealth and leisure time. This translated into a boom for choral organizations as amateurs flocked to their ranks.[1]

Churches also grew into prominent exponents of choral perform-ance. Some of the nation's most respected musicians worked for the church, especially in cultural centers like Boston and New York City, where Beach made homes. The list of organists and choirmasters who worked in these metropolitan areas reads like a venerable "who's who" of early American art music: Lowell Mason, Horatio Parker, George Whitefield Chadwick, Dudley Buck, T. Tertius Noble, John Knowles Paine, Charles Ives, Clarence Dickinson, and Beach's close friend David McKay Williams all left an indelible mark on the church and choral music in the early twentieth century. Before making his name as a conductor, even Leopold Stokowski began at St. Bartholomew's in New York City. Beach's output as a composer, specifically choral music, was deeply influenced by these cultural trends. Her output is tailored toward the rich resources of sacred institutions and the endless supply of singing organizations that cropped up throughout the United States.

Songs and choral works figure prominently among Beach's compos-itional output. Adrienne Fried Block reports that writing songs was a way to clear her mind at the end of the day. "Beach claimed that song writing was recreation for her; when she felt herself going stale while working on larger pieces, she would stop and finish the day's work by writing a song. 'It freshens me up,' she claimed. 'I really consider that I have given myself a special treat when I have written a song.'"[2] Beach surely felt this way while writing her choral works. Many of her choral works contain large vocal solos, creating a Victorian form of the traditional English verse anthem.

Beach was very sensitive to the range and requirements of the singers. In a letter dated April 10, 1907, she negotiated extreme notes in her music with her publisher Arthur P. Schmidt Co. to find more comfortable solutions. "The high A I can easily modify by choice notes if you would kindly return the manuscript." She went on to discuss low notes for the basses as well and clarified that she would like young singers to find the music "practicable."[3]

We can categorize Beach's works by their scope and by the context for which Beach wrote them. Her large-scale works include the Grand Mass in E-flat major and *The Canticle of the Sun*. Beach wrote medium-sized festival works such as the *Festival Jubilate*, *Wedding Cantata*, and *The Chambered Nautilus*. The rest of her works are small- to medium-scale works for the church and small secular choral works for male and female voices. The church works fall into two categories: small-scale works written in a modified motet or Anglican style with accompaniment and elaborate verse anthems that intermingle solo and choral sections. Her earliest choral compositions were a set of chorales written in 1882. Her last works in 1944 were compositions for women's chorus: "Pax nobiscum" and "The Ballad of the P. E. O." Choral music thus bookended her career.

These choral works were often an essential source of income in addition to being works of personal devotion. Block notes that late in Beach's life, *The Canticle of the Sun* and *Let This Mind Be in You* were her most performed compositions.[4] Beach's will bequeathed her royalties to the MacDowell Association, and these choral compositions provided the colony with an important source of revenue.[5] Her secular choral works, especially for male and female choruses, were written out of a sense of demand. Block writes, "The demand for women's choral music grew during the first decade of the new century. Men as well as women responded to that need, but women seem to have a special affinity for the medium. . . . [P]ublishers, including Schmidt and G. Schirmer, instituted women's choral series to serve the growing nationwide market."[6] When taken together, Beach's choral output includes thirty-six sacred works (including the large-scale Grand Mass) and thirty-five secular choral works. Only her solo songs rival this output. When the songs and choral works are combined, Beach's output comes into focus. She was a prolific composer for the human voice.

Religious Context

Amy Beach's beliefs in religion profoundly influenced her sacred music. These religious views were formed at an early age by her mother and religious upbringing. About her religious education, Block writes: "She attended Sunday School at the Central Congregational Church in Chelsea and fell in love with her teacher – the only teacher other than her mother that she would have during the next few years. At age five she took to reading the Scriptures aloud, which she did with the clarity and emphasis of an adult."[7]

She carried religion with her through the rest of her life. As a young adult, she was an active participant at Trinity Episcopal Church in Boston. Scholars have questioned her membership, reporting that she and her husband's names are not on the church's roll.[8] Despite this, we know that Phillips Brooks (1835–1893), rector of the church and famous for writing the hymn "O Little Town of Bethlehem," was very influential. Jean Reigles reports in her dissertation, "The Choral Music of Amy Beach," that "she and Brooks had frequent discussions regarding the topics of his sermons."[9] In 1911, after the death of her husband, she joined and was baptized at Emmanuel Church (Episcopal) in Boston.[10]

Upon moving to New York City in 1924, she immediately became established at St. Bartholomew's Church on Park Avenue. Her integration into the community and her friendship with music director David McKay Williams (1887–1978) led her to write some of her most interesting sacred choral compositions, many of which she dedicated to Williams. *Let This Mind be in You, Canticle of the Sun,* and *Christ in the Universe* all date to this inflection point in her career. Beach's works featured prominently in the church's centennial anniversary in 1935, and "Hearken unto Me" was written specifically for the celebration.[11]

Beach went on to say that her sacred choral music held a special place for her among her works. "I think my church music appeals to me more than anything I have done. I have written anthems and oratorios and a whole Episcopal Service with great joy, and they have become a part of me more than anything I have done, I am sure."[12] Her religious devotion continued to her death. Upon her death, Beach bequeathed her family jewels to Emmanuel Church in Boston, where she was baptized. Emmanuel Church declined the gift, so she offered them to St. Bartholomew's.[13] They hold a prominent place in the church to this day, having been ensconced in the church's prized communion chalice.

The Grand Mass in E-Flat Major

Amy Beach's most substantial choral composition was also her first major work. She began writing the Grand Mass in E-flat major in 1886. The project culminated in a premiere with the Handel and Haydn Society of Boston in 1892. Beach wrote the work for a quartet of soloists, full chorus, and orchestra.

A Grand Mass is a daunting proposition for a master composer, let alone an eighteen-year-old forced to educate herself after being denied even a composition teacher. A setting of the Mass proper, though, became a primary interest for Dr. Beach. He "incited her . . . to work on an audacious project, a mass for solo quartet, chorus, organ, and orchestra."[14] He believed this would solidify her reputation as a substantial American composer – a designation that would be more consistent with their social standing than just a performer or teacher.

Beach wrote the vocal and choral parts in 1886 and 1887. She worked on the orchestral score in 1889. Schmidt Publishing Company in Boston published the piano–vocal score before the premiere, which was uncommon. It allowed the work an opportunity to be reviewed by the *Boston Beacon* before it was performed. This led to interest in the work and its premiere in 1892. The Handel and Haydn Society of Boston, conducted by Carl Zerrahn, premiered the work. This would be the first time a major institution in the United States performed a multi-movement choral and orchestral work by an American female composer.[15]

The Mass was, by most accounts, a success. Philip Hale, music critic for the *Boston Times*, wrote, "the Mass is a work of long breath. It shows knowledge, skill, and above all application, patience, and industry."[16] Block writes, "In general most critics agreed that Beach's Mass was a noble work that placed her – as one said – 'among the foremost rank of American composers.'"[17] Despite this, the Schmidt Company never published the full score. The Mass lay dormant until renewed interest in the work commenced over a hundred years later. The only performing edition available was a facsimile reprint of the manuscript until A-R Publications produced the new edition prepared by this author in 2018.[18]

The Mass is written in the oratorio style, using a multi-movement structure for the Gloria and Credo. The Gloria is split into four movements: Gloria, Laudamus Te, Qui Tollis, and Quoniam. The Credo is a single movement, but the three sections that comprise the setting are formally and thematically distinct, giving it the character of a multi-movement setting. The Sanctus and Benedictus are also separate. The Kyrie, Graduale, and Agnus Dei are each single movements inclusive of the text.

Beach favors thematic development over traditional formal structure. For example, the Kyrie follows a ternary model, but the return of the theme is condensed. The Gloria and the Credo and Et Resurrexit are declamatory in style and eschew formal concerns for a more through-composed model, providing variations on the initial motive throughout the movement. The opening theme and fanfare-type gesture of mm. 65–67 make up the material for the entire opening movement of the Gloria. The orchestral openings of the Credo and Et Resurrexit are the impetus for these movements.

Solos play a prominent role in movements where the text is more introspective or devotional. The Et Incarnatus Est is an extended soprano solo. The Laudamus Te opens with a trio accompanied by strings and harp and is followed by an expressive alto solo. The Qui Tollis, Benedictus, and Agnus Dei are dialogues between soloists and the chorus.

The Graduale, a movement entirely for solo tenor between the Gloria and Credo, was a late addition to the Mass. It was composed at the behest of the Handel and Haydn Society for their star tenor Italo Campanini (1846–96). Even the orchestral parts were completed before the movement was written – it was inserted at the end of the book as opposed to its proper place after the Quoniam. It was never included in an updated piano–vocal score.

The choral writing is mainly homophonic with light touches of counterpoint. The lone fugue is the Quoniam movement – traditionally a fugue in large-scale Masses by classical composers. The fugue consists of multiple expositions that culminate in homophonic conclusions. After each section, an orchestral interlude creates a transition to the next exposition. This formal design results in a somewhat abrupt ending, but Beach compensates for this through sonic saturation by employing the entire performing forces, resulting in an exuberant conclusion.

Thematically the Mass is unified by the opening of the work. The first two measures of the Kyrie recapitulate at different moments in the Mass, most notably in the Sanctus and the Dona Nobis Pacem. The Sanctus begins with a direct quotation of the Kyrie theme. The Dona Nobis Pacem begins with the Kyrie theme in the bass (m. 172), after which the theme is part of the overall texture.

Other unifying devices occur in the transition to the Dona Nobis Pacem, including quotations of the Benedictus and the four-note gesture deployed extensively in the Credo (mm. 158–66). Beach avoids the practice of reprising the Hosanna at the end of the Benedictus. Instead, she writes a brief seven-measure conclusion in a more ethereal effect (mm. 124–31) than the exuberant Hosanna that ends the Sanctus (mm. 45–91).

Harmonically, the Mass is Romantic in nature, employing chromatic harmonies. Beach enjoys creating tension by moving through key centers using diminished and augmented-sixth chords. Beach's most common harmonic characteristic is her penchant for building to large climaxes, reminiscent of the English Victorian tradition. These climaxes appear in all the major movements, including the Kyrie (mm. 67–75), Gloria (mm. 246–74), Quoniam (mm. 120–53), Et Resurrexit (mm. 338–52), and Agnus Dei (mm. 112–28).

The orchestration is large, requiring a full complement of winds and strings, four horns, three trumpets in F (a common Romantic orchestration used by Bruckner and Mahler), three trombones, timpani, harp, and organ. The organ and harp parts are of particular interest. The opening sonority of the entire mass is an E-flat chord from the organ alone instead of the orchestra – a statement of individuality for the work and composer. The accompaniment of the Et Incarnatus Est was originally an organ solo for the entirety of the movement. The composer added strings later at the "crucifixus" text, as evidenced by an inserted handwritten page in the manuscript score. The harp plays an extensive cadenza at the opening of the Agnus Dei. A sublime cello solo accompanies the alto in the second half of the Laudamus Te. The overall effect of the orchestration is like that of the Requiems of Verdi and Berlioz: powerful in tutti sections, but economical and transparent for sensitive musical moments.

An immediate and intense conversation regarding the role of women in classical music, specifically in composition, followed the success of Beach's Mass. Artists such as Dvořák and Rubinstein made unfortunate comments regarding the ability of female artists. Beach's Mass stands in stark contrast to those opinions held by many at the time. Through her compositions, women's suffrage in classical music had a new, though unassuming, advocate in Beach – and this body of work would prove those who stood in opposition to female composers as foolish.

Early Period Sacred Works

Her marriage, while restrictive by modern-day standards, was generally remembered fondly by Beach. She presented Dr. Beach a song each year on his birthday, sometimes a setting of his poetry. In turn, he lavished jewels on her and provided her with a beautiful home filled with parties and music. While giving up her life as a concert artist was likely a struggle, she later remembered her switch to composition as a chance to become even more notable. She wrote, "Though I had not deliberately chosen, the work had chosen me. My compositions gave me a larger field. From Boston, I could reach out to the world."[19]

Regardless of how some people felt about women composing, Beach's notoriety increased after the success of the Mass. This newfound fame led to a major commission for the World's Columbian Exposition in 1893, which celebrated the anniversary of Columbus's famed voyage. Beach composed the *Festival Jubilate*, op. 17, to open the fair's Woman's Building on May 1, 1893. The work was deemed "dignified and elevated in style."[20] These words must have been well received by Beach since the festival organizers almost rejected the work solely due to her gender.[21]

The structure is sectional, dividing the motivic material and the musical texture by text. Psalm 100 has a myriad of opportunities for exuberance and introspection. Beach dramatically explores them all. The harmonic language, though Romantic, is more stable than the chromatic sections of the Mass. Modulations involve fewer diminished chords, favoring secondary dominants and more direct modulations. Beach may have used Baroque cantatas and odes for ideas regarding design by evidence of the largo maestoso opening and grave transition between the second fugue and the coda. These transitional largo sections remind us of festival odes written by Purcell and Handel.

The *Festival Jubilate* exhibits a significant maturation in contrapuntal technique. After a fanfare and orchestral introduction, the chorus presents a fugue on the opening verse of Psalm 100. Whereas the Mass' lone fugue is sectional with expositions being interrupted, the opening fugue to the *Jubilate* is more fluid as entrances connect more succinctly. One can sense that Beach felt more comfortable with her contrapuntal technique, treating the orchestra more colla parte (doubling the voices) and not relying on a separate texture to help keep the music moving forward. After a meditative section that contemplates the Lord's goodness, Beach employs a second fugue displaying similar maturity. Even in homophonic sections, Beach allows the voices more independence – though glimpses of the Mass' more declamatory style are present in the exuberant vivace (Schmidt edition, p. 14) and the ending "Gloria Patri" (Schmidt edition, p. 34).

Beach spent these early years focused on her larger concert works. However, she also wrote several smaller choral pieces used as service music. *O Praise the Lord, All Ye Nations*, op. 7, was composed in 1891 for the consecration of her close friend, Phillips Brooks, as Bishop of Massachusetts. She wrote three choral responses, including settings of the "Nunc Dimittis," "With Prayer and Supplication," and "Peace I Leave with You." Three anthems for feast days were produced in "Bethlehem" and "Peace on Earth" for Christmas and "Alleluia, Christ is Risen" for Easter.

These works show Beach at her most economical to date while not sacrificing her voice and creativity. *O Praise the Lord All Ye Nations* and the Three Responses date before the *Festival Jubilate*, and one sees the similarities. Beach uses common-tone relationships, as seen in mm. 63–67 of *O Praise the Lord All Ye Nations*. A C-sharp diminished chord is followed by a B-flat chord in second inversion, only to return to a D major in first inversion. This common-tone relationship gives Beach a varied vocabulary in her smaller works, while avoiding an inaccessible harmonic language. We see similar motions by common tone in "With Prayer and Supplication" and "Peace I Leave with You."

"Bethlehem" and "Alleluia Christ is Risen" remain in this economical style; however, we see Beach break out of these constraints in her Christmas anthem, "Peace on Earth." Beach sets the familiar text, "It Came Upon the Midnight Clear," with a fluid sense of homophony and polyphony that characterize her later works. Her sense of drama is also more profound, illuminating each verse with just the right texture and mood. "Peace on Earth" is also the first small church work where Beach uses a soloist and duet during the piece, a form she preferred in her later church music – a welcome addition to her compositional arsenal given her penchant for songwriting.

"Peace On Earth" also uses the organ in a more independent way than previous works. The work begins with a fifteen-measure organ introduction. It accompanies the choir for the first verse but then dialogues with the choir in subsequent sections. The organ accompaniment in the middle section partners perfectly with the soloists and allows Beach to display her capability in art song writing. In Beach's subsequent works, we will see the organ play a more prominent role, and her ability to write for this complicated instrument continues to improve.

That this piece is not in the standard repertoire for churches today is evidence that Beach sometimes suffers from a general lack of familiarity. "Peace on Earth" is worthy of performance by the most outstanding church choirs while accessible for any ensemble.

Beach concluded her early period with two ambitious choral works. *Help Us, O God!*, op. 50 (1903) is Beach's lone attempt at a sectional motet in the style of a Bach or Brahms motet. The Service in A, op. 63, is her first multi-movement work intended for a church service.

Help Us, O God! is one of Beach's few purely a cappella works, and one of her longest small-form sacred choral works. The work is comprised of texts from the book of Psalms and is designed in a sectional form that uses different voice textures in the style of Bach's "Jesu Meine Freude." The work is contrapuntally dense and harmonically progressive.

Despite the varied use of vocal texture, the lack of organ accompaniment restrains Beach from creating the dramatic contrasts found in earlier large-scale works. The primary device for this motet is the pure technique of composition. We see this in the fugue that ends the work – her most complex attempt at the form to date.

The Service in A embraces typical Anglican choral style. The primary responsibility of the choral parts is to proclaim the text in a melodic yet clear fashion. The organ features prominently as an equal partner with the voices. The harmonic language is decidedly Victorian. Beach deftly moves through keys without overly audacious sonorities – something that we do not expect in Anglican church music until the mature works of Herbert Howells (1892–1983). She employs suspension and augmented leading tones generously throughout the work.

As with the church works of Stanford, solos are important in these works. The "Te Deum" employs a soprano solo as an obbligato to the chorus. The slow section of the work uses a bass and alto solo. The "Magnificat" contains an extensive soprano solo, something common to settings of this text and likely a nod to Mary, who claims the text in the biblical story. The "Benedictus" and "Jubilate Deo" also contain extensive soprano solos, while the "Nunc Dimittis" uses a bass soloist.

Choral unison singing is another device Beach had not yet employed but is relatively common in Anglican service music. The "Te Deum" begins with an extended passage of choral unison singing, undoubtedly meant to illuminate the first moment of choral harmony on the word: "Holy!" (m. 47). The end of the "Te Deum," "Nunc Dimittis," and "Jubilate Deo" contain similar moments.

Each piece is unique based on the character of the text. In earlier compositions, Beach created contrasting dramatic effects to suit the text; but in these works, as we see in "Help Me, O God," she prefers a more unified character throughout, choosing instead to paint the text with compositional technique and ingenuity. While Anglican composers have sometimes created structural unity in service music through repeated motives, especially during the "Gloria Patri," Beach shows no such desire.

Despite this similarity to the preceding motet, the compositional language and style are much different, especially in Beach's use of counterpoint. The polyphony is almost nonexistent in these service pieces. Imitation is briefly used at the end of "Benedictus" and "Magnificat" during the text "as it was in the beginning." She forgoes this technique in the "Jubilate Deo" and "Nunc Dimittis," preferring unison writing.

It seems Beach regarded these works in a more serious style than her previous church works. Beach uses 4/2 meter, but labels it cut time which, like "Help Me, O God!," shows the influence of large works by Bach and Brahms. Both composers used this time signature in serious sacred works such as the B minor Mass, *Ein Deutsches Requiem*, and *Geistliches Lied*. Otherwise, the practice was uncommon until editors in the early twentieth century began using the meter to transcribe Renaissance music.

Early Period Secular Works

Beach's most significant contributions to concert works date from her early period. The "Gaelic" Symphony, Piano Concerto, and *Jephthah's Daughter* were all written before 1910. Her significant large-scale chamber works, except for the piano trio, were written before 1907. While she wrote secular choral music throughout her life, the most significant concert works – *Three Shakespeare Choruses*, op. 39; *Sylvania, A Wedding Cantata*, op. 46; *The Sea-Fairies*, op. 59; and *The Chambered Nautilus*, op. 66 – were also composed before 1907.

Beach often wrote her secular choral music for either all-female (SSA) or all-male choirs (TTB). There are sporadic secular works for SATB chorus, but the bulk of the works divide the genders, which is true even for the large-scale works. *Sylvania* is the only large-scale work of the four for SATB chorus – the rest are for SSA chorus. *The Sea-Fairies* and *The Chambered Nautilus* require orchestral accompaniment.

The *Three Shakespeare Choruses* were published in 1897. Written for treble voices, these pieces are the perfect fusion of English madrigal influence and nineteenth-century part songs. Romantic part songs were an important part of the European choral repertory in the nineteenth century. Schumann, Mendelssohn, and Schubert all contributed to this catalog, and these pieces exhibit this influence, especially in the decidedly early nineteenth-century Germanic harmonic language. However, Beach's sensitivity to the English text led her to include madrigal-style imitative writing and tone painting in these intimate and beautiful settings.

Sylvania: A Wedding Cantata was published in 1901 and is indicative of a light secular cantata. It was premiered in 1905 at a private performance in Chickering Hall. The *Boston Globe* warmly received the work. The reviewer wrote, "The work is illustrative of a sylvan wedding, and both lines and music are redolent throughout of the whisperings of the forest, the caroling of birds and songs of elves and fairies. Like a midsummer night's dream, it carries the auditor away into an age where all the world is young and innocent and beautiful."[22] Composed in five parts, the piece includes a cast of five soloists, a mixed chorus (her only large-scale secular work for SATB chorus), and an accompaniment for piano or orchestra. The text was "freely adapted from the German" by the Boston musician Frederick W. Bancroft (1856–1914).[23]

The Sea-Fairies and *The Chambered Nautilus* were Beach's most notable contributions to secular choral music, specifically to major works for treble chorus. Both pieces use four-part treble choirs and two soloists: soprano and contralto. The orchestral requirements for both works are almost the same: flutes, clarinets, horns, piano, and strings, though *The Chambered Nautilus* also requires bassoons. In both pieces, the piano plays an outsized role in the orchestration.

The Sea-Fairies is a single-movement piece in strophic form. The orchestra carries much of the thematic material while the chorus sings the text homophonically over the accompaniment's images of the sea. Arpeggios from the pianist abound while orchestral instruments add to the color and texture in static material. Beach relies heavily on the orchestration to paint pictures of undulating waves.

The Chambered Nautilus uses many of the same ideas as *The Sea-Fairies*, especially regarding orchestration, use of piano, harmonic ambiguity, and primacy of the text in both choral material and in how the orchestration paints the images of the poetry. However, Beach treats the choir much more independently. There are more individual lines, more imitation, and more development of thematic material.

The Chambered Nautilus was commissioned by Victor Harris of the St. Cecilia Club of New York. Beach finished the work during the summer of 1907, and the work's first performance was in 1908 by the St. Cecilia Club, who made it a staple of their repertoire in subsequent years.[24] A 1907 letter from American music theorist Percy Goetschius praised the work by contrasting it with modernist trends:

I have just spent a most delightful hour with your truly exquisite "Chambered Nautilus" and wish to tell you, warm from my first glowing impression, how keenly

I enjoyed it … in this day of dreadful disease … one might call the Debussy-disease – or Strauss or Max Reger-disease, … I am so glad that we have at least one *American* composer who is not affected by the plague. God bless you![25]

Goetschius' evaluation is humorous given the work's similarity to *La Mer* in its sea imagery.

Amy Beach's world was about to change in 1910, and her style and compositional focus changed with it. The death of her husband in 1910 saw Beach turn more toward the church and her faith. Her ability to travel outside of Boston gave her opportunities to vary her musical taste and influences. Her integration into different churches and relationships with more musicians inspired her to hone her skills as a composer of sacred choral music. During the second half of her life, her choral output would include her most performed works, some of the most important parts of her legacy, and some of her own favorite compositions.

Middle Period

After Henry Beach's untimely death in 1910, Amy Beach had the double-edged sword of a new life. Despite the freedom that Beach took advantage of through traveling and promoting herself as a composer and pianist, she was also grief-stricken. Block writes, "She would spend well over a year grieving before she could resume performing, and even then, she would find the life of a traveling pianist too stressful."[26] When studying her output, there is a notable gap between 1910 and 1915. Whether it was out of grief or necessity, her life was most certainly interrupted.

Amy Beach's choral compositions after her hiatus continued to display her love of writing for the voice. These works expand on the style she developed while writing the Service in A and "Peace on Earth." In the years ahead, she continued to treat each line sensitively but did away with the confinement of fugue and polyphony. Soloists were employed often, and the organ continued to be a prominent participant in the action. Beach's harmonic language continued to exploit borrowed chords and common-tone modulations, especially in her smaller works; however, in grand anthems and larger works, her chromaticism became more progressive and intense, especially in her choices of melodic material. Beach found her voice in these works, and she would speak with it through the rest of her career.

Her four-part setting of "All Hail the Power of Jesus' Name" has all the characteristics of a composer jumping back into the pool. Written with a secular text originally for the Panama–Pacific Exposition in California, the work was reissued with Edward Perronet's notable sacred text by Schmidt in 1915. The work is a delightful setting and the most accessible work thus far – its only modulations are two four-measure moves to the mediant, a noticeable departure from Beach's standard procedure before.

If "All Hail the Power of Jesus' Name" was Amy picking up her pen again, "Thou Knowest, Lord" was Amy being cathartic. The text by Jane Borthwick is hard to ignore, given Beach's life circumstance and her return to musical composition.

Thou knowest, Lord the weariness and sorrow
Of all sad hearts that come to Thee for rest;
Cares of today, and burdens of tomorrow,
Blessings implored and signs to be confessed;
We come before Thee at Thy gracious word,
And lay them at Thy feet:
Thou knowest, Lord!
Thou knowest all the past; how long and blindly,
Lost on the mountains dark, the wanderer strayed;
How the Good Shepherd followed,
And how kindly He bore it home,
upon his shoulders laid;
And healed the bleeding wounds and soothed his pain,
And brought back life, and hope, and strength again.

It is difficult not to think about Beach reading the last line of this second stanza and picturing herself returning to her former strength. The author of the poem goes on to speak of "future gleams of gladness" and finding "a hiding place, a rest, a home." "Thou Knowest, Lord," feels like a statement of reemergence for Amy.

The piece is a welcome return to the Beach we began to see at the turn of the twentieth century. Written in the verse anthem form, it is strophic, with each strophe alternating between soloist and chorus. The piece also employs a more progressive harmonic language, easily moving through keys and chromatic alterations, especially in melodic material.

The final verse speaks of the Lord's gentle call. Beach portrays this by having the chorus sing on a unison E-flat for twenty-one measures, only to give the chorus the tonic sonority for the final chord. During this chant, Beach provides the organist a recapitulation of melodic material. The effect of this texture is stunning, given the dense nature of the rest of the piece. It is as if Amy gives one last sigh of relief that her life is beginning to progress again.

Amy Beach seemed to be quite influenced by the texts she chose. When presented with an English poetic text, like "Thou Knowest Lord," she employed a Victorian expressiveness, using a verse anthem form and progressive chromaticism. However, when given a biblical text, she preferred writing in a more conservative form or older style. She often telegraphs this by writing the title in Latin, even though the piece's text is in English. Her *Four Canticles*, op. 78, display this practice.

Beach wrote her *Four Canticles* of 1916 for SATB chorus and organ. They are closer in style to the Service in A due to the easily discernible text setting. However, they still display Beach as an early twentieth-century American composer through her use of augmented leading tones and fluid chromaticism – frequently seen in many works of comparable composers from New England at the time.

Beach conceived the pieces as motets with organ accompaniment. Beach provides new music with each line of new text. She often uses imitation at the beginning of these new sections, but its deployment is brief. The preferred texture for these works is non-declamatory homophony. The lines retain independence, but Beach uses imitative counterpoint sparingly.

We also see this older style in the lack of solo writing. There is an obbligato soprano solo in "Bonum Est Confiteri," and "Benedic, Anima Mea" opens with a bass solo that is strikingly short when compared to "Thou Knowest, Lord." This lack of extended solos creates a clear contrast between the pieces Beach considers one part art song, one part choral work, and the pieces she conceives as strictly in anthem or motet form.

The raised fifth and flat-sixth, though certainly used before, become important harmonic devices for Beach. In the opening of "Bonum Est Confiteri," we see both in the organ part (mm. 3, 10, and 12). These chromatic alterations, and others like raised fourths and sevenths, can be found throughout the other Canticles. In the opening of "Benedic, Anima Mea," the raised fifth features prominently in measure 3. In "Deus Misereatur," fourths and sevenths are raised but often in triadic formulae, so they feel like raised fifths (mm. 1–2, 4–5, 7–10).

Whereas the organ part is a collaborative partner in Beach's Victorian verse anthems, the organ is much more subservient in these motet-style works. The organ's material matches the choir with more frequency. The introductions and interludes are sparser than in verse anthem-style compositions. The technical requirements are much less demanding. Notably, "Benedic, Anima Mea" contains Beach's only specific registration requirement in her works, asking that trumpet stops be used in the first two measures.

This contrast between the newer and older styles continues to appear, though on a smaller scale, with her subsequent two works, *Constant*

Christmas, op. 95, and *Benedictus Es Domine*, op. 103. *Constant Christmas* is a setting of a poem by Phillips Brooks, Bishop of Massachusetts and her longtime friend. Beach tempers her chromaticism, certainly a requirement of the text and possibly the performance context. It begins with an extended duet between alto and soprano. The chorus enters and concludes the piece in a simple homophonic fashion, proudly inviting us to run to the manger. *Benedictus Es, Domine*, displays the style used in the Canticle. The soloist occupies an obbligato role except for in the first six measures. Beach treats the choral parts more independently and uses imitative counterpoint at the end as she did in the Service in A. Both pieces use an economy of style that makes them delightful.

Beach's other sacred compositions from this period – *Lord of the Worlds Above*, op. 109; *Around the Manger*, op. 115; *Benedicte Omnia Opera*, op. 121; and the *Communion Responses*, op. 122 – also display these general characteristics. *Benedicte*, written for David McKay Williams, and the Communion Service, written for Raymond Nold,[27] contain some of Beach's most austere chromaticism until this point. These pieces' melodic material and harmonic instability prefigure the voice she will use in her serious works of the later period.

Amy Beach's most significant contribution to sacred church music is her anthem, *Let This Mind Be in You*, op. 105, along with *The Canticle of the Sun*, op. 123, her most performed and likely most lucrative sacred choral work. Beach wrote this piece in Victorian verse anthem style. The extended opening for bass and soprano solo shows Beach at her most expressive and secure. The chromaticism is accessible yet interesting, especially in the melodic material. The raised tones in the bass solo provide the perfect combination of well-written melodic construction and creativity (mm. 1–22).

The chorus' a cappella entrance is stark and subtle. The diminished chord and the following measure's conclusion on a half-diminished chord creates an ambiguity that prepares for the piece's satisfying conclusion (mm. 52–53). The final section contains some of Beach's most characteristic compositional ideas. The chorus sings mostly in unison for the text, "and that every tongue confess that Jesus Christ is Lord to the glory of God the Father." While the chorus is singing in unison, the organ deploys a dominant pedal point and thick sonorities in a sequential pattern. The result is reminiscent of the building of tension seen in the climactic portions of the Mass (m. 79). After the climax is achieved, the organ subsides. The chorus, still in unison, employs a flat sixth on the word God before allowing the piece to conclude with a luminous A-flat chord.

The energy Beach put into her sacred works, along with her busy performing schedule, must have taken their toll. Her secular choral music from this time is sparse – only five entries between 1915 and 1917. These consist mainly of small arrangements for children's choir, which were unpublished. The aforementioned *Panama Hymn*, op. 74, was reissued as a sacred piece. "The Candy Lion" is arrangements of solo songs for female chorus, leaving *Dusk in June*, op. 82, her only original secular choral composition from the middle period.

Beach's maturation as a composer is evident in these works from her middle period. These works contain a stylistic variety that morphed into a singular voice as she became more comfortable with her new life. This maturation subsequently flourished into some of her most substantial choral works. These works display wisdom and ingenuity while also being inspired by her new life in New York City, the church she invested herself in, and the people she would know as her closest and dearest friends.

Late Period

Beach began spending significant time in New York City in the 1920s. Her routine during touring was to split her time between the MacDowell Colony in New Hampshire and New York City. In 1930, Beach moved to New York City full time. Beach loved her constant encounters with art. She wrote to her friend Lillian Buxbaum, "The New York life never seemed more fascinating, and I never felt more enthusiasm."[28] She filled her schedule with concerts, theater, and social activities. The consistent stimulation must have been overwhelming and inspiring.

Beach also became a member of St. Bartholomew's on Park Avenue. St. Bart's was (and still is) a grand church known for its exemplary music and fine preaching. Preaching was always important to Beach. Robert Winkworth Norwood (1874–1932), rector of St. Bart's at the time, was a well-known theologian and author. Her attraction to him and the church is consistent with the spiritual nourishing she sought, especially after her husband's death.[29]

It was St. Bart's that provided the premiere of Beach's most well-known (at the time) choral composition, *The Canticle of the Sun*, op. 123, for chorus, SATB soloists, and an orchestra of strings, winds, four horns, two trumpets in F, and timpani, which was published and premiered in 1928 but composed several years earlier.[30] It is Beach's most operatic sacred choral work. It was an immediate hit, especially with the congregation at

St. Bart's, where the work was performed annually – though with organ accompaniment, as their tradition had been for all major works. Her publisher, Arthur P. Schmidt Co., also praised the work in a letter to Beach on June 29, 1928, calling it "most effective."[31]

The work is sectional and constructed around a four-note motive, reminiscent of a Renaissance cambiata, introduced as an ostinato in the bass in the first nine measures. The ostinato breaks off and then repeats itself up a third. This cell gives the work structural unity so that Beach can treat each new verse with a new texture and affect. The motive appears in the orchestration and melodic material – notably in solos and as a point of imitation over the words, "Bless ye the Lord," throughout the work. The effect is a multi-movement cantata that is through-composed.

Beach uses choral unison to prepare sudden dramatic chords in wide textural ranges and dissonant diminished sonorities. These sudden flourishes resemble the dramatic turns seen in the opening of Haydn's *Creation*. Beach treats the chorus as a homophonic instrument, preferring to bring out the text through clear declamation and dramatic intent outside of the point of imitation at the end and other rare occurrences.

The grandness of Beach's vision often overcomes the more subtle moments of the *Canticle*. However, the work ends with a great hush on the word "humility," showing that the text for Beach often consumed architecture. Whereas some composers would have preferred a vivacious ending to such an extroverted work and possibly reconfigured text or musical ideas to achieve this, Beach stays faithful to the requirements of the words. While the conclusion feels abrupt, one must respect Beach's authenticity and strength of ideal.

Beach's most substantial church works from this late period were written for the St. Bartholomew community, specifically her friend David McKay Williams, organist and choirmaster of the church. Block notes her attraction to Williams as a musician and person: "In church, Beach habitually sat on the left side of the sanctuary and as far back as possible so that she could watch Williams at the organ. She treasured every moment she spent with him, often recording in her diary the precise duration of their meeting or shared meal or evening of bridge and music."[32] The platonic relationship between the two was one Beach treasured, and it led her to write some of her most progressive sacred choral works.

Hearken Unto Me, op. 139, was written for the 100th anniversary of the church in 1934. In this seminal piece, Beach used an expanded version of the verse anthem form. After a dramatic organ introduction that includes a half-diminished chord on G as the first full sonority and concludes on an

E chord with an added seventh and ninth, the tenor cries "Hearken unto me!" as if he walked onto the stage at the Met. The entire composition feels like a mini opera sung in church. The chorus has a short interjection during the opening section, but the solo quartet generally dominates the piece. The chorus features more prominently at the end when they accompany the soaring soprano and tenor soloists. The range of these solos, along with the repeated triplet chords in the organ, gives the sense that we are listening to a new Amy Beach – one inspired by her surroundings: the theater; the fabulous singers at St. Bart's, including Ruth Shaffner, soprano soloist and the person that would become her trusted confidant; and David McKay Williams, the person who would champion her music for the rest of her career.

Other works would fall into this category. "O Lord God of Israel," op. 141, written in 1936, was one of the few works not published by Schmidt, existing only in facsimiled manuscripts in the library of St. Bart's and at the repository located at the University of New Hampshire. *I Will Give Thanks*, op. 147, written in 1939, appears to be more conservative in style but allows for Beach's more operatic impulses in the middle of the piece. A soprano soloist pierces the work's texture, relegating the choir to accompaniment while the soloist, through a melodic sequence, climbs to a high C.

Beach's last major choral composition in length and scope is *Christ in the Universe*, op. 132, written in 1932. Again dedicated to Williams, this is Beach's most complex and modern work. The text by Alice Meynell, a British writer and suffragist, is a striking example of twentieth-century mysticism. The opening line, "with this ambiguous earth, his dealings have been told us," handed Beach a blank canvas that she chose to paint with the most tonally ambiguous music she had written thus far. Beach does not establish a key until the chorus enters in m. 49. The key is fleeting as Beach slides back into an enchanting and progressive chromaticism that lasts throughout the work.

While rivaling the *Canticle* in length, *Christ in the Universe* is a sprawling fantasia instead of a sectional work. Material is linked together with organ interludes or additional vocal solos. Themes, though varied, are not different enough to merit the designation of a multi-movement cantata. This work is the ultimate expansion of her anthem form. The chorus, soloists, and organ are all equal partners in a lush work containing a plethora of harmonic twists and turns that would have made twentieth-century modernists quite proud. In her dissertation on Beach's choral music, Reigles notes: "The entire first 32 bars remind the listener Dr. William T. Allen[33] of

Debussy and Scriabin, the latter perhaps because of the piano patterns. According to Dr. Allen, 'we are still in tertian structure, and hanging on to tonality by our teeth,' by means of the implied leadings of dominant harmony."[34] Outside of its premiere on April 17, 1932, performances of this piece are undocumented.[35] The intense chromaticism may be a factor, but the work shows Beach at her most creative and harmonically extravagant.

Conclusion

Amy Beach's choral music makes up a significant portion of her output. The Grand Mass still endures as her most substantial composition – an amazing accomplishment for a young composer. Beach's church music explores a wide array of styles, from traditional Anglican church music to mini cantatas that bring operatic style to the Episcopal Mass. Her secular choral music includes significant contributions to women's choir repertoire. Her harmonic language progresses from Victorian uses of augmented leading tones and suspension to modernist deployments of ambiguous tonality. Her love of art song informs her use of the solo vocal line and the organ as an equal partner in the works' textures. Amy Beach's reemergence will only benefit from a continued and thorough examination of her as one of America's most important composers of sacred choral music.

Notes

1. Chester L. Alwes, "Choral Music in the Culture of the Nineteenth Century," in *The Cambridge Companion to Choral Music*, ed. Andre de Quadros (New York: Cambridge University Press, 2012), 29.
2. Adrienne Fried Block, *Amy Beach, Passionate Victorian* (New York: Oxford University Press, 1998), 146.
3. Letter to A. P. Schmidt Company, April 10, 1907, box 303, folder 5, A. P. Schmidt Company Archives, Music Division, Library of Congress.
4. Block, *Amy Beach, Passionate Victorian*, 257–58.
5. Block, *Amy Beach, Passionate Victorian*, 297.
6. Block, *Amy Beach, Passionate Victorian*, 164.
7. Block, *Amy Beach, Passionate Victorian*, 8.
8. Block, *Amy Beach, Passionate Victorian*, 325n3.
9. B. Jean Reigles, "The Choral Music of Amy Beach" (PhD diss., Texas Tech University, 1996), p. 9.
10. Block, *Amy Beach, Passionate Victorian*, 178.

11. Found in the commemorative program for St. Bartholomew's centennial celebration: January 13–20, 1935. Other pieces by Amy Beach performed as part of the centennial celebration include *Cantate Domino* and an excerpt from *The Canticle of the Sun*.

12. Reigles, "The Choral Music," 12.

13. Block, *Amy Beach, Passionate Victorian*, 296–97.

14. Block, *Amy Beach, Passionate Victorian*, 62.

15. The composer Constance Runcie (1836–1911) may have had a premiere in Missouri in the middle of the nineteenth century that would put this assertion in jeopardy; however, the performance is undocumented.

16. Quoted in Block, *Amy Beach, Passionate Victorian*, 71.

17. Block, *Amy Beach, Passionate Victorian*, 71.

18. Amy Beach, *Grand Mass in E-flat Major*, op. 5, ed. Matthew Phelps (Middleton, WI: A-R Editions, 2018).

19. Mrs. H. H. A. Beach, "Why I Chose my Profession," *Mother's Magazine* 9, no. 2 (February 1914): 7–8.

20. *Chicago Tribune*, quoted in Block, *Amy Beach, Passionate Victorian*, 82.

21. Block, *Amy Beach, Passionate Victorian*, 80.

22. Quoted in Reigles, "The Choral Music," 141.

23. The title page of the work spells the adapter of the text "Banckroft." The 1900 Federal Census records from Boston include two persons named "Frederick Bancroft": a 29-year-old postal clerk and a 44-year-old musician. The latter is presumably Beach's collaborator.

24. Block, *Amy Beach, Passionate Victorian*, 169.

25. Quoted in Block, *Amy Beach, Passionate Victorian*, 168.

26. Block, *Amy Beach, Passionate Victorian*, 179.

27. Block, *Amy Beach, Passionate Victorian*, 250.

28. Block, *Amy Beach, Passionate Victorian*, 233.

29. Block, *Amy Beach, Passionate Victorian*, 257.

30. See Block, pp. 363n38 and 39, on the date of composition.

31. Letter from A. P. Schmidt Company, June 29, 1928, box 303, folder 16, A. P. Schmidt Collection, Music Division, Library of Congress, Washington.

32. Block, *Amy Beach, Passionate Victorian*, 258.

33. William T. Allen (1926–2016) was a noted organist and writer on music.

34. Quoted in Reigles, "The Choral Music," 126.

35. Special thanks to my friend Paolo Bordignon for finding the premiere date in the archives of St. Bartholomew.

10 | Beach's Dramatic Works

NICOLE POWLISON

The final chapter of the analytical portion of this collection addresses three works that defy easy generic categorization. While the classification of "dramatic work" can be defined in multiple ways, for Amy Beach it encompasses a select few compositions over the course of her career: two dramatic unstaged arias for solo voice and orchestra, *Eilende Wolken, Segler der Lüfte* (1892), and *Jephthah's Daughter* (1903), and her only opera, *Cabildo* (1932).

It was not unusual for Romantic-era composers to create stand-alone vocal compositions in the style of nineteenth-century operatic *scena* ed *aria*. The drama of the scena's declamatory recitative and the contrasting tempos and styles of the multipart *aria* provide an appealing closed format for a composer such as Beach, with her talent for vocal composition. Beach's dramatic works are distinct from her cantatas and other church, choral, or solo voice works. The arias were originally for solo voice accompanied by orchestra and were published in a piano–vocal format shortly after their completion. *Cabildo* is a one-act chamber opera accompanied by piano trio. Premiered after Beach's death, *Cabildo* was not published, but it is still occasionally performed despite its manuscript format.

What Connects Beach's Dramatic Works?

Amy Beach's appreciation for opera is evident from the journals she kept throughout her life, enjoying performances of opera during her tours of Europe and while she lived in New York. Beach appreciated even quite modern dramatic works: she was very enthusiastic about the performance of her friend Marcella Craft (1874–1959) originating the title role in Richard Strauss's *Salome*,[1] and she found a performance of *Porgy and Bess* to be "thrilling, full of color and a haunting atmospheric spirit."[2] While she appreciated modern styles as an audience member, as a composer she was slower to absorb stylistic changes and explore new genres.

All three of Beach's dramatic works also share topics of history or biblical drama: relatively safe ground for a Bostonian composer who may have felt a subconscious reluctance to engage with works for the stage; a lingering skepticism from Boston's puritanical cultural roots that saw theater of any kind banned from the Revolutionary War through the end of the 1700s.[3] Beach's first major composition, her Grand Mass in E-flat major, was premiered by the Handel and Haydn Society, and her years of churchgoing and composing for St. Bartholomew's in New York also demonstrate that when she wrote dramatic works for voice they were often religious. But biblical figures and historical stories were safe territory for dramatic vocal works even by Beach's own estimation. Her music was harmonically adventurous and highly chromatic by the end of her career, but unlike some of the other operas composed by her contemporaries, Beach's subject matter did not venture into the experimental, political, or present-day.

The three dramatic works are united by the prominent central figure of a tragic female character. While a tragic female role is not an uncommon theme, the voices of the women in Beach's works are – if not empowered – powerfully dignified and claiming agency as they can. The popular historical figure Mary Stuart, Queen of Scots, is the voice of *Eilende Wolken*, nostalgic but unrepentantly sure of her identity despite her isolated imprisonment. The unnamed Jephthah's daughter reflects with a resigned dignity on what she stands to lose as a young woman fated to die before her time, a victim of circumstances beyond her control. Finally, while Lady Valerie dies before the events of *Cabildo* begin, she is the catalyst of the opera's plot: the mystery of her love for Pierre piques the newlywed Mary's interest, Valerie's commitment to Pierre's goodness saves him from himself (and political and historical ignominy), and in Mary's dream – or perhaps her vision of the past – Valerie is the one who frees Pierre, allowing him to save New Orleans and the United States.

Each of these dramatic works also reflects Beach's lifelong habit of collaborating with other female artists. Her partnerships with the singers C. Katie Alves and Marcella Craft, and with *Cabildo*'s librettist Nan Bagby Stephens, bring each of these works to life. Alves' commission of *Eilende Wolken* was Beach's first specially commissioned work, an endorsement from the singer who performed in the premiere of the Mass. Beach and Craft performed a number of her works while touring Europe to revive

Beach's solo career and promote her compositions. The powerful and challenging *Jephthah's Daughter* may have been among their concert repertoire. Craft's voice must have made quite an impression over the years of their European tour, as Beach mentioned Craft when she discussed ideas for opera in the early 1900s. When Beach did take on composing an opera in the 1930s, she chose a libretto by a female playwright and fellow MacDowell Colony artist Stephens.

Eilende Wolken, Segler der Lüfte, op. 18 (1892)

Amy Beach's first dramatic work, the scena and aria *Eilende Wolken, Segler der Lüfte* ("Wandering clouds, sail through the air") was also her first commission. In the spring of 1892, just a week after the premiere of her Grand Mass in E-flat major with the Handel and Haydn Society, one of the Mass soloists, C. Katie Alves (1862–1927), contacted Beach requesting a dramatic solo with orchestral accompaniment:

I have spoken continually since my return home, and intended to write and ask you whether you had written anything in the form of an aria suitable for my voice – you know how such little, for contralto, with orchestra we have for concert use – A grand dramatic Rec. and Aria – can range from the lower g to high B flat – I would be perfectly delighted to have such from your pen, as you so well understand how to write for the contralto voice.[4]

Beach chose a dramatic text from Friedrich Schiller's play *Maria Stuart* (1801), a dramatization of the final days of Mary, Queen of Scots, as she laments her imprisonment for treason by Queen Elizabeth I.[5] After she accepted the commission, recognition of Beach's compositional talent continued to roll in: she put the dramatic aria on hold to focus on her second commission, the *Festival Jubilate*, op. 17, to celebrate the opening ceremonies of the Woman's Building at the 1893 World's Columbian Exposition in Chicago. Finally, with Alves as the featured singer, *Eilende Wolken, Segler der Lüfte*, op. 18 (called *Mary Stuart* in the original orchestral manuscript),[6] was premiered on December 2, 1892. The premiere was conducted by Walter Damrosch and accompanied by the Symphony Society of New York, the first time that ensemble had performed the work of a female composer.[7]

Eilende Wolken begins with a brief orchestral overture followed by an introductory scena blending sections of recitative and arioso as the exiled queen reflects on her imprisonment. It is in this scene that the "Auld Rob Morris" folk theme first appears, a touch of Scottish color and a leitmotivic

Example 10.1 *Eilende Wolken, Segler der Lüfte*, mm. 79–95.

reference to the homeland of embattled royal Mary Stuart. "Auld Rob Morris" is introduced by the oboe (m. 79), establishing a brief call and response between the woodwinds and Mary singing "There, where yon misty mountains rise in grandeur, / I can my empire's border see" (Example 10.1).

Following the scena, the aria with the title text "Eilende Wolken, Segler der Lüfte" ["scudding clouds, sailors of air"] begins, and the "Auld Rob Morris" theme returns two more times. In a cabaletta-like section, a spirited *Vivace* with pictorial blasts of hunting horns, Mary reminisces about the freedom of hunting in the woods with her friends. The echoes of the horns remind her of a "well-remembered voice … resounding over the highlands," and the oboe reemerges with the "Auld Rob Morris" theme weaving through galloping triplets (mm. 233–40). Finally, the theme appears augmented in the strings as Mary reprises her "Eilende Wolken" aria and bids farewell to Scotland in the coda (mm. 296–301).[8]

This concert aria also represents a significant first in Beach's compositional style. The use of "Auld Rob Morris" is the first time Beach quotes folk music in her compositions, something she would come to do regularly throughout her career. Her works that borrowed from or were inspired by Gaelic folk songs and texts include her popular "Gaelic" Symphony, op. 32

(1897), *Five Songs* with texts by Robert Burns, op. 43 (1899), the piano character piece "Scottish Legend," op. 54, no. 1 (1903), "Shena Van," op. 56, no. 4 (1904), *The Fair Hills of Éiré, O!* op. 91 for piano (1922), and a later setting of the "Fair Hills" tune as her final published work and only composition for solo organ, *Prelude on an Old Folk Tune* (1943).[9]

Initial critical reception of *Eilende Wolken* was mixed. A correspondent for the *New-Yorker Staats-Zeitung* found the aria emotional and moving, a critic for the *American Art Journal* called it "a powerfully written work of decided dramatic feeling and expression and one that would do credit to any composer,"[10] and a reviewer for the New York *Sun* lauded it as "worthy of any but the very greatest composers."[11] Even international reviewers found plenty to appreciate, with a critic for the *Hamburger Fremdenblatt* providing a positive review of the vocal–piano score that was published promptly after the premiere. Praising the construction of the principal theme, the reviewer encouraged singers to seek out Beach's work for a satisfying challenge: "The aria demands for an adequate rendering the ripest knowledge and a wide vocal compass."[12] Other reviewers were more critical, with one from *Harper's Weekly* calling the aria "decidedly disappointing," noting Beach's apparent immaturity as a composer with her aria giving "evidence of more future promise than present fulfillment."[13]

After its premiere, *Eilende Wolken* was rarely programmed with full orchestra, but the piano–vocal version was given occasionally by Beach and others. After the premiere, Beach accompanied vocal soloists performing the work twice, in 1894 and 1903.[14] The Chromatic Club of Boston, founded by Beach's compatriot Edward MacDowell, performed the aria on a March 8, 1901, concert, where the Club made Beach an honorary member. On March 15, 1901, the Baltimore Symphony Orchestra conducted by Ross Jungnickel presented the "Woman in Music Grand Concert," sponsored by the United Women of Maryland. The program included Beach's *Eilende Wolken* – the second performance with orchestra – and the Graduale from her Grand Mass in E-flat major, as well as works by Margaret Ruthven Lang, Cécile Chaminade, and English composer Liza Lehmann.[15]

Jephthah's Daughter, op. 53 (1903)

Beach's second dramatic work was another aria, *Jephthah's Daughter*. The story of Jephthah's daughter is related in Judges 11: Jephthah vowed to sacrifice the first thing that came out of his house as an offering to God for victory over the Ammonites, but when Jephthah approached his home, his daughter and only child greeted him dancing and playing her tambourine. Doomed to be sacrificed, she requests time to mourn, and it is this mourning scene that Beach sets in her dramatic aria with orchestra. The French poet Charles-Louis Mollevaut (1776–1844) adapted the story of Jephthah's daughter in a biblical narrative poem published in 1824, and selections from the poem – in particular, the five stanzas appearing in Beach's *Jephthah's Daughter* – were reprinted in French poetic anthologies.[16] Beach translated Mollevaut's poem into English herself, remaining faithful to the rhyme scheme and overall structure of the original.[17] Her English lyrics were translated into Italian by Isidora Martinez, a colleague of Beach's.[18] The original manuscript presents the lyrics in the following order: French, Beach's English translation, and Martinez's Italian translation.[19] Martinez is uncredited in the manuscript, but acknowledged in the piano–vocal version – which presents only Beach's and Martinez's translations – published by Schmidt shortly after the aria was completed in 1903.

Jephthah's Daughter is in a recitative and aria form. This distinction between the two major sections is apparent from the musical setting but is particularly demarcated by the text. The recitative introduction (mm. 1–37) begins with a stark, unaccompanied entrance by the soprano soloist. Lyrics in the third-person perspective set the scene: this is the final evening of Jephthah's daughter, whose futile laments echo through "the desert wild" during her last sleepless night. The recitative continues with a disjunct and declamatory melody over churning chords in the accompaniment.

The aria section shifts to first-person perspective; now, we hear Jephthah's daughter herself. Beach's translation preserves the ABAB rhyme scheme of the original poetic text; the A rhyme changes in each stanza, but the B remains the same.[20] Subdivisions within the aria section are marked with changing tempos and styles, as Jephthah's daughter confronts the inevitability of her sacrifice and searches for emotional resolution. Beginning in F-sharp minor and marked *Largo con molto espressione*, the aria opens with accompaniment that evokes the descending tetrachord of lament arias such as Purcell's "Dido's Lament," as the singer mourns that she must die, comparing the impermanence of her life with a flower and reflecting that her friends will go on to have children but "Great Jephthah's name must die" with her.

Though this aria is through-composed, Beach creates a sense of structure through her adherence to the rhyming structure of the original poem and the return of the aria's opening melodic gesture (m. 45) throughout. Susan Mardinly and Clarissa Aaron have observed that while the aria's opening melody is "distinctly Near-Eastern … Aida-like,"[21] with a sense of

Example 10.2 *Jephthah's Daughter*, mm. 44–53.

"familiarity to the modern educated listener,"[22] suggestive of other works with somewhat Orientalist aesthetics, both scholars agree that this motive is neither a quotation of, nor inspired by, an existing melody (Example 10.2).

An abrupt transition in the middle of the aria, beginning in m. 89, accelerates the tempo and destabilizes the harmony as the singer strives for justification, to find sense in her death and pray for strength for her family. The climax of the aria is reached in Beach's setting of the final stanza, as the singer pleads for God to bless her father with the years that she would have lived. This selfless emotional plea ends with the singer peaking on the highest note of the aria, a *fortissimo* C flat held for three measures, over three-quarters of the way through the work (m. 158).

The aria closes in G-flat major with a return to the recitative-like qualities of the opening section, with a marking of *Largo* and declamatory, unaccompanied entrances. The singer's resolve in the text, satisfied that she shall "learn to die" as long as her death is not in vain, is reflected in the transformed major key and stabilized accompaniment.[23] Block posits that the overall "downward thrust" of the aria contributes to a sense of tragedy and futility, despite the major-key final resolution.[24]

While there is no known commission nor a dedication that hints at the occasion for this composition, Clarissa Aaron has observed that the particular challenges of this aria – the nearly two-octave range, dense accompaniment, and a lengthy and loud dramatic high note late in the work – would make it well suited for Beach's friend and collaborator Marcella Craft, or a singer with a voice like hers. The translation of the lyrics into Italian may also support this theory, as Craft was active as a performer in Germany and Italy.[25] *Eilende Wolken, Jephthah's Daughter,* and some of Beach's other important contemporary works, like her Violin Sonata, op. 34 (1896), Piano Concerto, op. 45 (1900), and Piano Quintet, op. 67 (1907), were part of Beach's European tour in the 1910s, where she was accompanied by Craft as a traveling companion and occasional performing partner. While *Jephthah's Daughter* was published as piano–vocal score promptly after its premiere, the manuscript copies of these works in full score were inadvertently left behind when Beach and Craft fled Europe at the start of World War I. Beach was eventually able to recover the manuscripts, but not until another European trip in the 1930s.[26]

Scholars have explored the possibility of biographical connections between Beach's life and her creative choices, especially when tantalizing parallels between her personal life and her musical subjects emerge. Adrienne Fried Block argues in favor of a potential biographical interpretation for *Jephthah's Daughter.* As in some of Beach's compositions in the early 1900s, especially the Piano Concerto, Block interprets *Jephthah's Daughter* as having a theme that points to potential strife in the relationships between Beach, her husband, and her mother. Block compares the "pathos" and the parallel relationship between a dead (or soon-to-be-dead) daughter and her father in *Jephthah's Daughter* to an earlier song by Beach, "Jeune fille et jeune fleur" (1885) that she made into a central motive in the Piano Concerto. Block supports this interpretation with an additional personal connection gleaned from a 1986 interview with David Buxbaum (son of Beach's close friend and collaborator, mezzo-soprano Lillian Buxbaum) when she observes, "the reference to Jephthah's daughter, who would die childless, had resonance for Beach's life: after seventeen years of marriage, there were still no children, nor would there be any, something she may have regretted."[27] Other scholars are more skeptical of a direct biographical interpretation of the aria. Aaron denies a biographical reading, pointing to an article published in *The Etude* where the interviewer William Armstrong states that, aside from occasional requests or commissions, "she composes when she feels the inclination moves her to it."[28] But, Aaron does allow for salient points of emotional camaraderie between Beach and Jephthah's daughter: "childlessness, namelessness, and resolve in the face of patriarchal control."[29]

Cabildo, op. 149 (1932)[30]

Beach was interested in American opera for many years before she started composing *Cabildo.* She mentioned in a 1915 interview that there was "a great deal of untouched material for musical inspiration in the works of our American poets," but lamented the lack of acceptable topics from events in American history "for the simple reason that it is all too recent for the necessary haze of romance to have been sufficiently drawn over it. How ridiculous it would be for example, to attempt to put Lincoln or Grant on the stage in an opera." She suggested a few alternatives:

There are, however, some picturesque moments in our history which might be made use of for opera texts, particularly those connected with Indian life and with the Spanish settlement of California, where many beautiful and suggestive incidents are to be found. But here of course we are dealing with something which is not typically American from the point of view of our generation.[31]

She may have had in mind some recent works by American composers, such as Mary Carr Moore's opera *Narcissa, or The Cost of Empire* (1909), about a massacre of Mormon missionaries set in the Oregon Territory, or even Puccini's *La fanciulla del West* (1910).[32] Beach's opinions, and the operas of her contemporaries, capture the many ways that white American composers were attempting to navigate the dual local and exotic qualities of African American and Native American music traditions in their efforts to locate a uniquely American musical identity. Native American and African American music traditions have the aesthetic advantage of sounding appealingly exotic to Beach's fellow New Englanders with British or German origins, while allowing composers to claim ownership of the music as representative of the United States by virtue of its origin within the geographic confines of North America. In the interview, Beach concluded that she did not believe that the future sound of American music would be significantly shaped by Native American and African American music and topics.[33]

Beach's concept of what is "typically American," while she did not clearly define it, seems to be founded on the Anglo–German–Dutch cultural roots of the Northeastern United States. Continuing her suggestions about more suitable topics for operas reveals her preference for stories that are connected to the Northeast:

On the other hand the old New York legends of Rip Van Winkle and Ichabod Crane and similar old American stories might make good material for opera, as they contain a great deal that is really American. The situations and character we can understand fully as they hail from the foundation of the modern American nation, whereas Indian and Spanish-California themes must ever remain to a great extent foreign to our innermost feelings.[34]

Both *Rip Van Winkle* and the *Legend of Sleepy Hollow* (whose main character is schoolmaster Ichabod Crane) had been used as subjects for English-language operas in the late nineteenth century: George Frederick Bristow's *Rip Van Winkle* (1855) and Max Maretzek's *Sleepy Hollow, or The Headless Horseman* (1879).[35] Beach clearly believed audiences in Europe and the (primarily Northeastern) United States could relate to foreign operas featuring ancient Roman and Egyptian royalty, or Italian peasants, but not to any characters or stories from African American or Native American culture presented in English.

Furthermore, while Beach's characterization of her suggested stories as "old New York legends" is a bit misconstrued, it is revealing. She clearly thinks of these stories as old legends because they have the feeling of stories that, in their topic and narrative, mimic some qualities of folklore. *Rip Van Winkle* (1819) and *The Legend of Sleepy Hollow* (1820) were stories published by American author Washington Irving (1783–1859). Both of Irving's stories make use of fairy-tale tropes – tricksters, ghosts, and pastoral settings – that are common in German, Scandinavian, English, and Irish tales seeded into American culture by European colonists. While the stories are closely related to North America's colonial era in time and sensibility, they do not quite constitute a US folklore.[36]

Beach may have been considering ways to write American opera as early as 1914. As she returned from a concert tour of Europe with her friend and collaborator Marcella Craft, the prima donna of the Munich Opera, a shipmate and reporter for *Musical America* asked Beach whether or not she was likely to write an opera.

"Shall you ever write operas?" I asked. Her face lit up . . . "How did you know about that?" she smiled. "If you looked among all that manuscript in my trunk in the hold, it's quite possible you might find some beginnings along that line. I want very much to write an opera some day and hear Miss Craft sing in it. That would be work worthwhile."[37]

Considering that Beach had just spent three years touring in Germany and Italy, reveling in what she described as the "tremendous respect"[38] of art music in the everyday lives of Europeans, it is likely that the opera she may have begun sketching for Craft would have been quite different in scope or topic from *Cabildo*.

She continued along these lines in a 1917 interview, also for *Musical America*, where she discussed the potential role of women composers in the postwar years. When asked about balancing her concert and composing activities, she admitted that in the summertime when she returns to New Hampshire to compose, she mostly creates smaller works:

For anything large scale I need a path quite clear of more or less distant concert duties and obligations. After a few more years of travel and recital-giving, I may settle down for a big, sustained effort – an opera, perhaps, if I can obtain a fine libretto. But I am much too enthusiastic a traveler yet to settle down, too fond of my audiences to give them up.[39]

By the time she arrived at her studio in the MacDowell Colony to begin her opera, with an apparently "fine libretto" in hand, decades had passed since her initial statements on the genre, and her concept of American identity and musical style had developed in response to the changing sonic landscape around her.

The source of *Cabildo*'s libretto was Nan Bagby Stephens' one-act play of the same name. Stephens (1883–1946) was a playwright, author, composer, and educator from Atlanta, Georgia, whose mentor and neighbor was author Joel Chandler Harris, better known by his pen name "Uncle Remus." Harris coached her in writing his style of African American dialect, a prominent feature of Stephens' novels and plays. The play *Cabildo* was premiered on September 28, 1926, by the workshop company at Le Petit Theatre Vieux Carré in New Orleans, a theater just across the across the street from the Cabildo building that served as the setting of the play.[40]

Cabildo was presented again on March 1, 1930, along with two other one-act plays as part of the student theater troupe's midwinter program at Agnes Scott College in Atlanta, where Stephens attended school and later taught playwriting. The College's yearbook, *The Silhouette*, provided program information and a photo of the performance (Figure 10.1). Since Agnes Scott was, and still is, a women's university, all the parts in this performance were played by the female students. The feature in *The Silhouette* provides additional information about the setting and staging. The "scene" is described as a "ground floor prison cell with courtyard beyond, the old Cabildo, New Orleans." The temporal shifts in the plot were described with the additional note that the stage was "darkened to denote the passage of time."[41]

Cabildo's single act is divided into three sections: a Prologue, set in the "modern day"; a main Scene set in January 1815, on the eve of a climactic

CABILDO

By NAN BAGBY STEPHENS

Characters as They Enter for the Prologue and Epilogue

MILDRED McCALIP . . . . *The Barker*
MARY LOUISE THAMES . . . . *Mary, a Bride*
PENELOPE BROWN . . . . *Tom, the Groom*
A Crowd of Sightseers

THE PLAY

SHIRLEY McPHAUL . . . . *Pierre La Fitte, a Pirate, Yet a Great Gallant*
MARY FRANCES TORRANCE . . . . *Dominique You, Another Pirate*
JULIA GRIMMET . . . . *The Gaoler of the Cabildo*
MARGUERITE GERARD . *Valerie, a Young Frenchwoman, in Love with Pierre*

Scene—Ground floor prison cell with courtyard beyond the old Cabildo, New Orleans.

Time—The present. Shortly before the Battle of New Orleans, January, 1815. The present.

The stage was darkened to denote the passage of time.

Figure 10.1 Program and Photo of *Cabildo* by Nan Bagby Stephens, presented by the Blackfriars of Agnes Scott College, 1930. *The Silhouette* vol. 27 (1930), pp. 108–109.

battle during the War of 1812; and a short Epilogue returning to the modern-day setting. After a brief overture, the Prologue introduces two newlyweds, Mary and Tom, on a tour of the Cabildo in the present day. The Barker, their melodramatic guide, tells the story of Pierre Lafitte and his escape, suggesting that the pirate may have had help from a mysterious lover. Mary's imagination is captured by the suggestion of a forbidden love story between a dashing pirate and noble lady, so she remains behind in Pierre's cell, falling asleep and dreaming of the events of 1815.

The lights dim and rise as the wails of imprisoned pirates sound through the Cabildo. After bribing the Gaoler, Pierre and his lieutenant Dominique You discuss their plans to free the pirate and the false accusations that led to Pierre's imprisonment. Pierre was accused of stealing a bracelet from Lady Valerie and then sinking the ship taking her to France to cover the crime. Pierre claims the bracelet was exchanged with Valerie as a promise of love, and he resolves to die to atone for his inability to save her. At this moment, she appears to him as an apparition, begging him to live and join the defense of New Orleans as a hero to clear his name. In the climactic scene, Pierre and Valerie sing a heartfelt love duet, and as her ghost departs, she lifts the latch on the cell, allowing Pierre to escape.

In the brief Epilogue, Tom returns to the cell to find Mary asleep. She awakens convinced that her dream is the true ending to the story of Pierre Lafitte and Lady Valerie. The opera closes with the two newlyweds singing about the power of love, both theirs and that of Pierre and Valerie.

While it is unclear how it came to be chosen as the opera's libretto, *Cabildo* and its author are aligned with Amy Beach's creative life. Stephens was a fellow MacDowell colonist, whose stories were set in the everyday life or historical events of the American South. *Cabildo* has appealing historical elements that fit within Beach's previously stated criteria for American opera: a plot rooted in American history (but not relying on Native American or African American themes), authored by an American, and with the additional assets of a light melodramatic romance and a setting that prompts the incorporation of distinctive folk songs. Beach likely would have found collaboration with Stephens to be both practical and satisfying, relying on their mutual creative respect and expertise to undertake this new endeavor.

Additionally, the potential for *Cabildo* to be developed as an opera suitable for a college or workshop seems designed from the outset. Perhaps in response to beginning this project during the Great Depression and acknowledging that demands for grand opera performances would have declined, Beach and Stephens may have speculated that the modest cast and accompaniment of *Cabildo* and prior success in workshops and colleges as a play could fulfill the needs of an emerging market serving college programs, opera workshops, and radio opera programming.

Amy Beach's record of composing *Cabildo* reveals elements of her regular compositional process at work. Beach borrowed from her own body of work for melodies, approached new folk tunes through harmonizing at the piano, and relied on the familiar backbone of piano and voice to produce an initial draft of the opera quickly. Spending part of each summer composing at a prodigious pace at the MacDowell Colony, she maintained a steady output of songs and smaller pieces, while her larger works could remain unpublished for years as she continued to refine them.

Beach recorded notes about her compositional process in her diaries. For many years, she kept five-year diaries that featured small spaces to write daily notes and reflections for the same day each year. Beach's entries commonly consist of brief notes of the work she did that day, the weather, performances, social visits, and – when at the MacDowell Colony – the types of birds she heard outside her studio. (For example, see Figure 10.2.) Beginning in the early 1920s, Beach visited the MacDowell Colony for at least a month every year. She frequently expressed that she was at her most productive while she was at the Colony; from her first visit in 1922 onward she sketched or completed nearly every work she published in a year during the month that she spent there each summer.[42] According to her diary entries for June 1932, Beach began work on the opera as soon as she arrived at the Colony.[43] She had received the libretto from Stephens before her trip and began working piecemeal on sections of the opera. With the freedom to focus entirely on composition, she completed the initial sketch of *Cabildo* in just eleven days.

Her entry for June 1, 1932, recorded that her first task for the day was working on *Cabildo*, starting with a love theme borrowed from her own works. She noted, "Began on opera (Nan's book). Took sop. aria first, using 'When Soul is joined.'"[44] This "aria," indicated for the soprano role of Valerie, would eventually become "Ah, love is a jasmine vine," the climactic scene of *Cabildo* sung by Valerie before she is joined in duet by Pierre. Beach continued to make progress and by June 3 turned her attention to the "scene between Pierre and Dominique." While she does not specify, it is potentially a reference to the expository scene explaining the circumstances of Pierre's imprisonment and the plan by Pierre's brother Jean and the Lafitte pirates to free him. Beach's record of compositional activities for June 4, "worked hard," is more vague, but she was most pleased to receive "Creole folk tunes and a *dear* letter" from Stephens.[45] She spent the next day having "great fun harmonizing Creole tunes." While there is no record of precisely which tunes Stephens sent to Beach, she incorporated several Creole folk tunes and dance rhythms throughout *Cabildo*, demonstrating her familiarity with their musical idioms.[46]

Throughout her career Beach borrowed a variety of folk tunes in her piano and chamber compositions.[47] She usually familiarized herself with new folk material by setting it for piano, or piano and voice, gaining a sense of its rhythm and style. Beach explained in a 1917 interview that her

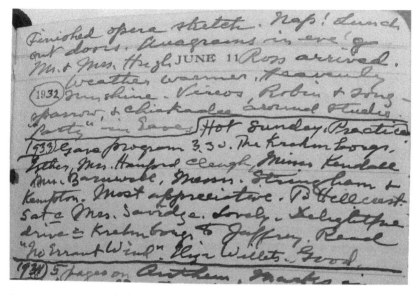

Figure 10.2 Amy Beach diary entry for June 11. The 1932 entry begins, "Finished opera sketch. Nap! Lunch outdoors. Anagrams in [evening]." Box 3, folder 5, Amy Cheney Beach (Mrs. H.H.A. Beach) Papers, 1835-1956, MC 51, Milne Special Collections and Archives, University of New Hampshire Library, Durham, NH.

autodidactic compositional techniques involved listening and score study in order not only to understand the style and construction of a work, but to integrate and internalize it to the point where she felt that it belonged to her and fit seamlessly into her own individual mode of expression.[48] Despite being her only opera, Beach's development of *Cabildo* is still representative of her process to create large works, including her lifelong habits of study and integration followed by composition.

Beach completed a sketch of the overture on June 7 and must have felt quite confident in what she had accomplished during her first week at the Colony, since the next day she asked Mrs. MacDowell for permission to invite Stephens to hear the early version of the opera later that month. Finally, on June 11, 1932, Beach cheerfully reported, "Finished opera sketch. Nap!" (Figure 10.2).

Stephens arrived at the Colony on the evening of June 25, and the next day Beach performed the opera for Stephens, who was "too delighted for words," "perfectly satisfied [with] [the] theatrical aspect of [the] work," and "adores the music." Pleased with the reception of this performance, Beach gave it again for approximately twenty-five people in her studio, to "much appreciation" from her audience. The next day, Beach and Stephens continued to work on the opera, with Beach remarking in her diary that it "grows better!" On the final day of Stephens's visit, June 28, Beach and Stephens toured the grounds of the MacDowell Colony and continued to work on the opera before Stephens left early the next morning. After completing the sketch and the "details" of her first opera in only a month, Beach left the MacDowell Colony for the summer on June 30, 1932. With the initial draft of the opera complete, Beach continued to compose out the orchestration to include violin and cello parts that mostly mirror similar lines in the piano.

Beginning in the 1940s, Beach and Stephens began to plan a premiere for *Cabildo* near Stephens's hometown of Atlanta, Georgia. In a letter to Beach, Stephens recounted a recital of the University of Georgia Glee Club accompanied by the chamber music ensemble, led by College of Music director Hugh Hodgson (1893–1969). In addition to performances by the chamber orchestra and some vocal soloists, the group also staged a one-act operetta, Gilbert and Sullivan's *Trial by Jury* (1875). Stephens said, "the more I heard, that night, the more convinced I was that Mr. Hodgson could give our opera a beautiful premiere,"[49] generous praise for a school that began student opera performances only in the 1930s. Afterwards, Stephens approached Hodgson about premiering the opera at the University of Georgia. She forwarded Hodgson's response to Beach, noting that he wished to see a score and – as a pianist himself – he was likely to be enticed by the prominent piano part in the accompaniment.

After Beach agreed to premiere *Cabildo* with Hodgson at the University of Georgia, Stephens wrote that she was thrilled at the progress, especially since Beach planned to attend the premiere, tentatively scheduled for March 1941. Stephens again lauded the quality of the student performers in the chamber music group, calling the instrumentalists "really outstanding."[50] Her praise hints that Hodgson was planning to request – or had already requested – permission from Beach to expand the original piano trio score for the premiere performance.[51] Stephens also offered to use her local contacts to increase the event's visibility. She wanted to approach other university music directors about *Cabildo* as soon as the premiere had been scheduled at the University of Georgia and discussed using her connections with the Atlanta arts scene to ensure that critics from local papers and national music periodicals would be able to attend and review the premiere to raise the profile of their opera.[52]

It soon became evident, however, that progress toward a premiere had stalled. Stephens wrote to Beach in March 1941 that Hodgson and the Glee

Club were on tour until the end of the month and that preparation for the premiere would start as soon as the group returned, but Hodgson had not given her firm production dates; Stephens hypothesized that they would be in late April or early May. Perhaps due to restrictions on funding, travel, or other scheduling conflicts within the university's music program, the opera would not be premiered at all that year.

Whatever the reasons, Hodgson was unable to arrange a premiere before Beach's death, and the first performance of the opera was given at the Pound Auditorium at the University of Georgia on February 27, 1945, just two months after Beach passed away from heart disease. The University of Georgia issued a press release announcing the premiere, and a short article promoting the performance appeared in the student newspaper, *The Red and Black*, on February 23, 1945. This article reported that *Cabildo*, paired with Pergolesi's comic intermezzo *La serva padrona* (1733), would be staged at the university's music department. This announcement also mentions Hodgson's expanded orchestration of *Cabildo* that included "sixteen stringed instruments and piano."[53] The evening's performance featured a mix of students, alumni, and faculty performing both on stage and in the accompanying orchestra.

A lengthy review of the opera, including photos from each performance, was published in the March 4, 1945, issue of the *Atlanta Constitution.* Reviewer Marguerite Bartholomew was impressed by the music department's staging of the premiere, describing the event as an "epoch-making success." Bartholomew also highlighted the local interest of the performance, describing Stephens as a "gifted musician and playwright of Atlanta."[54] Acknowledging Beach's recent death, Bartholomew provided a brief, eulogistic vita highlighting her accomplishments as "America's foremost woman composer" and confirming Beach's credentials in choral writing by calling attention to her anthem *Christ in the Universe,* op. 132, recently performed by Beach's church in New York, St. Bartholomew's Episcopal. Bartholomew described how Beach had completed the opera at the MacDowell Colony and credited Stephens with taking the lead to bring the opera to Hodgson's attention. She also confirmed that Beach gave permission to Hodgson to alter the score, adding "parts for viola, double-bass, and French horn, employing an instrumental ensemble of 16 in addition to the piano," although aside from naming a few instruments and the total number in the ensemble, she did not provide any more specific information about the instrumental performers. These parts have since been lost. The same chamber orchestra, under Hodgson's direction, provided accompaniment for both *Cabildo* and *La serva padrona.*

Bartholomew praised the "fine momentum" and "ecstatic climaxes in the dream scene" created by Beach's use of rhythm, melody, and harmony. She noted that the vocal declamation and harmony seemed reminiscent of Wagner and observed that several "old French [*sic*] folk songs that give attractive local color" had been woven throughout the score. Overall, the premiere was received as a success by the enthusiastic audience, with a "special ovation" for the librettist and guest of honor, Nan Bagby Stephens.[55]

Sometime in 1945, Hodgson returned the loaned manuscripts of *Cabildo* to the New England Trust Company in Boston, the executors of Beach's estate. Following Beach's death, Henry Austin from the Schmidt Company attempted to locate the *Cabildo* manuscript through Beach's close friend, the soprano Ruth Shaffner; evidently, when Hodgson returned the scores to the New England Trust, he had inadvertently stymied Austin's efforts to bring the scores to the Schmidt vaults in order to complete the publication of Beach's final works in the years following her death. Eventually, the manuscript scores and parts were sent to the MacDowell Colony according to the terms of Beach's will, which specified that they should benefit from her work. These manuscripts, and other archival materials of Beach's, were eventually purchased from the Colony by the University of Missouri–Kansas City in 1972, where they remain today.[56]

"Vital Peculiarity": Creole Music and Cabildo

Amy Beach combined musical material from several sources to craft the romantic, Creole-tinged setting of *Cabildo*. A few prominent themes appear for the first time in the Overture and Prologue sections, during the Barker's exposition of the legend of Pierre and Valerie, allowing the musical motives associated with the events of the story introduced at the beginning to be repeated and developed later in the Scene. Among the most frequently repeated motives are the ones based on Creole folk songs and dances, including themes associated with Pierre and the ball where Pierre and Valerie fell in love. These folk-based elements are woven together with music borrowed from Beach's own oeuvre and set within the advanced expressive and harmonic language Beach explored in her late works.

At some point Beach prepared a study of Creole folk music, focusing on distinctive rhythms and instruments. These "Notes on Creole Folk Music," which Beach may have presented to the local Hillsborough Music Club, consist of three typewritten pages with handwritten musical examples.[57] While these notes are filed in the Amy Beach Collection at Dimond Library

Example 10.3a Habanera rhythm written in Amy Beach's "Notes on Creole Folk Music."

Example 10.3b *Cabildo*, The "Governor's Ball" theme with the habanera rhythm in the bass, mm. 294–301.

at the University of New Hampshire in the same folder as the incomplete sketch of the opera dated June 1932, the "Notes" are undated.

In her "Notes," Beach commented that the "vital peculiarity of Creole folk music lies in its rhythms, the most frequently recurring of which is the rhythm of the habanera time."[58] Beginning with Spanish and French influences on the English contredanse, a popular social dance imported into European colonies in the Caribbean, the habanera developed through the early 1800s, picking up a distinctive dotted ostinato accompaniment introduced by Black musicians in Cuba (Example 10.3a). The habanera, or *contradanza habanera*, is named after Havana, where it was a popular dance among all classes. A dance for couples with slow and sensual movements, its influence can be found in other Latin American genres like the Argentine tango. In the late nineteenth century, the "exotic" style and unmistakable rhythm of the habanera were reexported to French and Spanish composers and made famous in works such as Bizet's opera *Carmen*.[59]

The habanera rhythm occurs multiple times throughout the score of *Cabildo* as an icon and an index of dance, appearing whenever characters mention the fateful Governor's Ball where Pierre and Valerie danced and fell in love (Example 10.3b). It is one of a few themes, aside from Lady Valerie's motive and Pierre's "noble pirate" motive, to occur in both the present-day Prologue and the 1815 Scene. This familiar dance rhythm becomes an indicator of the union between Pierre and Valerie, and between the diverse styles that have contributed to the music of the United States, persisting through time in both the past and present-day scenes of the opera.

Beach goes on to explain that "the origin of the habanera and of the syncopated waver in its rhythm is due to America having been settled by Spaniards, Portuguese, and French. Also the Indian has had something to do with influencing Creole music, and the African slaves have contributed some of their drum language to it," alluding to the multiple cultural influences present in the folk music of New Orleans.[60] Beach's final comments offer a generalization of the different themes that are prominent in the texts of Creole music:

> With the exception of a few nursery rhymes, the Creole knows only love songs. The few exceptions, hardly worth naming, are satirical songs, some comic darky tunes (even here a love theme is sure to be interwoven), [but] that is all. The only patriotic songs are the so-called national hymns of which there happen to be a few; the others are marches of stereotyped variety, and most of them have not a trace of national character. The love songs are sung by old and young, and are appreciated at a tender age by these people who mature so early.[61]

Even though her analysis now sounds simplistic or ethnocentric, Beach made use of many of these musical topics or themes in *Cabildo*. The first recognizable motive of the opera, which appears in the overture, is folklike and references a satire song of a fancy ball held by the upper class.[62] She also borrows the melodic and rhythmic contour of a love song, "Belle Layote," as Pierre Lafitte's primary musical motive. A generic anthemic- or patriotic-style topos, characterized by an ascending line leading to a sustained high note on the word "America" in the libretto, acts as another motive to indicate the patriotic defense of New Orleans by the pirates. The only directly quoted folk song is a translation of the Creole song "Quan' mo 'te d'un grand chimin," a tune with a folk or minstrel-like trope of a comic beggar, sung by the Gaoler.

In many ways *Cabildo* is consistent with Beach's style. The opera's tuneful melodic lines, rich harmonic colors, and sometimes unexpected key changes reflect the style that she had developed for herself throughout her career. When asked her opinion about modern trends in the new compositions of the twentieth century, Beach was dismissive of modernist works with "unceasing dissonance"[63] or the "purely intellectual ... of deep interest as problems ... but never for a moment touching our emotions."[64] Despite her reluctance to embrace the extended harmonies and techniques favored by ultramodernists and serialists, Beach never stagnated in a conservative Romantic milieu. She continued to be influenced – consciously or unconsciously – by the expressive potential of the modern music around her. Her late choral works, such as *Canticle of the Sun*, op. 123 (1924); *Christ in the Universe*, op. 132 (1931); and *Hearken Unto Me,* op. 139 (1934), utilize extended harmonic functions in vocal works for dramatic effect, pairing "progressive tonality" with an intended emotional resolution from struggle to transcendence.[65] *Cabildo* demonstrates this expressive approach to harmony and key relationships, eschewing traditional motions between key areas for dramatic effect, evoking composers such as Wagner, Strauss, and Mahler who used tonality for expressive, rather than structural, ends. G major and its closely related keys, with chromatic diversions interspersed, are the foundational key areas for the Prelude and Epilogue, while the dream sequence that makes up the majority of the opera explores distant harmonic territory, with the climactic moment of the opera arriving in the key of G flat.[66] The disjunction in time (or reality) between the outer scenes in the modern day and the past of Mary's dream is reinforced through the use of these distant keys.

Beach continued to develop her style in response to the music she heard around her, an ever-expanding world colored by jazz, Modernism, popular music, and the shifting definitions of what constituted art music. Initially, she had expressed reservations about the incorporation of jazz and non–Anglo-American folk music into compositions touted as "American," especially when it came to opera.[67] In *Cabildo*, however, Beach demonstrated a personal definition of American music that had expanded from her early comments about suitable sounds and subjects, to include traditional music of an iconically American place that was quite distant from her New England base, as well as a complex and expressive harmonic language that was not so distant from other modern composers' dramatic works.

Conclusion

While these dramatic works constitute only a small part of Beach's oeuvre, they represent landmarks in her lifelong creative and compositional process. Beach's infrequent choice to compose in dramatic genres – staged or unstaged – and conservative choices of text when she did, suggest a lingering Bostonian skepticism toward the theatrical, balanced by her prolific composition of chamber, choral, and church music. Nevertheless, her talent for vocal writing matched to dramatic texts, akin to her ballads and art songs, shines through.

Tracing the arc of these dramatic works through Beach's career reveals a steadily maturing composer wielding an ever-expanding harmonic vocabulary to great dramatic effect. Beginning with the first instances of "Auld Rob Morris" in *Eilende Wolken*, Beach's use of folk music for its distinctive colors and dramatic effects became a hallmark of her style, in addition to her economical borrowing and reinterpretation of her own previously composed songs. Despite her categorization as a primarily Romantic-era composer, the works she created during the twentieth century demonstrate that she continued to be cognizant of new musical styles and the tastes of performers and audiences, and that she made the effort to incorporate these into her compositions. The history of each of these dramatic works, and Beach's partnerships with Alves, Martinez, Craft, and Stephens, also correspond to Beach's work with female artists throughout her career. She supported, mentored, and created compositions with female poets, artists, composers, and performers throughout her life, forming an extended "family" of talented women who were shaping the future of American art.

Notes

1. Adrienne Fried Block, *Amy Beach Passionate Victorian: The Life and Work of an American Composer, 1867–1944* (New York: Oxford, 1998), 183.
2. Quoted in Susan Mardinly, "Amy Beach: Muse, Conscience, and Society," *Journal of Singing* 70, no. 5 (May 2014): 537.
3. David McKay, "Opera in Colonial Boston," *American Music* 3, no. 2 (Summer 1985): 138.
4. C. Katie Alves to Beach, February 15, 1892, box 1, folder 1, Amy Cheney Beach (Mrs. H. H. A. Beach) Papers, 1835–1956, MC 51, Milne Special Collections and Archives, University of New Hampshire Library, Durham, NH. Quoted in Randy Charles Brittain, "Festival Jubilate, op. 17 by Amy Cheney Beach (1867–1944): A Performing Edition" (DMA diss, University of North Carolina at Greensboro, 1994), 26.
5. Mary Stuart was a popular tragic subject for opera in the nineteenth century: Donizetti's *Maria Stuarda* (1835) also used Schiller's play as its source. Other Mary Stuart operas include Luigi Carlini's *Maria Stuarda, regina di Scozia* (1818); Carlo Coccia's *Maria Stuart, regina di Scozia* (1827); and Louis Niedermeyer's French grand opera *Marie Stuart* (1844).
6. Mrs. H. H. A. Beach, "Scena and Aria: Mary Stuart (Schiller)," unpublished orchestral score manuscript, [1892], New England Conservatory Library, accessed July 1, 2021 https://imslp.org/wiki/Mary_Stuart%2C_Op.18_(Beach%2C_Amy_Marcy).

7. Block, *Amy Beach, Passionate Victorian*, 73.

8. Block, *Amy Beach, Passionate Victorian*, 74. Block identified the "Auld Rob Morris" melody used by Beach in vol. 1 of *Scots Minstrelsie: A National Monument of Scottish Song*, John Greig, ed. (Edinburgh: T. C. & E. C. Jack, 1892–1895): 110–11.

9. Beach's use of folk song wasn't limited to Anglo-Saxon or Gaelic folk music. Throughout her career she explored German, Balkan, Native American, African American, and Louisiana Creole folk styles. For more on Beach's use of folk music, see Adrienne Fried Block, "Dvořák, Beach, and American Music," in *A Celebration of American Music: Words and Music in Honor of H. Wiley Hitchcock*, eds. Richard Crawford, R. Allen Lott, and Carol J. Oja (Ann Arbor: University of Michigan Press, 1990), 256–80.

10. "Zweite Symphonie Konzert," *New-Yorker Staats-Zeitung*, December 3, 1892, translated in "Theatres and Concerts," *Boston Daily Transcript*, December 7, 1892, and "New York Symphony Society," *American Art Journal* (December 10, 1892). Quoted in Block, *Amy Beach, Passionate Victorian*, 74.

11. Brittain, "Festival Jubilate," 27.

12. Reprinted in "Critical Reviews and Notices," *Mrs. H. H. A. Beach* (Boston: Arthur P. Schmidt, 1906), 77–78.

13. Quoted in Block, *Amy Beach, Passionate Victorian*, 74.

14. Block, *Amy Beach, Passionate Victorian*, 76. Block notes that "in May 1894 Beach gave a concert of her own works at Wellesley College at the invitation of Professor Junius Welch Hill, her former harmony teacher; the contralto Mrs. Homer E. Sawyer sang the Mary Stuart aria to Beach's accompaniment. The same singer repeated the work on March 18, 1903 at Steinert Hall, Boston, at Beach's annual recital, with the composer at the piano (S. C. Williams, "Musical Matters," *Boston Advertiser*, March 19, 1903, called the work "very significant"). The work received a lukewarm review when it was performed with piano accompaniment by Mme Hesse-Sprotte [Anna Ruzena Sprotte] in St. Paul, Minn. in October 1910: Caryl B. Storrs, "Sprotte-Bliss Recital," *Minneapolis Star Tribune*, October 19, 1910, p. 12.

15. Block, *Amy Beach, Passionate Victorian*, 173–75.

16. Clarissa E. Aaron, "A Story of Feminine Sacrifice: The Music, Text, and Biographical Connections in Amy Beach's Concert Aria Jephthah's Daughter" (Thesis, Seattle Pacific University, 2018), 19. Aaron also discovered that the same section of Mollevaut's poem, translated into English, appeared in the *Yale Literary Magazine* in 1841, another source Beach may have been able to access.

17. Aaron, "A Story of Feminine Sacrifice," 20–21. Beach had at least a working knowledge of important languages related to the study of music, including French and German. She translated musical treatises like Berlioz's treatise on orchestration, and as a teenager enjoyed completing

her language studies while doing daily drills on the piano. Block, *Amy Beach, Passionate Victorian*, 29.

18. Block, *Amy Beach, Passionate Victorian*, 347. Martinez was "a singer, conductor, and linguist, of Boston, who translated Italian, French, and German texts [for Beach] beginning with op. 51."

19. Mrs. H. H. A. Beach, "Jephthah's Daughter: Aria for Soprano," op. 53, unpublished orchestral score manuscript [1903], New England Conservatory Library, accessed July 1, 2021 https://imslp.org/wiki/Jephthah's_Daughter%2C_Op.53_(Beach%2C_Amy_Marcy).

20. Aaron, "A Story of Feminine Sacrifice," 9.

21. Mardinly, "Amy Beach: Muse, Conscience, and Society," 535.

22. Aaron, "A Story of Feminine Sacrifice," 11.

23. Aaron, "A Story of Feminine Sacrifice," 18.

24. Block, *Amy Beach, Passionate Victorian*, 156.

25. Aaron, "A Story of Feminine Sacrifice," 4n16.

26. Block, *Amy Beach, Passionate Victorian*, 256.

27. Block, *Amy Beach, Passionate Victorian*, 156n28. The note about Beach possibly regretting not having children comes from Block's interview with David Buxbaum, Chebeague Island, ME, August 21, 1986. David's mother, Lillian, was a mezzo-soprano and collaborator of Beach's who inherited the composer's home in Centerville.

28. William Armstrong, "New Gems in the Old Classics: A Talk with Mrs. H. H. A. Beach," *The Etude* 22, no. 2 (February 1904): 51.

29. Aaron, "A Story of Feminine Sacrifice," 31–32.

30. The present author contributed a more extensive discussion on *Cabildo*, including detailed musical analysis and contextualization of the work within English-language opera in the United States, to the American Women Composer Pianists conference featuring scholarship on the works of Beach and Teresa Carreño, among others.

31. Edwin Hughes, "The Outlook for the Young American Composer: An Interview with the Distinguished American Composer, Mrs. H. H. A. Beach," *The Etude* 33, no. 1 (January 1915): 14.

32. Both *La fanciulla del West* and later Charles Wakefield Cadman's *Shanewis* were premiered at the New York Metropolitan Opera under the Music Director Giulio Gatti-Casazza. *Shanewis* and *Narcissa, or The Cost of Empire* were both winners of the David Bispham Memorial Medal, a prize established in 1921 to support composers of opera in English, most of whom used American librettists and subjects.

33. Hughes, "The Outlook for the Young American Composer," 14.

34. Hughes, "The Outlook for the Young American Composer," 14.

35. Maria F. Rich, et al. s.v. "Opera," *The New Grove Dictionary of American Music* v. 3, 415.

36. Folklore (n.) "the traditional beliefs, legends, and customs, current among the common people; the study of these." *Oxford English Dictionary Online* (accessed June 17, 2022). The interpretation of which stories, actions, or traditions constitute folklore is flexible, but most definitions place emphasis on transmission, specifically oral and informal transmission; the communication of cultural values; and the group authorship of the traditions by community members.

37. Clare P. Peeler, "American Woman Whose Musical Message Thrilled Germany," *Musical America* 20, no. 24 (October 17, 1914): 7.

38. Hughes, "The Outlook for the Young American Composer," 13.

39. H. F. P., "Believes Women Composers Will Rise to Greater Heights in World Democracy," *Musical America* 25, no. 25 (April 21, 1917): 3.

40. The Cabildo is now part of the Louisiana State Museum. Frederick Lamar Chapman, "A History of Le Petit Theatre du Vieux Carré" (PhD dissertation, Tulane University, 1971), 143.

41. Agnes Scott College, "Blackfriars Presents," *The Silhouette*, vol. 27, edited by Margaret Ogden (Decatur, GA: Agnes Scott College, 1930), 108–109. https://archive.org/stream/silhouette193027agne#page/108/mode/2up.

42. Mrs. H. H. A. Beach, "Twenty-Fifth Anniversary of a Vision," *Music Teachers National Association Proceedings* 27 (1932), 45–46.

43. Amy M. Beach Diary 1931–1935, box 3, folder 5, Beach Papers, University of New Hampshire.

44. "When Soul is Joined to Soul," op. 62 (1905), an art song by Beach. The text is a poem by Elizabeth Barrett Browning (1806–61).

45. Amy M. Beach Diary 1931–1935. Emphasis by Beach.

46. There are several earlier potential sources for the Creole folk tunes that appear in *Cabildo*, although no one collection contains all of the referenced melodies: George W. Cable, "The Dance in Place Congo," *Century Magazine* 31, no. 4 (February 1886): 517–31; George W. Cable, "Creole Slave Songs," *Century Magazine* 31, no. 6 (April 1886): 807–27; Clara Gottschalk Peterson, *Creole Songs from New Orleans in the Negro Dialect* (New Orleans: L. Grunewald, 1902); Maud Cuney Hare, *Six Creole Folk-Songs* (New York: Carl Fischer, 1921).

47. Arthur Wilson, "Mrs. H. H. A. Beach: A Conversation on Musical Conditions in America," *Musician* 27, no. 1 (January 1912): 10. The origins of the *Variations on Balkan Themes*, op. 60, *Eskimos*, op. 64, and *Suite for Two Pianos Founded upon Old Irish Melodies*, op. 104, among many others, were similar in that Beach was exposed to a collection or presentation of folk music and took on study of it to explore themes and styles.

48. Harriette Brower, *Piano Mastery: Talks with Master Pianists and Teachers*, Second ser. (New York: Stokes, 1917), 187.

49. Letter from Nan Bagby Stephens to Amy Beach, June 4, 1940, box 1, folder 14, Beach Papers, University of New Hampshire.

50. Letter from Stephens to Beach, September 23, 1940, box 1, folder 14, Beach Papers, University of New Hampshire.

51. Marguerite Bartholomew, "Opera Librettoed by Atlantan Thrills Athens at Premiere," *Atlanta Constitution* (March 4, 1945) p. A11.

52. Letter from Stephens to Beach, March 23, 1941, box 1, folder 14, Beach Papers, University of New Hampshire. Stephens specifically mentions wanting to contact Paul Weaver at the Eastman School of Music, and connections at *Musical America, Musical Courier,* and *Musical Digest*; critical reviews of *Cabildo's* 1944 premiere do not appear in these publications.

53. Joe Conckle, "'Cabildo,' Short Opera Produced by Students, To Have Premiere Here," *The Red and Black* (February 23, 1945): 1.

54. Bartholomew, "Opera Librettoed by Atlantan Thrills Athens at Premiere," p. A11.

55. Bartholomew, "Opera Librettoed by Atlantan Thrills Athens at Premiere," p. A11.

56. Leslie Petteys, "*Cabildo* by Amy Marcy Beach," 12. MacDowell is an artists' colony, not an archive. While MacDowell does maintain the James Baldwin Library (formerly the Savidge Library), which contains many donated works by MacDowell fellows, it is primarily for published versions of works created or completed at the Colony, not for the preservation of archival material from former fellows.

57. Letter from Rita Morgan (Fuller Public Library) to Leslie Petteys, April 13, 1981, box 9, folder 6, Adrienne Fried Block Papers, Milne Special Collections and Archives, University of New Hampshire Library, Durham, NH.

58. Amy M. Beach, "Notes on Creole Folk Music," [1], box 6, folder 12, Beach Papers (Fuller Public Library deposit), University of New Hampshire.

59. Frances Barulich and Jan Fairley, s.v. "Habanera," *Grove Music Online*, Oxford Music Online.

60. Beach's notes on Creole music lack references or citations, but the statement about the habanera is a close paraphrase of Henry Krehbiel's analysis of the dance in his book *Afro-American Folksongs: A Study in Racial and National Music* (New York: Schirmer, 1914), 115–16.

61. Beach, "Notes on Creole Folk Music," 3.

62. Block, *Amy Beach, Passionate Victorian*, 276. George W. Cable, "The Dance in Place Congo," *Century Magazine* 31, no. 4 (February 1886): 528.

63. Mrs. H. H. A. Beach, "Mission of the Present-Day Composer," *Triangle of Mu Phi Epsilon* (Feb 1942): 71.

64. Mrs. H. H. A. Beach, "Emotion vs Intellect in Music," *Proceedings of the Music Teachers National Association* (1931): 18.

65. Block, *Amy Beach, Passionate Victorian*, 266–68. Block also wrote frequently on Beach's use and reuse of identifiable musical themes and analysis of her late works, including: "Amy Beach's Music on Native American Themes," *American Music* 8, no.2 (Summer 1990): 141–66; "Dvořák, Beach and

American Music," in *A Celebration of American Music: Words and Music in Honor of H. Wiley Hitchcock*, eds. Richard Crawford, R. Allen Lott, and Carol J. Oja (Ann Arbor, WI: University of Michigan Press, 1990), 256–80; "On Beach's *Variations on Balkan Themes*, op. 60," *American Music* 11, no. 3 (Fall 1993): 368–71; "A 'Veritable Autobiography'? Amy Beach's Piano Concerto in C-Sharp Minor, op. 45," *Musical Quarterly* 78, no. 2 (Summer 1994): 394–416; and her critical edition of Beach's *Quartet for Strings (in One Movement)*, op. 89, *Music in the United States of America*, vol. 3 (Madison, WI: A-R Editions, 1994).

66. G flat is also the original key of "When Soul is Joined to Soul," the song that became the climactic love duet. Beach's color-key associations are often discussed along with her music; that the prominent key area of the Prologue and Epilogue, G major, is associated with red, and a prominent key area explored in the dream section is D flat, associated with violet, seems more coincidental than symbolic.

67. Hughes, "The Outlook for the Young American Composer," 14.

## PART III

Reception

11 | Phoenix Redivivus: Beach's Posthumous Reputation

E. DOUGLAS BOMBERGER

When Beach died in December 1944, her circle of supporters had grown smaller but no less loyal. The pair of concerts in Washington's Phillips Gallery in honor of her seventy-fifth birthday was a testament to the range of her musical output and the determination of violinist Elena de Sayn to share it with a wide audience.[1] Beach's many friends from the MacDowell Colony remembered her fondly despite her absence in recent years. Her circle of younger female musician friends remained intensely loyal. But by this time most of her works were out of print and performances were rare, as it seemed likely that Beach's name would soon disappear from American music.

Fast forward to 2022, and Beach is more prominent than ever. In a documentary in the series "Now Hear This" that aired on PBS in April 2022, violinist Scott Yoo calls her "a first-rate genius," "America's greatest Romantic composer," and "the towering equal of the greatest European composers."[2] To borrow a quaint New England expression that Beach would probably have recognized, "You can't get there from here." The story of Beach's renaissance can be told in two separate but related streams: one focused on scholarship and the other on performance and recording. In order to place these in context, however, we will need to examine the reasons for her decline, which have as much to do with changing musical tastes and historical events as they do with her music.

Beach's Decline

The pinnacle of Beach's fame was achieved in the mid-1910s. She had cannily taken advantage of her European reviews to build a national reputation upon her return to the United States in 1914. For three years after her return, she performed extensively until personal circumstances led her to reduce her schedule in 1918. By the time she was ready to resume an active career in the early 1920s, the postwar arts climate was shifting with the rise of Modernism in art music and the widespread popularity of jazz, which had burst onto the scene in 1917.[3]

As Kara Anne Gardner has chronicled, the decades before and after 1900 witnessed the growing influence of women as performers and patrons in American music. By 1922 there was a backlash, prompting critic Deems Taylor to write of the "feminization" of musical culture and its deleterious effect on the status of serious musical composition.[4] Gardner identifies Beach's skill at connecting with the emotional needs of her female audience as both a strength and a weakness for her long-term reputation, noting: "When modernists redefined their 'erratic tendencies' toward experimentation as independent and American, Beach's musical style began to be viewed as anachronistic."[5] Furthermore, in her study of avant-garde American music in the 1920s, Carol Oja provides ample evidence of the misogynism of modern music in the later decades of Beach's life. Women played crucial roles as organizers, editors, and patrons of modern music, but they were not welcomed as composers or conductors. Critics from Paul Rosenfeld to Deems Taylor were dismissive of female composers on principle, and composers from George Antheil to Virgil Thomson were jealous of competition from women composers. The modernist clique was even more of a "boys club" than the Second New England School had been a generation earlier. As a consequence, Oja points out that the only successful female American modernists were Marion Bauer and Ruth Crawford Seeger.[6] Although a few of Beach's late works – notably the String Quartet, op. 89, and the Five Improvisations, op. 148 – adopt some of the harmonic techniques of Modernism, she was still a Romantic at heart.

In similar fashion, Beach showed no interest in exploring the possibilities of jazz style. Throughout her life, she had been open to incorporating exotic influences in the form of melodies and harmonies. The "Gaelic" Symphony; the *Variations on Balkan Themes*, op. 60; *Eskimos*, op. 64; and even the Hermit Thrush pieces showed her willingness to find melodic interest in a wide range of source materials. Jazz presented a different challenge, however, as those who embraced it were drawn to its audacious rhythms and raucous timbres. To a Romantic like Beach, these parameters were not the ones that she wished to explore, as even her most harmonically adventurous late works remain firmly grounded in traditional rhythms and timbral combinations.

Beach also experienced frustration in later years as her works gradually fell out of print. She had enjoyed the benefits of a twenty-five-year exclusive relationship with Arthur P. Schmidt during her husband's lifetime, when some of her most ambitious works were written. The publisher was a close friend and medical patient of Dr. Beach, who clearly did what was necessary to keep Schmidt actively engaged in his wife's career. After his death, however, the relationship quickly cooled. The correspondence files in the Library of Congress' Arthur P. Schmidt Company Archives contain numerous examples of Beach asking why her works were not more easily available and Schmidt or his successors making a series of excuses. She grew so dissatisfied that she turned to Schmidt's rival, Schirmer, while in Europe and did not return to her first publisher until after the owner's death in 1921. Now, though, she could no longer count on having all her new works accepted, and instead she needed to convince Schmidt's successors to accept each work on its merits and to open negotiations with other publishers. More to the point, however, she discovered belatedly that the company was allowing the copyrights of some of her best early works to go unrenewed at the end of their initial twenty-eight-year terms. A particularly troublesome illustration of this was the company's failure to renew the copyright on her Balkan Variations, op. 60, which I believe was her motivation for the hastily prepared revised edition of 1936.[7] Though Schmidt has been hailed as a champion of women and American composers, his company's copyright record book shows that the company rarely bothered to renew copyrights by female composers.[8]

Compounding the lack of availability of publications for performers was a lack of documentary evidence for scholars. When Beach died, she bequeathed her home and its contents in Centerville, Cape Cod, to her close friend Lillian Buxbaum. Although she recognized her obligation to preserve the letters, diaries, and other manuscripts that she had inherited, Beach's friend also wished to spread her mentor's fame by sharing their contents with interested parties. This led her to loan a large cache of primary source materials in 1950 to Walter S. Jenkins, a young composer Beach had befriended at the MacDowell Colony who wanted to write her biography. Despite numerous urgent pleas, he never returned these items to Buxbaum, leading her son to write in 1993,

My mother allowed him to take many items, with the understanding that he would return them to her. To the best of my knowledge, she never saw him or the aforementioned items again. She was very upset about this and often talked about it with me, because she wanted my sister and my wife and me to have all of the items which were in "Aunt Amy's" home.[9]

The items finally made their way to the University of New Hampshire Special Collections in 1994 after Jenkins' biography was published posthumously, where they joined other manuscripts that had followed similarly circuitous paths. These include the documents in Beach's Hillsborough apartment at her death, which had lain unnoticed for decades in the Hillsborough Public Library, as well as various manuscripts donated by Beach's other "kittens": Ruth Shaffner, Eugenie Limberg Dengel, and Virginia Duffey Pleasants.[10] For researchers, though, the documentary evidence for telling Beach's story was largely inaccessible for decades after her death.

Scholarship

As a subject for scholarly research, Beach was "rediscovered" initially by writers of dissertations working primarily from published scores. E. Lindsey Merrill completed a dissertation entitled "Mrs. H. H. A. Beach, Her Life and Music" in 1963 in fulfillment of a requirement of the PhD in music theory at the University of Rochester.[11] The title is deceptive, as it looked only briefly at her life but examined her music in depth using the theories of his adviser, Allen McHose. In this system, works are analyzed statistically to determine frequency of chord usage, a method that yielded valuable insights when applied by McHose to the chorales of J. S. Bach but was perhaps less enlightening when applied to the late-Romantic harmonic vocabulary of Beach. Merrill (1925–95) was appointed dean of the University of Missouri–Kansas City School of Music in 1975, where he continued to promote Beach's music. UMKC staged a production of *Cabildo* in conjunction with the 1982 MTNA convention, established an important collection of primary sources related to Beach, and hosted a scholarly conference on Amy Beach in April 1989. Myrna Garvey Eden's 1977 dissertation for Syracuse University looked at Beach's aesthetic orientation as a reflection of the cultivated tradition in America, which flourished 1865–1920. She drew parallels to the work of sculptor Anna Hyatt Huntington (1876–1973) in their cultural backgrounds and aesthetic ideals.[12] Eden's work explicitly showed the significance of Boston as a center for the dominant trend in late nineteenth-century American high culture. Her dissertation was published as a book by Scarecrow Press in 1987.

Beach later became recognized as a fruitful subject for DMA dissertations, presumably because her cosmopolitan musical style bore similarities to the European works that performance students know best. Marmaduke Miles completed a dissertation on Beach's solo piano works at Peabody Conservatory in 1985, backing up his scholarly work with public performances. In 1992, two dissertations on the solo songs by Patricia J. Bracken and Katherine Kelton appeared, along with concerts and recordings. Jeannell Wise Brown completed a dissertation on the chamber works at the University of Maryland in 1993 that was subsequently republished as a book by Scarecrow Press.[13] The remainder of the 1990s saw a virtual flood of new scholarship in the form of dissertations.

To bring a composer to public attention, however, dissertations have limited impact. In the case of Beach, her reputation was secured primarily through the efforts of one dedicated scholar: Adrienne Fried Block (1921–2009). She began her musicological career with a dissertation on Renaissance music, but her publication with Carol Neuls-Bates of *Women in American Music: A Bibliography of Music and Literature* (1979) set her career on a decisive new path. Described in a memorial tribute by Ellie Hisama as "Feminist Scholarship as a Social Act," Block's research was shaped by the feminist scholarship and activism of her era.[14] Over the next two decades, she brought a missionary zeal to promoting the life and music of Beach, the dogged research skills of a musicologist to locating and analyzing source materials, and the creative imagination of a social historian to reimagining Beach's cultural significance. As the culmination of her decades of research, she published the biography *Amy Beach, Passionate Victorian*, which won the Society for American Music's Lowens Award for best book in American music for 1998. Along the way, she published a series of important scholarly editions of out-of-print works, contributed liner notes to new Beach recordings, wrote numerous articles on specific aspects of Beach's life and works, and delivered a plethora of conference papers. On one occasion she confided to me that all this activity in Beach research amounted to a "cottage industry" for her.

Among the many significant accomplishments of Block's decades of service to Beach scholarship was the organization of two scholarly conferences. The first, entitled "Amy Beach and Her Times," took place at the University of New Hampshire on October 28, 1998. The event brought together an eclectic group of scholars and performers to celebrate Beach in conjunction with the release of Block's biography. A highlight of the program was a discussion with Eugenie Limberg Dengel about recollections of her friend and mentor. The second conference, "The Music of Amy Beach: A Cross-Disciplinary Conference," was hosted by the Mannes School of Music in December 1999. Participants at this conference analyzed and performed a diverse range of musical works from a wide variety of theoretical and performance perspectives.[15]

Block was of course not the only scholar interested in Beach, but she was part of a cohort of female scholars who actively sought to center women in a musicological canon that had previously ignored them. Judith Tick, whose pioneering work on Ruth Crawford Seeger unfolded parallel to Block's on Beach, recalled the radical agenda of their work: "When I remember the beginnings of the scholarship around Amy Beach, 'rediscovery' does not capture the various efforts necessary to launch a scholarly investigation into her legacy. The words that come to mind are 'rehabilitation' and 'radical revisionism.' . . . To get to first base meant reclaiming her identity on the most basic level."[16] One of the strategies they employed was to rechristen the composer's public persona as "Amy Beach," the name she had used in private settings and during her European tour, but not in her professional life in the United States. This was the central act of revisionism that freed Beach from the shadow of her husband and Victorian stereotypes, rehabilitating her as a woman appropriate for a new feminist generation in the late twentieth century.

Performance

Turning to performance and recordings, the acceleration of interest has been even more impressive. As noted, Beach's works had largely fallen out of print by the end of her life, a trend that only continued after she was no longer available to remind the Schmidt Company of her desires. In 1959, the company was sold to the Summy-Birchard Company, Inc., of Evanston, Illinois. David Sengstack, president of the successor company, had the foresight to donate the music manuscripts, correspondence, and selected financial records of the Schmidt Company to the Library of Congress, where they were preserved for scholars and performers.[17] This allowed most of Beach's scores to be readily accessible when interest began to revive in the 1970s. In particular, Da Capo Press took advantage of lapsing copyrights to publish facsimile editions of piano, vocal, and chamber works.[18]

Piano was integral to Beach's entire professional career, and it is not surprising that the Beach "rediscovery" was spearheaded by two female pianists. Mary Louise Boehm and Virginia Eskin were each professional pianists looking to broaden their repertoire in the 1970s. Eskin became acquainted with the music of Beach around 1971, and she has been playing it ever since. She had the distinction in 1976 of playing the first Boston-area performance of the Beach Piano Concerto, op. 45, since Beach's 1917 performance with the BSO.[19] She recalled that when she first signed with Columbia Artists in 1977, they tried to dissuade her from playing women and American composers on her concerts. Her persistence eventually led to her reputation as a specialist in women composers, which was then promoted by Columbia.[20] Eskin also created a niche for herself with recordings of Beach, starting with a 1975 album of Beach solo works for Genesis. She went on to record four more albums devoted in part or in full to the music of Beach on the Musical Heritage Society, Northeastern, and Koch International labels. Almost simultaneously with Eskin's initial efforts, Mary Louise Boehm (1924–2002) began recording Beach as well. With her husband Kees Kooper, Boehm released a recording of the Piano Quintet in 1974. She recorded the Piano Concerto with Siegfried Landau and the Westphalian Symphony Orchestra in 1976. Because both of these recordings were on the Vox Turnabout label, they have been rereleased in multiple anthologies and box sets in subsequent years. Boehm later released an important recording of the *Variations on Balkan Themes*, op. 60.

Following in the footsteps of these pioneering pianists, many performers have taken up the task of recording Beach's solo works in the age of the compact disc. Joanne Polk recorded a three-volume anthology of the piano works (Arabesque, 1996–98). She subsequently recorded several CD recordings of songs, chamber works, and the piano concerto. Pianist Kirsten Johnson recorded a four-volume anthology of the piano works (Guild, 2007–11). The result of all this recording activity is that all of Beach's major solo works have been recorded by at least four different pianists each, allowing listeners to compare and contrast the interpretations.

With the ice broken by these female pianists, Beach's music began to attract the attention of male musicians as well. Violinist Joseph Silverstein and pianist Gilbert Kalish released a recording of the Violin Sonatas of Beach and Arthur Foote on the New World Records label in 1977 that has seldom been equaled in refinement and never surpassed in Romantic intensity. Pianist Alan Feinberg included Beach works on two of his albums (*American Romantic*, 1990, and *American Virtuoso*, 1991). He subsequently played the solo part of Beach's Piano Concerto with Kenneth Schermerhorn and the Nashville Symphony (Naxos, 2003). The "Gaelic" Symphony proved to be especially attractive to male conductors, including Karl Krueger and the Royal Philharmonic (Society for the Preservation of the American Musical Heritage, 1968), Neeme Järvi and the Detroit Symphony Orchestra (Chandos, 1991), and Kenneth Schermerhorn and the Nashville Symphony Orchestra (Naxos, 2003).

As these professional performances and recordings raised awareness of Beach among the general public, her works also made inroads with students. A 1977 interview with Mary Louise Boehm entitled "Where Was Amy Beach All These Years?" was published in *Clavier Magazine*, the leading periodical for piano teachers.[21] The years since then have seen a host of articles on her piano music aimed at teachers and students, most recently in the Summer 2022 issue of *Piano Magazine*, the journal of the Frances Clark Center at the New School for Music Study.[22] The *Journal of Singing*, the publication of the National Association of Teachers of Singing, published a substantial article by Katherine Kelton in 1996 and another by Susan Mardinly in 2014.[23] Pedagogical editions of easier piano works were published by Alfred Publishing Company (edited by Maurice Hinson), Hal Leonard and Mel Bay (Gail Smith), and Dover Publishing. The International Music Score Library Project (imslp.org)/Petrucci Music Library has made free downloads of most of Beach's public domain scores easily accessible online. As a result of these efforts, Beach's music is now heard regularly on programs in music schools throughout the country.

Naturally, there were detractors in the face of Beach's newfound prominence. For reviewers who view the classical music canon as a zero-sum game, the addition of new music from previous eras can seem like a threat to the existing order. Critic Allan Kozinn explored this issue in a 1998 review of a Beach piano concert by Joanne Polk. He rather cynically assessed the Beach revival at that time:

> There are reasons to cheer along the Beach revival. One is a desire to extend American musical history from the Copland generation backward into the 19th century. Beach fits that bill. She lived from 1867 to 1944, established herself as a pianist and composer before she was 18, composed prolifically – her catalogue includes more than 300 works, most published under the name Mrs. H. H. A. Beach – and had works performed by major orchestras in her lifetime. She is equally useful, of course, to anyone trying to construct a repertory of female composers. But those reasons, however well-intentioned, are historical and political, not musical, and if room is to be found in the standard repertory for Beach's music, only musical reasons will matter.[24]

While he admitted that it was tempting to "join the growing Beach appreciation society," he offered two principal objections, both of which were founded on subjective reasons. First, as reviewers have been doing since the early nineteenth century, he claimed that European influences were too pronounced and "overshadowed her own voice." Throughout American musical history, American critics have been slow to appreciate cosmopolitan music by their compatriots because it sounded too – well, cosmopolitan. Second, Kozinn claimed that Beach's Romantic style did not speak to listeners of his era: "There is a grandiose quality to Beach's music that rings false to late-20th-century ears. Huge chordal flourishes, bombastic themes, chordal figures running up and down the keyboard and other varieties of sheer Romantic steaminess were meant to make music majestic, yet beneath all the clatter, much of it was a not particularly durable variety of salon music." This bias against Romantic music is a relic of the anti-Romantic campaign of 1920s Modernism, which was useful for young composers trying to carve a niche beside the seemingly unassailable Edward MacDowell but can now be recognized as a limiting factor to a full appreciation of the musical history of the United States.

Significance of the Beach Revival

Recent years have confirmed the growth of Beach's reputation on multiple fronts. Since 2014, the Women's Philharmonic Advocacy has maintained an informative website devoted to news and information about Amy Beach (www.amybeach.org). The brainchild of Dr. Liane Curtis of Brandeis University, the site was begun in anticipation of the sesquicentennial of Beach's birth in 2017 but has continued since that time. Curtis led a group of scholars in planning another conference on Beach in September 2017, this time in conjunction with the centennial of Teresa Carreño's death. The event took place at the University of New Hampshire and was covered by the *New York Times* and other national publications.[25] The growth of music streaming services has expanded the audience for Beach's music. Subscribers who may not attend concerts but like to listen to classical music as they work, travel, or relax at home are given a variety of musical selections in a particular genre suited to their tastes. The music of Beach is similar enough to cosmo-politan music in the European classical tradition to sound familiar while still being new in origin and inspiration.

Beach has been the subject of two recent documentary films. New Hampshire filmmaker John Gefroerer created a historical introduction to Beach's life entitled *Composer: Amy Beach* that was first aired on Vermont Public Television in Fall 2021.[26] Featuring interviews with musicologist Sarah Gerk of Binghamton University and pianist Virginia Eskin, the film traced the composer's life with archival documents and compelling visual images from New England. Particularly stunning was a juxtaposition of the sight and sound of a live hermit thrush superimposed over Eskin's perform-ance of the *Hermit Thrush at Morn*, demonstrating the source of Beach's inspiration. The second film aired on public television stations nationwide in April 2022 as part of the series *Great Performances: Now Hear This*. Entitled *Amy Beach: American Romantic*, the film was hosted by violinist Scott Yoo in the context of concerts performed at the Festival Mozaic in California. It is not so much a historical overview as a passionate defense of the artistic qualities of Beach's music. In rehearsal sequences with other chamber musicians, he urges them to promote Beach as the equal of better-known contemporaries, stating, "This is a first-rate genius, and if people get that, then we've done our job."[27] He clearly feels a strong emotional connection to the works of Beach, and he also argues that their constructive complexity makes them worthy of attention from today's audiences. In keeping with efforts to promote diversity, equity, and inclusion, Yoo unabashedly demands a place for Beach in the canon of classical music.

In twenty-first-century America, questions of canon are perhaps less relevant than to generations past. The former primacy of classical music has been eclipsed by both scholarly study and critical acceptance of the range of styles that used to be designated "popular." As the audience for European classical music continues to shrink, what is the relevance of an American composer whose reputation is clearly holding its own, if not growing? As noted by Judith Tick, the reimagining of Amy Beach was an inherently political act led by feminist scholars who saw her as a viable symbol for their movement in the 1970s. But that advocacy does not explain the persistence of her music itself and its ability to attract new advocates in the twenty-first century. It seems that Kozinn's ambivalent 1998 assessment was premature, as the emotional sincerity and construct-ive integrity of Beach's music continue to draw supporters as diverse as Gefroerer, Yoo, and Curtis. Beach's reputation in the third decade of the twenty-first century has exceeded anything she could have imagined as her career neared its end in the 1940s.

Notes

1. Programs, clippings, and correspondence related to this event on November 27–28, 1942, may be found in the De Sayn/Eversmann Collection, Music Division, Library of Congress, Washington, DC.
2. "Amy Beach: American Romantic," in *Great Performances: Now Hear This* (Public Broadcasting Service, 2022), https://video.alexanderstreet.com/watch/amy-beach-american-romantic.
3. For a discussion of the changes that jazz brought to American musical culture after the first national release of a jazz record in April 1917, see E. Douglas Bomberger, *Making Music American: 1917 and the Transformation of Culture* (Oxford: Oxford University Press, 2018).
4. Quoted in Kara Anne Gardner, "Living by the Ladies' Smiles: The Feminization of American Music and the Modernist Reaction" (PhD dissertation, Stanford University, 1999), 11.

5. Gardner, "Living by the Ladies' Smiles," 77.

6. See especially Carol J. Oja, "Women Patrons and Activists," in *Making Music Modern: New York in the 1920s* (New York: Oxford University Press, 2000), 201–27.

7. E. Douglas Bomberger, "Motivic Development in Amy Beach's *Variations on Balkan Themes*, op. 60," *American Music* 10, no. 3 (Fall 1992): 326–47.

8. Box 440, A. P. Schmidt Company Archives, Music Division, Library of Congress. See especially pp. 660–76.

9. David Buxbaum to William E. Ross, November 2, 1993, collection files, Amy Cheney Beach (Mrs. H. H. A. Beach) Papers, 1835–1956, MC 51, Milne Special Collections and Archives, University of New Hampshire Library, Durham, NH.

10. The story of this documentary odyssey will be told in detail in a forthcoming article by retired UNH archivist William E. Ross.

11. Lindsey E. Merrill, "Mrs. H. H. A. Beach: Her Life and Music" (PhD dissertation, University of Rochester, 1963).

12. Myrna Garvey Eden, "Anna Hyatt Huntington, Sculptor, and Mrs. H. H. A. Beach, Composer: A Comparative Study of Two Women Representatives of the American Cultivated Tradition in the Arts" (PhD dissertation, Syracuse University, 1977).

13. Marmaduke Miles, "The Solo Piano Works of Mrs. H. H. A. Beach" (DMA dissertation, Peabody Conservatory, 1985); Patricia J. Bracken, "A Guide for the Study of Selected Solo Vocal Works of Mrs. H. H. A. Beach (1867–1944)" (DMA dissertation, Southern Baptist Theological Seminary, 1992); Mary Katherine Kelton, "The Songs of Mrs. H. H. A. Beach" (DMA dissertation, University of Texas at Austin, 1992); Jeannell Elizabeth Wise Brown, "Amy Beach and Her Chamber Music: Biography, Documents, Style" (PhD dissertation, University of Maryland at College Park, 1993).

14. Ellie Hisama, "Feminist Scholarship as a Social Act: Remembering Adrienne Fried Block," *American Music Review* 39, no. 1 (Fall 2009): 1, 3.

15. Liane Renee Curtis, "The Music of Amy Beach: A Cross-Disciplinary Conference (Mannes College of Music, December 5, 1999)," *IAWM Journal: International Alliance for Women in Music* 6, nos. 1–2 (2000):15–16.

16. Email communication, Judith Tick to E. Douglas Bomberger, July 23, 2022.

17. "Provenance," in *A. P. Schmidt Company Archives: Guides to Special Collections in the Music Division of the Library of Congress* (Washington: Music Division, Library of Congress, 1994), p. 5.

18. Quintet in F-sharp minor for Piano and Strings, op. 67 (New York: Da Capo, 1979); Piano Music (New York: Da Capo, 1982); Sonata for Violin and Piano, op. 34 (New York: Da Capo, 1986); Twenty-Three Songs (New York: Da Capo, 1989).

19. William S. Goodfellow, "Piano Music of Amy Beach Finds a Strong Advocate in Virginia Eskin," *Deseret News*, November 26, 1989.

20. Quoted in Goodfellow.

21. Dean M. Elder, "Where Was Amy Beach All These Years? (Interview with Mary Louise Boehm)," *Clavier* 15, no. 9 (1976): 14–17.

22. "Discovering Amy Beach," *Piano Magazine* 14, no. 2 (Summer 2022).

23. Mary Katherine Kelton, "Mrs. H. H. A. Beach and her Songs for Solo Voice," *Journal of Singing* 52, no. 3 (January/February 1996): 3–23; Susan Mardinly, "Amy Beach: Muse, Conscience, and Society," *Journal of Singing* 70, no. 5 (May/June 2014): 527–40.

24. Allan Kozinn, "Is it Artistry or Wishful Thinking?" *New York Times*, September 22, 1998, p. E3.

25. William Robin, "Even So, Her Works Have Persisted: Celebrating the Composer Amy Beach on Her 150th Birthday," *New York Times*, September 3, 2017, p. AR7.

26. A description of the film may be found on Gefroerer's website: www.accompanyvideo.com/amybeach.

27. "Amy Beach: American Romantic," in *Great Performances: Now Hear This* (Public Broadcasting Service, 2022) https://video.alexanderstreet.com/watch/amy-beach-american-romantic.

Appendix: List of Works

Works with Opus Numbers

1/1–4 *Four Songs:* "With Violets" (K. Vannah); "Die vier Brüder" (F. von Schiller); "Jeune fille et jeune fleur" (F. R. Chateaubriand); "Ariette" (P. B. Shelley), 1885–87

2/1–3 *Three Songs (H. H. A. Beach):* "Twilight"; "When Far from Her"; "Empress of Night," 1887–91

3 Cadenza to Beethoven, Piano Concerto No. 3, op. 37, 1st mvt., 1888

4 *Valse-Caprice,* 1889

5 Grand Mass in E-flat major, 1890
"Graduale: Thou Glory of Jerusalem," 1892 (insertion in Mass in E flat, 1890)

6 *Ballad* for piano, 1894

7 *O Praise the Lord, All Ye Nations* (Ps. 117), 1891

8/1–3 *Choral Responses:* "Nunc dimittis" (Luke 2.29); "With Prayer and Supplication" (Philippians 4.6–7); "Peace I Leave with You" (John 4.27), 1891

9 *The Little Brown Bee* for women's chorus (M. Eytinge), 1891

10/1–3 *Songs of the Sea:* "A Canadian Boat Song" (T. Moore); "The Night Sea" (H. P. Spofford); "Sea Song" (W. E. Channing), 1890

11/1–3 *Three Songs* (W. E. Henley): "Dark Is the Night!"; "The Western Wind"; "The Blackbird," 1889–90

12/1–3 *Three Songs* (R. Burns): "Wilt Thou Be My Dearie?"; "Ye Banks and Braes O' Bonnie Doon"; "My Luve Is Like a Red, Red Rose," 1887

13 *Hymn of Trust* (O. W. Holmes), 1891

14/1–4 *Four Songs:* "The Summer Wind" (W. Learned); "Le Secret" (J. De Resseguier); "Sweetheart, Sigh No More" (T. B. Aldrich); "The Thrush" (E. R. Still), 1890

15/1–4 *Four Sketches:* "In Autumn"; "Phantoms"; "Dreaming"; "Fireflies," 1892

16 *The Minstrel and the King:* Rudolph von Hapsburg (F. von Schiller), 1890

17 *Festival Jubilate* (Psalm 100), 1891

18 *Eilende Wolken, Segler der Lüfte* (F. von Schiller), 1892

19/1–3 *Three Songs:* "For Me the Jasmine Buds Unfold" (F. E. Coates); "Ecstasy" (A. M. Beach); "Golden Gates," 1893

20 *Villanelle: Across the World* (E. M. Thomas), 1894

21/1–3 *Three Songs:* "Chanson d'amour" (V. Hugo); "Extase" (Hugo); "Elle et moi" (F. Bovet), 1893

22 *Bal Masqué* (orchestral version 1893; piano 1894)

23 *Romance* for violin and piano, 1893

24 *Bethlehem* (G. C. Hugg), 1893

25/1–6   *Children's Carnival*, 1894

26/1–4   *Four Songs*: "My Star" (C. Fabbri); "Just for This" (Fabbri); "Spring" (Fabbri); "Wouldn't That Be Queer" (E. J. Cooley), 1894

27   *Alleluia, Christ is Risen* (after M. Weisse, C. F. Gellert, T. Scott, T. Gibbons), 1895

28/1–3   *Trois morceaux caractéristiques*: "Barcarolle"; "Minuet Italien"; "Danse des fleurs," 1894

29/1–4   *Four Songs*: "Within Thy Heart" (A. M. Beach); "The Wandering Knight" (Anon.); "Sleep, Little Darling"; (Spofford) "Haste, O Beloved" (W. A. Sparrow), 1894

30   *The Rose of Avon-town* (C. Mischka), 1896

31/1–3   *Three Flower Songs* (M. Deland): "The Clover"; "The Yellow Daisy"; "The Bluebell," 1896

32   Symphony in E minor, "Gaelic," 1894–96

33   *Teach Me Thy Way* (Ps 86.11–12), 1895

34   Sonata in A minor for piano and violin, 1896

35/1–4   *Four Songs*: "Nachts" (C. F. Scherenberg); "Allein!" (H. Heine); "Nähe des Geliebten" (J. W. von Goethe); "Forget-me-not" (H. H. A. Beach), 1896

36/1–5   *Children's Album*: Minuet, Gavotte, Waltz, March, Polka, 1897

37/1–3   *Three Shakespeare Songs*: "O Mistress Mine"; "Take, O Take Those Lips Away"; "Fairy Lullaby," 1897

38   *Peace on Earth* (E. H. Sears), 1897

39/1–3   *Three Shakespeare Choruses*: "Over Hill, over Dale"; "Come unto These Yellow Sands"; "Through the House Give Glimmering Light," 1897

40   *Three Compositions* for violin and piano: "La Captive"; "Berceuse"; "Mazurka," 1898

41/1–3   *Three Songs*: "Anita" (Fabbri); "Thy Beauty" (Spofford); "Forgotten" (Fabbri), 1898

42   *Song of Welcome* (H. M. Blossom), 1898

43/1–5   *Five Burns Songs*: "Dearie"; "Scottish Cradle Song"; "Oh Were My Love Yon Lilac Fair!"; "Far Awa'"; "My Lassie," 1899

44/1–3   *Three Browning Songs*: "The Year's at the Spring"; "Ah, Love, but a Day"; "I Send My Heart up to Thee," 1900

45   Concerto for Piano and Orchestra in C-sharp minor, 1899

46   *Sylvania: A Wedding Cantata* (F. W. Bancroft, after W. Bloem), 1901

47   Summer Dreams for piano four hands, 1901

48/1–4   *Four Songs*: "Come, Ah Come" (H. H. A. Beach); "Good Morning" (A. H. Lockhart); "Good Night" (Lockhart); "Canzonetta" (A. Sylvestre), 1902

49   *A Song of Liberty* (F. L. Stanton), 1902

50   *Help Us, O God* (Pss. 79.9, 5; 45.26), 1903

51/1–4   *Four Songs*: "Ich sagete nicht" (E. Wissman); "Wir drei" (H. Eschelbach); "Juni" (E. Jansen); "Je demande à l'oiseau" (Sylvestre), 1903

52   *A Hymn of Freedom: America* (S. F. Smith), 1903 (rev. with text "O Lord our God Arise," 1944)

53   *Jephthah's Daughter* (Mollevaut, after Judges 11.38, It. trans., I. Martinez, Eng. trans., A. M. Beach), 1903

54/1–2   "Scottish Legend"; "Gavotte fantastique," 1903

55   *Invocation* for violin and piano, 1904

56/1–4   *Four Songs*: "Autumn Song" (H. H. A. Beach); "Go Not Too Far"
(F. E. Coates); "I Know Not How to Find the Spring" (Coates); "Shena Van"
(W. Black), 1903–4

57/1–2   Women's Choruses: "Only a Song" (A. L. Hughes); "One Summer Day"
(Hughes), 1904

59   *The Sea-Fairies* for women's chorus (A. Tennyson), 1904

60   *Variations on Balkan Themes*, 1904

61   "Give Me Not Love" (Coates), 1905

62   "When Soul is Joined to Soul" (E. B. Browning),1905

63   Service in A: "Te Deum"; "Benedictus"; "Jubilate Deo"; "Magnificat"; "Nunc
dimittis," 1905–6

64/1–4   *Eskimos*, Four Characteristics Pieces: "Arctic Night"; "The Returning
Hunter"; "Exiles"; "With Dog-teams," 1907

65/1–5   *Les rêves de Colombine: Suite française:* "La Fée de la fontaine"; "Le prince
gracieux"; "Valse amoureuse"; "Sous les étoiles"; "Danse d'Arlequin," 1907

66   *The Chambered Nautilus* (Holmes), 1907

67   Quintet for Piano and Strings in F-sharp minor, 1907

68   "After" (Coates), 1909

69/1–2   *Two Mother Songs*: "Baby" (G. MacDonald); "Hush, Baby Dear"
(A. L. Hughes), 1908

70   "Iverniana" for two pianos (1910, lost)

71/1–3   *Three Songs*: "A Prelude" (A. M. Beach); "O Sweet Content" (T. Dekker);
"An Old Love-Story" (B. L Stathem), 1910

72/1–2   *Two Songs*: "Ein altes Gebet" (Anon.); "Deine Blumen" (L. Zacharias), 1914

73/1–2   *Two Songs* (Zacharias): "Grossmütterchen"; "Der Totenkranz," 1914

74   *Panama Hymn* (W. P. Stafford), 1915

74   *All Hail the Power of Jesus' Name* (E. Perronet), 1915 (alternate text for
Panama Hymn)

75/1–4   "The Candy Lion" (A. F. Brown); "A Thanksgiving Fable" (D. Herford);
"Dolladine" (W.B. Rands); "Prayer of a Tired Child" (Brown), 1914

76/1–2   *Two Songs*: "Separation" (J. L. Stoddard); "The Lotos Isles" (A. Tennyson),
1914

77/1–2   *Two Songs*: "I" (C. Fanning); "Wind o' the Westland" (D. Burnett), 1916

78/1–4   *Canticles*: "Bonum est, confiteri"; "Deus misereatur"; "Cantate Domino";
"Benedic anima mea," 1916

79/1–3   *Three Songs*: "Meadowlarks" (I. Coolbrith); "Night Songs at Amalfi" (S.
Teasdale); "In Blossom Time" (Coolbrith), 1917

80   *Theme and Variations for Flute and String Quartet*, 1916

81   *Prelude and Fugue* for piano, 1917

82   *Dusk in June* for women's chorus (S. Teasdale), 1917

83   *From Blackbird Hills* for piano, 1922

84   *Te Deum* for men's chorus, 1921

85   *In the Twilight* (Longfellow), 1922

86   *May Eve* for chorus, 1921

87   *Fantasia fugata* for piano, 1923

88   *Spirit Divine* (A. Read), 1922

89   *Quartet for Strings in One Movement*, 1929

90   *Pastorale* for flute, cello, and piano, 1921

91   *The Fair Hills of Éiré, O!* (Old Irish melody) for piano, 1922

92/1–2   "The Hermit Thrush at Eve"; "The Hermit Thrush at Morn" for piano, 1921

93   *Message* (S. Teasdale), 1922

94   *Three School Songs:* "The Arrow and the Song" (H. W. Longfellow); "Clouds" (F. D. Sherman); "A Song for Little May" (E. H. Miller), 1922

95   *Constant Christmas* for women's chorus (P. Brooks), 1922

96   *The Lord Is My Shepherd* (Ps 23), 1923

97/1–5   *From Grandmother's Garden* for piano: "Morning Glories"; "Heartsease"; "Mignonette"; "Rosemary and Rue"; "Honeysuckle," 1922

98   *I Will Lift Up Mine Eyes* (Ps 121), 1923

99/1–4   *Four Songs:* "When Mama Sings" (A. M. Beach); "Little Brown-Eyed Laddie" (A. D. O. Greenwood); "The Moonpath" (K. Adams); "The Artless Maid" (L. Barili), 1923

100/1–2   *Two Songs:* "A Mirage" (B. Ochsner); "Stella Viatoris" (J. H. Nettleton), 1924

101   *Peter Pan* for women's chorus (J. Andrews), 1923

102/1–2   "Farewell Summer"; "Dancing Leaves" for piano, 1924

103/1–2   "Benedictus es, Domine"; "Benedictus," 1924

104   *Suite for Two Pianos Founded upon Old Irish Melodies,* 1924

105   *Let This Mind Be in You* (Philippians 2.5–11), 1924

106   *Old Chapel by Moonlight* for piano, 1924

107   *Nocturne* for piano, 1924

108   *A Cradle Song of the Lonely Mother* for piano, 1924

109   *Lord of the Worlds Above* (I. Watts), 1925

110   *The Greenwood* for chorus (W. L. Bowles), 1925

111   *From Olden Times: Gavotte* for piano, lost

112   *Jesus My Saviour* (A. Elliot), 1925

113   *Mine Be the Lips* (L. Speyer), 1921

114   *By the Still Waters* for piano, 1925

115   *Around the Manger* for chorus (Davis), 1925

116   *Tyrolean Valse-Fantasie* for piano, 1926

117/1–3   *Three Songs* (M. Lee): "The Singer," "The Host," "Song in the Hills," 1925

118/1–2   *Two Children's Choruses:* "The Moon Boat" (E. D. Watkins); "Who Has Seen the Wind" (C. Rossetti), 1938

119/1–6   *From Six to Twelve:* "Sliding on the Ice"; "The First May Flowers"; "Canoeing"; "Secrets of the Attic"; "A Camp-fire Ceremonial"; "Boy Scouts March," 1927

120   *Rendez-vous* (L. Speyer), 1928

121   *Benedicite omnia opera Domini* (Daniel 3.56–68), 1928

122   *Communion Responses:* "Kyrie"; "Gloria Tibi"; "Sursum corda"; "Sanctus"; "Agnus Dei"; "Gloria" (supplement to Service in A), 1928

123   *The Canticle of the Sun* (St. Francis), 1928

124   *Springtime* (S. M. Heywood), 1929

125/1–2   *Two Sacred Songs:* "Spirit of Mercy"; "Evening Hymn: The Shadows of the Evening Hours" (A. Procter), 1936

126/1–2   "Sea Fever" (J. Masefield); "The Last Prayer" for men's chorus, 1931

127   *When the Last Sea Is Sailed* for men's chorus (J. Masefield), 1931

128/1–3   *Three Pianoforte Pieces:* "Scherzino: A Peterborough Chipmunk"; "Young Birches"; "A Humming Bird," 1932

129	*Drowsy Dreamtown* for women's chorus (R. Norwood), 1932	
130	*Out of the Depths* for piano, 1932	
131	*Dark Garden* (L. Speyer), 1932	
132	*Christ in the Universe* (A. Meynell), 1931	
133	Four Choral Responses (J. Fischer), 1932	
134	*God Is Our Stronghold* (E. Wordsworth)	
135	*To One I Love* (S. R. Quick), 1932	
136	*Fire and Flame* (A.A. Moody), 1932	
137/1–2	*Two Mother Songs:* "Baby" (S. R. Quick); "May Flowers" (A. Moody), 1933	
139	*Hearken Unto Me* (Isaiah 51.1, 3; 43.1–3; 40.28, 31), 1934	
140	*We Who Sing Have Walked in Glory* (A. S. Bridgeman), 1934	
141	*O Lord God of Israel* (1 Kings 8.23, 27–30, 34), 1936	
142	*I Sought the Lord* (Anon.), 1937	
143	*I Shall Be Brave* (K. Adams), 1932	
144	*This Morning Very Early* for women's chorus (P. H. Hills), 1937	
145	*April Dreams* (K. W. Harding), 1935	
146	*Lord of All Being* (O. W. Holmes), 1938	
147	*I Will Give Thanks* (Ps 111), 1939	
148	*Five Improvisations* for piano, 1938	
149	*Cabildo*, one-act opera (N. B. Stevens), 1932	
150	*Trio for Piano, Violin, and Violoncello*, 1939	
151	*Pastorale* for woodwind quintet, 1942	
152	*Though I Take the Wings of Morning* (R. N. Spencer), 1941	

Works Without Opus Numbers

"Mamma's Waltz," 1872

"Air and Variations," 1877

"Menuetto," 1877

"Romanza," 1877

"Petite valse," 1878

"The Rainy Day" (H. Longfellow), 1880

Four Chorales: "Come Ye Faithful"; "Come to Me"; "O Lord, How Happy Should We Be"; "To Heav'n I Lift My Waiting Eyes," 1882

St. John the Baptist (*Matthew, Luke*), 1889 (Libretto)

Three movements for piano four hands, before 1893

"An Indian's Lullaby" for women's chorus (Anon.), 1895

Three Flower Songs: "The Clover"; "The Yellow Daisy"; "The Bluebell," 1896

Thou Knowest, Lord, 1915

Balloons (L. A. Garnett), 1916

Friends (Brown), 1917

A Song of Liberty, 1918

Caprice, The Water Sprites, for flute, cello, and piano, 1921

Around the Manger, 1925
A Bit of Cairo for piano, 1928
Mignonnette, 1929
Birth (E. L. Knowles), 1929
A September Forest, 1930
Fragment: Prelude for violin, cello, and piano, 1931
My Love Came through the Fields, 1932
A Light That Overflows, 1932
Evening Song, 1934
A Bumblebee Passed by My Window for women's chorus, 1935
The Deep-Sea Pearl (E. M. Thomas), 1935
Jesus, Tender Shepherd, 1936
Pax Nobiscum for chorus (E. Marlatt), 1939
Hymn: O God of Love, O King of Peace (H. W. Baker), 1941
Prelude on an old Folk Tune for organ ("The Fair Hills of Éiré, O"), 1943
The Ballad of the P. E. O., 1943
If Women Will Not Be Inclined, n.d.
Lento espressivo, n.d.
Singing Joyfully (J. W. Chadwick), n.d.
The Heart That Melts, n.d.
The Icicle Lesson, n.d.
Time Has Wings and Swiftly Flies, n.d.

Arrangements of Works by Others

Beethoven: Piano Concerto No. 1, 2nd mvt., piano four hands, 1887
Berlioz: *Les Troyens*, act 1, scene 3, piano solo, 1896
Richard Strauss: *Serenade* (Transcription of "Ständchen"), piano solo, 1902
On a Hill: Negro Melody (trad.) for violin and piano, 1929
"Whither" (W. Müller) (accompaniment: Chopin, *Trois nouvelles études*,
     no. 3), song, ca. 1878

Select Bibliography

Recent Beach editions

The Canticle of the Sun. Ed. Betty Buchanan. Recent Researches in American Music, vol. 57. Madison, WI: A-R Editions, 2006.

The Chambered Nautilus, op. 66. Bryn Mawr, PA: Hildegard, 1994.

Children's Carnival, op. 25. Ed. Sylvia Glickman. Bryn Mawr, PA: Hildegard, 1990.

Festival Jubilate. Ed. Randy C. Brittain. Bryn Mawr, PA: Hildegard, 1995.

Five Songs on French and German Texts. Ed. Ruth C. Friedberg. San Antonio, TX: Southern Music Company, 1994.

Grand Mass in E-Flat Major, op. 5. Ed. Matthew Phelps. Recent Researches in American Music, vol. 84. Madison, WI: A-R Editions, 2018.

The Life and Music of Amy Beach, "The First Woman Composer of America." Compiled and ed. Gail Smith. Pacific, MO: Creative Keyboard Publications, 1992.

Music for Violin and Piano. Ed. Sylvia Plaut. Bryn Mawr, PA: Hildegard, 1994.

Piano Concerto, op. 45. Ed. Martha Furman Schleifer. Bryn Mawr, PA: Hildegard, 1995.

Piano Music. New Introduction by Sylvia Glickman. New York: Da Capo Press, 1982.

Piano Music. Ed. Adrienne Fried Block. Mineola, NY: Dover, 2001.

Quartet for Strings (in One Movement), op. 89. Ed. Adrienne Fried Block. Music of the United States of America (MUSA), vol. 3. Madison, WI: A-R Editions, 1994.

Quintet in F-sharp Minor, for Piano and Strings, op. 67. Ed. Adrienne Fried Block. New York: Da Capo Press, 1979.

The Sea-Fairies, op. 59. Ed. Andrew Thomas Kuster. Recent Researches in American Music, vol. 32. Madison, WI: A-R Editions, 1999.

Sonata in A Minor for Violin and Piano, op. 34. Ed. Rose-Marie Johnson. New York: Da Capo Press, 1986.

Suite for Two Pianos Founded upon Old Irish Melodies, op. 104. Ed. Adrienne Fried Block. Bryn Mawr, PA: Hildegard Publishing, 2000.

Symphonie ("Gaelic") in E moll für grosses Orchester, op. 32. Intro. by Phillip Brookes. Munich, Germany: Musikproduktion Höflich, 2015.

Symphony No. 2 [sic] in E minor ("Gaelic"), op. 32. Boca Raton, FL: Kalmus, [n.d.].

Theme and Variations for Flute and String Quartet, op. 80. Ed. Adrienne Fried Block. Bryn Mawr, PA: Hildegard Publishing, 1996.

Three Movements for Piano Four-Hands. Ed. Adrienne Fried Block. Bryn Mawr, PA: Hildegard Publishing, 1998.

Twenty-Eight Songs. Huntsville, TX: Recital Publications, 1985.

Twenty-Three Songs. Ed. Mary Louise Boehm. New York: Da Capo Press, 1991.

Variations on Balkan Themes, op. 60. Boca Raton, FL: Masters Music, 1995.

Young People's Album, op. 36. Ed. Maurice Hinson. Van Nuys, CA: Alfred: 2003.

Young People's Carnival, op. 25. Ed. Maurice Hinson. Van Nuys, CA: Alfred: 1994.

Beach writings

"New Gems in the Old Classics: A Talk with Mrs. H. H. A. Beach, Reported by William Armstrong." *The Etude* 22, no. 3 (February 1904): 51.

"Common Sense in Pianoforte Touch and Technic." *The Etude* 34, no. 10 (October 1916): 701.

"Emotion Versus Intellect in Music." *Music Teachers National Association Proceedings* 26 (1931), 17–19.

"How Music Is Made." *Keyboard* (Winter 1942): 11, 38.

"The Mission of the Present-Day Composer." *The Triangle of Mu Phi Epsilon* 36, no. 2 (February 1942): 72.

"Music after Marriage and Motherhood." *The Etude* 27, no. 8 (August 1909): 520.

"The Outlook for the Young American Composer: An Interview . . . by Mr. Edwin Hughes." *The Etude* 33, no. 1 (January 1915): 13.

"A Plea for Mercy." *Music Teachers National Association Proceedings* 30 (1935), 163–65.

"To the Girl Who Wants to Compose." *The Etude* 36, no. 11 (November 1918): 695.

"The Twenty-Fifth Anniversary of a Vision." *Music Teachers National Association Proceedings* 27 (1932), 45–48.

"Why I Chose My Profession." *Mother's Magazine* (February 1914): 7–8. Reprinted in *Music in the USA: A Documentary Companion*. Ed. Judith Tick. Oxford and New York: Oxford University Press, 2008. Pp. 323–29.

"Work Out Your Own Salvation." *The Etude* 36, no. 1 (January 1918): 11.

"The World Cries Out for Harmony." *The Etude* 62, no. 1 (January 1944): 11–12.

Books and Articles

Beckerman, Michael. "Henry Krehbiel, Antonín Dvořák, and the Symphony 'From the New World.'" *Notes* 49, no. 2 (Dec. 1992): 447–73.

Beckerman, Michael. *New Worlds of Dvořák: Searching in America for the Composer's Inner Life*. New York: W. W. Norton, 2003.

Blair, Karen J. *The Torchbearers: Women and Their Amateur Arts Associations in America, 1890–1930*. Bloomington: Indiana University Press, 1994.

Block, Adrienne Fried. "Amy Beach." In *Women Composers: Music Through the Ages*, vol. 7, *Composers Born 1800–1899: Vocal Music*, ed. Sylvia Glickman and Martha Furman Schleifer. New York: G. K. Hall, 2003. Pp. 492–528.

Block, Adrienne Fried. "Amy Beach as Teacher." *American Music Teacher* 48, no. 5 (April/May 1999): 22–25.

Block, Adrienne Fried. *Amy Beach, Passionate Victorian: The Life and Work of an American Composer.* New York: Oxford University Press, 1998.

Block, Adrienne Fried. "Amy Beach's Music on Native American Themes." *American Music* 8, no. 2 (Summer 1990): 141–66.

Block, Adrienne Fried. "Arthur P. Schmidt, Music Publisher and Champion of American Women Composers." In *The Musical Woman: An International Perspective*, vol. 2, *1984–1985*, ed. Judith Lang Zaimont, Catherine Overhauser, and Jane Gottlieb. Westport, CT: Greenwood Press, 1987. Pp. 145–76.

Block, Adrienne Fried. "Boston Talks Back to Dvořák." *Institute for Studies in American Music Newsletter* 18, no. 2 (1989): 10–11, 15.

Block, Adrienne Fried. "Dvořák, Beach, and American Music." In *A Celebration of American Music: Words and Music in Honor of H. Wiley Hitchcock*, ed. Richard Crawford, R. Allen Lott, and Carol Oja. Ann Arbor: University of Michigan Press, 1990. Pp. 256–80.

Block, Adrienne Fried. "Early Federation Connections with Amy Beach: Amy Beach and the Federation – An Affair of the Heart." *Music Clubs Magazine* 78 (Winter 1998): 8–9.

Block, Adrienne Fried. "How to Write an American Symphony: Amy Beach and the Birth of the 'Gaelic' Symphony." American Composers Orchestra, www .americancomposers.org/beach_article.htm, accessed June 1, 2014.

Block, Adrienne Fried. "'A Veritable Autobiography'? Amy Beach's Piano Concerto in C♯ Minor, Op. 45." *Musical Quarterly* 78, no. 2 (Summer 1994): 394–416.

Block, Adrienne Fried. "Why Amy Beach Succeeded as a Composer: The Early Years." *Current Musicology* 36 (Fall 1983): 41–59.

Bomberger, E. Douglas. "Amy Marcy Cheney Beach." In *Women Composers: Music Through the Ages*, vol. 6, *Composers Born 1800–1899: Keyboard Music*, ed. Sylvia Glickman and Martha Furman Schleifer. New York: G. K. Hall, 1999. Pp. 351–70.

Bomberger, E. Douglas. "Edward MacDowell, Arthur P. Schmidt, and the Shakespeare Overtures of Joachim Raff: A Case Study in Nineteenth-Century Music Publishing." *Notes* 54, no. 1 (September 1997): 11–26.

Bomberger, E. Douglas. *An Index to Music Published in The Etude Magazine, 1883–1957.* MLA Index and Bibliography Series, No. 31. Lanham, MD: Scarecrow Press, 2004.

Bomberger, E. Douglas. *MacDowell.* New York: Oxford University Press, 2013.

Bomberger, E. Douglas. *Making Music American: 1917 and the Transformation of Culture.* New York: Oxford University Press, 2018.

Bomberger, E. Douglas. "Motivic Development in Amy Beach's *Variations on Balkan Themes*, op. 60." *American Music* 10, no. 3 (Fall 1992): 326–47.

Bomberger, E. Douglas. "The Nineteenth Century." In *From Convent to Concert Hall: A Guide to Women Composers*, ed. Sylvia Glickman and Martha Furman Schleifer. Westport, CT: Greenwood, 2003. Pp. 153–216.

Brooks, Benjamin. "The 'How' of Creative Composition: A Conference with Mrs. H. H. A. Beach." *The Etude* 61, no. 3 (March 1943): 151.

Brower, Harriet. "Mrs. H. H. A. Beach: How a Composer Works." In *Piano Mastery*, Second Series. New York: F. A. Stokes, 1917. Pp. 179–87.

Brown, Jeanell Wise. *Amy Beach and Her Chamber Music: Biography, Documents, Style*. Metuchen, NJ: Scarecrow Press, 1994.

Buchanan, Betty. "Connection: A Medieval Text and Twentieth-Century Expressionism in 'Canticle of the Sun' by Amy Beach." *Choral Journal* 41, no. 10 (May 2001): 9–19.

Burton, Anthony. "Amy Beach: America's Thwarted Great." *BBC Music* 25, no. 6 (March 2017): 60–63.

Cipolla, Wilma Reid. "Arthur P. Schmidt: The Publisher and His American Composers." In *Vistas of American Music: Essays in Honor of William K. Kearns*, ed. Susan L. Porter and John Graziano. Warren, MI: Harmonie Park Press, 1999. Pp. 267–81.

Cook, Susan C., and Judy S. Tsou, eds. *Cecilia Reclaimed: Feminist Perspectives on Gender and Music*. Urbana: University of Illinois Press, 1994.

Corn, Wanda M. *Women Building History: Public Art at the 1893 Columbian Exposition*. Berkeley: University of California Press, 2011.

Croly, J[ennie] C. *The History of the Woman's Club Movement in America*. New York: H.G. Allen, 1898.

Curtis, Liane Renee. "The Music of Amy Beach: A Cross-Disciplinary Conference (Mannes College of Music, December 5, 1999)." *IAWM Journal: International Alliance for Women in Music* 6, nos. 1–2 (2000): 15–16.

De Graaf, Melissa J. "'Never Call Us Lady Composers': Gendered Receptions in the New York Composers' Forum, 1935–1940." *American Music* 26, no. 3 (2008): 277–308.

DeVenney, David P. *Source Readings in American Choral Music*. Missoula, MT: College Music Society, 1995.

Eden, Myrna G. *Energy and Individuality in the Art of Anna Huntington, Sculptor and Amy Beach, Composer*. Metuchen, NJ: Scarecrow Press, 1987.

Elder, Dean M. "Where Was Amy Beach All These Years? (Interview with Mary Louise Boehm)." *Clavier* 15, no. 9 (1976): 14–17.

Ellison, Cori. "A Woman's Work Well Done." *New York Times*, May 7, 1995, p. H29.

Elson, Arthur, and Everett E. Truette. *Woman's Work in Music*. Boston, MA: L. C. Page, [1931].

Faucett, Bill F. *Music in Boston: Composers, Events, and Ideas, 1852–1918*. Lanham, MD: Lexington Books, 2016.

Feldman, Ann E. "Being Heard: Women Composers and Patrons at the 1893 World's Columbian Exposition." *Notes* 47, no. 1 (1990): 7–20.

Flatt, Rose Marie Chisholm. "Analytical Approaches to Chromaticism in Amy Beach's 'Piano Quintet in F-Sharp Minor.'" *Indiana Theory Review* 4, no. 3 (1981): 41–58.

Fletcher, Alice. *A Study of Omaha Indian Music.* Cambridge, MA: Peabody Museum of American Archaeology and Ethnology, 1893.

Friedberg, Ruth C. "Selected Settings of European Texts by American Song Composers." *Journal of Singing* 71, no. 5 (May/June 2015): 559–71.

Gates, Eugene. "Mrs. H. H. A. Beach: American Symphonist." *The Kapralova Society Journal* 8, no. 2 (Fall 2010): 1–7; 9–10. www.kapralova.org/journal15.pdf

Gerk, Sarah. "'Common Joys, Sorrows, Adventures, and Struggles': Transnational Encounters in Amy Beach's 'Gaelic' Symphony," *Journal of the Society for American Music* 10, no. 2 (May 2016): 149–80.

"Glickman to Appear with Merion Orchestra." *The Philadelphia Public Ledger*, March 2, 1978, p. 17.

Goetschius, Percy. *Mrs. H. H. A. Beach.* Boston: A. P. Schmidt, 1906. https://imslp .org/wiki/Mrs._H._H._A._Beach_(Goetschius%2C_Percy).

Gottlieb, Lynette Miller. "Composing Oneself: Amy Beach, Ruth Crawford, and Their Declarations of Independence." *Women of Note Quarterly* 9, no. 1 (2005): 18–23.

Hisama, Ellie. "Feminist Scholarship as a Social Act: Remembering Adrienne Fried Block." *American Music Review* 39, no. 1 (Fall 2009): 1, 3.

Holland, Bernard. "A Composer Who Made Her Timely Choice." *New York Times*, May 15, 1995, p. C15.

Horowitz, Joseph. "Beach, Chadwick: New World Symphonists: Native New World Symphonies." *New York Times*, October 27, 1991, p. H25.

Horowitz, Joseph. "Reclaiming the Past: Musical Boston Reconsidered." *American Music* 19, no. 1 (2001): 18–38.

Howard, John Tasker. *Our American Music.* New York: Crowell, 1931.

Howe, Mark Anthony DeWolfe. *The Boston Symphony Orchestra: 1881–1931.* 2nd ed. Revised and extended in collaboration with John N. Burk. Cambridge, MA: The Riverside Press, 1931.

Hughes, Rupert. *Famous American Composers.* Boston, MA: L. C. Page and Co., 1900.

Jenkins, Walter S. *The Remarkable Mrs. Beach, American Composer: A Biographical Account Based on Her Diaries, Letters, Newspaper Clippings, and Personal Reminiscences.* Ed. John H. Baron. Michigan: Harmonie Park Press, 1994.

Kandell, Leslie. "A Composer at Last Comes into Her Own." *New York Times*, March 14, 1999, p. NJ14.

Kelton, Mary Katherine. "Mrs. H. H. A. Beach and Her Songs for Solo Voice." *Journal of Singing* 52, no. 3 (January/February 1996): 3–23.

Kinney, Edith Gertrude. "Mrs. H. H. A. Beach." *The Musician* 4, no. 9 (September 1899): 355.

Kinscella, Hazel Gertrude. "Play No Piece in Public When First Learned, Says Mrs. Beach." *Musical America* 28, no. 19 (September 7, 1918): 9.

Kozinn, Allan. "Is It Artistry or Wishful Thinking?" *New York Times*, September 22, 1998, p. E3.

Latham, Edward D. "Gapped Lines and Ghostly Flowers in Amy Beach's 'Phantoms,' op. 15, no. 2." In *Analytical Essays on Music by Women Composers, Secular & Sacred Music to 1900*. Ed. Laurel Parsons and Brenda Ravenscroft. New York: Oxford University Press, 2018. Pp. 228–42.

Ledeen, Lydia Hailparn. "Remembering Amy Beach: A Conversation with David Buxbaum." *IAWM Journal: International Alliance for Women in Music* 6, nos. 1–2 (2000): 17.

Logan, Jeremy. "Synaesthesia and Feminism: A Case Study on Amy Beach (1867–1944)." *New Sound: International Magazine for Music* 46 (2015): 130–40.

MacDonald, Claudia. "Critical Reception and the Woman Composer: The Early Reception of Piano Concertos by Clara Wieck Schumann and Amy Beach." *Current Musicology* 55 (Fall 1993): 24–55.

Malawey, Victoria. "Strophic Modification in Songs by Amy Beach." *Music Theory Online* 20, no. 4 (December 2014): 1–15.

Mardinly, Susan. "Amy Beach: Muse, Conscience, and Society." *Journal of Singing* 70, no. 5 (May/June 2014): 527–40.

McGlinchee, Claire. "American Literature in American Music." *Musical Quarterly* 31, no. 1 (January 1945): 101–19.

Orr, N. Lee, and W. Dan Hardin. *Choral Music in Nineteenth-Century America: A Guide to the Sources*. Lanham, MD: Scarecrow Press, 1999.

Peeler, Clare P. "American Woman Whose Musical Message Thrilled Germany." *Musical America* 20, no. 24 (October 17, 1914): 7.

Pendle, Karin, and Melinda Boyd. *Women in Music: A Research and Information Guide*. 2nd ed. Routledge Music Bibliographies. New York: Routledge Taylor and Francis Group, 2010.

Petteys, M. Leslie. "'Cabildo' by Amy March Beach." *Opera Journal* 22, no. 1 (1989): 10–20.

Pisani, Michael V. *Imagining Native America in Music*. New Haven, CT: Yale University Press, 2005.

Radell, Judith. "Sphere of Influence: Clara Kathleen Rogers and Amy Beach." In *Essays on Music and Culture in Honor of Herbert Kellman*. Ed. Barbara Helen Haggh. Paris: Minerve, 2001. Pp. 503–17.

Rausch, Robin. "The MacDowells and Their Legacy." In *A Place for the Arts, The MacDowell Colony 1907–2007*. Ed. Carter Wiseman. Lebanon, NH: University Press of New England, 2006. Pp. 50–132.

Reynolds, Christopher. "Documenting the Zenith of Women Song Composers: A Database of Songs Published in the United States and the British Commonwealth, ca. 1890–1930." *Notes* 69, no. 4 (June 2013): 671–87.

Reynolds, Christopher Alan. *Motives for Allusion: Context and Content in Nineteenth-Century Music*. Cambridge, MA: Harvard University Press, 2003.

Robin, William. "Even So, Her Works Have Persisted: Celebrating the Composer Amy Beach on Her 150th Birthday." *New York Times*, September 3, 2017, p. AR7.

Shadle, Douglas W. *Orchestrating the Nation: The Nineteenth-Century American Symphonic Enterprise*. New York: Oxford University Press, 2016.

Smith, Gail. "Amy Beach: Celebrating 150 Years." *Clavier Companion* 9, no. 2 (March/April 2017): 46–49.

Smith, Joseph. "Amy Beach: Out in the Cold." *Piano Today* 27, no. 1 (Winter 2007): 7–19.

Sonneck, Oscar G. "American Composers and the American Music Publisher." *Musical Quarterly* 9 (January 1923): 122–44.

Sparkhall, Olivia. "Amy Beach: 'St. Paul's Benediction' (1891)." *Women & Music* 24 (2020): 127–29.

Spitzer, John. *American Orchestras in the Nineteenth Century*. Chicago: University of Chicago Press, 2012.

Stevens, Clare. "Choral Music of Amy Beach and Randall Thompson." *Choir & Organ* 10, no. 6 (November/December 2002): 82–83.

Strauss, William, and Neil Howe. *Generations: The History of America's Future, 1584–2069*. New York: William Morrow, 1991.

Thompson, Berenice. "Music and Musicians: Mrs. Beach's Songs." *Washington Post*, January 17, 1904, p. E11.

Tick, Judith. "Passed Away Is the Piano Girl: Changes in American Musical Life: 1870–1900." In *Women Making Music: The Western Art Tradition, 1150–1950*. Ed. Jane Bowers and Judith Tick. Urbana: University of Illinois Press, 1986. Pp. 325–48.

Tick, Judith. "Women as Professional Musicians in the United States, 1870–1900." *Anuario Interamericano de Investigacion Musical* 9 (1973): 95–133.

Tsou, Judy. "Unpublished Song by Amy Beach Discovered." *Society for American Music Bulletin* 37, no. 1 (Winter 2011): 1–4.

Tuthill, Burnet C. "Mrs. H. H. A. Beach," *Musical Quarterly* 26, no. 3 (July 1940): 297–310.

Upton, George P. *Woman in Music*. Boston: J. R. Osgood, 1880.

Valdivia, Hector. "Amy Beach." In *Women Composers: Music Through the Ages*, vol. 8, *Composers Born 1800–1899: Large and Small Instrumental Ensembles*. Ed. Sylvia Glickman and Martha Furman Schleifer. New York: G. K. Hall, 2006. Pp. 369–95.

Vernazza, Marcelle Wynn. "Amy Beach and Her Music for Children." *American Music Teacher* 30, no. 6 (1981): 20–21.

"Very Good for an American": Essays on Edward MacDowell. Ed. E. Douglas Bomberger. Hillsdale, NY: Pendragon Press, 2017.

Von Glahn, Denise. "American Women and the Nature of Identity." *Journal of the American Musicological Society* 64, no. 2 (2011): 399–403.

Von Glahn, Denise. *Music and the Skillful Listener: American Women Compose the Natural World*. Bloomington: Indiana University Press, 2013.

Ward, Lucile Parrish, *A Musical of 100 Years: A History of the National Federation of Music Clubs*. Greenville, SC: A Press, 1995.

Webster, Daniel. "Welcome Revival for Amy Cheney." *The Philadelphia Public Ledger*, April 24, 1977.

Whitesett, Linda. "Women as 'Keepers of Culture': Music Clubs, Community Concert Series, and Symphony Orchestras." In *Cultivating Music in America: Women Patrons and Activists since 1860*, ed. Ralph P. Locke and Cyrilla Barr. Berkeley: University of California Press, 1997. Pp. 65–86.

Wilson, Arthur. "Mrs. H. H. A. Beach: A Conversation on Musical Conditions in America." *The Musician* 17, no. 1 (January 1912): 9.

Wilson, Jennifer C. H. J. "Conference Report: 'American Women Pianist-Composers: A Celebration of Amy Beach and Teresa Carreño." *Society for American Music Bulletin* 44, no. 1 (Winter 2018): 14–15.

Wilson Kimber, Marian. "Women Composers at the White House: The National League of American Pen Women and Phyllis Fergus's Advocacy for Women in American Music." *Journal of the Society for American Music* 12, no. 4 (November 2018): 477–507.

Women Making Music: The Western Art Tradition, 1150–1950. Ed. Jane Bowers and Judith Tick. Urbana: University of Illinois Press, 1986.

Wright, David. "A Lady, She Wrote Music Nonetheless." *New York Times*, September 6, 1998, p. AR23.

Theses and Dissertations

Aaron, Clarissa E. "A Story of Feminine Sacrifice: The Music, Text, and Biographical Connections in Amy Beach's Concert Aria Jephthah's Daughter." Thesis, Seattle Pacific University, 2018.

Alfeld, Anna Poulin. "Unsung Songs: Self-Borrowing in Amy Beach's Instrumental Compositions." MM thesis, University of Cincinnati, 2008. http://rave .ohiolink.edu/etdc/view?acc_num=ucin1217521725

Baker, Monica Schultz. "Amy Beach for the New Generation: The Effects of Increased Interest in Beach's Works on the Current Place in the Performance Canon of Concerto for Piano and Orchestra in C-Sharp Minor, op. 45." DMA dissertation, University of Alabama at Tuscaloosa, 2019.

Blunsom, Laurie K. "Gender, Genre, and Professionalism: The Songs of Clara Rogers, Helen Hopekirk, Amy Beach, Margaret Lang and Mabel Daniels, 1880–1925." PhD dissertation, Brandeis University, 1999.

Bracken, Patricia J. "A Guide for the Study of Selected Solo Vocal Works of Mrs. H. H. A. Beach (1867–1944)." DMA dissertation, Southern Baptist Theological Seminary, 1992.

Brittain, Charles. "Festival Jubilate, op. 17 by Amy Cheney Beach (1867–1944): A Performing Edition." DMA dissertation, University of North Carolina at Greensboro, 1994.

Brown, Jeannell Elizabeth Wise. "Amy Beach and Her Chamber Music: Biography, Documents, Style." PhD dissertation, University of Maryland at College Park, 1993.

Buchanan, Elizabeth Moore. "The Anthems and Service Music of Amy Beach Published by the Arthur P. Schmidt Company." MA thesis, American University, 1996.

Burgess, Stephanie J. "Finding the 'Indian' in Amy Beach's Theme and Variations for Flute and String Quartet, op. 80." MM thesis, University of North Texas, 2007. https://pqdtopen-proquest-com.proxy-etown.klnpa.org/doc/304828770.html?FMT=AI&pubnum=1452035

Burnaman, Stephen Paul. "The Solo Piano Music of Edward MacDowell and Mrs. H. H. A. Beach: An Analysis." DMA dissertation, University of Texas–Austin, 1997.

Clark, Donna Elizabeth Congleton. "Pedagogical Analysis and Sequencing of Selected Intermediate-Level Solo Piano Compositions of Amy Beach." DMA dissertation, University of South Carolina, 1996.

Eden, Myrna Garvey. "Anna Hyatt Huntington, Sculptor, and Mrs. H. H. A. Beach, Composer: A Comparative Study of Two Women Representatives of the American Cultivated Tradition in the Arts." PhD dissertation, Syracuse University, 1977.

Gallagher, Ruth. "A Stylistic Examination of Shakespeare's Texts Set for Solo Voice by Amy Beach, Elizabeth Maconchy and Madeleine Dring." MA thesis, Waterford Institute of Technology, 2013. https://repository.wit.ie/2734/1/Final%20doc.pdf

Gardner, Kara Anne. "Living by the Ladies' Smiles: The Feminization of American Music and the Modernist Reaction." PhD dissertation, Stanford University, 1999.

Gearheart, Madelyn Spring. "The Life and Solo Vocal Works of Amy Marcy Cheney Beach (1867–1944)." EdD dissertation, Columbia University Teachers College, 1998.

Gerk, Sarah Rebecca. "Away O'er the Ocean Go Journeymen, Cowboys, and Fiddlers: The Irish in Nineteenth-Century American Music." PhD dissertation, University of Michigan, 2014. http://hdl.handle.net/2027.42/110488

Gerk, Sarah. "A Critical Reception History of Amy Beach's Gaelic Symphony." MA thesis, California State University–Long Beach, 2006.

Hung, Yu-Hsien Judy. "The Violin Sonata of Amy Beach." DMA dissertation, Louisiana State University, 2005.

Indenbaum, Dorothy. "Mary Howe: Composer, Pianist and Music Activist." PhD dissertation, New York University, 1993.

Kelton, Mary Katherine. "The Songs of Mrs. H. H. A. Beach." DMA dissertation, University of Texas at Austin, 1992.

Kuby, Dathryn Amelia. "Analysis of Amy Cheney Beach's *Gaelic Symphony*, op. 32." DMA dissertation, University of Connecticut, 2011.

Laemmli, Amy. "Amy Beach: The Victorian Woman, the Autism Spectrum, and Composition Style." MA thesis, University of Missouri–Columbia, 2012. https://mospace.umsystem.edu/xmlui/bitstream/handle/10355/15276/research .pdf?sequence=2&isAllowed=y

Llewellyn, Sharon. "Amy Beach and Judith Lang Zaimont: A Comparative Study of Their Lives and Songs." DMA dissertation, Arizona State University, 2008.

Merrill, Lindsey E. "Mrs. H. H. A. Beach: Her Life and Music." PhD dissertation, University of Rochester, 1963.

Miles, Marmaduke. "The Solo Piano Works of Mrs. H. H. A. Beach." DMA dissertation, Peabody Conservatory, 1985.

Miller, Carla Anita. "A Pedagogical Perspective on Selected Piano Music of Amy Beach." Master's thesis, Western Carolina University, 1996.

Petracca, Eleanor Frances. "From the Parlor to the Stage: Women Composers and the 1893 World's Columbian Exposition in Chicago." MM thesis, California State University–Long Beach, 2012.

Piscitelli, Felicia Ann. "The Chamber Music of Mrs. H. H. A. Beach (1867–1944)." MM thesis, University of New Mexico, 1983.

Powlison, Nicole. "Amy Beach's *Cabildo*: An American Opera." PhD dissertation, Florida State University, 2017.

Reigles, B. Jean. "The Choral Music of Amy Beach." PhD dissertation, Texas Tech University, 1996. http://hdl.handle.net/2346/19154

Rich, Erin Marie. "Accent Patterns in Text and Music in the Songs of Amy Beach, Richard Strauss, and Camille Saint-Saëns." MA thesis, University of Iowa, 2016.

Robinson, Nicole Marie. "'To the Girl Who Wants to Compose': Amy Beach as a Music Educator." MM thesis, Florida State University, 2013. https://diginole .lib.fsu.edu/islandora/object/fsu:183883/datastream/PDF/view

Rushing, Katrina Carlson. "Amy Beach's Concerto for Piano and Orchestra in C-Sharp Minor, op. 45: A Historical, Stylistic, and Analytical Study." DMA dissertation, Louisiana State University, 2000. https://digitalcommons.lsu.edu /cgi/viewcontent.cgi?article=8225&context=gradschool_disstheses

Schnepel, Julie. "The Critical Pursuit of the Great American Symphony, 1893–1950." PhD dissertation, Indiana University, 1995. UMI 96–08607.

Schultz, Geralyn. "Influences of Cultural Ideals of Womanhood on the Musical Career of Mrs. H. H. A. Beach." MA thesis, University of Wyoming, 1994.

Sears, Elizabeth Ann. "The Art Song in Boston, 1880–1914." PhD dissertation, the Catholic University of America, 1993.

Song, Chang-Jin. "Pianism in Selected Partsong Accompaniments and Chamber Music of the Second New England School (Amy Beach, Arthur Foote, George

Whitefield Chadwick, and Horatio Parker), 1880–1930." PhD dissertation, Ball State University, 2005.

Song, Yoon. "Amy Beach Piano Quintet, op. 67." DMA dissertation, Manhattan School of Music, 2011.

Streety, Jule Josef. "The Second New England School and Helen Hopekirk: A Case Study in American Music Historiography." MM thesis, University of Arizona, 2019. https://repository.arizona.edu/bitstream/handle/10150/634378/azu_etd_17396_sip1_m.pdf?sequence=1&isAllowed=y

Treybig, Carolyn Marie. "Amy Beach: An Investigation and Analysis of the Theme and Variations for Flute and String Quartet, op. 80." DMA dissertation, University of Texas, 1999.

Walker, Tammie Leigh. "The Quintet for Piano and Strings, op. 67 by Amy Beach: An Historical and Stylistic Investigation." DMA dissertation, University of Illinois at Urbana-Champaign, 2001. http://hdl.handle.net/2142/85696

Yang, Ching-Lin. "An Analytical Study of the Piano Concerto in C-Sharp Minor, Op. 45, by Amy Beach." PhD dissertation, University of Northern Colorado, 1999.

Zerkle, Paula Ring. "A Study of Amy Beach's Grand Mass in E flat Major, Op. 5." PhD dissertation, Indiana University, 1998.

Index

Aaron, Clarissa, 206, 207, 208
Abell, Arthur, 13
Adams, Katharine, 42
African American dialect, 211
African American music, 103, 108, 113, 114, 142, 156, 157, 165, 174, 209
Agnes Scott College, 211
Aldrich, Thomas Bailey, 123, 125
Alfeld, Anna Poulin, 159, 161
Alfred Publishing Company, 238
Allen, William T., 198
Alves, C. Katie, 203
American musical identity, 158
American Pen Women, 112
American Women's Association Clubhouse, 32
Amphion Club, 25
Andrée, Elfrida, 122
Antheil, George, 232
Apollo Club of Chicago, 181
Armstrong, William, 208
Asia, 43
Atlantic Monthly, 123
"Auld Rob Morris," 203
Austin, Henry, 16, 62, 63, 111, 218

Bach, Johann Sebastian, 3, 12, 234
Baermann, Carl, 4, 72
Baltimore Symphony Orchestra, 27, 205
Bancroft, Frederick W., 191
Bartholomew, Marguerite, 217
Bartók, Béla, 147
Bauer, Marion, 26, 42, 44, 232
Bavarian Opera, 106
Bayreuth, 40
Beach, Amy
    American history, views on, 209
    Asian influences, 207
    autobiographical influences, 208–9
    autodidact, 8, 9, 102, 121, 160, 161, 215
    Biblical texts, 64, 84, 86, 114, 187, 189, 194, 205
    child prodigy, 3, 19, 71, 93
    childhood, 3–5

chromaticism, 95, 108, 125, 128, 138, 144, 173, 186, 192, 194, 195, 199, 202
commissions, 11, 22, 23, 25, 26, 108, 123, 154, 187, 191, 202, 203, 207, 209
compositional process, 159–60, 164, 165, 174, 214
cosmopolitan influences, 125
cosmopolitan style, 10, 234, 238
critical responses, 5, 12–14, 15, 155, 162, 163, 172, 191, 205, 217
death, 217
dissertation topic, 234
European influences, 238
female collaborators, 17, 22–34, 202, 222
folk music influences, 76, 78, 82, 104, 125, 151, 164, 165, 168, 173, 204, 214, 218, 222
hands, 5, 15
health, 18
heart condition, 46
impressionistic influences, 111
marriage, 7, 9, 11, 187, 208
name, 12, 236, 238
nature, inspiration of, 38, 42, 43, 45, 82, 85, 89, 96
opera, 210
pianist, 5, 71
poetry in songwriting, 95
publishers, 50–65
reception history, 170–73
recitals, 4, 7, 10, 12, 14, 33, 73, 211, 223
religious faith, 108, 113, 192
religious views, 183
Romantic style, 144, 221, 239
royalties, 46, 182
sesquicentennial, 239
singing, 93
song accompaniments, 100, 102, 111
song anthologies, 99
song forms, 102
songs, 10, 13
songwriting, 93, 103, 156, 159, 199
songwriting as recreation, 10, 96, 181–82

songwriting process, 97
synesthesia, 3, 98, 140, 148, 227
translations, 98, 206, 223
Victorian style, 189, 194
Victorianism, 186
vocal ranges, 182
widowhood, 39
works
　"Ah, Love, but a Day!," 25, 26, 29, 98
　"All Hail the Power of Jesus' Name," 192
　"Allein," op. 35 no. 2, 148
　"Alleluia Christ is Risen," 188
　Around the Manger, op. 115, 59, 195
　Bal Masqué, 74, 90, 155, 161–64, 167
　"Ballad of the P.E.O., The," 33, 182
　Ballade, op. 6, 73, 89
　Benedicte Omnia Opera, op. 121, 195
　Benedictus Es Domine, op. 103, 195
　"Bethlehem," 188
　"Birth," 110
　Bit of Cairo, A, 85
　"Blackbird, The," op. 11 no. 3, 96
　Browning Songs, op. 44, 11, 24, 52, 104,
　　114
　Burns Songs, op. 43, 86, 205
　By the Still Waters, op. 114, 84
　Cabildo, 18, 110, 202, 209–18, 234
　Cadenza to Beethoven Concerto No. 3, 73
　Canticle of the Sun, The, op. 123, 17, 62,
　　182, 183, 197, 200
　Canticles, op. 78, 194
　"Canzonetta," op. 48 no. 4, 105
　Chamber Pieces, op. 40, 122, 133–34
　Chambered Nautilus, The, op. 66, 26, 54,
　　182, 191–92
　"Chanson d'amour," op. 21, no. 2, 105
　Characteristic Pieces, op. 64, 54
　Children's Album, op. 36, 75, 76
　Children's Carnival, op. 25, 75, 177
　Christ in the Universe, op. 132, 86, 183,
　　198–99, 217
　Communion Responses, op. 122, 195
　Constant Christmas, op. 95, 195
　Cradle Song of the Lonely Mother, A, op.
　　108, 61, 84
　Danse des fleurs, 72
　"Dark Is the Night," op. 11, no. 1, 166
　Dusk in June, op. 82, 196
　"Ecstasy," 10, 98, 103, 114
　Eilende Wolken, Segler der Lüfte, 202,
　　203–5
　"Ein altes Gebet," 108, 114
　"Elle et moi," op. 21 no. 3, 105

Eskimos, op. 64, 54, 78, 148, 232
Fair Hills of Éiré, O!, The, op. 91, 42, 82,
　205
Fantasia fugata, op. 87, 81
Far Awa', 86, 88
"Far Awa'!", 104
Festival Jubilate, op. 17, 11, 25, 123, 161,
　182, 187, 203
From Blackbird Hills, op. 83, 81
From Grandmother's Garden, op. 97, 16,
　83
From Olden Times, op. 111, 84
From Six to Twelve, op. 119, 60, 85
"Gaelic" Symphony, 8, 13, 15, 22, 26, 27,
　75, 155, 164–67, 204, 232, 237
Grand Mass in E-flat major, op. 5, 8, 22,
　25, 51, 161, 182, 184–86, 199, 203
Hearken unto Me, op. 139, 183, 197
Help Us, O God!, 188–89
Hermit Thrush pieces, 16, 42, 62, 82, 83,
　232, 239
Hymn of Welcome, op. 42, 11
"I send my heart up to Thee," op. 44 no. 3,
　114
"I Sought the Lord," op. 142, 114
I Will Give Thanks, op. 147, 198
Improvisations, op. 148, 63, 87, 232
"In the Twilight," op. 85, 62, 111
"Indian Lullaby, An," op. 57 no. 3, 143
Invocation, op. 55, 122, 133
Iverniana for two pianos, op. 70, 88, 141
"Je demande á l'Oiseau," op. 51 no. 4, 105
Jephthah's Daughter, op. 53, 205–9
"Jesus my Saviour," op. 112, 59
"Jeune fille et jeune fleur," 8, 105, 168
"June [Juni]," op. 51 no. 3, 105, 114
Let this Mind be in You, op. 105, 182, 183,
　195
"Light that overflows, A," 110
Little Brown Bee, 51
Lord of the Worlds Above, op. 109, 195
"Lotos Isles, The," op. 76, 86, 108
Magnificat, 113
Mamma's Waltz, 71
"Meadowlarks," op. 78 no. 1, 96
Menuet italien, 72
"Message, A" op. 93, 110
"Mignonette," 110
"Mine be the Lips," op. 113, 57
"Mirage, A.," 44
Morceaux caractéristiques, op. 28, 10, 74
"Morning Glories," op. 97 no. 1, 148
Mother Songs, 62

Beach, Amy (cont.)
"My Love came through the Fields," 110
"My Star," op. 26 no. 1, 114
Nocturne, op. 107, 61, 84
"O Lord God of Israel," op. 141, 198
O Praise the Lord, All Ye Nations, op. 7, 187
Old Chapel by Moonlight, op. 106, 61, 84
"On a Hill," 62, 113
Out of the Depths, op. 130, 85, 86
Panama Hymn, op. 74, 11, 14, 27, 40, 196
Pastorale for Woodwind Quintet, op. 151, 63, 122, 148
"Pax nobiscum", 182
"Peace on Earth", 188
"Peter Pan," op. 101, 44, 59
Piano Concerto, op. 45, 9, 10, 13, 15, 26, 40, 155, 167–70, 208, 236, 237
Piano Pieces, op. 102, 83
Piano Pieces, op. 128, 85
Piano Pieces, op. 54, 76
Piano Quintet, op. 67, 9, 13, 15, 26, 54, 122, 134–41, 144, 237
Piano Trio, op. 150, 63, 122, 148–51
Prelude and Fugue, op. 81, 55, 57, 79
Prelude on an Old Folk Tune, 88, 205
Quartet for Strings, op. 89. *See* String Quartet, op. 89
"Rainy Day, The," 7, 59, 100
Rêves de Colombine, Les: Suite française, op. 65, 41, 54, 79
Romance in A major, op. 23, 122, 123–25
Rose of Avon-town, The, op. 30, 26
"Scottish Legend," op. 54 no. 1, 205
Sea-Fairies, The, op. 59, 22, 26, 31, 44, 191
"Secret, Le," op. 14 no. 2, 105
"Separation," 108
September Forest, A, 86
Serenade, 75
Service in A, op. 63, 189–90, 195
Shakespeare Choruses, op. 39, 190
Shakespeare Songs, op. 37, 11
"Shena Van," op. 56 no. 4, 98, 104, 205
Sketches, op. 15, 10, 73, 178
"Song of Liberty, A," op. 49, 99
Songs, op. 100, 26
Songs, op. 14, 123
Songs, op. 71, 54
Songs, op. 73, 108
Songs, op. 75, 108
Songs, op. 78, 57
Songs, op. 100, 26
"Spirit Divine," op. 88, 59

"Stella Viatoris," 44
String Quartet, op. 89, 17, 122, 145–47, 232
Suite for Two Pianos, op. 104, 17, 61, 122, 142–43
Summer Dreams, op. 47, 52, 87
"Sweetheart, Sigh No More," 123
Sylvania: A Wedding Cantata, 182, 191
Te Deum, op. 84, 59
Theme and Variations for Flute and String Quartet, op. 80, 55, 57, 64, 122, 143–45
"Thou Knowest, Lord," 193
"Though I Take the Wings of Morning," op. 152, 63, 114
"Thrush, The," op. 14 no. 4, 96
"To One I Love," op. 135, 110
Trois morceaux caractéristiques. See Morceaux caractéristiques, op. 28
Tyrolean Valse-Fantaisie, op. 116, 79
Valse Caprice, op. 4, 73
Variations on Balkan Themes, op. 60, 10, 76, 77, 143, 232, 233, 237
Variations on Balkan Themes, op. 60, for two pianos, 88
"Villanelle: Across the World," op. 20, 114
Violin Sonata, op. 34, 9, 12, 15, 33, 122, 125–33, 237
"Wandering Knight, The," op. 29 no. 2, 114
Water-Sprites, The, op. 90, 81
"When Soul is joined to soul," op. 62, 11, 214, 225
"With Violets," op. 1, no. 1, 7, 52
"Wouldn't That Be Queer," 162
"Year's at the Spring, The," 24, 26, 29, 99, 105
writings, 159
Beach, Dr. H.H.A., 6, 7, 10, 11, 20, 39, 52, 102, 178, 184, 233
death, 54, 192
poet, 102
restrictions on Amy, 73, 160, 186
Beck, Lily Adams, 43
Beethoven, Ludwig van, 4, 13, 57, 121, 171
"Pathétique" Sonata, op. 13, 7, 102
Piano Concerto No. 3, 51
Berlin Philharmonic, 13
Better Homes and Gardens, 29
Birchard, C. C., 63
birdsong, 82, 96, 214
Bizet, Georges
Carmen, 219

Black Crook, The, 161
Black, William, 104
Block, Adrienne Fried, 4, 11, 123, 148, 161, 167, 208, 235
Boas, Franz, 78
    Central Eskimo, The, 151
Boehm, Mary Louise, 236, 237
Bomberger, E. Douglas, 161, 167
Bordignon, Paolo, 180, 200
Borthwick, Jane, 193
Boston, 202, 221
Boston Browning Society, 25
Boston Herald, 103
Boston MacDowell Club, 14
Boston Music Company, 56
Boston Pops Orchestra, 163
Boston Symphony Orchestra, 5, 7, 8, 15, 51, 52, 160, 168, 236
Boulanger, Nadia, 33
Boyd, Charles, 171
Bracken, Patricia J., 234
Brahms Quintet, 26
Brahms, Johannes, 12, 107, 122, 125, 156
    Clarinet Sonata in F minor, op. 120 no. 1, 127
    Clarinet Trio, op. 114, 128
    Double Concerto, op. 102, 127
    Intermezzo, op. 76 no. 4, 127
    Piano Concerto No. 2, 168
    Piano Quintet, op. 34, 9, 130, 134
    Symphony No. 4, op. 98, 129
    Violin Sonata in D minor, op. 108, 127
    Violin Sonata No. 2 in A major, op. 100, 151
Braille, 99
Brandeis University, 239
Bristow, George Frederick, 157
    "Arcadian" Symphony, 157
    Rip Van Winkle, 210
Britain, Radie, 175
Broekhoven, John
    Suite Creole, 157
Brooks, Phillips, 20, 183, 188, 195
Brown, Jeannell Wise, 235
Browning Society of Boston, 104
Browning, Elizabeth Barrett, 11, 225
Browning, Robert, 105, 160
Bruckner, Anton, 186
Buck, Dudley, 181
Buffalo Orchestra, 27
Buffalo Twentieth-Century Club, 26
Bulgaria, 10, 76
Burns, Robert, 86, 104, 205
Busch, Carl, 171

Busoni, Ferruccio, 74
Buxbaum, David, 208, 224
Buxbaum, Lillian, 32, 33, 113, 196, 224, 233

Cadman, Charles Wakefield, 27
Caecilia Ladies' Vocal Society of Brooklyn, 26
California, 40
Campanini, Italo, 185
Carnegie Hall, 142
Carpenter, John Alden, 57
Carreño, Teresa, 122, 239
Cassatt, Mary, 123
Centerville, MA, 11, 17, 33, 46, 233
Central Congregational Church, 183
Chadwick, George Whitefield, 9, 27, 53, 58, 67, 154, 181
Chaminade, Cécile, 24, 27, 121, 205
Cheatham, Kitty, 108
Chelsea, MA, 4
Cheney, Charles Abbot, 4
Cheney, Clara Marcy, 4, 8, 12, 19, 54
Cheney, John Vance, 82
Chicago, 32
Chicago Musical College, 32
Chicago Musician's Club of Women, 27
Chicago Symphony Orchestra, 172
Chicago World's Fair. See World's Columbian Exposition
Chopin, Frédéric, 4, 5, 52, 128
    Nocturne in G minor, op. 15 no. 3, 128
Chromatic Club of Boston, 25, 205
chromatic saturation, 110, 148
Church, John, 60
Church, John Company, 50, 60–61
Cincinnati May Festival, 181
Civil War, 50
Clavier Magazine, 238
Cleveland, Grover, 122
Cochrane, Josephine, 123
Coghill, Walter L., 50, 61
College Club, 25
Colum, Padraic, 42
Columbia Artists, 236
Composers Press, 63
Cooley, Elsie Jones, 162
Copland, Aaron, 170, 238
    Appalachian Spring, 175
copyright, 115
Cordon Club, 27
Cowen, Frederic Hymen
    "Welsh" Symphony, 166
Craft, Marcella, 12, 106, 108, 201, 208, 210
Crane, Ichabod, 210

Creole folk songs, 218–20
Crosby, Harry B., 62
Cuba, 219
Curtis, Liane, 239

d'Indy, Vincent, 94
Da Capo Press, 236
Damrosch, Walter, 203
Daniels, Mabel, 44, 54
Dawson, William
    Negro Folk Symphony, 170
de Sayn, Elena, 18, 231
De Wolf, Jessica, 22
Debussy, Claude, 94, 107, 108, 192, 199
Degas, Edgar, 123
DeLamarter, Eric, 172
Deland, Margaret, 24
Delius, Frederick, 170
dell'Acqua, Eva, 105
Dengel, Eugenie Limberg, 234, 235
Detroit, 31
Detroit Symphony Orchestra, 237
Dett, Nathaniel, 170
Dickinson, Clarence, 181
Ditson, Oliver Company, 50, 59
Duffey, Virginia, 32
Duparc, Henri, 108
Dvořák, Antonín, 8, 65, 103, 125, 134, 156
    "New World" Symphony, 142, 164, 167,
        169, 174
    folk music inspiration, 158
Dyckman, Helen, 44

Eden, Myrna Garvey, 234
Eiffel Tower, 123
Elson, Louis, 169, 173
Emery, Florence J., 62
Emmanuel Church (Episcopal), 183
England, 41
Eskin, Virginia, 236, 239
Etude, The, 24, 59, 80, 159, 208
Europe, 85
Exposition universelle of 1889, 123

Faelten, Carl, 15
fairy tales, 210
Farrenc, Louise, 122
Farwell, Arthur, 143
Faulkner, Anne Shaw, 29
Fauré, Gabriel, 107
Feinberg, Alan, 237
female composers, 15, 154, 186, 233
feminist scholarship, 235, 240

Fergus, Phyllis, 27, 31
Ferris Wheel, 123
folk music, 156, 157, 168, 170
folksong, 107, 113
Foote, Arthur, 53, 61, 237
Foster, Stephen, 58
France, 31
Franck, César, 134, 170, 171
Fry, William Henry, 157
    Santa Claus: Christmas Symphony, 157

Gardner, Kara Anne, 232
Gaynor, Jessie, 27
Gefroerer, John, 239
Gehrkens, Karl W., 60
General Federation Magazine, 28
General Federation of Women's Clubs, 22, 24,
    26, 28, 44
Genesis Records, 237
George, Stefan, 138
Gericke, Wilhelm, 5, 8, 160, 168
Gerk, Sarah, 161, 165, 239
Germany, 4, 12, 14, 40, 44, 51, 55, 56, 58, 79,
    106, 107, 211, 236
Gershwin, George
    Porgy and Bess, 202
Gilbert and Sullivan
    Trial by Jury, 216
Gilbert, Henry, 170
Glass, Philip
    "Heroes" Symphony, 156
Glazunov, Alexander, 171
Goetschius, Percy, 11, 133, 191
Gottschalk, Louis Moreau, 157,
Gounod, Charles, 105
Gray, H. W., 63
Great Depression, 45, 63, 99, 111
Grieg, Edvard, 104, 173
Griffes, Charles T., 57

habanera, 219
Hadley, Henry, 57
Hal Leonard, 238
Hale, Philip, 53, 61, 169, 184
Hamilton, Clarence G., 60
Handel and Haydn Society, 8, 25, 181,
    184, 202
Harper's Magazine, 103
Harris, Joel Chandler, 211
Harris, Victor, 26, 191
Harvard University, 6
Haubiel, Charles T., 63
Haverhill, MA, 33

Haydn, Franz Joseph, 3, 159
   Creation, The, 197
Hayes, Roland, 114
Heine, Heinrich, 148
Heinrich, Anthony Philip, 156
Henniker, NH, 4
Hensel, Fanny, 27, 121
hermit thrush, 239
Hier, Ethel Glenn, 44
Hill, Junius Welch, 8, 223
Hillsboro. *See* Hillsborough, NH
Hillsborough Music Club, 32, 219
Hillsborough, NH, 15, 17, 31, 33, 80, 85, 234
Hinson, Maurice, 238
Hisama, Ellie, 235
Hoberg, Margaret, 44
Hodgson, Hugh, 216
Hofmann, Josef, 73, 74
Hood, Helen, 52
Hopekirk, Helen, 52
Hopkinson, Francis, 63
Howells, Herbert, 189
Hughes, Rupert, 103
Hugo, Victor
   Les Orientales, 133
Huntington, Anna Hyatt, 234

Impressionism, 94, 95
Industrial Revolution, 181
International Copyright Law, 55
International Music Score Library Project,
   94, 238
International Standardizing Organization
   (ISO), 102
Inuit music, 145, 148
Irish folk music, 82, 88, 142, 165,
   166, 171
Irving, Washington, 210
   Legend of Sleepy Hollow, The, 210
   Rip Van Winkle, 210
Italy, 107
Ives, Charles, 181

Jackson, Eileen, 158, 174
Jaëll, Marie, 122
Järvi, Neeme, 237
jazz, 27, 57, 221, 232
Jenkins, Walter S., 233
Jewett, Sarah Orne, 24
Joachim, Joseph, 121
Johnson, Kirsten, 237
Journal of Singing, 238
Jungnickel, Ross, 205

Kalish, Gilbert, 237
Kelton, Katherine, 238
Kneisel Quartet, 134
Kneisel, Franz, 9
Koch International, 237
Kooper, Kees, 237
Kozinn, Allan, 238, 240
Krehbiel, Henry, 166, 171, 226
Krueger, Karl, 237

Lafitte, Pierre, 212
Lamartine, Alphonse de, 74
Landau, Siegfried, 237
Lang, Margaret Ruthven, 205
Lee, Gerald Stanley, 4
Lehmann, Liza, 205
Library of Congress, 56, 94, 236
Limberg, Eugenie, 32
Liszt, Franz, 3, 48, 56, 72, 79, 125, 132
   Piano Sonata, 132
Longfellow, Henry Wadsworth, 7, 111
   Song of Hiawatha, 143
Los Angeles Symphony Orchestra, 26, 172

MacDowell Association, 182
MacDowell Colony, 16, 17, 26, 31, 32, 33,
   38–47, 82, 84, 85, 87, 110, 196, 211, 213,
   214, 233
   Allied Members of the MacDowell Colony, 45
   Amy Beach Fund, 46
   Colony Hall, 41
   hurricane, 45
   Nubanusit Tea Room, 38
   Regina Watson studio, 41, 46
MacDowell Society, 27
MacDowell, Edward, 13, 16, 25, 27, 38, 39, 41,
   53, 205, 239
   Indian Suite, op. 48, 143
MacDowell, Fanny, 39
MacDowell, Marian, 16, 26, 38, 39, 44, 85, 215
Mahler, Gustav, 11, 186, 221
Malipiero, Gian Francesco, 17
Mannes School of Music, 235
Manuscript Society of New York, 162
Mardinly, Susan, 206, 238
Maretzek, Max
   Sleepy Hollow, or The Headless Horseman,
   210
Martinez, Isidora, 206
Mary Stuart, Queen of Scots, 202, 203
Mason, Daniel Gregory, 170
Mason, Lowell, 181
Massachusetts General Hospital, 6, 7

McHose, Allen, 234
Mel Bay, 238
Melodist Club, 27
Mendelssohn Club of Pittsburgh, 181
Mendelssohn(-Bartholdy), Felix, 3, 5
  "Scottish" Symphony, 166
  Cello Sonata in D major, op. 58, 130
Merrill, E. Lindsey, 234
Meynell, Alice, 198
Miles, Marmaduke, 234
Modernism, 27, 110, 221, 232, 239
Mollevaut, Charles-Louis, 206
Moody, Dwight, 60
Moore, Mary Carr
  Narcissa, or The Cost of Empire, 209
Moresby, Elizabeth Louisa, 43
Moscheles, Ignaz, 5, 72
Mozart, Wolfgang Amadeus, 3, 7
Mu Phi Epsilon, 17, 27, 32
Mulligan, Charlotte, 26
Murkland, Margaret, 25
music clubs, 22–34, 156
Music Publishers Association of the United
  States, 61
music streaming services, 239
Music Teachers National Association, 17, 31,
  42, 157, 234
Musical America, 211
Musical Courier, 13
Musical Heritage Society, 237
Musical Monitor, 25, 27
Musical Quarterly, 56

Nashville Symphony Orchestra, 237
National Association of Teachers of Singing,
  238
National Federation of Music Clubs, 24, 25, 31,
  40, 41
National League of American Pen Women, 24,
  29, 44
nationalism, 27
Native American music, 81, 142, 143, 145, 209
nature, 27, 178
Neuls-Bates, Carol, 235
Nevin, Ethelbert, 27
New England, 209, 231, 239
New England Conservatory, 32, 72, 107
New Hampshire Federation of Women's
  Clubs, 24
New Hampshire's Daughters, 24
New Orleans, 211
New School for Music Study, 238
New World Records, 237

New York Herald, 142
New York Times, 239
Noble, T. Tertius, 181
Nold, Raymond, 195
Northeastern Records, 237
Norwood, Robert Winkworth, 196

Ochsner, Mrs. Albert J., 32
Oja, Carol, 232

P.E.O., 33
Paeff, Bashka, 42
Paine, John Knowles, 53, 181
Palmer, Bertha Honoré, 123
Panama-California Exposition, 14, 107, 108
Panama-Pacific International Exposition, 11,
  14, 27, 40, 172, 192
Parker, Horatio, 181
passaggio, 100, 102
Patti, Adelina, 7
Paur, Emil, 170
Perabo, Ernst, 4, 72
Pergolesi, Giovanni Battista
  La serva padrona, 217
Perronet, Edward, 193
Peterborough Pageant, 40
Pfohl, Ferdinand, 13
Phelps, Ellsworth
  "Emancipation" Symphony, 157
Philadelphia, 31
Philadelphia Orchestra, 15
Phillips Gallery, Washington, DC, 231
Piano Magazine, 238
pitch standard, 102
Pittsburgh Orchestra, 171
player-pianos, 57
Pleasants, Virginia Duffey, 234
poetry, 95
Polk, Joanne, 237, 238
Powell, Maud, 123
Presser, Theodore, 58
Presser, Theodore Company, 50, 58
Price, Florence
  Songs of the Oath, 175
Pro Musica, 27
Puccini, Giacomo
  La fanciulla del West, 209
Purcell, Henry
  "Dido's Lament," 206

Rachmaninoff, Sergei, 3
Ralston, Frances Marion, 26, 44
Raudenbush, George King, 173

Reger, Max, 192
Reigles, Jean, 183
Rip Van Winkle, 209
Robb, Graham, 134
Robinson, Edwin Arlington, 42
Rodin, Auguste, 123
Rogers, Clara Kathleen, 52
Romanticism, 94, 95
Roosevelt, Eleanor, 31, 85
Rosenfeld, Paul, 232
Rosenthal, Moritz, 74
Royal Philharmonic, 237

Saint-Saëns, Camille
    Piano Concerto No. 2 in G minor, 171, 172
Samaroff, Olga, 83
San Diego Exposition. *See* Panama-California
    Exposition
San Francisco Century Club, 27
Sanborn, Kate, 24
Sankey, Ira D., 61
scena ed aria, 201
Schermerhorn, Kenneth, 237
Schiller, Friedrich, 222
    Maria Stuart, 203
Schirmer, E. C., 56
Schirmer, G., 13, 50, 107, 233
Schirmer, Gustav Sr., 55
Schirmer, Gustave Jr., 56
Schirmer, Rudolph, 56, 58
Schmidt, Arthur P., 11, 12, 13, 16, 27, 38, 50, 51,
    61, 107, 122, 163, 182, 184, 232
    orchestral scores, 154
    promotion of Beach, 93, 99
Schoenberg, Arnold, 132, 146
    Drei Klavierstücke, op. 11, 138
    Second String Quartet, op. 10, 138
Schott's Söhne, 13
Schubert, Franz, 148
    "Erlkönig," 112
    "Trout" Quintet, 156
Schumann, Clara, 27, 121, 148
Schumann, Robert, 134, 171
    Piano Quintet, op. 44, 9
Schumann-Heink, Ernestine, 108
Scott, Ida Gray, 28
Scriabin, Alexander, 199
Second New England School, 34, 232
Seeger, Ruth Crawford, 232, 236
Sengstack, David, 236
Shaffner, Ruth, 17, 32, 33, 113, 115, 198,
    218, 234
Shawe, Elsie, 22

Sibelius, Jan, 171
Silver Burdett, 63
Silverstein, Joseph, 237
Sinding, Christian, 171
Sleeper, William Washburn, 76
Smith, Alice Mary, 122
Smith, Gail, 238
Smyth, Ethel, 122
Society for American Music, 235
Society of American Women Composers, 17,
    29, 45
Sonneck, Oscar G., 56
Sousa, John Philip, 60
Southern, Eileen. *See* Jackson, Eileen
Spanish flu, 57
Spencer, Robert Nelson, 114
Spiering, Theodore, 13
St. Bartholomew's Church, 17, 33, 113, 180,
    183, 196, 202, 217
    100th anniversary, 197
    communion chalice, 184
St. Cecilia Club of New York, 26, 191
Stanford, Charles Villiers, 171
Steele, Mrs. William Delaney, 28
Stephens, Nan Bagby, 18, 211, 213, 218
    Cabildo, 211
Still, William Grant, 170
Stock, Frederick, 172
Stokes, Richard L., 172
Stokowski, Leopold, 15, 173, 181
Stratford-on-Avon, 40
Strauss, Johann, 163
Strauss, Richard, 12, 94, 105, 107, 169, 192, 221
    Salome, 202
    Ständchen, op. 17, no. 2, 75, 105
Summy-Birchard Company, 236
Sundstrom, Ebba, 173
Sutro, Rose and Ottilie, 17
Svendsen, Johan, 171
Symphony Society of New York, 203

tango, 219
Taylor, Deems, 232
temperance, 23
Tennyson, Alfred, 86, 108
Thiede, Alexander, 173
Thomas, Rose Fay, 25
Thomas, Theodore, 5
Thompson, Berenice, 94, 154
Thoms, William, 163
Thomson, Virgil, 232
Three Choirs Festival, 181
Thursday Morning Musical Club, 25

Tick, Judith, 236, 240
Ticknor, Howard, 169
Transcendentalists, 42
Trans-Mississippi International Exposition, 11
Triangle of Mu Phi Epsilon, 32
Trinity Episcopal Church, 183
tuning. *See* Pitch Standard
Tuthill, Burnet C., 18

Uncle Remus. *See* Harris, Joel Chandler
United Women of Maryland, 27, 205
University of Chicago, 174
University of Georgia, 217
University of Georgia Glee Club, 216
University of Missouri-Kansas City, 218, 234
University of New Hampshire, 198, 219, 233, 235, 239
Unverhau, Mrs. Heinrich, 24
Upton, George P., 9

Vannah, Kate, 7
Vermont Public Television, 239
Victorianism, 96
Vienna, 87
Vox Turnabout, 237

Wagner, Richard, 107, 125, 169, 171, 218, 221
Washington, DC, 18, 30, 31, 45
Watson, Dorothy DeMuth, 44
Watson, Regina, 41

Wa-Wan Press, 143
Westphalian Symphony Orchestra, 237
White House, 31, 33, 85
Whiting, George E., 157
whole-tone scale, 110
Williams, David McKay, 17, 113, 181, 183, 195, 197, 198
Wolf, Hugo, 11, 105, 107, 148
    "Auf ein altes Bild," 108
Woman's Club of Evanston, Illinois, 27
Woman's Symphony Orchestra, 173
Women's Philharmonic Advocacy, 239
Women's Press Association, 25
women's suffrage, 23, 25, 186
Women's Symphony of Chicago, 27
Women's Symphony Society of Boston, 173
Woodman, Clarence A., 60
World War I, 14, 27, 40, 44, 50, 57, 58, 62, 107, 111, 172, 208
World War II, 18, 111, 114, 115
World's Columbian Exposition, 11, 25, 122, 187
    Woman's Building, 123, 187, 203

Yandell, Enid, 123
"Yankee Doodle," 156
Yoo, Scott, 231, 239

Zerrahn, Carl, 184

Milton Keynes UK
Ingram Content Group UK Ltd.
UKHW032057010124
435325UK00003B/5